MW00638407

Knowledge and Politics in Plato's *Theaetetus*

The *Theaetetus* is one of the most widely studied Platonic dialogues because its dominant theme concerns the significant philosophical question, what is knowledge? In a new interpretation of this dialogue, Paul Stern provides the first full-length treatment of its political content, particularly its relationship with the epistemological theme. Stern argues that this approach sheds significant light on the distinctiveness of the Socratic way of life, with respect to its initial justification and its ultimate character. More specifically, he argues that Socrates' revolutionary decision to subject political life to philosophic reflection, the decision that leads directly to his trial and execution, is his awareness of the elusiveness of comprehensive knowledge and the implications of that elusiveness for the validity of philosophic inquiry. This view of Socrates' rationale has important consequences for our understanding of political philosophy and of the desirability of the life of reason.

Paul Stern is professor of politics at Ursinus College. He is the author of *Socratic Rationalism and Political Philosophy: An Interpretation of Plato's "Phaedo."*

Knowledge and Politics in Plato's *Theaetetus*

PAUL STERN
Ursinus College

CAMBRIDGE UNIVERSITY PRESS
Cambridge, New York, Melbourne, Madrid, Cape Town, Singapore, São Paulo, Delhi

Cambridge University Press
32 Avenue of the Americas, New York, NY 10013-2473, USA

www.cambridge.org
Information on this title: www.cambridge.org/9780521884297

First published 2008

Printed in the United States of America

A catalog record for this publication is available from the British Library.

Library of Congress Cataloging in Publication Data

Stern, Paul
Knowledge and politics in Plato's Theaetetus / Paul Stern.
p. cm.
Includes bibliographical references (p.) and index.
ISBN 978-0-521-88429-7 (hardback)
1. Plato. Theaetetus. 2. Knowledge, Theory of. 3. Political science – Philosophy. I. Title.
B386.S79 2008
121–dc22 2007027751

ISBN 978-0-521-88429-7 hardback

To Lisa

Contents

Acknowledgments

The seeds of this book were planted in a course given by Joseph Cropsey at the University of Chicago some thirty years ago. His illuminating examination of the dialogue provided questions that have ever after guided my reading. My understanding of the issues raised in the dialogue has been shaped since that time in conversations with Don Brand, Paul Franco, and Rick Sorenson. Their friendship has been a lifelong source of encouragement and pleasure.

Many colleagues read and usefully commented on the manuscript. Chief among these is Rick Sorenson, who read the entire manuscript with his characteristic acuity. Jeff Church, Darrell Dobbs, Bernard Dobski, Paul Franco, Paul Kirkland, Eric Petrie, and David Roochnik also provided insightful readings of portions of the manuscript. Thanks also to Scott Hemmenway and an anonymous reviewer for Cambridge University Press for their very helpful advice. Comments from animated audiences at Temple University, The College of the Holy Cross, James Madison College at Michigan State University, and Assumption College helped me sharpen my argument. Cathy Bogusky helped me prepare the manuscript for publication.

I have done all the work on the book while teaching at Ursinus College. I am grateful to the students in my several seminars on the *Theaetetus* for their willingness to engage wholeheartedly with this often befuddling dialogue. I can only hope that our common effort to seek clarity benefited them as much as it did me. At Ursinus I have also found colleagues and friends who inspire by their vision of liberal education. Steve Hood, Robert Dawley, Dallett Hemphill, and Stewart Goetz have fashioned Ursinus into an environment where the Socratic questions are essential to the daily lives of both teachers and students. Such an environment does not occur without the support of an unusually enlightened administration, which we have in President John Strassburger and Dean Judith Levy. Their efforts have helped transform Ursinus into a home for teacher-scholars. Thanks to these efforts I received a grant from the Mellon Foundation (administered by Ursinus) that afforded me much-needed time to study the *Theaetetus*.

Finally, I wish to express my gratitude to my wife, Lisa. Her intense interest in the work and her ceaseless encouragement sustained me in the many years it took to complete the book. More importantly, she created a home for me and for our sons, Ben and Alex, in which thinking about these issues seems a very worthwhile thing to do. I dedicate the book to her.

1

Knowledge, Politics, and Midwifery

Introduction

My interpretation of Plato's *Theaetetus* aims to give full weight to the political substance of the dialogue. Readers will be excused for thinking this aim should have produced a work considerably shorter than the one they now hold in their hands. It assuredly is not due to its political insight that the *Theaetetus* ranks among the most studied of Plato's dialogues. The dialogue earns that privileged place because of its penetrating examination of no less a question than what is the meaning of knowledge. In the rarefied atmosphere of such a question my consideration of the dialogue's political teaching may seem an unwelcome, because unwise, lowering of our sights. But I do not recommend that we look at politics *instead* of knowledge. Rather, I hope to show that Plato's treatment of the *Theaetetus*' pervasive theme can only be properly understood through careful attention to the dialogue's political character. To begin to establish the plausibility of my thesis I want to sketch the more prominent political features of the *Theaetetus*. I start with the dialogue's conclusion because it locates the *Theaetetus* as a whole in an eminently political context.

At the dialogue's end, Socrates makes this portentous announcement: "But now there's something I need to go and face in the courtyard of the king-archon, in response to the indictment which Meletus has drawn up against me (210d2–4)."[1] With Socrates' walk to the courtyard he begins his inexorable

[1] I have relied on the translations by Joe Sachs, *Plato's Theaetetus* (Newburyport, MA: Focus Publishing Company, 2004) and Seth Benardete, *The Being of the Beautiful* (Chicago: University of Chicago Press, 1984). I have also consulted the translations by John McDowell, *Plato "Theaetetus"* (Oxford: Clarendon Press, 1973); Robin Waterfield, *Plato, "Theaetetus"* (London: Penguin, 1987); and M. J. Levett in Myles Burnyeat, *The "Theaetetus" of Plato* (Indianapolis, IN: Hackett Publishing Company, 1990). I have used the Greek text of W. F. Hicken in E. A. Duke et al, eds., *Platonis Opera*, vol. I (Oxford: Clarendon Press, 1995). Page and line references refer to this edition. All references within the text refer to the *Theaetetus*. Texts not attributed to an author are by Plato.

march to death in an Athenian cell. The political character of the *Theaetetus* would be an issue worth pursuing if for no other reason than to discern why Plato has the knowledge-obsessed *Theaetetus* initiate the series of dialogues through which he weaves the story of Socrates' political trial.[2] Approaching the *Theaetetus* with this broad dramatic context in mind must already prompt us to ask what connection Plato might intend between the dialogue's abstract theme and this concrete political outcome. Other prominent passages make this question even more salient. To use Socrates' oft-repeated phrase, let's begin again at the beginning.

The dialogue actually begins with a Prologue set some thirty years after Socrates' death.[3] In it, two Megarian philosophers, Euclides and Terpsion, reminisce about Socrates. They recall the extraordinarily stimulating discussion he had with the young Theaetetus in the days prior to Socrates' death. What prompts the Megarians' reminiscences of Socrates and his death is Euclides' chance encounter with the now-mature Theaetetus as he is carried back to Athens, having been wounded in battle. Thus, the Prologue ensures that the specter of politically hued deaths hovers over the subsequent proceedings.

The looming presence of Socrates' trial continues to cast its shadow as the dialogue moves from the Prologue to the conversation about knowledge. Well before the culminating lines of the *Theaetetus* Socrates expresses awareness of the community's disdain for his activity, acknowledging also the likely consequence of that disdain. Through the famous image of the midwife, Socrates makes clear that challenging conversation with promising youth about the community's constitutive opinions plays a crucial role in his philosophic activity. He does not pretend that these conversations have any other result than to generate perplexity in these future leaders. Neither does he blink the fact that this result earns him his fellow citizens' denunciation.

In addition to the *Theaetetus*' beginning and conclusion, politics is most powerfully present in the dialogue's very heart. Here Socrates provides what may properly be regarded as a brief for his upcoming trial. This central passage of the dialogue contains a vigorous defense of the philosopher's life as superior to the politician's. It is perhaps too vigorous – and in other ways too subtle – a

[2] Insightful treatments of the series of dialogues involved in Socrates' political-philosophic trial can be found in Joseph Cropsey, *Plato's World: Man's Place in the Cosmos* (Chicago: University of Chicago Press, 1997) and Jacob Howland, *The Paradox of Political Philosophy: Socrates' Philosophic Trial* (Lanham, MD: Rowman and Littlefield, 1997).

[3] There is some controversy concerning the date of Theaetetus' death. At issue is the exact battle in which Theaetetus was wounded. The only battles that fill the bill occurred in 369 BCE and 394 BCE. I have accepted the later date following Benardete's suggestion that the earlier date "would seem to condense Theaetetus' achievements into too short an interval." Benardete, *Being of the Beautiful*, I.84. For arguments supporting the earlier date see Debra Nails, *The People of Plato: A Prosopography of Plato and Other Socratics* (Indianapolis, IN: Hackett Publishing Company, 2002), 276. For a brief overview of the participants in this long-standing debate, see Timothy Chappell, *Reading Plato's Theaetetus* (Indianapolis, IN: Hackett Publishing Company, 2004), 30.

defense to be effective in court. But for just these reasons it contains one of the most enlightening treatments of the central issue of Socrates' trial found anywhere in the entire saga.

Together, these passages provide a basis on which to speak sensibly of the dialogue's political character. Furthermore, given their prominence, they substantiate the need at least to consider the connection between the meaning of knowledge and this political character in any comprehensive interpretation of the dialogue. Precisely this prominence, however, raises an immediate question for any new interpretation of this much-studied dialogue. If through these conspicuous passages Plato does place this connection squarely before the reader, why have so many thoughtful readers managed to overlook it?

The common scholarly reaction to the central passage of the *Theaetetus*, usually called the Digression, provides sufficient evidence of this neglect. Until very recently this passage has received little sustained scholarly attention.[4] Those theorists that are most interested in the *Theaetetus*, those preoccupied by the meaning of knowledge or by what is sometimes called "Plato's epistemology," find the Digression philosophically inconsequential.[5] Those who do think it of some value often believe, following Schleiermacher, that its rehearsal of apparently familiar Platonic themes simply means to provide reassurance that, despite the dialogue's skepticism, the stable Platonic world remains firmly in place.[6] This assessment, however, judges the Digression as at best auxiliary to the central theme. Characterizing its content as extraneous, another more recent commentator maintains that the Digression contains material "which in a modern book might be served by footnotes or an appendix."[7] There is, in short, a broad consensus that the Digression "does not contribute to the main inquiry."[8]

In my treatment of the Digression I argue against this last assessment at some length. Nevertheless, here I would affirm that such conclusions are perfectly understandable. The political theme of the Digression does seem to spring up abruptly from this intensely abstract discussion between Socrates and two mathematicians concerning the meaning and even possibility of knowledge. Its confident praise of the philosophic life does sit uneasily in the heart

4 Two recent exceptions are Scott R. Hemmenway, "Philosophical Apology in the *Theaetetus*," *Interpretation* 17 (1990): 323–46 and Rachel Rue, "The Philosopher in Flight: The Digression (172c–177c) in Plato's *Theaetetus*," in *Oxford Studies in Ancient Philosophy, vol. 11*, ed. C. C. W. Taylor (Oxford: Clarendon Press, 1993), 71–100.

5 Without necessarily meaning to affirm the judgment as his own, Chappell refers to "what many take to be the philosophical backwater of the Digression." Chappell, *Reading Plato's "Theaetetus,"* 19. For examples of such treatment see McDowell, *Plato "Theaetetus,"* 174–5 and David Bostock, *Plato's "Theaetetus"* (Oxford: Clarendon Press, 1988), 98–9.

6 Friedrich Schleiermacher, *Introductions to the Dialogues of Plato*, trans. William Dobson (New York: Arno Press, 1973), 197–8. See also Francis M. Cornford, *Plato's Theory of Knowledge* (1935; repr., Indianapolis, IN: Bobbs-Merrill Company, 1957), 89.

7 McDowell, *Plato "Theaetetus,"* 174.

8 Burnyeat, *The "Theaetetus" of Plato*, 36.

of this most skeptical of dialogues. Socrates does identify the passage, at least once, as a digression. The dialogue itself, then, makes the passage seem anomalous, its political theme detachable from the dialogue's main business. So although Plato does undeniably place the political character of the *Theaetetus* squarely before us, it would be most accurate to say that the dialogue's surface poses the connection between politics and the meaning of knowledge *as a question*.

This being the case, the most prevalent scholarly reaction to the dialogue provides a key to Plato's intent in the dialogue, although not in the usual manner. For, the reluctance of many commentators to engage this question mirrors the disposition of the interlocutors Plato provides Socrates within the dialogue. In this conversation about knowledge, Socrates converses with Theodorus, an older geometer, and Theaetetus, his young, brilliant student. They too resist the invitation to reflect on the dialogue's political themes. They too abstain from the examination of the connection between the dominant theme of the dialogue, the meaning of knowledge, and its political character. These theorists much prefer the more serious and lofty examination of knowledge to the mundane, and perhaps more uncertain, consideration of political life.

However, in his portrayal of these theorists Plato begins to reveal the inner connection between these issues by showing the cost of such neglect. In particular, their unwillingness to examine rationally political and ethical matters leaves these mathematicians unable to defend the good of their own theoretical activity. Plato's portrayal of this inability directs us to the heart of the dialogue's concern. Connecting politics and the meaning of knowledge is this question: is it good to pursue knowledge?[9] It is a question that properly introduces the story of one who forfeits his life for this pursuit.

Contrary to his interlocutors' neglect of this concern, Socrates' philosophic inquiry concentrates unceasingly on the human meaning of the pursuit of knowledge. The reaction of his fellow citizens to that pursuit doubtlessly helped affirm for Socrates its questionable character. Yet, this reaction, so I will argue, was an effect not a cause. Socrates' philosophic pursuit embroiled him in political controversy to an unprecedented extent as a consequence of a theoretical insight. He saw more clearly than did his predecessors the partiality of our knowledge and the question raised by that partiality for the validity of the knowledge-seeker's pursuit. This theoretical insight heightens the danger of Socratic inquiry because, as I also argue, in response to it Socrates sees the

[9] This intertwining of the question of good with politics may seem pertinent only to nonliberal political orders. Yet liberalism too can be understood as embodying a notion of a right way of life. For an example of such an understanding, see William Galston, *Liberal Purposes: Goods, Virtues, and Diversity in the Liberal State* (Cambridge: Cambridge University Press, 1991). However, even more specifically pertinent to the *Theaetetus*, part of Socrates' refutation of the notion that knowledge is perception involves showing that the relativism (and conventionalism) that underlies liberal neutrality is itself animated by a notion of good. See esp. Chapter 5.

need to place the philosophic study of politics at the center of philosophy as a whole. More specifically, to state the central claim of this study, the *Theaetetus* shows that only through this study can Socrates attain the self-knowledge that both justifies philosophic inquiry and guides it toward knowledge properly understood.[10]

If this claim is true, then it is the essential requirement of Socrates' distinctive philosophic activity that brings about Socrates' trial and execution. In this case, it would clearly be a mistake to regard either these political events or the political character of the *Theaetetus* as merely a dispensable dramatic frame for Plato's presentation of Socratic philosophy. Neither would it be sufficient to conclude that Socrates' study of politics is only a matter of prudence for the self-protective philosopher. Again, I wish to substantiate the more comprehensive claim: this study is, for Socrates, central to philosophic inquiry itself. As such, it does most profoundly "contribute to the main inquiry" of the *Theaetetus*. With its apparently anomalous juxtaposition of political and epistemic themes, the very surface of the dialogue invites us to consider their relationship and work through for ourselves the reasons for their paradoxical connection. The interpretation contained herein seeks to respond to this invitation.

Plato exhibits the significance of this connection through the lamentable result of its neglect. Through the reluctance of these knowledge-seeking interlocutors to engage this same connection, Plato exhibits as well the imposing barriers to its consideration. But the effort to surmount these barriers remains worthwhile. The invitation still deserves a response because the issue to which Socrates' novel approach responds also persists. We are acutely aware of the critique of reason, expressed powerfully by Nietzsche and Heidegger. One compelling strand of that critique charges that the choice to seek guidance from reason is itself dogmatic, and so not truly rational.[11] This critique renders reason's capacity to provide the most vital knowledge – the knowledge that might guide life – dubious. As Plato makes clear in the drama of Theaetetus and Theodorus, this incapacity cannot help but rebound on any and all claims for reason's efficacy. In this light, the concerns of the *Theaetetus* remain our concerns.

Through the consideration of the *Theaetetus*' political character that follows, I undertake to show that the dialogue can help us respond to this critique. It

[10] See Leo Strauss, "The Problem of Socrates: Five Lectures" in *The Rebirth of Classical Political Rationalism: An Introduction to the Thought of Leo Strauss* (Chicago: University of Chicago Press, 1989), 126.

[11] See, e.g., Friedrich Nietzsche, *The Birth of Tragedy*, trans. Walter Kaufmann (New York: Vintage Books, 1967), 95–6 and Friedrich Nietzsche, *Beyond Good and Evil*, trans. Walter Kaufmann (New York: Vintage Books, 1989), 2. With respect to Heidegger, I deal with this issue as it bears on the *Theaetetus* in Chapter 7 where I briefly consider his treatment of the *Theaetetus* in Martin Heidegger, *The Essence of Truth: On Plato's Cave Allegory and "Theaetetus,"* trans. Ted Sadler (London: Continuum, 2002), 109–236.

does so in its articulation of an approach that offers the possibility of a reasoned defense of the good of philosophic inquiry. Socrates formulates this defense in full awareness of the limits of reason because it is prompted precisely by this awareness. *Midwifery* is the distinctive name Socrates gives to this distinctive approach. Through this practice, which takes its bearings from the political opinions of his interlocutors, Socrates inquires into all things, including the prerequisites, theoretical and practical, of his own inquiry. Is Socratic midwifery still viable? Any response to this question requires first an interpretation of this dialogue in which Socrates explores these prerequisites. But it is at least some measure of midwifery's viability that such an investigation is best undertaken with the kind of self-awareness characteristic of this practice. We cannot afford to succumb to the fate of the self-forgetting theorist when the question is no less than whether reason can guide life.

Interpretations

A perception shared by otherwise divergent interpretations of the *Theaetetus* is that the dialogue possesses a profoundly skeptical tenor. Several prominent features of the dialogue make this an apt characterization. First, the dialogue ends in explicit aporia. Referring to the dialogue's three great attempts to define knowledge, Socrates employs the imagery of midwifery to ask Theaetetus: "Then our art of midwifery declares that all these things came into being as wind-eggs and are not worth rearing? (210b8–9)." Theaetetus responds: "Absolutely (210b10)." With one additional speech by Socrates, the dialogue thus concludes. Also contributing to the dialogue's skeptical tone is the absence of the doctrines of the Forms and Recollection which, in other dialogues, provide a guarantee of ultimate intelligibility. Their absence is especially conspicuous because in an examination of the meaning of knowledge we would have expected them to occupy center stage. Add to these facts an unusually self-critical and cognitively humble Socrates, and we have clear justification for the characterization rendered in the preceding text.[12]

From this shared perception, however, interpretations of the *Theaetetus* diverge according to their reactions to this skeptical character. As David Sedley has shown, the main strands of these competing interpretive reactions were already present in antiquity.[13] The most general division among the interpretations lies between those that take the dialogue's aporetic conclusion at face value and those that do not. Two distinct considerations place interpreters in the former camp. The first, more characteristic of ancient than of contemporary

[12] Sedley provides a useful list of the problems posed by the *Theaetetus* with respect to its skepticism. David Sedley, "Three Platonist Interpretations of the *Theaetetus*," in *Form and Argument in Late Plato*, eds. Christopher Gill and Mary Margaret McCabe (Oxford: Clarendon Press, 1996), 84–5.

[13] Ibid.

interpreters, is the possibility that in the *Theaetetus* Plato is found "retracting or undermining the confident manifesto of knowledge presented in the *Republic*."[14] In this way, he reveals himself finally as a thoroughgoing skeptic. More evident in contemporary skeptical interpretations, however, is the judgment that in the *Theaetetus* Plato seeks to formulate a defensible definition of knowledge but fails. Accordingly, we are to take the dialogue's conclusion as Plato's sincere confession of failure.[15]

Any refutation of this position must obviously contend with Socrates' reference to the several definitions of knowledge as "wind-eggs" and "not worth rearing." Such a refutation might begin from the recognition that these phrases occur in a *question* posed to Theaetetus not in a statement made by Socrates. But even if Socrates did pronounce this judgment as his own we would still need to consider whether the position belongs also to the author of the dialogue. The more general point is that a determination of these phrases' meanings rests on a coherent account of the whole rather than a particular statement (or question) voiced by one of the characters.[16]

In adopting this interpretive stance, I follow the widespread view that the dialogues are more akin to dramas than treatises. Given this form, the dialogue yields its meaning only to the reader willing to consider the import of all its details. Accordingly, I strive to conceive how such considerations as the interlocutors' characters and deeds, not only their sound arguments but also their faulty arguments, might all contribute to the fulfillment of the author's intent. I hold that we must, in short, attend as carefully as possible to the world of the dialogue in all its particularity. Such attention is especially demanded in the case of the *Theaetetus*, for in its opening pages we learn that a contributing

[14] Ibid., 84. On the skeptical interpretation in general see ibid., 86–9.

[15] See, e.g., W. G. Runciman, *Plato's Later Epistemology* (Cambridge: Cambridge University Press, 1962), 57; Jacob Klein, *Plato's Trilogy* (Chicago: University of Chicago Press, 1977), 145; and Bostock, *Plato's "Theaetetus,"* 13–14.

[16] On the interpretive approach that I have adopted, consider first Jacob Klein, *A Commentary on Plato's "Meno"* (Chapel Hill: University of North Carolina Press, 1965), 3–10. The literature concerning the proper approach to the Platonic dialogue has become voluminous in the last few decades. Some fruitful places to consider the issues are Charles Griswold, ed., *Platonic Writings/Platonic Readings* (University Park: The Pennsylvania State University Press, 2001); James Klagge and Nicholas D. Smith, eds., *Methods of Interpreting Plato and His Dialogues, Oxford Studies in Ancient Philosophy*, suppl. vol. (Oxford: Clarendon Press, 1992); Gerald A. Press, *Plato's Dialogues: New Studies and Interpretations* (Lanham, MD: Rowman and Littlefield, 1993); Francisco J. Gonzalez, *The Third Way: New Directions in Platonic Studies* (Lanham, MD: Rowman and Littlefield, 1995). On the particular question of treating Socrates as another character in the dialogues, rather than simply Plato's mouthpiece, see the articles in Gerald A. Press, ed., *Who Speaks for Plato? Studies in Platonic Anonymity* (Lanham, MD: Rowman and Littlefield, 2000) and Ruby Blondell, *The Play of Character in Plato's Dialogues* (Cambridge: Cambridge University Press, 2002), 18–21. For an alternative view, see Richard Kraut, "Introduction to the Study of Plato," in *The Cambridge Companion to Plato*, ed. Richard Kraut (Cambridge: Cambridge University Press, 1992), 25–30.

author of the forthcoming conversation edited the transcript with a view to suppressing these particulars. But this fact as well is one of the particulars to which we must attend.

My initial rationale for adopting this approach is that it enables the greatest degree of openness to such intricacies of the text's manifest literary form. However, at several points in the *Theaetetus*, and thus in my interpretation, the philosophic significance of the dialogic form becomes thematic. This should not be surprising. Given the pervasive themes of the *Theaetetus* – how we come to know, how we learn – we might expect this text to provide enlightenment regarding the philosophic judgments underlying Plato's choice of the form in which he instructs his readers. These judgments explicate further the rationale underlying the dialogue form and thus substantiate further the interpretive approach adopted herein.

It is noteworthy, however, that numerous commentators adhering to a variety of interpretive approaches recognize that the *Theaetetus* yields its meaning only to the active reader. Perhaps owing to the desire to account for the dialogue's anomalous skepticism, there is extensive recognition that the paradoxical aspects of the dialogue are not simply Platonic shortcomings but rather provocations aimed to engender in us our own reflections.[17] Such a reader, one who regards the dialogue's outcome as only apparently negative, would still need to explain why Plato omits the doctrines of the Forms and Recollection, and why he portrays such a skeptical Socrates. This reader would, in sum, need to articulate the positive meaning of those dialogic elements that make the skeptical interpretation plausible. The other two strands of interpretation noted by Sedley take up this task.

Sedley calls the first of these an "object-related interpretation," so designated because it takes the *Theaetetus* to be concerned with the appropriate objects of knowledge.[18] More specifically, through its concentration on sensible objects rather than the Forms it shows us what the objects of knowledge are *not*.[19] Most famously expressed by Francis Cornford, this interpretation

[17] Ellen Haring writes, "the dialogue itself licenses and encourages active interpretation." E. S. Haring, "The *Theaetetus* Ends Well," *Review of Metaphysics* 35 (1982): 510. Myles Burnyeat's commentary on the dialogue makes such interpretation thematic. He holds that Plato intentionally sets before the reader two interpretations, designated by Burnyeat as Reading A – generally speaking a version of the Cornfordian approach (see following text) – and Reading B – Burnyeat's own interpretation that is again, generally speaking, a Revisionist account (see following text). Given this conception of Plato's intention, the dialogue yields its meaning only to the reader who is willing to engage in the dialectic between these two readings. Burnyeat, *The "Theaetetus" of Plato*, passim. In his own book-length commentary Sedley endorses Burnyeat's view and sees the need for the reader to go beyond the dialogue to "rear" those thoughts engendered by the dialogue. David Sedley, *The Midwife of Platonism* (Oxford: Clarendon Press, 2004), 5–6. See also Rosemary Desjardins, *The Rational Enterprise: Logos in Plato's "Theaetetus"* (Albany: State University of New York Press, 1990), 4–8.

[18] Sedley, "Three Platonist Interpretations," 90

[19] Ibid.

maintains that we are meant to see "in the failure of all attempts to extract knowledge from sensible objects" that "knowledge has for its objects things of a different order – not sensible things but intelligible Forms and truths about them."[20] Accordingly, we are to understand the Forms as separate from any material instantiation, unchanging and imperishable.[21] The dialogue's failure thus provides a positive argument for the necessity of the Forms so understood.

Cornford's line is especially attractive to those Platonic scholars sometimes called Unitarians. These commentators argue that neither the *Theaetetus*, nor any other of what are called late dialogues, represent a substantial departure from the doctrines for which Plato is most famous.[22] Again, in the case of the *Theaetetus*, it is rather that its unresolved perplexities point us precisely to the necessity of these doctrines. Or, to use the title of the most recent version of this understanding, Plato has Socrates serve here as "the midwife of Platonism," permitting the reader to see that the inadequacies of his understanding can be remedied by Platonic metaphysics.[23]

In introductory typologies of *Theaetetus* interpretations, such as the one I am now offering, the Unitarians are often opposed to the Revisionists.[24] As the name suggests, the latter group regards the *Theaetetus* as a rejection, or at least a substantial revision, of the orthodoxies of Platonic metaphysics.[25] However, I want to indicate briefly why I think it is misleading to consider the dialogue through the lens of the Unitarian-Revisionist alternative. In this way, I can show why I regard the third strand of interpretation noted by Sedley as providing a more appropriate approach to the *Theaetetus* than does the preceding object-related interpretation.

Confining ourselves to the Unitarian-Revisionist alternative begs many questions: Can we determine the order of the dialogues? Do we know enough to speak sensibly about Plato's "development"? Just what should we understand by Plato's metaphysics?[26] Still more problematic, however, is that this

[20] Cornford, *Plato's Theory of Knowledge*, 162–3.

[21] Ibid.

[22] For another example of Unitarianism, see W. D. Ross, *Plato's Theory of Ideas* (Oxford: Oxford University Press, 1953).

[23] Sedley, *The Midwife of Platonism*, 8–13.

[24] For a recent example, see Chappell, *Reading Plato's Theaetetus*, 16–21.

[25] Both McDowell's and Bostock's commentaries express this view. A seminal paper in this regard is G. E. L. Owen, "The Place of the *Timaeus* in Plato's Dialogues," in *Studies in Plato's Metaphysics*, R. E. Allen, ed. (New York: Humanities Press, 1965), 313–38. Given its use of the Forms it becomes important to the Revisionist thesis to place the *Timaeus* earlier in Plato's career than was previously thought. For a defense of the Unitarian thesis on this ground see Harold Cherniss, "The Relation of the *Timaeus* to Plato's Later Dialogues" in Allen, *Studies in Plato's Metaphysics*, 339–78.

[26] In the course of interpreting 186c7–e12, McDowell argues that it is unlikely that Plato has in mind here the Theory of Forms because the passage lacks the features of "the typical expositions of the Theory of Forms." To this claim, Chappell, a committed Unitarian responds, "We could ask, pedantically maybe, whether Plato offers us even one *exposition* of the

alternative directs our attention to an issue that is extrinsic to the dialogue's concern. My point is illustrated when, early in the dialogue, Socrates rejects one of Theaetetus' attempts to define knowledge just because it does take its bearings from the *object* of knowledge. To this attempt Socrates retorts, "but what was asked, Theaetetus, was not that, what things knowledge is about, or how many pieces of knowledge there are; for we didn't ask it because we wanted to count them but in order to discern knowledge itself – whatever that is (146e7–10)." The guiding question of the dialogue directs us not to the object of knowledge, not to what knowledge is *of*, but to the requirements of knowing, out of which the character of the object emerges.[27] To the extent that a picture of the object of knowledge does emerge in the dialogue, it does so as a response to these requirements. These requirements stand at the heart of its concern; hence the emphasis throughout the dialogue on the activities of learning and of inquiry.

For this reason, the third group in Sedley's typology of ancient interpretations of the *Theaetetus* is particularly significant. This group comprises commentators who sought to provide a "subject-related interpretation."[28] Such interpretations do consider the crux of the *Theaetetus* to be its examination of those requirements of knowing that shape the available objects of knowledge. They do not presuppose the character of those objects from the start. My interpretation shares this orientation. However, to avoid an anachronistic and potentially misleading understanding of the term *subject* in this regard, I must immediately add that I do not subscribe to the view that Plato means *only*, in Sedley's words, to "[define] knowledge in terms of the knowing subject's own state."[29] This state undoubtedly forms part of the picture. But the requirements of knowing pertain not only to our psychic apparatus but also to what the beings must be insofar as they are knowable in the ways that they are. The requirements of knowing are not as clearly separable as the subject-object distinction would imply. Apart from this significant caveat, however, my interpretation does agree with this third line of interpretation regarding the *direction* of the dialogue's inquiry. The *Theaetetus*' consideration of knowledge

Theory." Chappell, *Reading Plato's "Theaetetus,"* 148 (emphasis in original). The question is not merely pedantic. Coming especially from a staunch proponent of an orthodox view of Plato's metaphysics, it illustrates the difficulties of summarizing accurately that orthodoxy. On the related difficulties of discerning Plato's philosophic development from the chronology of the dialogues see Jacob Howland, "Re-reading Plato: The Problem of Platonic Chronology," *Phoenix* 45 (1991): 189–214 and Charles H. Kahn, *Plato and the Socratic Dialogue* (Cambridge: Cambridge University Press, 1996), 42–8.

27 Bostock, *Plato's "Theaetetus,"* 243, makes this point explicitly against Cornford. In so doing he follows Gilbert Ryle, "Logical Atomism in Plato's *Theaetetus*," *Phronesis* 35 (1990): 22–3, 44–6. (The article is a transcript of a talk delivered by Ryle in 1952.) For another cogent expression of this view see Mitchell Miller, "Unity and *Logos*: A Reading of *Theaetetus* 201c–210a," *Ancient Philosophy* 12 (1992): 88.

28 Sedley, "Three Platonist Interpretations," 94.

29 Ibid.

begins with reflection on how we really do come to know. From this standpoint, if the dialogue does have a positive outcome it concerns the understanding of the requirements of knowledge discussed therein.

What, then, does the *Theaetetus* tell us about the character of these requirements and how complete is its understanding?[30] With respect to its completeness, some commentators argue that the dialogue provides a definitive account of the meaning of knowledge when read in a philosophically engaged manner.[31] I do not wholly affirm this view for reasons that emerge more fully in my discussion of the last definition of knowledge.[32] In any case, more central to my concern, and to this present effort to differentiate my interpretation from its predecessors, is the former issue of the character of the requirements of knowing. I wish to show that it is with respect to this issue that attention to the political substance of the dialogue pays dividends. If the requirements of knowing provide the context from which the object of knowledge emerges, it is clearly of the utmost importance to map that context as accurately as possible. Only on the basis of such an understanding can we hope to discern what an object of knowledge can be for us. Yet a decisive element of that context has been overlooked due to the relative neglect of the dialogue's political character. It is decisive because it bears on the beginnings of inquiry, which, if we fail to see them clearly, may distort all that follows. By giving the political substance of the dialogue its due attention, I aim to discern as completely as possible the picture of the human context of knowing provided to us in the *Theaetetus*.

30 The discussion that focuses on the objects of knowledge occurs in other dialogues, but these discussions would certainly have to take into account the requirements of knowledge developed in the *Theaetetus*. Whether the Forms as understood by Cornford would satisfy those requirements is at least a question.

31 Among full-length commentaries see, e.g., Desjardins, *The Rational Enterprise*, 7 and Ronald Polansky, *Philosophy and Knowledge: A Commentary on Plato's "Theaetetus"* (Lewisburg, PA: Bucknell University Press, 1992), 237–8. Sedley thinks the dialogue comes very close to achieving this outcome. Sedley, *The Midwife of Platonism*, 5.

32 This incompleteness hinges on the fact that the cognitive capacity, *nous*, by which in other Platonic works we are said to grasp the ultimate object of knowledge as a whole, is absent from the *Theaetetus*. This absence, I will argue, helps Plato focus the discussion on the context of knowing, the beginning of inquiry, rather than on the apprehension of the completed object of knowledge.

2

The Prologue

Introduction

How a work begins – its title, first words, and opening passages – are often taken to be particularly clear indications of an author's intent. The material an author places at the beginning occurs before a plot or an argument exerts constraints. It is reasonable to believe, therefore, that with this greater latitude the author speaks more directly to us, in a manner more reflective of his or her choice. Because of his authorial anonymity such signs are especially valuable to Plato's readers.[1] In these choices the veil of anonymity is for a moment less opaque, affording a glimpse of Plato's authorial hand.

A particular feature of the *Theaetetus* reinforces this need to fix our attention on the dialogue's opening passages. Throughout the dialogue Socrates insists that Theaetetus must reexamine the beginning of the argument in recognition of the extent to which the starting point of reflection shapes all that follows. As active readers of the dialogue we appropriately apply Socrates' advice to the dialogue in which it occurs.

Heeding this advice, we must pay careful attention to the dialogue's Prologue. Such care is not misplaced. For the remarkable Prologue with which Plato begins the *Theaetetus* does shape in discernible ways the subsequent conversation between Socrates and the mathematicians.

Plato uses the device of a prologue in other dialogues, but the *Theaetetus*' Prologue is distinctive in several respects. The scholarly reaction to it helps us appreciate its unusual character. Again, with some notable exceptions, the most prevalent scholarly view regards the Prologue as thoroughly

[1] On the philosophic importance of Platonic anonymity see Charles L. Griswold Jr., "Plato's Metaphilosophy: Why Plato Wrote Dialogues" in *Platonic Writings, Platonic Readings*, ed. Charles L. Griswold Jr. (New York: Routledge, 1988), 160–4 and Diskin Clay, *Platonic Questions: Dialogues with the Silent Philosopher* (University Park: The Pennsylvania State University Press, 2000), 3, 11, 17, 90, 145, 268.

dispensable.[2] Pursuing this line, some contemporary commentators pick up on a report of the ancient anonymous commentator that an alternative version of the Prologue existed. From this report, they conclude that the Prologue in its present form does not even belong to the dialogue proper.[3] More usual than this outright dismissal, however, is either a cursory treatment or simple neglect. Some of this treatment reflects, no doubt, an eagerness to get beyond the merely "dramatic" interplay of the Prologue and into the meaty "epistemological" arguments of the dialogue. Certainly, the Prologue does not appear to have any material nearly as philosophically engaging as the upcoming arguments. Seemingly, it could be removed without affecting the subsequent conversation, which could easily stand on its own as a nonnarrated dialogue.

However, it is just this apparently adventitious character that makes the Prologue, not only in its content but also in its very existence, particularly suggestive of Plato's intent. Just because the apparent requirements of the argument do not include the Prologue, its presence is more clearly a matter of Plato's choice. Seeing how this choice contributes to the dialogue's intention provides the most persuasive response to those who would hasten past the Prologue.

Why does Plato make the reader of the dialogue pass through the antechamber of the Prologue before entering the great hall of the argument? If it afforded unfettered passage, this device *would* seem little more than an authorial affectation, providing a note of "dramatic reality" to the proceedings. But Plato fills this foyer with information that cannot be ignored as we enter into the main argument of the dialogue. What we learn in this corridor substantively shapes our judgment of that argument.

To begin to examine the *Theaetetus*' Prologue, it is helpful to compare it with the Prologue of the *Phaedo*, the concluding chapter in the story of the trial and death of Socrates. The two Prologues share some distinctive features. In the *Phaedo* we listen to the story of Socrates' deathday told by Phaedo, some indeterminate but apparently substantial time after the event (57a6–b2). Phaedo was present in Socrates' cell on his deathday, but he was not Socrates' main interlocutor. Phaedo tells his story to Echecrates and other philosophically interested students at Echecrates' school in Phlius. Likewise, in the Prologue of the *Theaetetus*, we listen to the conversation between Euclides and Terpsion, two adherents of the Megarian school of philosophy, both of whom were also present in Socrates' cell on the day of his death. These two converse not in Athens but in their hometown of Megara.[4] Their conversation

[2] Neither Cornford, McDowell, or Bostock find anything of philosophic import in the Prologue.

[3] See, e.g., Klein, *Plato's Trilogy*, 75. On the sources of this report, see Cornford, *Plato's Theory of Knowledge*, 15; and Sedley, *The Midwife of Platonism*, 1n2. My view that the Prologue as we have it is the one Plato intended depends finally on the strength of the substantive links I draw between the Prologue and the rest of the dialogue.

[4] Diogenes Laertius, *Lives of Eminent Philosophers* (Cambridge, MA: Harvard University Press, 1980), ii, 106–12, notes that Plato was said to have gone to Megara after the execution

occurs some thirty years after Socrates discussed the meaning of knowledge with Theaetetus.[5] Euclides' chance meeting with Theaetetus causes him to recall the conversation that Socrates, now long dead, had with the then young boy.

These Prologues, attached to the opening and closing chapters of the drama of Socrates' trial and execution, occur distanced in space and time from Socrates' life and death. In both cases we depend on a relatively undistinguished acquaintance of Socrates for our access to his thought. Both situate us in the atmosphere of the philosophic school. Plato thus affords us the opportunity to hear how Socrates' thought would be treated after his death by students, disciples, and epigones.[6] He shows us how Socrates' life and thought become a story, a tradition transmitted to subsequent generations.

Philosophic reflection, like all knowledge, is subject to the necessarily unpredictable vagaries of time, place, and individual capacity. But for such reflection to become a tradition, an accepted and largely unchallenged view must strike at the very heart of an activity that aims at complete wakefulness. In this light, there is something oxymoronic and disconcerting about referring to "the Socratic tradition." Through the Prologue of the *Theaetetus*, however, Plato acknowledges this danger and directs us to its antidote. By raising this issue of transmission Plato means exactly to highlight the human context of philosophy, those particular preconditions that generate and orient its concerns. A central theme of the subsequent conversation is the need for persistent attention to this context as crucial to philosophic activity. Careful consideration of the Prologue provides training in the kind of attention required.

Like all contexts, the one that the Prologue imposes on Socrates' conversation with Theaetetus is woven out of disparate strands. Three of these strands seem particularly important because, on the one hand, they bear decisively on our assessment of the subsequent conversation, but, on the other, we would be unaware of them without the Prologue. I refer specifically to the following three items of information: (1) Euclides' modification of the transcript from indirect to direct discourse, (2) the sight of the mortally wounded Theaetetus dying in the service of Athens, and, finally, (3) Socrates' avid interest in preserving his conversation with Theaetetus. Plato weaves together these seemingly unrelated facts to provide the context for the examination of the meaning of knowledge. We must determine why together they provide the appropriate prelude to this conversation.

of Socrates. With respect to their names, Andrew Ford writes, "When the son of 'Good Fame' presents a text to 'Pleasure', we may suspect a deliberate revision of traditional oral transmission as represented by Homer." See Andrew Ford, "Protagoras' Head: Interpreting Philosophic Fragments in Theaetetus," *American Journal of Philology* 115 (1994): 216n30. This observation is especially pertinent to my interpretation of the Digression which I regard as an episode in Socrates' contest with Homer.

5 See Chapter 1, n. 3.

6 On this point, see Polansky, *Philosophy and Knowledge*, 35.

The First Strand: The Megarians and the Problem of Knowledge

Why does Plato choose Euclides and Terpsion as the curtain raisers for the dramatic portrayal of Socrates' last days? As I mentioned, in the *Phaedo* Plato notes that Terpsion as well as Euclides, representatives of the Megarian school of philosophy, were present at the philosophic convention in Socrates' cell on his very last day.[7] But as I also noted, even prior to Socrates' deathday Euclides visited him often as he sat in his cell awaiting the ship from Delos and death. The admiration that prompted these visits persists even thirty years after Socrates' demise. No doubt, this admiration, shared by Terpsion, arises in part from what every student of philosophy must feel for the intrepid philosopher. In the Megarians' case, however, its roots reach to a more specific philosophic similarity with Socrates.[8] This similarity sets the stage for the problem Socrates faces in the question explored in his conversation with Theaetetus, what is knowledge?

As the Prologue begins, Terpsion finally meets up with Euclides whom he had been expecting to see earlier in the city. Euclides explains that his unwonted absence was due to a chance meeting with Theaetetus, wounded in battle at Corinth and suffering from dysentery, as he was being carried home to Athens. Euclides accompanied Theaetetus on part of his journey, unable to persuade him to remain in Megara rather than continue the grueling trip to Athens in his debilitated condition (142a1–b3).[9] Moved by these events, Euclides and Terpsion recall Socrates' conversation with this same Theaetetus many years before.

Neither Euclides nor Terpsion heard that conversation firsthand. But Euclides does possess a transcribed reconstruction of it, a document that was produced by a rather intricate process. During Euclides' numerous visits to Socrates' cell, Socrates would relate portions of this conversation to him. After each visit, on his return home, Euclides would immediately write up reminders of what Socrates had said and later, at his leisure, turn these notes into a more complete account. On his subsequent visits Euclides would show Socrates this work-in-progress, with Socrates providing corrections for further editing (142c8–a5).[10]

Now Terpsion and Euclides are tired from the day's meanderings and wish to relax. Having stated this desire they are at once present at Euclides' house where the text in question is produced. Euclides directs a slave-boy to read

7 Ronna Burger, *The "Phaedo": A Platonic Labyrinth* (New Haven, CT: Yale University Press, 1984), 59c2.

8 Jane Harrison, "Plato's Prologue: *Theaetetus* 142a–143c," *Tulane Studies in Philosophy* 27 (1978): 112–15, best brings out this philosophic affinity.

9 Chappell notes that the word for Euclides' escort services – *propempein* – is also the word for accompanying a corpse to its burial. Chappell, *Reading Plato's "Theaetetus,"* 26n18.

10 In the *Phaedo* (58c5) we are told that because of Athens' ceremony recalling Theseus' slaying of the Minotaur, Socrates spent a "long time" in prison between his trial and death. Euclides says he asked Socrates "again and again" about what he didn't remember (143a4).

the transcript of the conversation among Socrates, Theaetetus, and Theodorus. Thus, we join our fellow auditors, Euclides and Terpsion (143a8–c7).

By this contrivance Plato obstructs our immediate view of the conversation, not only by the insertion of space and time but also by the intervening characters of the Megarian philosophers. Plato makes both the form and the content dependent particularly on Euclides. In this way, he interposes a screen between us and Socrates' thought; hence, the temptation to remove that screen, to proceed directly to the main conversation.

The mediocrity of Euclides makes this temptation all the more acute. Neither he nor Terpsion seems a remarkable intelligence. If Euclides had been more promising, Socrates would no doubt have engaged him in conversation rather than employing him as an amanuensis of uncertain talent; Euclides himself indicates that his memory certainly does not rank with Socrates' (143a1). As for Terpsion, he had known about the transcript for some thirty years but only now asks to hear it. Once the reading begins we never again hear from either character. Neither of them interrupts the slave-boy's reading with a single question or comment, the exertion of the day perhaps having taken its toll.

Rather than worthy models of critical intelligence, Euclides and Terpsion seem to embody Socrates' worries about writing, presenting as they do a picture of ossified philosophy.[11] Yet, before wholly endorsing Socrates' indictment of written philosophy, we should note first that Plato portrays Socrates himself as having a hand in the production of this transcript (a point I explore further in the following text). Plato presents the conversation as available to Euclides and Terpsion, and us, only because of Socrates' efforts. Perhaps late in his life Socrates concluded that written philosophy need not be inert. Certainly, Plato's writing is anything but inert, at least if we as readers respond to its provocations.[12] In the present case, this requires us to take the silent assent of the Megarians as an admonitory example, a spur to ask the questions they leave unasked. Again, careful attention to the Prologue prepares us for just this task.

In this undertaking we can begin from the recognition that the Megarians' influence, especially that of Euclides, persists throughout the dialogue.[13] The Prologue thus highlights our dependence on the particular capacities and views of this specific individual. But how should we interpret this dependence? Although the effect of Euclides' intellectual limitations on the transcript's accuracy may be incalculable, we can assess the meaning and import of

[11] *Phaedrus* 274b6–277a5. See, also, Andrea Tschemplik, "Framing the Question of Knowledge: Beginning Plato's *Theaetetus*," in *Plato's Dialogues: New Studies and Interpretations*, ed. Gerald A. Press (Lanham, MD: Rowman and Littlefield Press, 1993), 174.

[12] With respect to the "living" character of Plato's writing see Charles L. Griswold Jr., *Self-Knowledge in Plato's "Phaedrus"* (New Haven, CT: Yale University Press, 1986), 219–26.

[13] See Blondell, *The Play of Character*, 306–7 on the limitations of these Megarians.

Euclides' most significant modification of the conversation: his editorial decision to transform Socrates' reported conversation from indirect to direct discourse, as if it were occurring immediately in the present.

Euclides explains his preference for direct discourse as an avoidance of trouble (143b8–c1). Specifically, he is reluctant to include the many "he said's" in his transcript (143c1–6). But it is not simply laziness, or some other character defect, that underlies this reluctance. Rather, what makes this preference of utmost interest is its connection to the most famous of the Megarians' philosophic views. We need to consider that view to understand fully the significance of this preference and thus the appropriateness of the Megarians' presence in the Prologue.

Aristotle's brief account of the Megarian school in his *Metaphysics* is one of the few sources for our understanding of its view. His account is especially useful for our purposes because of its resonances with the *Theaetetus*, the most important of which concerns the idea of potential.[14] Plato makes this idea prominent in the Prologue's comparison of the mature Theaetetus with the young boy who was so full of promise thirty years ago.[15] Euclides expresses wonder at Socrates' prophecy that the youthful Theaetetus would "become renowned if he reached maturity (142d1–3)." It is all the more striking then that their denial of the reality of potential constitutes the Megarians' most famous philosophic position. Aristotle notes that this Megarian view leads to absurdities, and Plato depicts these absurdities in the tension between the Megarians' words and deeds that we will consider in the following text. Yet despite its nonsensical consequences, Aristotle, like Plato, considers the view of sufficient philosophic importance to bring to our attention. There must be something serious about such an apparently implausible view, if only the philosophic motivation that leads to its adoption.

As Aristotle notes, one consequence of the Megarians' denial of the distinction between actuality and potentiality is that they "eliminate motion and generation."[16] If there is only actuality, there is no explaining how anything

14 My understanding of Aristotle's treatment of the Megarians is informed especially by Stanley Rosen, "Dynamis, Energeia, and the Megarians," *Philosophical Inquiry* 1 (1979): 105–19; Charlotte Witt, "Powers and Possibilities: Aristotle vs. The Megarians," in *Proceedings of the Boston Area Colloquium in Ancient Philosophy*, vol. XI, eds. John J. Cleary and William Wians (Lanham, MD: University Press of America, 1995), 249–66; Arthur Madigan, S. J., "Commentary on Witt" in *Proceedings of the Boston Area Colloquium in Ancient Philosophy*, vol. XI, eds. John J. Cleary and William Wians (Lanham, MD: University Press of America, 1995), 267–73; and Stephen Menn, "The Origins of Aristotle's Concept of *energeia*: *energeia* and *dunamis*," *Ancient Philosophy* 14 (1994): 73–114.

15 Menn notes Aristotle's criticism that Plato does not clearly formulate the actual-potential distinction. But as Menn also shows, the distinction is implicit in the *Euthydemus* at 280b5–282a6 in its distinction of possession and use, and in the *Theaetetus* at 197a8–c8 in the distinction between merely possessing and actually having, or taking hold of, knowledge. See Menn, "The Origins," 73–5, 81–7, 112–13.

16 Aristotle *Metaphysics* 1047a14.

could come to be *where* or, more importantly for the dialogue, *what* it is not now.[17] It is not difficult to appreciate the failure of such a view to account for the world as we experience it, a world in which there is both constant movement and development. As one of several examples of this failure, Aristotle cites the impossibility of explaining on Megarian grounds our acquisition of an art and thus, by implication, any learning whatsoever.[18] He also addresses the consequences for beings in general, maintaining that on the Megarians' view "nothing will have the potency of being cold or hot or sweet or in general of being sensed unless it is being sensed."[19] Aristotle concludes that in this case the Megarians turn out to be "asserting the doctrine of Protagoras" that nothing is in itself.[20] Both these difficulties prove to play significant roles in the dialogue, as does "the doctrine of Protagoras."

But the ease with which Aristotle, or anyone, might pile up the absurdities consequent on the Megarian view simply makes more pointed the question of why the view deserves his, or Plato's, philosophic attention. Aristotle's treatment of the Megarians indicates that the answer to this question lies in the difficulty of explaining change in general and potential in particular.

When speaking of change or generation we necessarily speak of that which *is not* – the log burned in the fire is no more; the infant now exists where one did not before. Yet the log cannot simply pass into nothing nor the child come from nothing. Were this prohibition not in place, were it possible for something to come to be from or pass into nothing, there would be in principle no limits regarding what cause might lead to what effect. Any being might come from, or change into, any other being. Such beings or kinds of beings would have nothing whatsoever determinate about them. The very notion of a kind of being, of a being having this or that character, would be undermined. Lacking determinacy, knowledge of the beings would be impossible. We would not be able to say *what* they are.

In light of this outcome, the Eleatics, philosophic mentors to the Megarians, balked at the idea of potential because it necessarily invokes the notion of not-being: what is only potentially is not what it is actually. And speech and thought about not-being must, they insisted, be avoided at all costs.[21] The premise of this prohibition against not-being asserted by the Eleatics, and shared by

[17] Menn notes that "what the Megarians were denying was neither change nor possibility . . . but Aristotle's analysis of change and possibility in terms of active and passive capacities and their exercise." He draws this conclusion from the use of the word *energeia* in the passage that refers to activity rather than actuality. But Menn does note here that "*energeia* sometimes means merely 'actuality'." Moreover, later in his article he writes that in *Metaphysics*, ix, where the reference to the Megarians occurs, Aristotle avoids the term *entelexeia* and uses *energeia* for "actuality" as freely as for "activity." Menn, "The Origins," 94n31, 105.

[18] Ibid., 1046b36–1047a4.

[19] Ibid., 1047a4–6.

[20] Ibid., 1047a6–7.

[21] On the connection between the Megarians and the Eleatics, see Campbell, *The "Theaetetus" of Plato*, xi–xii and W. D. Ross, *Aristotle's "Metaphysics"* (Oxford: Clarendon Press, 1970), 244.

the Megarians, derives from the deeper prohibition against something coming from or passing into nothing. And both, in turn, rest on reflection, by those most intent on knowledge, concerning the necessary conditions of intelligibility.

To preserve intelligibility, the Megarians' Eleatic precursors – most famously, Parmenides – were led to "say that the One and the whole of nature is immovable not only with respect to generation and distinction (for this was an old belief and agreed upon by all) but also with respect to every other change."[22] That is, thinkers such as Parmenides denied not only that nature as a whole undergoes change but also that the particulars do so. Thus what we take to be coming into being and passing away reflects changes only in the affections. As when someone becomes noble, we do not say that he is generated in the full sense or that he perishes in the full sense if he loses this quality because he persists as an underlying subject.

Yet this response leaves a problem as well, one that leads to the requirement that not only the underlying nature or subject be inalterable but also its affections. For it leaves open the question of how this underlying subject relates to what does change. If we cannot explain this relationship we still cannot account for how a being might undergo a far-reaching change from, say, ignobility to nobility or from boyhood to manhood. Again, the intelligibility of the beings is left dubious.[23] Accordingly, in their effort to preserve intelligibility, the Megarians insist that what is not yet, what is only potentially, cannot be decisively different from that which actually is. The desire to circumvent the difficulty of explaining change and generation motivates the Megarians' assertion that only that which is actual is. Intelligibility, they concluded, demands the paradoxical claim that all change is illusory, including change in the particular beings.

Given that particulars as such must change, however, the ultimate result of this claim would seem to be a denial of particularity and thus of the way in which we experience the world. Euclides' editorial activity is a direct product of this denial. For the Megarians we live in an eternal "now," a conception that avoids acknowledging the flux of particulars as part of our experience. Thus, as Jane Harrison notes, when Euclides translates the conversation from indirect to direct discourse, he "forces the listener to hear the thirty year old interchange as though it were going on 'just now,'" the words with which the dialogue begins.[24] With this modification, Euclides eliminates the temporal context preserved by narrativity. He closes that temporal gap between the account and the event, the existence of which could remind us that our knowledge is subject to the vagaries of flux.[25]

[22] Aristotle *Metaphysics* 984a31–b1.

[23] I owe this point to David Bolotin, "The Eleatic Stranger and Parmenides in Plato's *Sophist*." Lecture delivered at St. John's College, Santa Fe, New Mexico, January 14, 2004, 5–9.

[24] See Harrison, "Plato's Prologue," 106.

[25] On the distinction between performed and narrative dialogues, see Leo Strauss, *The City and Man* (Chicago: University of Chicago Press, 1977), 58–9. Regarding the implications of narrativity see David M. Halperin, "Plato and the Erotics of Narrativity," in *Oxford Studies in Ancient Philosophy*, suppl. vol., ed. Julia Annas (Oxford: Clarendon Press, 1992), 102–4.

Euclides' editorial efforts aim as well, and for the same reason, to eliminate particularity altogether. The Megarians insisted that what has reality can be found only in speech – specifically, speech that is immediate and explicit in the manner of direct discourse.[26] So when Euclides says that he edits the conversation to avoid, as he puts it, "trouble," he refers also to the things (*pragmata*), the deeds or particulars which, in their particularity and consequent flux, fall outside the Megarians' theoretical premise (143c1, 143b5–c5). Accordingly, he omits as unreal whatever gestures, comments on intonation, characterization of posture, in sum, whatever deeds Socrates might have noted in the indirect discourse of his narration.[27]

Euclides' editorial abstractions lose the context of the speeches. Most telling in this regard is how little heed he pays to the fact that Socrates recounts his conversation while in his cell awaiting execution (142c5–6). Euclides' editorial efforts bespeak a desire to neglect all these considerations. He wishes to treat the participants as disembodied *logoi* rather than as embodied individuals who must be known not only through speech but also by the joint lived experience that Socrates calls "association" (142c7).[28]

I have already referred to the absurdities generated by the abstractions of the Megarian position. Plato makes us aware of these absurdities throughout the Prologue by displaying the numerous discrepancies between the Megarians' theoretical orientation and the manner in which they conduct their daily lives, that is, between their words and their deeds. Such discrepancies abound, as they must, in light of a view that finds reality only in that which is fully actual right now as expressed in speech. Such a view reduces life to disconnected moments. It is incapable of "connecting the dots," of tracing the arc of change characteristic of our experience. In this result it is indistinguishable from its opposite, the doctrine of radical flux, which occupies so much of the forthcoming conversation. Both views deny the essential characteristic of a specifically human life, namely, its capacity for being seen *as a life*, as a whole comprising all the inevitable changes and thus as somehow partaking of both stability and flux.

However, this means that merely by living their lives Euclides and Terpsion must violate their own theoretical orientation: they do distinguish between past and present, regard not only Theaetetus but also one another as having sustained identities, have expectations of one another, and, most tellingly, invoke the notion of potential (e.g., 142a1, a2–3, c3–5). A few of the numerous examples of these theoretical violations suffice to make the point.

Speaking of Theaetetus, Terpsion exclaims, "What a man (*andra*) you say is in danger (142b6)!" This phrase, "what a man," carries with it the implication

[26] See Aristocles *De Philosophia* vii in Eusebius. *Praeparatio Evangelica*. xiv. VII.1. I owe this reference to Harrison, "Plato's Prologue," 106n13.

[27] On this point, see Benardete, *Being of the Beautiful*, I.86.

[28] I deal with the significance of the word *association* in Chapter 3.

that individuals of a certain type might be more and less of what they are. It implies, in short, that manliness is not an all-or-nothing condition, that it partakes of degrees, the various examples of which we measure against some standard. Still more explicit in this regard, however, is Euclides' account of Socrates' prophecy, mentioned in the preceding text, in which he reports Socrates saying there "is every necessity that [Theaetetus] become renowned if he reaches maturity (142d2–3)." Necessarily implied by the notion of reaching maturity must be some enduring idea of fulfillment that, at each interim point, Theaetetus would both be and not be. Euclides expresses wonder at Socrates' prophetic power; he does not charge him with invoking an unreal notion.

The Megarians' view then leaves a great discrepancy between their theoretical outlook and the world in which they live. If knowledge requires an accurate account of "what is," then this gap between word and deed suggests the Megarians' view falls short of knowledge.[29] Yet before dismissing the Megarians out of hand, we must ask whether there is a theoretical explanation that would dispel the Megarian absurdities even now available.

It is not clear that invoking the notion of potential, as the Megarians were reluctant to do, resolves the issue. Aristotle takes this step, but his account does not dispel all difficulties. Aristotle appeals to the distinction between the potential and the actual to account for the unity of "those things that have more than one part, and of which the sum is not like a heap but a whole that is something over and above the parts."[30] Given this difference, the elements of the whole only constitute it as its parts by virtue of the addition of some unifying principle. Unless and until such a development occurs, they are that whole only in a manner of speaking. Put otherwise, they both are and are not that whole.[31]

The specific difficulty addressed by the potential-actual distinction concerns the perplexed relationship between the elements of the whole and that unifying principle that accounts for the elements' transformation into parts of the whole. From its beginning, the *Theaetetus* too links the notion of potential and the being of wholes. Throughout the dialogue the difficulty of accounting for their being stands as *the* expression of the problem of knowledge.[32] Unfortunately, regarding this transformation as an actualization of a potential does

[29] See Benardete, *Being of the Beautiful*, 87–8 and Chappell, *Reading Plato's "Theaetetus,"* 29–30.

[30] Aristotle *Metaphysics* 1045a9–10.

[31] For a discussion of this issue, see Stewart Umphrey, *Complexity and Analysis* (Lanham, MD: Lexington Books, 2002), 65–6.

[32] Desjardins makes the notion of what she terms "emergent wholes" the centerpiece of her interpretation of the *Theaetetus*. I agree regarding the importance of this kind of whole. I think it is at least important, however, to understand the dialogue's teaching regarding the human significance of such wholes in general and their bearing on the character of philosophic inquiry in particular.

not perfectly resolve the question. As Aristotle states, "what is in potency and what is in activity are *in a certain way one thing*."[33] The necessary implication is that in a certain way they are *not* one thing.[34] Aristotle's ambiguity in this formulation preserves this problem of accounting for wholes.

Admittedly the gap between experience and its theoretical account is more yawning in the Megarians' case than in Aristotle's. But throughout the *Theaetetus* we see Socrates himself struggle to provide theoretical explanations of such undeniable aspects of our experience as error and falsehood, identity and change.[35] For Socrates, too, there is an abiding discrepancy between what we think and the being of the world. In the *Theaetetus*, the aforementioned gap between the being of wholes and our knowledge of them underlies this discrepancy.

From this standpoint, the Megarians' orientation becomes more understandable. Their insistence on crediting only the actual, the fixed and stable – akin to their philosophic uncles, the Eleatics – does lead to absurdities, but it does so in the name of preserving the availability of a stable object of knowledge. That which we can characterize most accurately, that which we can know best, is that which most endures as itself. Accordingly, it is held that the most knowable is that which is one, which is at rest.

It can be argued that Socrates also embraces this notion, at least in part, in his claim that the intelligible, the Forms, although multiple, are unchanging.[36] To someone like Socrates, intent on gaining knowledge, the philosophic allure of the Megarian view – and behind it the Parmenidean view – is clear. Socrates' veneration of Parmenides, as well as his emulation of the Megarians' eristic deployment of an absolute distinction between being and not-being, suggests such affinity. Yet those famous doctrines of the Forms and Recollection, which together might assuage some skeptical anxieties, are absent from the *Theaetetus*. Neither is it clear, even at the end of his life, that Socrates regarded these doctrines as demonstrable.[37] The character of the object of knowledge, in any case, remains problematic to the *Theaetetus'* very end.

Thus although the Megarians may share with Socrates a view of the hoped-for character of knowledge, they lack his willingness to take the momentous step that led him away from his predecessor's rigidities. They lack his willingness to confront the possibility that the world may not be constructed to

33 Aristotle *Metaphysics* 1045b21, 1048a30 (emphasis added).

34 See Rosen, "*Dynamis*, *Energeia*, and the Megarians," 115–19 and Madigan, "Commentary on Witt," 269–72.

35 This same difficulty is, arguably, pointed to in the very title of the work in its commemoration of a mathematician whose discoveries regarding irrational numbers suggest a permanent discrepancy between what we can think and the constitution of the empirical world. See Cropsey, *Plato's World*, 27–9.

36 Campbell, *The "Theaetetus" of Plato*, xi–xii presents Euclides' thought as a hybrid of Parmenides and Socrates.

37 *Phaedo* 76d7–e7, 100d5–6.

answer to this hope, his willingness to confront the implications of our distance from "what is." Such willingness is evident throughout the *Theaetetus* in Socrates' numerous expressions of cognitive humility and in his self-criticism. Like the Megarians, he strives for knowledge of "what is," but he is intent on avoiding their absurdities. Socrates aims, in particular, to avoid adopting a view that makes the world as we experience it inexplicable, an outcome indicative of a dogmatically asserted rationalism. Crucial to achieving this aim is precisely an understanding of the problem of knowledge which, as I will argue, makes Socratic inquiry possible and necessary. The distinctiveness of Socrates' inquiry is best displayed through an examination of its decisive differences from those with whom he has much in common. Plato appropriately chooses the Megarians to introduce this examination.

Socrates has a most pressing reason to avoid the Megarian path. This examination is, for him, no idle inquiry. As he relates his conversation with Theaetetus to Euclides, he sits in a cell awaiting execution for living a life in pursuit of knowledge. Can knowledge understood as partial, and perhaps even ultimately problematic, justify paying this ultimate price? Were we wholly dependent on Euclides' account we would not know of the practical and very particular bearing of this abstract question. But Plato's Prologue frees us from such dependence through making explicit that deed by which Euclides omits mention of the deeds. Plato thus alerts us to our task throughout the dialogue: to consider the practical, particular meaning of the abstract problem of knowledge which drives Socrates' inquiry on.

In making us aware of the difference between the event of Socrates' conversation and Euclides' account of it, Plato makes the reader experience the discrepancy between "what is" and an account of "what is." He makes us experience an instance of the problem of knowledge. In rendering us explicitly dependent on Euclides he lets us see that in the face of that problem we can meliorate distortion in our understanding only if we begin by considering the bearing of particulars – of capacity, orientation, and circumstance – as they shape our knowing. Accordingly, the question now before us is, among the multiplicity of particulars available for consideration, which are most critical for the question of knowledge? Plato responds to this question with the second strand of the context woven by this Prologue.

The Second Strand: Political Life and the Problem of Knowledge

The Prologue directs our attention to two exceedingly dramatic particulars: the impending death of Theaetetus and the long-ago death of Socrates.[38] But why should these deeds be so central to our grappling with the problem of knowledge? Perhaps it is that death is the deed par excellence in that it

[38] The political significance of the two deaths is recognized by Polansky, *Philosophy and Knowledge*, 35.

most clearly underscores our particularity. If we grasp all that this particularity entails we might then understand why we must seek knowledge rather than possessing it immediately.

Although true, this explanation is incomplete. It leaves out the profoundly political character of both deaths. The bearing of particularity on knowledge may be the issue, but we need to recognize that Plato makes this particularity available to us in a political mode. This raises a more specific question: why should we need, above all, to consider these political deeds or, more generally, the political context in examining the problem of knowledge? The details of the Prologue sketch the answer that is explored in the rest of the dialogue.

The lens through which Plato gives us our first glimpse of Theaetetus is undeniably political. Theaetetus' circumstances reflect the most dramatic and concrete of political facts: he is a soldier dying in the service of his community. Again, Euclides tells of Theaetetus, wounded and suffering from dysentery, being carried from the battle at Corinth where he acquitted himself courageously. Near death, he insists on pressing homeward for Athens, heedless of Euclides' protests regarding his condition (142a6–b3). Plato portrays Theaetetus as a war hero, a patriot willing to lay down his life fighting for Athens, so attached to his city that he risks hastening death to ensure dying at home.

Such patriotism does not figure into the portrayal of the young Theaetetus. As a youth his notoriety derives instead from his intellectual promise especially in mathematics, a promise borne out by the mathematical discoveries to which his name is attached.[39] Yet when Euclides and Terpsion praise him it is his civic virtue rather than his mathematical accomplishments, which they do not specifically mention, that earns Theaetetus their praise. Such is his virtue that even these non-Athenians accord him the traditional Greek characterization of the perfect gentleman, referring to Theaetetus as *kalon te kai agathon*, noble (or beautiful) and good (142b7). Although this phrase is not at all unusual in the Platonic corpus, the frequency of its usage cannot be taken as an index of the clarity of its meaning. The phrase carries with it significant difficulties that bear on the present inquiry.

Most basically, the compound character of the phrase raises the question of the relationship between the beautiful and the good. To repeat, this phrase is traditionally used to characterize the perfect or complete gentleman, the citizen who goes beyond fulfillment of the basic requirements of citizenship to epitomize the virtues his community admires, especially selfless devotion to that community. The addition of "beautiful" to "good" aims to capture

[39] Theaetetus is referred to as a child (*pais* or *paidion*) at 162d3, 166a3, 166d8, 184d1, and 209e7 and as a lad (*meirakion*) at 142c6, 143e5, 144c8, 146b2, and 168e3. His age is approximately fifteen at the time of the conversation. Thomas Heath writes that Theaetetus laid the foundation of the theory of irrationals as we find it in Euclid, *Elements*, bk. X. He also contributed to Euclid's *Elements*, bk. XIII, which concerns the construction of the five regular solids. See Thomas Heath, *Greek Mathematics* (New York: Dover, 1963), 133–4.

this self-transcendent aspect of the formula: the aspiration that looks beyond what is merely advantageous or useful, that aspires to something more than that which pertains to us as finite individuals. On one understanding of the beautiful, it is precisely awareness of this finitude, of our mortality, that moves us to seek in beauty a compensation for these limits.[40] Whether this will be Socrates' understanding remains to be seen. The present point is that the idea of the beautiful or noble answers to our sense that the wholeness or fulfillment of human life requires something more than the satisfaction of those mundane necessities concomitant with our individual existences.

Theaetetus' plight seems to evoke exactly this sense in Euclides and Terpsion. It is, apparently, what moves the former to diverge from his usual habits and the latter to ask to hear the thirty-year-old conversation although he has long known of its existence (142a2–3, 143a6–7). They are moved, moreover, to assess the meaning of Theaetetus' life as a whole, its significance and its worth – and perhaps wonder about their own. In so doing, the Megarians violate their own theoretical premises for they thereby treat Theaetetus' life not as a series of disconnected moments but as a human life, that is, as a whole lived in the light of some idea of fulfillment. Furthermore, in reacting this way to Theaetetus' impending death, they express the idea of specifically human mortality that permeates the dialogue from the beginning. Such mortality is characterized not only by a concern to remain in existence but also a concern for the significance of that existence.[41] Being aware that human life as a whole has an end, they, and we, can perhaps not help but wonder about its meaning as such.

Theaetetus' activity can be regarded as an archetypal example of an aspiration for the noble, an act that seeks to transcend particularity through devotion to something beyond oneself. He overcomes the very basis of self-concern for the sake of his beloved Athens. In the same act, however, Theaetetus illustrates most vividly the tension expressed in the traditional formula, "beautiful and good"; these praiseworthy noble deeds have him at death's door. Terpsion's previously mentioned exclamation – "what a man you say is in danger" – encapsulates this same tension (142b6). Theaetetus' nobility – "what a man" – places him "in danger" and so threatens the undeniable good of his survival. In what way is that which is beautiful or noble also good for the individual performing the noble deed? This is the unavoidable question when the desire to live in a beautiful or noble manner, to be a real man (*andra*) as defined by one's community, jeopardizes the satisfaction of the desire simply to be.

[40] For a treatment of the issues raised by the phrase, "beautiful and good" see Mark Lutz, *Socrates' Education to Virtue: Learning the Love of the Noble* (Albany: State University of New York Press, 1998), 92–110.

[41] Erineos, the place to which Euclides accompanied Theaetetus (143b1), is the location from which Hades abducted Persephone. See Hesiod, *Theogeny*, 773. Walter Burkert writes that through the Persephone story "a dimension of death is introduced to life." See Walter Burkert, *Greek Religion* (Cambridge, MA: Harvard University Press, 1985), 161.

There may be some view of nobility or beauty or, to speak more generally, of human fulfillment that would reconcile this conflict and be truly good for the individual. Yet as we will see throughout the *Theaetetus*, the meaning of beauty remains a question.[42] This questionableness is evident already in the Prologue's ambiguity about the meaning of human fulfillment. Theaetetus developed into a distinguished mathematician and a war hero. Which constituted the fulfillment of his potential? Was it his intellectual accomplishments or the manliness that enabled him to defend his homeland? By showing us the mature Theaetetus before we see the boy, Plato sets this question before us.

There is hardly a more appropriate place for this question than the beginning of the *Theaetetus*. The question of how one ought to live goes to the core of the Socratic story that the *Theaetetus* initiates. In juxtaposing these two lives, or rather deaths, the Prologue depicts the difficulty in understanding human fulfillment, the decisive issue of Socrates' trial, most incisively. The endeavors of both Theaetetus and Socrates are highly praised and regarded as beautiful, but the political outcome of their lives makes clear how opposed these endeavors are. The city for which Theaetetus gives up his life is the same city that executes Socrates. Through understanding this juxtaposition we can begin to grasp why Plato would focus on political deeds in this Prologue to a dialogue whose theme, the problem of knowledge, seems far from any political concern.[43]

These deaths illustrate the conflicts, internal and external, characteristic of political communities. In these conflicts, people may even stake their lives. By introducing an investigation into the meaning of knowledge with this evocation of political conflicts, Plato points most obviously to one urgent aim of the quest for knowledge. Divergent practices result in the deaths of Socrates and Theaetetus, the former executed for impious and corrupt philosophizing, the latter defending his homeland. Given this divergence, either Theaetetus or Socrates (or both) must have given his life for something less than the highest cause. Where one's very life is at stake one must want to know for sure which way is right. It is, therefore, urgently important to know what exactly constitutes human fulfillment in order to find some guidance for our most critical choices.

Equipped with such knowledge, it is perhaps even possible that the conflicts that engendered events as lamentable as Theaetetus' war and Socrates' execution might well be avoided. Such hopes fuel our quest for knowledge. Yet, regrettably, even today these conflicts remain unfortunate but not unusual

42 Although Theaetetus is praised as beautiful by Euclides and Terpsion, later in the dialogue Theodorus judges him second only to Socrates in ugliness (143e8–9). Still later, Socrates once again calls Theaetetus "beautiful and good," this time for his beautiful speeches rather than deeds, the ground also of Socrates' prophecy regarding Theaetetus' success (185e3–5; see also 209b10–c3 and 210d1–2).

43 Polansky, *Philosophy and Knowledge*, 36, notes "the surprising political context" of the Prologue. See also Tschemplik, "Beginning Plato's *Theaetetus*," 175.

features of political life. Force, as well as deliberation, still plays a role in the resolution of political controversy.

This persistence of conflict, however, may point beyond this practical need for knowledge to a still deeper connection between the problem of knowledge and political life. When we reflect on this persistence, in conjunction with the previous reflections on the phrase "beautiful and good," we must consider this troubling possibility: further knowledge regarding human nature may not yield the peace and harmony we seek. A clearer understanding of humanity might rather reveal that politics remains a scene of conflict precisely due to the imperfect reconcilability of human desires expressed in the "noble (beautiful) and good" formula. It is perhaps not corrigible ignorance that underlies the enduring conflict of political life but the problematic nature of the human whole.

The political strand of the context provided in the Prologue brings this problematic character of our nature squarely into view. The nexus between this strand of the context and the previous strand lies at the difficulty of knowing a human being, including oneself. The Prologue initially directs us to this point through its allusions to just how elusive such knowledge is. Terpsion's expectations of Euclides, the many's expectations of Theaetetus, and Socrates' prophecy regarding Theaetetus are each characterized as matters of wonder (142c4, a3, b9).[44] Each pertains to the possibility of knowing a particular human being sufficiently well so as to predict future behavior.

The problem of knowledge is most particularly perplexing, and vexing, regarding that whole with which we are most concerned – namely, the human whole. We can well wonder whether our own prophecy for Theaetetus' future would be any more accurate, any less qualified than Socrates'. When we are finished with the text we might still hesitate to claim that we know Theaetetus' soul, the examination of which is the object of the entire conversation. Plato's desire to keep this difficulty before us may explain the very particular title he gives to this very abstract dialogue.[45] He intends us, as I said, to see knowledge *as a problem*, but one that arises more specifically from the most basic and compelling questions about ourselves.

Through the device of the Prologue and through the examples used throughout the dialogue, Plato makes clear that it is the problem of knowing Theaetetus that exemplifies this issue. To put the question from the standpoint of the Megarians' concerns, how is it that an individual can be in such diverse ways

44 On these occurrences of wonder see Polansky, *Philosophy and Knowledge*, 35 and David Roochnik, "Self-Recognition in Plato's *Theaetetus*," *Ancient Philosophy* 22 (2002): 42–4.

45 The titles of the two dramatically subsequent dialogues in the trilogy do refer to more abstract terms. By having us think of these asymmetrical titles together Plato may intend for us to reflect more generally on the philosophic practice of Socrates and the Eleatic Stranger. My own view is that the Eleatic becomes ever more Socratic so that the object of philosophy is ultimately best designated by the title of the *Theaetetus*, the problem of knowing an individual soul.

over time, such that, for example, the immature Theaetetus can become the dying war hero and still be Theaetetus? To weave these two strands of the Prologue together even more tightly, we can ask, what must the beings be, and what must we be, such that whether an individual fulfilled his or her potential stands as a question for us?

The alternative deaths of Theaetetus and Socrates, and the political conflicts these represent, epitomize the problematic character of human fulfillment or wholeness. This problematic wholeness compels the question of whether there is some unifying principle, or perhaps some greater whole, that might resolve the discord within. Socrates explores this question of our wholeness, the question of the unity of virtue, in numerous dialogues. In the *Protagoras*, for example, he famously recommends knowledge as the ground of the unity of the apparently heterogeneous virtues. In examining the meaning of knowledge Socrates' conversation in the *Theaetetus* may be seen as furthering the investigation begun in the *Protagoras*. Certainly, no intellectual figures more prominently in the *Theaetetus* than does Protagoras. But the hope that the *Theaetetus* would provide a resolution to the conundrum of the *Protagoras* needs to be tempered in light of the Prologue's first strand: knowledge will be investigated as itself a problem.

It is a problem, as I have suggested and as will be ever more evident in the dialogue, of knowing wholes, of knowing any whole including the whole of knowledge. In pursuing this often quite abstract investigation, however, it is exceedingly important to recall the Prologue's lesson regarding the origin of the problem. As revealed above all in the conflicts inherent in political life, it originates in the urgent practical need to know a human being, whether oneself or another. Later in the dialogue, Socrates locates the origin of philosophy in wonder, but as just seen, we first encounter that wonder in the Prologue's references to knowing the human whole (155d2–4). Beyond displaying the urgent practical need for knowledge, political life connects to the problem of knowledge in this still deeper way. Through its endemic conflicts political life expresses the perplexities of that object of knowledge that we most yearn to know and that most eludes our understanding: our nature and our good.

This last consideration is of special pertinence to Socrates as he sits in his cell reflecting on the way of life that brought him to this end. In particular, such self-knowledge may provide a clearer understanding than that possessed by his predecessors of why, even with this outcome, philosophic inquiry should be regarded as essential to a fulfilled life. This possibility helps explain the last vital piece of information conveyed in the Prologue: Socrates' intense interest in the preservation of this conversation.

The Third Strand: The Deed of Socrates and the Deed of Plato

As I have mentioned, what we are about to have read to us is presented by Plato as a transcript of an earlier conversation. Although the transcript bears the marks of Euclides' hands, this should not obscure the fact that it is produced with the active involvement of Socrates.[46] Socrates knew what Euclides was up to, knew that his cooperation with his admirer would produce some sort of written document (142c8–a5). Near the end of his life Socrates did relax his famous animadversions against the written word, composing a hymn to Apollo and setting some Aesopian fables to verse.[47] But through his collaboration with Euclides he also helped produce a text more evidently related to his lifelong philosophic practice than these efforts. By providing us with this provenance Plato inclines us to regard the conversation in the *Theaetetus* as more directly expressive of Socrates' views than other dialogues. Certainly, a similar claim could be made for those dialogues that Socrates narrates. It could also be made for a dialogue such as the *Phaedo* whose conversation he must have known would be passed on to others. Yet only in the case of the *Theaetetus* does he take the further step of overseeing the production of a written transcript. We are thus provided a record, however modified, of a conversation, which Plato wants us to know, that Socrates was intent on preserving. As such, notwithstanding Euclides' modifications, the text provides as close to a Socratic self-portrait as occurs in any dialogue.[48] Perhaps it should not be surprising that he should produce such a valedictory expressing the heart of his self-understanding as he contemplated his fast-approaching death.

As a self-portrait, however, it raises at least as many questions as it answers. As I have noted, the doctrines of the Forms and Recollection, often regarded as central to his thought, are both absent despite their obvious pertinence to the central theme of the *Theaetetus*. As I have also noted, the dialogue culminates, famously, in explicit aporia (210b8–9). The self-portrait lacks photographic clarity. Socrates' valedictory leaves a legacy of perplexity.

Yet this is the conversation Socrates wished to preserve. As such, he must intend it to play a significant role in others' posthumous assessments of him, especially those he seemed to care most about, the potential Socratic philosophers in any future audience. In considering the conversation that follows we must constantly ask why Socrates would want this or that detail included, or excluded, as part of his surviving self-presentation. Beyond the presence and absence of details we must also ask why Socrates omits his most famous doctrines. Plato puts us in the proper frame of mind to ask these questions with the "distanced" character of the Prologue. Like the participants in the Prologue, remote in space and time, we can assess the conversation as a vehicle for

[46] Sedley, *The Midwife of Platonism*, 28, writes that the transcript "has Socrates' own approval and imprimatur." In the *Symposium* (173b4–6) Apollodorus says that he asked Socrates to verify the account he had heard from Aristodemus. But unlike the process described in the *Theaetetus* he seems only to have asked once.

[47] *Phaedo* 60c8–61b7.

[48] On the vividness of the portrait of Socrates see A. A. Long, "Plato's Apologies and Socrates in the *Theaetetus*," in *Method in Ancient Philosophy*, ed. Jyl Gentzler (Oxford: Clarendon Press, 1998), 115–16.

transmitting Socrates' thought to those living after his death. In so doing we engage in the activity Socrates wished to preserve, as we become interlocutors not mere auditors.[49]

Only through Plato's appending of the Prologue, however, do we know of Socrates' contribution to the production of the text. Again, in confiding this fact to us, Plato narrows the most manifest difference between himself and his creation – namely, Socrates' aforementioned opposition to writing. In his *Phaedrus*, Plato makes the philosophic issues at stake in this difference thematic. He thus requires us to reflect similarly on what reasons might explain Socrates' modification of his lifelong policy.

Socrates writes, as does anyone, as a partial antidote to his own finitude and thus to the transience of his thought.[50] Through writing, he can reach that ideal student that might live decades or centuries and more after his own death. Yet the fact of that transience or, more generally, the bearing of particularity on our thinking was available to Socrates well before he became an imprisoned author. After all, Socrates locates the distinctiveness of his philosophy in its unusual orientation to death.[51] It was thus also clear well before his imprisonment that steps need to be taken to address this transience. From this standpoint, the Prologue's information might constitute the beginning of a Platonic critique of his Socrates for not fully appreciating the bearing of particularity on thought.

Without denying this possibility I want to suggest another consideration that might also bear on our understanding of Plato's point. Specifically, the transience that Plato's writing aims especially to forestall concerns the justification of the philosophic life. Stated otherwise, Plato writes to make available to others this practice, this way of life. It is reasonable to infer from this deed that Plato regards the practice as good. His writing might thus be said to be animated by justice, providing others a good that they might enjoy, even as we now do, long after his own life ends. The key point is that the premise of his act is that this way of life is good. Perhaps, then, that most evident difference between Socrates and Plato reflects a division of labor or, better, a necessary sequence of tasks. For, clearly, we cannot know what good we should do for others until we have evidence of what is good. It is just this question, the question of the good of the philosophic life, that Socrates spent his life pursuing.[52] In light of these considerations, the conversation in the *Theaetetus* takes on added importance insofar as it is the one conversation that Plato presents Socrates as taking steps to preserve and so make available to others.[53] The

49 See Chappell, *Reading Plato's "Theaetetus,"* 13.

50 I am aware that Socrates does not truly write anything. The question remains as to why Plato portrays him as assisting in this writing.

51 *Apology* 29a2–b6.

52 Ibid., 23b4–c1.

53 Whereas in the *Symposium* it is Apollodorus' initiative to secure Socrates' confirmation of Aristodemus' report, in the *Theaetetus* (142c8–d1) it is Socrates who takes the initiative to recount the entire conversation to Euclides.

possibility I am suggesting is that in this conversation Socrates establishes to his satisfaction that the philosophic life is good and so can rightly be shared. This task, taken up by Socrates at the end of his life, is only fulfilled by Plato. However, by indicating the unique character of the forthcoming conversation Plato steps out of the shadows in this Prologue perhaps to suggest that this conversation provides the impetus to his own lifelong task.

Providing some additional evidence for this speculation is that it is the question of the good of the philosophic life that weaves together the three strands of the Prologue. The Prologue has introduced the fact that the forthcoming conversation deals with knowledge *as a problem*. In the face of that problem, Plato directs us to the importance of the consideration of the particulars that shape our knowing by alerting us precisely to Euclides' efforts to remove them. The Prologue suggests the further possibility that this problem might lead the self-critical philosopher, in contradistinction from his predecessors, to regard political life with utter seriousness. Again, in the face of the problematic status of knowledge the investigation of what justifies a life spent seeking it becomes crucial to such a philosopher. That investigation calls for the self-knowledge particularly available, for reasons made clearer in the following text, through reflection on political life. Through these reflections Socrates will show that his distinctive form of inquiry is a practical necessity and a theoretical possibility. Accordingly, we can well understand why, in his last moments, in a jail cell awaiting execution, he took steps to record a conversation that would induce others to live, and so preserve, the life he knows is good. With this context in mind, we are now prepared to consider that conversation.

3

Socratic Midwifery

Introduction

Of the three definitions of knowledge in the *Theaetetus*, the first examined in detail – that knowledge is perception – occupies fully half of the dialogue.[1] Preceding this definition is a discussion between Theodorus and Socrates, and eventually including Theaetetus, the pervasive theme of which is teaching and learning. The discussion culminates in Socrates' introduction of the midwife image to describe his characteristic activity. The image aims, most obviously, to encourage Theaetetus in his attempts to say what knowledge is. It succeeds, inducing Theaetetus to offer the definition that "knowledge is nothing else than perception (151e2–3)." Any assessment of this definition and its vital role in the dialogue requires an examination of the vivid, not to say outlandish, image that prompts its generation.[2]

However, something more than the image's rhetorical effectiveness links the midwife image and Theaetetus' definition. There is a deep substantive relationship between the image and the definition, albeit an antithetical one. Following the exposition of the definition, Socrates explicitly opposes the two, maintaining that if Theaetetus' definition is correct then his own philosophic activity must be rejected as "nonsense" (161e7–162a2). Specifically subject to this verdict is his midwifery, his teaching through "conversation" that seeks "to examine and try to refute the appearances and opinions of one another (161e5, e6, e7–8)." Socrates thus makes the midwife image the bearer of his flag in a contest whose outcome may entail the wholesale rejection of his philosophy.

1 As we see in the following text, Theaetetus does offer a previous definition (146c7–d3) that, however, is regarded by Socrates as a series of examples rather than a definition.

2 Howland, *The Paradox of Political Philosophy*, 295n12, notes the aptness of the word *outlandish* to describe Socrates more generally. He borrows this characterization from Carl Page, "Philosophy and the Outlandishness of Reason," *Journal of Speculative Philosophy* 7 (1993): 206–25.

Recalling, in addition, Socrates' editorial oversight of the transcript, we can conclude that this image expresses what Socrates thinks is distinctive about his activity. In what follows we see that the image does express something essential concerning the character of philosophy, for it considers the meaning of the very object of that activity – namely, wisdom, especially as it is distinguished from knowledge. This distinction emerges from the discussion of teaching and learning that provides reasons to regard knowledge, as understood by Theodorus and Theaetetus, to be problematic. Through that discussion, the wisdom expressed in and through midwifery comes to light as that which both grasps knowledge as a problem and reflects on the implications thereof. I begin my consideration of the practice of midwifery with this discussion of teaching and learning from which the image arises and to which it responds.[3]

Two Teachers Talking (143d1–144d7)

The slave-boy begins reading the transcript. Curiously, even though subject to his editorial scrutiny, the transcript commences with Socrates and Theodorus in midconversation rather than at the beginning or even at some natural break-point in their discussion. The intensely reflexive character of the dialogue as a whole – not surprising given its theme – prompts the thought that such a beginning requires us, from the start, to fill in the blanks, to think what is not there immediately before us. Just as we might wonder whether the slave-boy understands this conversation when he finishes reading it, so hearing these words alone may not suffice for our understanding. Effort is required.

Acting on this requirement, we can extrapolate from Socrates' initial recorded speech that he must previously have asked his fellow teacher, Theodorus, whether he knew of any promising students. In response, Theodorus must have mentioned students from his own hometown of Cyrene, which elicits Socrates' initial words: "If I cared more about things in Cyrene, Theodorus, I'd ask you about things there and about the people, whether there are any of the local young people who pay attention to geometry or to any other sort of philosophy. But as things are, I love them less than those who are here and I'm more eager to know which of our young people are considered likely to make a decent showing (143d1–6)." Commencing at just this point, the text gives prominence to Socrates' intense interest in the teacher-student relationship. The conversation about knowledge begins with the theme of learning. Commencing in just this way, the text provides a model of how to read the subsequent speeches, attending to both their form and content. With respect to Socrates' initial speech, the form and content converge on the issue of how it is that we come to know. This heightened attention on the approach to knowledge rather than on its purported object pervades the rest of the conversation.

[3] On the *Theaetetus* as a final representation of Socrates, see Long, "Plato's Apologies," 113–36. I do not, however, share Long's view that Socrates is superseded by the Eleatic Stranger.

The theme throughout concerns how that approach shapes what the object of knowledge must be.[4]

Socrates' initial reflections on teaching are quite concrete. He simply insists, as just seen, that his care happens to be directed much more to the Athenian students than to others. We should not take this statement as merely an attempt to cover himself posthumously with a patriotic cloak. His care, after all, is for the philosophically inclined Athenian youth rather than for Athens. Moreover, Socrates unabashedly admits that he turns over those students disinclined to philosophy to sophists such as Prodicus. He does not claim to return them to the ancestral ways (151b5–6). As this opening passage progresses, it becomes clearer that Socrates' affection for Athenian rather than Cyrenian youth proves rather to be connected with the distinctive character of his pedagogical activity whose character emerges especially through contrast with that of Theodorus. The most striking fact about this beginning is that in this dialogue so expressive of his philosophic distinctiveness, Socrates begins with, and thus spotlights, his pedagogical efforts.

Given his circumstances, Socrates' purpose in asking about promising students is not immediately clear. Earlier in his life it made sense to seek long-term students with the possibility that they might even become equal partners in his search. But now, aware of his age and of his impending trial, it is unlikely that Socrates thinks such an outcome could be feasible with a youth of Theaetetus' age (143e5).[5] Yet, given the provenance of this text, Theaetetus need not be its only addressee. This is one dialogue in which not only Plato but also his Socrates has a wider audience in mind, one that will hear his speeches after his death. Ideally, this audience would comprise not only those such as Euclides and Terpsion but also those potential Socratic philosophers who might live, and so work to maintain, the life Socrates cherishes.

The pertinent question then is why *this* discussion of teaching and learning, undertaken with *these* participants, should be particularly important to set before potential Socratic philosophers. Two considerations would make it so: first, if it somehow conveys to them what is most distinctive about Socratic philosophy; and, second, if it addresses the paramount obstacles that impede

[4] As I noted in Chapter 1 (p. 11 and n25), Gilbert Ryle recognizes the distinction between defining knowledge by reference to its objects versus defining the activity of knowing. He sees the *Theaetetus*' emphasis on the latter as an implicit critique of the *Republic*. As such, it plays a role in the wider debate concerning the presence or absence of the Forms in the dialogue and in the still wider debate between the Unitarian and Revisionist interpretations of the Platonic corpus. My views on the former issue, the issue of the Forms, emerge through the argument in the text. See Ryle, "Logical Atomism," 23.

[5] Benardete, *Being of the Beautiful*, I. 88–9 follows Campbell's suggestion and compares the situation in this dialogue with that in the *Charmides*, a point much earlier in Socrates' life. Benardete suggests that Theaetetus' nonphilosophic nature may have had something to do with what he calls Socrates' "suicidal defense" in the *Apology*. See Campbell, *The "Theaetetus" of Plato*, 6n1.

this philosophic pursuit. Accomplishing these goals, this conversation would do as much as possible to ensure that, through his future interlocutors' properly informed efforts, Socrates' way of life might endure. A look at Socrates' immediate interlocutors shows how the conversation fulfills these tasks.

Who is Theodorus and who, therefore, is his student likely to be?[6] In the course of the conversation, Theodorus proves often to be a passive, reluctant, and even oblivious participant (e.g., 146b3–4, 162a4–b9). These characteristics are connected with a piece of indirect discourse Euclides does report prior to the reading of the transcript: Socrates refers to Theodorus as a "geometer" (143b8). In the same reference, Socrates mentions Theaetetus but does not assign him a comparable appellation, emphasizing the importance Theodorus' profession holds for Socrates. Socrates thus designates Theodorus as a representative of a kind of knowledge that possessed and continues to possess a special prestige and authority.

Far from denying the worth of such knowledge, Socrates relates in the *Republic* that geometry holds a special place in the curriculum of the potential philosopher. Specifically, it aids in turning the soul from becoming to being as it enables the student to see the fluctuating visible world as an image of an invisible but stable and intelligible world.[7] Yet, ultimately, geometry is but a preparation for philosophy, a "prelude" rather than "the song itself."[8] The source of Socrates' reluctance to identify geometry with dialectic or philosophy helps explain the importance of Theodorus as his interlocutor.

Socrates makes clear that what Glaucon refers to as "geometry and its kindred arts" do not examine the hypothetical character of their own foundations.[9] Therefore, they do not appreciate what dialectical inquiry would reveal – namely, the necessarily partial character of their principles, the extent to which these principles depend on unexamined and even unstated premises. Instead, the strong inclination of the *technai*, which geometry expresses in refined form, is to proceed deductively from their principles to explain the visible world rather than to strive for a more comprehensive view.[10] And, as is indicated by Glaucon's association of geometry and *techne*, the goal is not only to explain but also to manipulate that world.[11] Like thinkers nearer our own

[6] For more on Theodorus in the dialogue, see Howland, *The Paradox of Political Philosophy*, 57; and Blondell, *The Play of Character*, 186–7, 277–81. On Theodorus in connection with Plato, see Diogenes Laertius *Lives* 3.6, 2.102.

[7] *Republic* 527b5–c10.

[8] *Republic* 531d7–e1; *Euthydemus*. 290b10–c6.

[9] Ibid., 511b1–2.

[10] *Republic* 510d5–511a8. For further discussion, see Mitchell H. Miller Jr., *The Philosopher in Plato's "Statesman"* (The Hague: Martinus Nijhoff, 1980), 4.

[11] My understanding of *techne* in Plato as a whole is indebted to David L. Roochnik, *Of Art and Wisdom: Plato's Understanding of Techne* (University Park: The Pennsylvania State University Press, 1996).

time, Plato thus recognizes the connection between mathematical knowledge and the mastery of the visible world that such knowledge affords.[12]

By asking the geometer Theodorus about his students Socrates should expect to hear of one that sought out a mathematician as a teacher to satisfy his yearning for that stable knowledge and perhaps for the greater promise it holds forth.[13] In examining such a student Socrates can learn for himself – and when we read this transcript, teach us – what it is that moves him to seek such knowledge. The soul of the young knowledge seeker is of acute interest, especially if this young soul is poised at the point where, to use the image of the "Divided Line," it may either turn its attention to the visible world below or ascend the path of dialectic.[14] Already noted for his mathematical prowess, and also the beneficiary of an education in many of the subjects taken to be propaedeutic to philosophy in the *Republic*, Theaetetus seems the model of such a soul.[15] It is difficult to imagine a conversation more appropriate for review by other potential philosophers than one such as this that speaks directly to their most crucial decision. Such students, much like Theaetetus, would be those who have already shown, and understand themselves to have shown, a devotion to knowledge. The key question for them now is what kind of knowledge they should seek.

Socrates may well see in those young seekers of knowledge a resemblance to himself as a young man when he was "wondrously desirous of that wisdom they call inquiry into nature."[16] Again, Theaetetus himself acquired a reputation for brilliance at a young age. We might surmise that the physical resemblance between Socrates and Theaetetus, mentioned several times in the dialogue, extends to deeper, less visible similarities (143e8–9, 209c1–3). In fact, some commentators have regarded Theaetetus as a new Socrates or, to use one intriguing formulation, as a "philosopher-prince" soon to ascend the throne.[17] We should recall, however, that Socrates' reported prophecy concerning Theaetetus' success is heavily qualified and even somewhat ambiguous. It promises renown rather than wisdom (142d2). I think it is safer, and more accurate, to see such similarities as pertaining to Socrates in his youth and especially to the decision he made at that precise point which he relates in

[12] See Jacob Klein, *A Commentary on Plato's "Meno"* (Chapel Hill: University of North Carolina Press, 1965), 116–22. See also Rene Descartes, *Discourse on the Method*, trans. John Cottingham, Robert Stoothoff, and Dugald Murdoch (Cambridge: Cambridge University Press, 1998), 29, 47.

[13] Polansky, *Philosophy and Knowledge*, 39, sees the similarity between this feature of the dialogue and the central books of the *Republic*.

[14] *Republic* 511b3–c2.

[15] Ibid., 522a2–531e5, 536d5–8.

[16] *Phaedo* 96a6–8.

[17] See Blondell, *The Play of Character*, 252–60. Blondell's examination of the characters in the *Theaetetus* (and other dialogues) is particularly insightful, although I differ from her assessment of Theaetetus as will appear in the following text.

his intellectual autobiography in the *Phaedo*. The intellectual kinship joining Socrates and Theaetetus is most intimate at the point just prior to that decision.

This point is most clearly expressed in the *Theaetetus* just after Theaetetus holds that the "soul itself through itself" examines its objects apart from the body. This, states Socrates, "*was* my opinion too" (185e6–9, emphasis added).[18] Socrates also once longed for pure knowledge untainted by the particular. But, as we will see, it is exactly when he comes to terms with the unavailability of such knowledge that Socrates undertakes his distinctive brand of philosophizing. With Theaetetus Socrates can replicate the circumstances of his own internal conversation that yielded the insight launching him on his novel philosophic voyage. More specifically, in speaking about knowledge with those committed to this mathematical understanding, he can better distinguish and defend his own theoretical activity from this much more prevalent, and perhaps more obviously attractive, notion of what constitutes such activity.

We should understand the difference between geometry and philosophy, which Socrates suggests in his initial speech, in precisely this light. He speaks first of students that might be interested in "geometry or some other philosophy (143d3)." Subsequently, however, he omits this reference to philosophy saying it is "for geometry and all the rest" that students seek out Theodorus (143e1–2). Socrates does not deny that geometry is a form of knowledge worth learning. It is "right" that students seek Theodorus (143e1). He refuses, however, to assimilate geometry and philosophy. He regards this distinction of such importance that he preserves this conversation involving these mathematicians rather than the young, politically ambitious types that populate many of his other conversations. And he elucidates this distinction by examining the extent to which his interlocutors appreciate the partial character of even mathematical knowledge.[19] This accounts, in particular, for the dialogue's attention to those wholes whose irreducible character may thwart the comprehensive aspiration of the mathematically oriented theorist. It is this appreciation of enduring partiality that animates the scrutiny of presuppositions characteristic of Socratic inquiry, the activity Socrates aims to perpetuate.

By recording this conversation, Socrates also provides insight regarding the greatest threat to his characteristic theoretical activity. The participation of these particular interlocutors suggests that, perhaps contrary to our initial impression, the threat may not lay in future head-on collisions between philosophers and the political community. Such collisions presume the existence of that Socratically inclined philosopher who would scrutinize political

[18] For a contrary assessment of this passage see Martin Heidegger, *The Essence of Truth: On Plato's Cave Allegory and "Theaetetus,"* trans. Ted Sadler (New York: Continuum, 2002), 140–4. As I make clear in subsequent chapters, I do not mean to suggest that Socrates denies the distinctive power of the soul – quite the contrary. Rather, I maintain that only he realized the implications of that discovery for the possibility of comprehensive wisdom. I deal with Heidegger in more detail in Chapter 7.

[19] See Miller, *Plato's "Statesman,"* 4–5.

life. More threatening would be the prevalence or dominion of non-Socratic theorists who, in their self-forgetting assurance, would neglect to consider this crucial question: if knowledge is a problem, is the seeking of it good? Failing to consider the validity of their own activity they would reduce philosophy to what we would call ideology. Conflict with the political community would then dissipate because the incendiary question would not be asked. Along with the diminution of such conflict, the self-understanding of the philosophic inquirer would also fade. With these participants then, Socrates aims not to elevate the sights of political types to the importance of theory but rather to make theorists aware of the importance of ethical-political questions for their theoretical activity. It is these questions that may, in some, turn the soul from the certainties of geometry to the perplexities of dialectic.

Yet Socrates' task in confronting geometry is daunting. The attraction of such knowledge is great, especially in comparison with the apparent futility of dialectics. Geometry holds out the promise of certainty. Certainty by itself, however, does not yet account for its attractiveness. Rather, its allure lies in the hope that such certainty will grant power, specifically, the power to achieve what we most yearn for; hence the association of geometry with the *technai*. But Socrates rarely lacks for resources. In this passage leading up to the midwife image, Socrates employs the discussion of teaching and learning to question exactly whether technical knowledge should be regarded as comprehensive. The presuppositions of learning, to which Socrates alludes in the educational scene he sketches at the outset, strikingly convey the partial character of our knowledge. Reflection on these presuppositions opens up the question of what we are, what the world is, such that we must seek knowledge. It thus bears directly on the premises that inform Socrates' own inquiry. We need to reflect, and not for the last time, on what Socrates' portrayal tells us about these presuppositions of learning.

Socrates depicts students of varying capacities and interests. In seeking to learn, they pursue similarly diverse teachers (143d1–e3). They seek out teachers based on their hopes of what they might learn from them (143d8). Such behavior presupposes a need on the part of these students and an awareness of that need that moves them to remedy this self-perceived defect. Their deeds presuppose the further awareness that they cannot supply this remedy themselves, and so they seek others who can. Student activity thus presumes the power of self-reflection that somehow grants a premonitory sense, far from infallible, of what knowledge they lack and who, therefore, they should seek to remedy this lack. Gaining such knowledge, fulfilling one's potential in this sense, depends on this mysterious capacity to know what one lacks. It depends as well on the chance that we will find those other humans most adequate to respond to this need, and that we have the capacity to recognize them when we meet them.

Do we yet understand with precision this capacity for self-assessment that guides the student toward fulfillment? Do we understand the specific talents distinguishing the worthy from the unworthy teacher? The disparate results, even in Socrates' classroom, along with the enduring controversy regarding the means and ends of education, suggest that our knowledge in this regard falls short of being apodeictic. Socrates' focus on learning underscores the complexity of human potential, first raised in the Prologue, that underlies this perplexity.

The students' activity indicates that there is complexity and perplexity too, on the side of the *mathemata*, that which is to be learned. The students' recognized need for teachers and their inability to remedy their defect themselves both testify to the difficulty of learning, to the extraordinary effort it can require. It must be that the objects to be learned do not immediately disclose themselves to the student. If we had only to open our eyes to know, such efforts, such study, would not be required. The beings must be sufficiently complex as to require these efforts to ascertain the truth about them. This complexity, expressed, for example, in the distinction between being and seeming, like that on the side of the learner, also perplexes our understanding.

We will have to make our own effort to keep these perplexities in view because the definition of knowledge that receives the lengthiest scrutiny – that knowledge is perception – eliminates them on the side of both the knower and the known. As a consequence it makes learning unintelligible. For the present, however, it is important to note that were Theodorus to reflect on his own activity as a professor he might be less assured that his geometric understanding sufficed to explain his own doings. Plato makes this point even more emphatically as Socrates distinguishes the nature of his own teaching from Theodorus'. This distinction emerges from an invitation to Theodorus to assess his best Athenian student.

Speaking as a teacher, Socrates indicates that his "care" directs him to be more avidly interested in the youth of Athens and what it is they make their "concern" than he is in the youth of Cyrene (143d1–5).[20] He wishes to know which of the former "are expected to make a decent showing (143d5–6)." Socrates does not inquire solely into the students' intellectual capacity. Recognizing that care, which arises from that passionate concern, guides his own reflections, Socrates well understands that the desires, passions, and more generally, the character of students play significant roles in directing their concerns. The students' community has already put its stamp on this character. Such character formation arguably constitutes the chief occupation of

[20] On reasons for Socrates' care in addition to those mentioned in the text, see Polansky, *Philosophy and Knowledge*, 40 and Howland, *The Paradox of Political Philosophy*, 56. Cropsey makes the notion of Socrates' care a major theme in his book. One point I make in this chapter is that this care is not simply the product of benevolence (although it may have that effect) but is based most deeply on self-concern, on Socrates' desire for clarity about the good of the philosophic way of life. Such clarity is the prerequisite of him benefiting others.

the community. For Socrates, unlike the itinerant Theodorus, students are Athenians and Cyrenians rather than isolated individuals inhabiting some state of nature.[21] Therefore it matters a great deal where they come from, especially given the themes pervading the philosophic education pursued by Socrates.

Socrates' themes also dictate a divergence from Theodorus in pedagogical approach. Later, Theodorus explicitly disavows any familiarity with, or inclination to become familiar with, the conversational approach for which Socrates is famous (146b3–4). His own pedagogical strategy appears in the present context when, in response to Socrates' question about his student, Theodorus says "it is for me to say and you to hear" (143e4–5). Conversely, Socrates' approach is explicitly conversational. In the following text I will have more on the connection between Socrates' conversational approach and his philosophic focus. For now, it suffices to note that the kinds of questions in which Socrates was most interested, questions regarding the human soul, are inherently controversial. They resist resolution through measurement.[22] Such questions, moreover, emphatically evoke those passions previously mentioned. One purpose of inquiry through conversation is to ensure that numerous perspectives will be considered regarding these controversial, many-sided issues. Without such inquiry, a more comprehensive understanding might be lost under the influence of a single unchallenged passion. Examination of such issues is clearly not a matter of simply conveying information from the all-wise teacher to the passively attentive student.

Socrates uses a specific vocabulary here, and again in the midwife passage, to capture his much more intricate relationship with students. These words – translated as "association" or, more literally, "being-with" – designate a range of interactions, from simply spending time in another's presence to a sexual relationship (*sungignomai*, 143d8; *suneimi*, 150d2, d4, e5, 151a2, a4, a5).[23] In using these words, Socrates indicates that the student-teacher relationship is not delimited by the verbal conveyance of information but may also include indirect teaching by nonverbal means – a form of teaching that requires more than a day. This requirement provides yet another reason why Socrates directs his care to those with whom he can stay in extended contact. Insofar as learning involves not only the conveyance of information but also the education of the passions or the formation of character, long-term association will be required. In this way, Socrates acknowledges what all communities recognize as the

[21] In its generality it would seem that writing neglects this particularity. But the Platonic dialogue may be a kind of writing constructed with this concern in mind. See Griswold, *Plato's "Phaedrus,"* 221–6. It is also worth mentioning that the conversation Socrates comes closest to writing has as one of its chief aims to induce in those attracted to hyperabstraction an appreciation of the irreducibly heterogeneous nature of things.

[22] *Euthyphro* 7b6–d6; *Phaedrus* 263a2–b9.

[23] The word is first used by Euclides, apparently quoting Socrates' description of his time spent with Theaetetus.

requirements for such character formation.[24] And his language also recognizes, rather provocatively, the formal similarity between his own soul-shaping efforts and those of the community. Because Socrates' philosophic education thus confronts the results of this civic education, he must be intimately familiar with the character of those students already formed by the community.

These characteristics of the teacher-student relationship make it resistant to codification in a set of hard and fast rules. In making education his theme, Socrates draws the attention of the geometer, Theodorus, to a realm he is quite unused to reflecting on. It is a realm navigated with cognitive means geometry may not supply. In his lengthy assessment of Theaetetus, we see the results of Theodorus' need to rely on nongeometric modes of understanding. From this assessment by his teacher, we also learn much about the influence by which Theaetetus has been formed.

Theodorus begins his assessment of Theaetetus from the surface, calling attention to the boy's ugliness (143e6–9). It is not maliciousness that animates his comments but a desire to guard against any hint of impropriety in his own pedagogical activity. Theodorus worries that some, hearing him praise the boy so effusively, might conclude that Theodorus is a smitten lover and thus besmirch his reputation – with deleterious effect on his livelihood (143e6–7). The voice of public opinion, which determines the standards of impropriety, strikes fear in Theodorus' heart. It is this voice that guides the practical judgments of this ostensibly cosmopolitan, free-thinking mathematician. Contrarily, Socrates speaks of his affection for Athenian youth, of students wishing to "be with" teachers, of the way in which the teacher-student relationship in general is bound up with the fulfillment of powerful needs on both sides. In this way, Socrates is much less heedful of "public opinion" than is Theodorus. But such human desires are, to say the least, not Theodorus' primary area of expertise.

Theodorus further exemplifies his deficient understanding of his fellow humans as he now comments on Socrates' appearance. He tells Socrates that Theaetetus shares with him the unattractive combination of a snub nose and bulging eyes, adding "thoughtfully," however, that Theaetetus possesses these to a lesser degree than does Socrates (143e8–144a1). Theodorus confides this comment on Socrates' ugliness having first requested that Socrates not be annoyed with him as he speaks "fearlessly" (144a1). On display in this exchange is an important element of Theodorus' dimness regarding his fellow humans, one that he will be seen to share with his friend, Protagoras. I refer to his vast overestimation of the power of speech (162b5–9, 176a2–4).

[24] See Kevin Robb, "*Asebeia* and *Sunousia*. The Issues behind the Indictment of Socrates," in *Plato's Dialogues: New Studies and Interpretations*, ed. Gerald A. Press (Lanham, MD: Rowman and Littlefield Publishers, 1993), 77–106, on the institution of *sunousia*, which is the vehicle by which the community aimed to reproduce itself. Specifically, it refers to those means, verbal and nonverbal, by which old Athens sought to hand down its ways, especially from fathers to sons.

Theodorus' geometric expertise has not equipped him to reflect on the range of human motivations, in himself or others, which includes those motives that do not respond to reason alone. The result is a pose of autarchy especially unwarranted in one who, in truth, responds mainly to urges and passions that are not reflected on.[25] In particular, Theodorus exhibits the kind of vanity and attendant fear of ridicule engendered by overwhelming self-concern (143d8–e1, 144a2).

Theodorus begins his assessment of Theaetetus claiming, "no one I have perceived is thus wonderfully well-natured (144a2)."[26] He follows this initial judgment with several other indications of Theaetetus' comparative superiority: his learning capacity is "hard for anyone else to match"; he is "exceptionally gentle"; and he is "manly beyond anyone whatsoever" (144a3–5). What is most wondrous to Theodorus is the way in which Theaetetus' soul somehow combines these qualities of intelligence, gentleness, and manliness. He wonders, in particular, that one can be intelligent without also being given to bursts of anger.[27] This possibility proves to be of central importance when Socrates distinguishes himself not only from the sophists but also from his philosophic predecessors.

For now, however, I am most interested in the cognitive basis of Theodorus' knowledge of Theaetetus. Theodorus concludes that such an amalgam of characteristics as are found in Theaetetus "doesn't occur" because "I don't see it occurring (144a5–6)." How then does Theodorus know Theaetetus? He relies on experience rather than on some abstract general principle under which he subsumes this particular person. His practice coincides with Aristotle's judgment that it is experience that provides our access to that which is individual.[28] Theodorus' use of comparatives indicates that he has judged Theaetetus in comparison with other students he has known. And far from using some definition, he admits he would not have predicted that one such as Theaetetus exists. When it comes to understanding humans, even someone so given to abstraction as Theodorus does not ignore the resistance of the particulars to subsumption under a universal.

Necessary to understanding such an object is a cognitive capacity open to such resistance. Reasoning deductively from first principles does not suffice. Such a capacity is necessary when considering the discrepancy between what we should mean by humankind, on the one hand, and the many diverse individual expressions of humanity, on the other. Still, it is doubtful that Theodorus'

[25] See Miller, *Plato's "Statesman,"* 4–5; and Howland, *The Paradox of Political Philosophy*, 66–7.

[26] In light of the forthcoming thesis that knowledge is sense-perception, it should be noted that this first use of the word pertains to knowing something that is not fully visible: another person's nature. I have altered the translation to make it more literal.

[27] See Kenneth Dorter, *Form and Good in Plato's Eleatic Dialogues: The "Parmenides," "Theaetetus," "Sophist," and "Statesman"* (Berkeley: University of California Press, 1994), 69.

[28] Aristotle *Metaphysics* 981a15–16.

reliance in practice on such an alternative approach ever leads him to reflect on what his reliance means regarding the character of knowledge. Such reflections might have given him to see that this knowledge, insofar as it is of particular individuals, requires learning, spurred by an awareness of need in this regard. In addition, his reliance on experience might have awakened an awareness of the extent to which there is something unalterably particular about knowledge. It might have enabled Theodorus to reflect on himself as a student and as a teacher.

Theodorus' strikingly paradoxical phrase, "wonderfully well-natured," expresses this imperfect harmony of universal and particular. This phrase recalls the issue in Euclides' and Terpsion's earlier assessment of Theaetetus – namely, how a being can be of this kind or nature, and thus share something decisive with all others of its kind, yet have this nature so emphatically as to cause wonder. It is the problem perfectly captured in Terpsion's exclamation: "What a man (142b6)!" Apparently, with respect to humankind the individuals or particulars resist universalization such that even the long experience of Theodorus does not suffice to exhaust the possibilities of which humankind is capable. There is a vast diversity of individual humans, still identifiable as such and thus comprehensible within humankind. Theodorus' wonder at Theaetetus thus carries forward an issue present from the first to the last page of the *Theaetetus*, the problem of knowing wholes, wholes in general and the human whole in particular. But again, Theodorus will not permit himself to appreciate what his deed, his reliance on experience, implies about the extent to which knowledge is problematic.

In his continuing efforts to convey the wonder of Theaetetus' soul, Theodorus adopts another strategy. He devises two images. One image expresses the usual character of most brilliant students, while the other aims to capture Theaetetus' peculiar character. Claiming that high intelligence is normally inversely proportional to congeniality, Theodorus represents this bright but mercurial and irritable type as an unballasted ship, a vessel buffeted about by forces, all of which are external to it. However, Theodorus imagines Theaetetus' rare combination of high intelligence and gentleness as a stream of olive oil flowing effortlessly (144a8–9, b4–5).

Before we consider the content of these images, we need to note the implications of Theodorus' reliance on images in his assessment. As a geometer, Theodorus would use images in his work. The geometer employs diagrams – a circle, a triangle, a square – that are taken as images of invisible entities. Specifically, such diagrams, although available to our senses, are taken as images of, and thus less real than, the invisible entities that are more knowable than the former images. These invisible entities are the *mathemata*, those things that are most learnable because they are unchanging, precisely not dependent on the fluctuating sensible world. They possess fixed structures that are what they are in an enduring way and thus can be known as such.

Theodorus' use of images in the present passage differs, however, from his usual practice. The object Theodorus attempts to portray is infinitely more complex than any line or triangle. Here, accordingly, Theodorus' images are likewise more complex. Furthermore, the invisible object he portrays in the present case is not accessible in the same way as the geometric entity. Whereas the triangle could be expressed in a nonimagistic manner, in a general formula of the kind found in a geometric proof, the same cannot be said of the soul. In this latter case, our understanding of the object depends on the image in a way that is not the case for the geometric entity.

The point is not that such images are dispensable. On the contrary, Socrates portrays the soul through images throughout the Platonic corpus. And upcoming in this dialogue are the famous psychic images of the wax block and the aviary, and the midwife. Rather the point pertains to the need to reflect on the implications of our necessary reliance on such images.

One such implication is that this reliance makes us depend to a significantly greater extent on Theodorus' imagination. The striking asymmetry of the negative first image and the positive second image makes this last point especially evident.[29] The negative aspect of the first image lies in its representation of a life wholly in the sway of forces beyond its control. We might then think that the image representing the opposite way of life would be the *ballasted* ship. Such an image would represent a life with some degree of stability, and thus of control, while still acknowledging those forces over which our power is imperfect. Instead, Theodorus juxtaposes to the unballasted ship the stream of olive oil. Theodorus' praise of Theaetetus as the wholly unresisting student expresses the teacher's desire for a wholly unimpeded life, a wholly free life.

This asymmetry between an unballasted ship and a stream of olive oil suggests that Theodorus lacks a firm grasp on the intelligible object he is trying to depict. Clearly, a triangle would not admit of being imaged in such heterogeneous ways. Again, it is also clear that the triangle could be expressed with precision in a nonimagistic way, in the kind of general formula found in the geometer's proofs. Precisely because of the elusiveness of the latter, the image of the triangle is dispensable in a way that the image of Theaetetus' nature is not. Because of this elusiveness there is also latitude to devise varying images or hypotheses to represent this nature – as various as the unballasted ship and the stream of olive oil. Moreover, this latitude permits room for diverse motives animating the generation of these images, a possibility especially worth monitoring when we are concerned with wholes of acute importance to us, wholes such as ourselves. Because of the elusiveness of these wholes, the constellation of one's desires, passions, and view of good can and does impinge on our understanding of them.

Consider Theodorus' two images once again in this light. Behind these images we can glimpse his view of good. Again, in juxtaposing to the unballasted ship the stream of olive oil, Theodorus seems to want to reject the

[29] Benardete, *Being of the Beautiful*, I.90 recognizes this asymmetry but offers a different explanation of it.

fettered life for the life of total freedom, an aspiration that goes well beyond the moderate, partially restrained hopes that would be expressed by the ballasted ship. Theodorus' hopes have shaped his understanding as Socrates' care does his. Distinguishing the two teachers, however, is the degree to which each is aware of this influence and of why it can exert the power it does over our understanding.

Socrates' reaction to Theodorus' rather lengthy assessment of Theaetetus' nature is exceedingly terse. He tells Theodorus simply, "You report well (144b7)."[30] Nevertheless, Socrates has learned something significant about Theaetetus from Theodorus, if only indirectly. In particular, he has a better sense of the influence by which the boy has been shaped, information that he immediately puts to use in his forthcoming examination of Theaetetus' soul. Socrates prefaces that examination with a series of questions for Theodorus about Theaetetus' background. These seemingly superficial exchanges, apparently mere gossip, gain in significance as the dialogue proceeds, especially as they bear on the Digression where Socrates explicitly compares the philosopher and the politician. But, first, they deserve scrutiny as examples of alternative ways by which we know another human being or any other being.

With these inquiries, Socrates shows himself immersed in the details of life in the community, details of which Theodorus seems largely oblivious. His first question about Theaetetus is a political one: who's his father? – or, literally, "of which citizen is he? (144b8)." Theodorus does not remember the father's name nor at this point has he even mentioned Theaetetus' name. But just now Theodorus sees Theaetetus approaching with his friends freshly oiled from the wrestling school (144c1–3). No sooner does Theodorus speak of this stream of olive oil than Plato has Theaetetus himself appear as the very embodiment of this image! No wonder Theodorus has an elevated conception of his power of speech. Asked by Socrates to urge Theaetetus to join them, Theodorus confidently affirms that "these things will be (144d7)." Theodorus points out that Theaetetus is the one in the middle – an observation dependent on more than perception alone – thus suggesting that he is the leader of the group, the one the others want to be near.

Socrates acknowledges that he does "recognize (*Gignosko*)" Theaetetus but does not know his name (144c5, c8). A brief look at the verb of knowing employed in this context is useful. In his study of Plato's use of verbs of knowing, John Lyons shows that Plato goes out of his way to distinguish *gignoskein* from *epistasthai*, the verb more closely related to *epistamai*. He shows further that Plato uses *gignoskein* as the verb of knowing when the object

[30] For a discussion of the unusual character of this phrase, rare in the Platonic corpus, see Fritz Gregor Herrmann, "Wrestling Metaphors in Plato's *Theaetetus*," *Nikephoros* 8 (1995): 83–91. He argues that it is used as a quasitechnical term in the context of agonistic contests to proclaim the victor. Its use in the present context would thus enhance the impression of a contest between the two teachers.

is a person or personal pronoun.[31] *Episteme*, at least potentially, refers to a kind of knowledge characterized by precision and certainty. It is also worth noting that *gignoskein* covers a range of meanings that includes a less precise kind of knowing so that the word is often translated as "to recognize." In his study of Plato's *Phaedrus*, Charles Griswold states that this usage raises the question as to whether there is a "sense of self-knowledge that tells us 'what it is to be human' without transforming the soul into a special type of abstract object."[32] It is significant that throughout the *Theaetetus* this word will be used with reference to knowing wholes including the soul.

We have heard Theodorus' account of Theaetetus based on experience. Socrates has indicated that knowledge of Theaetetus might also need to include knowledge of his genesis. Now it has been suggested that there is a kind of knowledge, recognition, that lets us identify someone as the particular being he is without constituting comprehensive knowledge of him. Socrates' still-partial knowledge includes neither Theaetetus' name nor the analysis of Theaetetus' soul that constitutes the bulk of the dialogue. "Recognition" consists in a kind of knowledge that is not yet complete knowledge. These seemingly innocuous exchanges prepare us to consider which form – or, as seen in the final definition, which *forms* – of knowledge best captures how we should understand the soul, or any being, as a whole. In what follows, this question is directed at knowledge itself as a whole. This issue provides the explicit focus of Socrates' examination of Theaetetus. That examination begins just after we learn a few more telling details about the boy.

Unlike Theodorus, Socrates does know the name of Theaetetus' father – and much more besides. He indicates that, contrary to Theodorus' judgment of the rarity of Theaetetus' soul, the father possessed these same qualities (144c5–7). In a strand of rhetoric that will soon intensify, Socrates questions the adequacy of Theodorus' assessment in such a way as to diminish Theodorus' authority in Theaetetus' eyes. That authority, and its power over Theaetetus, becomes more important in light of the piece of information Socrates adds regarding Theaetetus' patrimony. The young boy is fatherless and so has already inherited much property (*ousia*, 144c7–8). Much of this property, however, was squandered by the young boy's trustees or guardians (144d1–2). Nevertheless, Theodorus adds, he is still amazingly liberal with his funds – perhaps a subject of interest to this teacher (144d2–4). In sum, Theaetetus is an exceedingly intelligent, but also exceedingly vulnerable, boy whose trust has been betrayed.

This background plays a role in Theaetetus' attraction to what Theodorus has to offer: the promise of a trustworthy, indisputable, even perfect kind of knowledge. A sense of vulnerability and a concomitant desire for security are, however, hardly the province of fatherless boys alone, and so Theaetetus'

[31] John Lyons, *Structural Semantics, An Analysis of Part of the Vocabulary of Plato* (Oxford: Blackwell, 1969), 177, 179, 179n2, 196–8, 220–3.

[32] Griswold, *Plato's "Phaedrus,"* 6.

yearnings are of more general interest. Such hopes drive many of us to conceive of knowledge in a Theodoran manner. Knowledge, so conceived, neglects its own limitations. Discussing teaching with the teacher, Theodorus, Socrates learns of Theodorus' unwitting reliance on a cognitive capacity distinct from his geometric expertise. He also exhibits the way in which the implied imprecision of understanding, especially as regards the souls of his students, permits Theodorus' own passions to shape his views. Socrates thus takes us along the first steps toward the need for wisdom understood as midwifery, a path he continues to travel as he now turns his attention to Theaetetus.

Getting Theaetetus to Talk (144d8–146c6)

Socrates' conversation with Theodorus has revealed the geometer as one who believes technical knowledge to be *the* form of knowledge, willfully oblivious of its limitations. Socrates puts this information to use as he begins to interrogate Theaetetus. In particular, he challenges this notion of *techne*'s comprehensiveness by assailing the authority Theodorus holds for Theaetetus. Such authority must be great especially for someone whose life is precarious. Theodorus employs this authority to bring Theaetetus over to talk and Theaetetus places himself near Socrates. Theaetetus thus begins his "association" with Socrates whose focus is, as many have noted, less on Theaetetus' property (*ousia*) than his being (*ousia*), a distinction reflective of alternative views of good.[33] We begin to learn why Socrates should be so interested in this boy.

Socrates initiates a bond with Theaetetus intended to create an alliance in opposition to Theodorus. He immediately tells Theaetetus that Theodorus has likened his face to Socrates' (144d9–e1). This cannot be welcome news for Theaetetus. He must see that such a comment could not have been meant as a compliment. It will be some time before Socrates tells Theaetetus that Theodorus followed this insult with effusive praise. Instead, Socrates allows this wound to fester, as it must in this insecure boy who is dependent on his venerable teacher's good opinion. In a further exhibition of his own insensitivity, Theodorus says nothing that might assuage Theaetetus' hurt feelings. By the time Socrates does mention Theodorus' praise he will have considerably relaxed Theodorus' grip over Theaetetus. These tactics surely do make clear that for Socrates the student-teacher relationship involves something more than merely the conveyance of information. We will see what justifies such stratagems in what follows.

Engaging Theaetetus in a discussion that directly challenges Theodorus' authority, Socrates asks him, in what exactly is Theodorus an expert (145a4–9)? Eventually, this line of questioning makes explicit that the issue between

33 This double meaning is noted and interpreted by several commentators including Polansky, *Philosophy and Knowledge*, 41n5 and Eugenio Benitez and Livia Guimaraes, "Philosophy as Performed in Plato's *Theaetetus*," *Review of Metaphysics* 47 (1993): 308–9.

Socrates and Theodorus concerns the kind of knowledge available regarding the soul. Socrates prepares the ground for this outcome by first interrogating Theaetetus about Theodorus' judgment in two other areas of study, music and graphic art.

Socrates asks Theaetetus this complicated question: "if each of the pair of us had a lyre and he [Theodorus] said they had been similarly tuned, would we straight off trust him, or would we go on to examine whether he's speaking as one who is skilled in music? (144e1–3)." With this artful question Socrates touches on several points vital to his examination of Theaetetus' soul. First, he casts himself along with Theaetetus as fellow lyre owners. In this capacity they are compared with one another by Theodorus, thus preserving the sting of that earlier comparison and further cementing the bond between them. Moreover, using the dual form, Socrates speaks of how the two of them should react. He makes the character of their response turn on trust in the declarations of others, something about which, we now know, the boy must care deeply. Finally, with this question Socrates shifts the locus of authority from Theodorus to expertise in music. Socrates and Theaetetus sit in judgment of Theodorus, trusting his word only if he can be trusted to know that which is truly trustworthy, musical expertise. Socrates makes this choice explicit for Theaetetus when, to repeat, he asks, "would we straight off trust Theodorus' word or would we see whether he's skilled in music? (144e2–3)." Theaetetus chooses the latter option and thus makes the assessment of different forms of knowledge the focus of the discussion. More importantly, we see the attraction for Theaetetus of what expertise can offer, stronger even than the attraction of a venerable teacher. For him, the criterion of knowledge is trustworthiness. His attraction to expertise as *the* form of knowledge directly reflects the high value he sets on this quality.[34]

Socrates has placed himself and Theaetetus in the position of judging the expertise of others. It might be surprising to Theaetetus that he is called on to judge others' expertise when he lacks it himself – and he must lack it, else why seek a teacher of these subjects? Whether or not he is struck by his anomalous position, one familiar from such dialogues as the *Laches* and the *Meno*, it prepares him to judge concerns about which there may be no expert. The progress from music, to graphic art, to the soul, describes a movement toward precisely such a concern.

Socrates turns to the second stage of this movement, which involves the comparison of faces. He insists, even less plausibly than with respect to tuning lyres, that here too expertise is required.[35] Socrates maintains, specifically, that one must be a skilled graphic artist to make such comparisons, a point rightly met with something less than an enthusiastic endorsement by

[34] There are numerous words in this passage that have the *-ikos* ending denoting them as forms of *techne*. See Lyons, *Structural Semantics*, 143–4, 163–4.

[35] See Roochnik, "Self-Recognition," 42, 42n7.

Theaetetus (145c3). But Socrates presses forward toward his goal. He asks of such graphic skill, as he had not asked of music, whether Theodorus even possesses this expertise. Socrates' question enables Theaetetus to explicitly deny a kind of knowledge to his teacher, which he may be just as happy to do given the subject matter. In any case, Socrates plants the thought that there may be kinds of knowledge outside of Theodorus' ken and, moreover, that Theodorus may be a bit of a boaster, making pronouncements on topics about which he lacks expertise. In whittling away the scope of Theodorus' knowledge, Socrates goes so far as to ask whether Theodorus is a geometer at all (145a6). With Theaetetus' emphatic insistence that he is, Socrates has reached the limit of Theaetetus' willingness to distance himself from his teacher. He has also found the nerve of Theaetetus' attraction to Theodorus in his belief in the importance of geometry. As the paradigm of certain knowledge, it must provide a source for Theaetetus in which he can reliably place his trust.

Socrates now lists the other areas in which Theodorus is skilled: "astronomy, logistic, and music, and so much as is connected with education (145a8–9)."[36] From this positive list, Socrates draws the negative conclusion that "if he praises us or blames us with regard to the body it's not worth paying him any mind (145a11–13)." We might think that what remains in Theodorus' pedagogical repertoire concerns the soul. Yet we have already seen reason to doubt this conclusion in Theodorus' exaggerated concept of the soul's freedom. In casting doubt on his teacher's scope of expertise, Socrates places Theaetetus in the position of having to examine his own soul for himself. A crucial part of this self-examination, itself particularly revelatory of Theaetetus' soul, is whether Theaetetus will be willing to undertake it.

After this lengthy preface, Socrates finally comes to the soul. There are distinct asymmetries between his treatment of the first two subjects and his treatment of the soul. In the first two examples, the question was whether Theodorus, or anyone, had the expertise to render the judgment in question. The answer to this question was to be determined by examining the expert. The procedure differs regarding the soul. Here, the one who hears the praise of the soul – presumably whoever hears it – should be eager to examine the one praised. Moreover, the one praised must be eager to display himself. Socrates does not mention an expert regarding the soul (145b1–4). Theodorus' scope has been drastically limited. His expertise does not pertain to the body, and there is no expert on soul. Why should this be the case?

Those things of which there can be expertise are those objects that are determinate. Being determinate, they can be known with precision and certainty. Their determinacy also makes it possible to clearly demarcate the field of knowledge pertaining to each of them and so provide distinct areas in which

36 Surprisingly, Theaetetus answers somewhat tentatively to this list, perhaps because, as we later learn, he knows there are important subjects left out of Theodorus' curriculum.

one might then become an expert. These areas of expertise are the distinct *technai* that correspond to these objects.

Mathematics is central to *technai* in providing number, the basis of all determinacy, and in the clarity and thus knowability of its objects.[37] It is this precision and certainty that makes possible the activity from which the *technai* derive their great prestige – namely, their ability to manipulate the world, exercising some control over forces that otherwise might lead to our ruin. Those who grasp the clearly delineated rational principles of a particular *techne* do not hesitate to present themselves explicitly as knowers and as teachers capable of conveying these principles to others. Those concerned with gaining such control – and there are few who do not share this concern with the orphan Theaetetus – might well find such knowledge coterminous with knowledge itself.

With respect to the soul, it is especially the requirement of determinacy that makes doubtful the soul's eligibility as an object of expertise. As capable of self-reflection and self-motion, as capable of learning, the soul is not a passive, stable object waiting to be known. The present conversation, for example, will alter Theaetetus unpredictably depending on his own self-reflection and self-motion, on whether, as Socrates continually urges him, he will be eager to examine himself. This capacity for self-relational activity makes the being of the soul elusive.

If, concerning self-motion, a soul has an active and a passive part, we would need to ask what must again be divided to explain its initial motion? If, in addition, one part of the soul reflects on another, we would need to ask whether there must not be another part that reflects on the reflecting in order to have an awareness of this possibility.[38] Insofar as it both acts and reflects on acting, the soul's wholeness eludes us. For this reason, every reference to soul in the dialogue, beginning with the first, refers to its being at least complex and usually in internal conflict.

Unlike the objects of *techne* or expertise, intrinsic to the study of soul is a question about what it is and thus also what its good might be. The soul then lacks the determinacy of those objects that can be objects of *techne*. The question raised is how the soul might be known if not by technical understanding. Socrates soon points to this issue in pressing the question of the distinction between knowledge and wisdom. However, first, in an effort that displays an expertise-denying character itself, he must overcome a manifestation of self-relation in Theaetetus' reluctance to pursue understanding of his own soul.

Socrates reveals to Theaetetus that the point of the preceding discussion was to induce him to display his soul (145b6–9). Only now does he bring up Theodorus' praise. He uses it as leverage to elicit Theaetetus' participation in the examination that now occurs on Socrates' terms. Socrates has made it more

[37] Roochnik, *Of Art and Wisdom*, 36–9.
[38] On self-relation see ibid., 117, 125.

difficult for Theaetetus to wriggle out of the examination, as he continues to try to do, by insisting that Theaetetus has made a solemn agreement to participate and by offering the first of many words of encouragement (145c2–5).

As a last resort, Theaetetus suggests that perhaps Theodorus' praise was made in jest. Socrates responds bluntly, "that's not Theodorus' way (145c2)." How can Socrates be so confident of this judgment? He himself jests throughout the Platonic corpus and is extraordinarily playful in this dialogue too. Socrates' confidence seems related to the comment he adds to his denial of Theodorus' playfulness. Using the language of the courts Socrates connects being playful with suffering political consequences (145c3–5). By linking Theodorus' avoidance of political trouble with his disinclination to joke, Socrates points to a connection between his own political fate and his playfulness. Let's consider this link.

If Theodorus were capable of joking he would, in the present context, be assigning Theaetetus characteristics that he does not possess. He would pretend that things are as they are not. For this claim to work effectively as a joke, those hearing must not immediately grasp this discrepancy between how things are and how they are made to seem. The joke depends on the existence of the difference between seeming and being, and on the inability of the hearers to know instantaneously that there is a difference between what is and the account of what is. Joking is possible insofar as we are all immersed in the problem of knowledge. This problem comprises not only the possibility of a gap between how things are and how they are said to be, between what is and what appears to be, but also the fact that the discrepancy often requires effort to uncover. In this regard, Socrates' irony may reflect the notion that the world itself is ironic. With these observations in mind, two questions emerge: how can Socrates assert so confidently that Theodorus does not joke? How is joking related to political affairs?

Socrates' confident pronouncement about Theodorus' humorlessness derives from Theodorus' occupation as a mathematician. I hasten to add that this is not to say that mathematicians are uniformly devoid of humor. More importantly, I am not claiming that mathematics does not by itself raise issues connected with the distinction between being and seeming. Its use of images would suffice to raise such issues. Still, raising them is not the same thing as addressing them. I am suggesting that mathematics as such may not be able to explore those distinctions fully while maintaining its prestige as the paradigm of intelligibility, especially if intelligibility is identified with certainty. Joking might involve Theodorus in reflections that would threaten the notion of knowledge to which he is most strongly drawn. His reluctance to joke is of a piece with his reluctance to engage in examination of those objects that may only properly proceed conversationally.[39]

39 Socrates later attributes similar seriousness to Protagoras. Both are serious about securing their own, in the face of which Socratic playfulness seems irresponsible, childish, and thus

To come to the second question, why does this reluctance exempt Theodorus from those perils of political life in which Socrates' playfulness embroils him? There is no doubt that Socrates' often transparent irony can be irritating. Yet in connecting this ironic playfulness with politics, Plato has a deeper point to make. The point already introduced in the Prologue is that his awareness of the problem of knowledge, which makes possible joking and irony, requires Socrates to examine politics more seriously and thus more intimately than thinkers less acutely aware of this problem. His theoretical insight requires that he risk the dangers of close political analysis. Theodorus' reluctance to joke indicates his insufficient awareness, willing or unwilling, of knowledge as a problem. Socrates can therefore predict with confidence that because Theodorus does not examine this problem, neither would he see the need to investigate political life with the dangers that this investigation brings.

Seeing his last escape route blocked, Theaetetus grudgingly agrees to go along. He regards his participation as compelled by the opinion of his teachers.[40] Although he is reluctant to examine his own soul, Theaetetus proclaims that he is an eager student of the things that Theodorus teaches (145d3). In this way, Theaetetus shows a tacit recognition of the difference between types of knowledge, a difference he will, however, explicitly deny in his forthcoming identification of knowledge and wisdom. Socrates announces that he too is eager for such knowledge, but in a rare profession of competence says that he has these Theodoran subjects down "fairly well (145d4–6)." This claim enables Socrates to point to the same distinction in the objects of knowledge implicit in Theaetetus' comment. For, despite Socrates' claimed expertise, he immediately announces he is in perplexity about the subject of learning. The point brought home is that it is possible to know competently the things that Theodorus teaches and nevertheless be profoundly perplexed by others. Furthermore, these other things might have such significance that one would devote one's life to seeking knowledge of them rather than of the Theodoran matters.

Socrates' initial statement of his perplexity does concern that same issue with which he began the conversation, the issue of learning. This perplexity is in a sense more comprehensive than the meaning of knowledge on which he

immature. Socrates thus makes much of his Protagoras' insistence that he and Theodorus, being elderly, should act seriously. The appropriate conception of human maturity is in question in these passages (168c8–e3).

40 Having listed the subjects in Theodorus' repertoire, Socrates provides Theaetetus a list of subjects he learns from Theodorus. The chief difference between the two lists is the inclusion in the former of the phrase "and everything connected with education (145a9)." In question is whether Theodorus can be said to provide the most needful education, whether he or anyone else can teach these most needful things. Perhaps Theodorus' failure to joke (*paizon*) brings also into question his credentials as a source for a true education (*paideias*). That there may be an important distinction in the kind of things these two teachers aim to teach emerges in what follows.

eventually focuses. Socrates suggests the possibility that knowledge, at least as understood in the Theodoran manner, may not exhaust what is learnable. We need to keep in mind Socrates' initial perplexity regarding learning in considering the forthcoming examination of the meaning of knowledge. This perplexity keeps alive what proves to be the distinction between knowledge and wisdom. The meaning of knowledge, rather than of learning, becomes the featured issue only because Theaetetus does not make this distinction. Socrates makes our task easier, however, with his continual recurrence to the issue of learning.

Socrates asks the student, Theaetetus, to reflect on his own activity: what does he learn when he learns (145d7–8)? Socrates' question designates the object of learning as wisdom rather than knowledge: "to learn is to become wiser in whatever one learns" and "the wise are wise by virtue of wisdom (145d11)." With Theaetetus' assent to both these propositions, Socrates asks of wisdom: "And this doesn't differ at all does it from knowledge? (145e1)." Socrates could have said that to learn is to become more knowledgeable and then have proceeded directly to his perplexity about the meaning of knowledge. Instead, he makes Theaetetus decide on the relationship between wisdom and knowledge. But Theaetetus does not understand Socrates' question. Socrates asks Theaetetus about the relationship between wisdom and knowledge three separate times in this passage (145e1, e3–4, e6). After Theaetetus' first uncertainty about his meaning, Socrates makes his question more acceptable to Theaetetus by treating wisdom not as something unitary as he had done previously – "the wise are wise by virtue of wisdom" – but as plural. He does so in accord with the list of sciences just agreed to by Socrates and Theaetetus. He therefore now says it is "just those things in which they [the wise] are knowledgeable that they are wise (145e3–4)." Referring as it does to a plurality, this proposition is more in line with the way Theaetetus conceives of knowledge, as the many *technai*. So when Socrates asks one more time whether knowledge and wisdom are the same, Theaetetus affirms their identity.

We, however, should pause to take advantage of one of the opportunities Socrates provides to question this identity. Given the way in which Socrates secures Theaetetus' assent, we can well ask whether wisdom should not be distinguished from the many knowledges previously listed. His initial discussion with Theodorus alone prompts this question. Moreover, Socrates has just indicated that extraordinarily significant issues remain to be investigated – the present perplexity, for example – even after one has attained professional competence in these knowledges. Nor does Socrates treat the forthcoming attempt to understand the meaning of knowledge as itself just another of the knowledges in which one can gain expertise. Given its aporetic ending, it is certainly not clear that the result of the present examination is "epistemology," understood as a knowledge of knowledge.

The point is that Socrates keeps open the question that Theaetetus closes. He does so by insisting that they explore what Socrates, unlike his interlocutors, has long been perplexed about: whatever *is* knowledge as a whole? In this deeply reflexive dialogue, Socrates' attempt to understand knowledge as a whole illustrates the problem of knowledge related to the knowledge of all wholes. In focusing on this perplexity about knowledge, Socrates thus enables us to examine wisdom insofar as it gives access to this perplexity, and accordingly is distinguishable from knowledge. In the subsequent course of the dialogue he thus lets the orienting object of his life emerge in all it distinctiveness.

Prior to examining his perplexity, Socrates dwells on how their investigation should proceed. He says that the perplexity must be examined "with you and these here (145d6–7)." Socrates does not specifically ask Theodorus, his contemporary and an accomplished educator, about this perplexity. Nor does he ask Theaetetus whether he has learned of it from Theodorus as he had asked about geometry. Socrates marks off this perplexity from the things one might learn from the experts. The investigation into it will be conducted jointly, notwithstanding the fact that several of those present are boys about whom Socrates knows little, either of their training or competence. This approach diminishes the importance that expertise plays in the forthcoming investigation. Socrates displays the singularly unmethodical character of his method by breathlessly asking a series of questions: "Whatever is knowledge? Can we really say it? What do you all say? Who would be the first of us to speak? (145e9–146a2)."

Becoming ever more playful, he likens what they are doing to a game in which "the one who makes a mistake will, as children playing ball, take his seat, an ass" while "the one who prevails without a mistake, he'll be our king and enjoin us to answer whatever he wants (146a2–5)."[41] Socrates' playfulness should not obscure the very serious connection he draws here between a notion of knowledge and a notion of rule. This "quiz show" conception of their endeavor squares with the notion of knowledge as inerrancy, possessing the one right answer available for each question. In Socrates' scenario the one who possesses these answers rightly controls those who do not. He exerts his power to whatever end he pleases.

In this game, Socrates gestures toward a connection between *techne* and tyranny, which he presents more elaborately in other contexts. One such presentation is found in the *Charmides*, where the future tyrant, Critias, dreams of the error-free life made possible by the proper deployment of *techne* in

[41] The word used here, *basileus*, is used in the *Republic* to denote the conjunction of rule and knowledge in the philosopher-king (*Republic* 473c11–d3). Blondell writes that Socrates' intention is to suggest that "whoever excels in the argument will be entitled dialectical kingship like the Republic's philosopher-ruler." See Blondell, *The Play of Character*, 256, 256n24. I regard the kingship offered in the present context as reflective instead of the serious Critian hopes for the combination of power and knowledge and thus in opposition to the kind of human community desired by the playful philosopher.

the hands of the ruler.[42] Associated with Socrates' inquiry into perplexity is a much different view of human community. From his inquiry comes eagerness "to make us converse and become friends and mutually agreeable (146a7–8)." Here, the result is not one absolute ruler commanding us to do his bidding but the formation of a community based on agreement. Connecting the meaning of knowledge to the issue of rule, Socrates alerts us that how we conceive of knowledge bears on how we organize our lives together – and perhaps vice versa. This is an intensely practical issue, which involves and elicits our strongest passions. Requiring conversation on this matter again acknowledges the danger of solitary reflection on such issues in which passion-driven beliefs might go unchallenged by the countervailing views of others.

Theodorus balks when asked to join in this conversation. His refusal is most significant. It betokens a more general reluctance to engage in conversation at all as a means of inquiry (146b3–4). Such reluctance means that he does not see, or does not wish to see, the existence of inherently controversial issues such as the one Socrates has just alluded to, the views of justice and rule associated with the meaning of knowledge. Neither, apparently, does he care to achieve that mutuality and friendship available only through discussion. His view retains a distinctly coercive or controlling character that Theodorus, and the view of knowledge to which he clings, values more than truly shared understanding. There is a bond between the apolitical mathematician and the tyrant Critias.

Socrates points to Theodorus' reluctance by calling attention to the silence of the group as a whole. Socrates had addressed his questions to the entire group, including Theodorus to whom the younger students would defer. Who would dare speak up on such a weighty matter when his teacher was there? Theaetetus, we know, regards Theodorus as knowledgeable in many things. Theodorus' silence in this Socrates-engineered context must be deafening to his students.

Having revealed Theodorus' incapacity, Socrates asks if he is himself being boorish. Theodorus responds with the self-revelatory comments I have already mentioned regarding his resistance to this or any other conversation. He urges Socrates to engage one of the lads instead. It would, he says, be fitting for them "and they would improve much more, for youth is truly open to improvement in everything (146b4–5)." With this explanation, Theodorus points to a crucial distinction between himself and Socrates. Being "open to improvement in everything," the youth exemplify the peculiarly omni-directional character of the human soul's potential (146b5–6). Socrates' conversational approach is dictated by his focus on the soul as an object of study for it is, above all, through speech that the soul displays itself. Failing to see the importance of this study, Theodorus rejects the "conversation of this sort (146b3)." He also thus rejects the need to study those things about which there is no expertise, and so

[42] *Charmides* 171a6–172c3.

distinguishes himself from the Socratic philosopher.[43] Following Theodorus' declaration Socrates pointedly asks Theaetetus: "Do you hear, Theaetetus, what Theodorus is saying? (146b8)."

Theaetetus begins to participate under what, for him, is the compelling fear of disappointing his elders. He says he will answer but if he makes a mistake they will correct him. Socrates responds that they will correct him, if they are able (146c6). If only Theaetetus had the right answer at his fingertips he could, as Socrates says, rule all the others and never have to endure shame.

The State of Theaetetus' Soul (146c7–148e6)

Theaetetus' first answer to the question of the meaning of knowledge reflects lessons learned under Theodorus' tutelage. Knowledge is, for Theaetetus, whatever one learns from Theodorus, including especially geometry. However, in a revealing remark, Theaetetus adds to his list, "shoemaking and the other arts (*technai*) of the rest of the craftsmen (146d1–2)." In equating geometry with these applied knowledges Theaetetus confirms that for him knowledge is, or certainly includes, expertise or *techne*, the knowledge of a determinate object that can produce something useful for humanity. As it came later to be stated, knowledge is power, a view Socrates has Protagoras endorse later in the *Theaetetus* (166d4–7, 167b7–c4). Yet here Theaetetus does not provide such a unified conception of knowledge, leaving us only with a multiplicity of examples.

Theaetetus' usage in this context suggests the means by which he avoids this issue of the wholeness of knowledge. Having listed the examples of knowledge, he adds, "*all and each of them*, are nothing else than knowledge (146d2–3, emphasis added)." This highlighted phrase presumes no difficulty in moving from the particulars to the whole. Each particular is as wholly knowledge as the whole of knowledge comprising them. Theaetetus' locution reflects an arithmetical way of conceiving the world in which the homogeneous units taken together yield a sum, understood simply as these units taken together. Now, even in the case of number it is not clear that the units when taken together *are* in the same way as when separate. Socrates refers in the *Theaetetus*, and throughout the dialogues, to his difficulty in thinking of how one and one yield "two," a whole that has properties not found in either of its constituents.[44] This situation is, however, even more evident with respect to the many knowledges because, as Theaetetus' plurality of names for them attests, they are significantly heterogeneous. In particular, Theaetetus does not explain how these many knowledges can be identified as many, and thus distinct, and yet

43 Thus, when Socrates now tells Theaetetus that it is against *Themis* to disobey a wise man, it is not exactly clear to whom he is referring (146c1–2).

44 See, e.g., *Phaedo* 96e6–97b6. This issue regarding numbers becomes more explicit at 204a11–205a7.

somehow constitute a one. In what follows, Socrates makes Theaetetus' avoidance of this difficulty ever more difficult.

Socrates "praises" Theaetetus' answer for offering not only many when asked for one but also "complex instead of simple (146d5)." In adding this second opposition, Socrates introduces the possibility of four different types of response to his question. The most intriguing of these is that although a valid definition ought to provide for unity, that unity need not be simple. Clearly, if a definition leaves a plurality or a many, it seems it has not yet finished its work. On the basis of such a "definition" we would be unable to grasp the thing as the one kind of thing it is, a familiar Socratic complaint.[45] However, the possibility presented by Socrates' typology is of a unity that is not simple but complex. To connect this possibility with the previous reflections, should the parts of a whole not constitute that whole in some seamless, unproblematic way then it could be the case that the whole is, as such, a unity but in a complex manner, because it is not simply conceivable as the sum of its parts.[46] Socrates now begins to explore this possibility.

Explaining his critique of Theaetetus' response, Socrates first complains that Theaetetus has told him not what knowledge is but rather of what there is knowledge: "but the question, Theaetetus, was not this, of what things there's knowledge nor how many knowledges there are either. For we didn't ask because we wanted to count them but to get to know (*gnonai*) knowledge, whatever it itself is (146e7–10)."[47] Socrates wants to grasp knowledge as a whole but Theaetetus, in focusing on what knowledge is *of*, leaves a plurality corresponding to the many heterogeneous objects of knowledge. Yet Theaetetus' answer is not entirely wrongheaded. The number and kinds of knowledge do provide some knowledge of knowledge, some knowledge of the parts that somehow constitute the whole.[48] But in the preceding statement,

45 See, e.g., *Euthyphro* 6d9–e2; *Meno* 72a6–d1. On the momentous effect of Socrates' "what is" questions, see Gerasimos X. Santas, *Socrates: Philosophy in Plato's Early Dialogues* (London: Routledge, 1978), 6; Leo Strauss, *Natural Right and History* (Chicago: University of Chicago Press, 1968), 121–6; and Leo Strauss, "On Classical Political Philosophy," in *The Rebirth of Classical Political Rationalism*, ed. Thomas L. Pangle (Chicago: University of Chicago Press, 1989), 59–60. It is important to add that Socrates' orientation on this question does not presuppose comprehensive intelligibility. As I discuss here and in subsequent chapters, this orientation carries with it its own abiding perplexities.

46 This issue becomes most explicitly thematic in the treatment of the last definition of knowledge, but it is present throughout the dialogue. As I have indicated, Desjardins makes it the focal point of her interpretation of the dialogue but does not, in my view, adequately connect this issue to the question of the wholeness of the soul.

47 See Chapter 1, 12 and 12n24.

48 Both Bostock and McDowell recognize that examples can be informative. Moreover, by directing the reader to *Philebus* 12c1–18d2, McDowell acknowledges that Socrates understands this as well. See Bostock, *Plato's "Theaetetus,"* 32–3 and McDowell, *Plato "Theaetetus,"* 115. Nevertheless, we still want to distinguish defining a thing, saying what it is, from clarifying examples.

where Socrates distinguishes the issue of how many knowledges there are from what they are of, Socrates indicates that the greater problem is how this heterogeneous many can cohere as a whole. Socrates' complaint is more than simply an exhortation to look to the one whole instead of the many parts. He is also urging Theaetetus to consider how a heterogeneous many can be a one. In this way, Socrates makes more prominent the obstacles to such a movement from the many to the one. These obstacles are the implicit theme of the example Socrates now asks Theaetetus to consider, an example that, he suggests, elaborates what he has already stated (147a1). Elaborated in particular are the perplexities involved in knowing a whole.

Socrates illustrates his point with the example of mud.[49] Apparently, he has overcome his youthful reluctance to consider such ignoble examples. He is now willing to consider objects lacking in the perfection and purity of the loftiest things. The wonder that generates philosophy can arise from very mundane sources.[50] Socrates asks, "if we were asked to give a definition of mud and offered a list of different kinds of mud, wouldn't we be ridiculous (147a2–5)"? He then offers two separate reasons for their regarding themselves in this way. We need to consider these reasons in themselves and in relation to one another.

With respect to the first reason, Socrates asks whether it would be ridiculous because whenever we say the word "mud" we must already know what it is without enumerating the kinds of mud. Presumably, it cannot be the case that "someone understands some name of something if he doesn't know what it is (147b2–3)." Yet if by this claim Socrates means that understanding the referent of a name entails complete knowledge of that thing, the claim seems dubious on its face. The dialogue has given us reason to doubt it; Socrates calls Theaetetus by name without pretending that he knows the boy's soul prior to examining it. Furthermore, in the immediate context, Socrates twice mentions the possibility of "saying nothing," the implication being that one can utter words and names with less than complete understanding (146d7, 146e10). Later in the dialogue, Socrates points out that all along he and Theaetetus have been using the word *knowledge* without having yet succeeded in defining it (196d11–e7). Clearly, Socrates recognizes that to name a thing is not to understand it completely, and that we cannot avoid speaking on the basis of less than comprehensive knowledge. Why then does he make such a dubious claim in the present context? As we see in the subsequent exchange, the reason is related to the status and possibility of such partial knowledge.[51]

49 *Parmenides*. 130c1–e4. Benardete, *Being of the Beautiful*, I.94 calls attention to the connection with this dialogue.

50 It is probably too fanciful to point out that sea and earth are the parents of both wonder and mud. See Hesiod *Theogeny* 237.

51 One way to put the point is this: Socrates here intentionally confuses "a common sense and a paradoxical claim of epistemic priority, corresponding to the distinction between a weak and a strong sense of knowing." He does this to induce reflection on the prerequisites of partial

Socrates asks, whether one who "*does not know* science does not understand the science of shoes either (147b5–6, emphasis added)." Practicing shoemakers will be surprised to learn that to pursue their craft they must first grasp what perplexes even Socrates. In response to Theaetetus' puzzlement Socrates repeats this unusual question but with a crucial alteration. He asks, "so whoever's *ignorant* (*agnoei*) of science does not understand the leathermaking science or any different art either (147b8–9, emphasis added)." In the first iteration, not-knowing could include partial knowledge, but the second version, insisting on ignorance, precludes any knowledge whatsoever. This replacement thus points to what is dubious in Socrates' initial statement regarding names. In that initial statement, like the second version of his question, Socrates neglects the possibility of partial knowledge. He propounds instead an all-or-nothing view of knowledge – one either knows something fully or not at all – that explicitly dominates much of the dialogue. Why should this view be such an important part of Socrates' discussion with Theaetetus?

If I am correct in regarding the *Theaetetus* as Socrates' gift to his potential successors, then the possibility of partial knowledge rightly occupies a prominent place within it. This possibility, and the concomitant denial of the validity of the "all-or-nothing" view, is crucial to the Socratic way of life. On this possibility rests the possibility and necessity of Socratic inquiry. On it, too, rests the knowledge of ignorance, which is that inquiry's spur, and its chief result. Yet who would deny the existence of such knowledge, which seems to characterize our everyday existence? Why would one adopt instead the all-or-nothing view previously mentioned? As the dialogue has indicated, and as will become ever clearer, such a denial reflects Theaetetus' persistent inclination. Many, including the younger Socrates, share this inclination and its underlying source.[52] It constitutes an important obstacle to Socratic inquiry especially among those who understand themselves as seekers of knowledge. Accepting as their goal only the knowledge that is perfect and pure, they do not see the perplexities that make inquiry both possible and necessary. Or, more accurately, they do not wish to see these perplexities for it is less theoretical incapacity than an affective disposition that accounts ultimately for this neglect. To accept the need for such inquiry, and especially that its outcome might be partial knowledge, means to relinquish hope for an object wholly perfect, a demand of particular severity when the object in question is the good one desires for oneself.

For the key audience of the *Theaetetus*, the potential Socratic philosophers, it is important to think through the prerequisites, pertaining to knower and

knowledge. Kahn, *Plato and the Socratic Dialogue*, 157–64 and the material cited therein. This issue of the status of our initial cognition, present throughout the dialogue, returns most explicitly in the examination of the final definition of knowledge.

52 I refer to Socrates as a youth, not to the character "young Socrates" who appears in the *Sophist* and *Statesman*.

known, of such knowledge as we experience every day. For although it permeates our experience, the possibility of such partial knowledge proves exceedingly difficult to explain and even more difficult to defend as a desired goal. Soon Socrates will devise the midwife image expressly to respond to these difficulties. For now, we need to recognize that by supplanting partial knowledge with an apparently more theoretically straightforward, and more defensible, view of knowledge, Socrates ensures that only those willing and able to look beyond the straightforward view will work to discern the premises of that kind of knowledge with which we are most familiar. The justification for such intentional obscurity is above all pedagogical. It may be the case that only by making such a discovery for oneself could one accept partial knowledge and its persistent perplexities as inquiry's goal, a goal defensible to oneself and to others.

In this light, the initial answer regarding the varieties of mud is not as ridiculous as Socrates suggests. If we can distinguish between knowing a thing's name and knowing it wholly, then the former must be a kind of partial knowledge, which we must take steps to make more complete. Again, Socrates' movement from Theaetetus' name to an analysis of his soul instructs how to proceed. Similarly, the whole expressed by the name *mud* must also be analyzed, its parts considered, to move from the initial recognition of such a whole toward a full understanding of mud. A consideration of its many uses does seem an important part of such an analysis.

The second reason Socrates offers for the initial answer being ridiculous suggests, however, that such an analysis is not by itself sufficient. He says they could have answered in a "trivial and simple" way that mud is the product of earth "kneaded with a liquid" rather than consider the various kinds of mud (147c3–6). Why would this answer be ridiculous? Socrates' point here is that Theaetetus' answer is ridiculous because it offers an endless list of components when a brief and straightforward answer is available. Nevertheless, as with the preceding argument, Socrates' claim here too leaves something to be desired. The analysis that yields earth and liquid as mud's constituents does not yet provide comprehensive understanding of mud. To use the present example, without some sense of the whole, one does not know the proper proportions in which to mix earth and liquid. Neither, as Socrates' use of *liquid* instead of *water* suggests, does one thereby know whether the liquid used should be water or something else. Should one make mud with earth and mercury? The point is that analysis alone is insufficient because the parts come to light as parts only on the basis of their contribution to a whole.

For Theaetetus to know the whole of mud, or of knowledge, or any whole whatsoever, he must have a sense of the whole and an understanding of that which the whole comprises. To draw on Socrates' earlier categories, a whole can be both a unity and complex. This requirement leaves open the question that Theaetetus avoided in the case of knowledge: how do the parts and whole relate to one another? Answering this question seems crucial if we are to have knowledge of any whole, of what makes it the whole that it is. But this question proves more difficult if wholes are not wholly what they are throughout their parts, that is, if they are not uniformly what they are as wholes. For such wholes it is not the case that, as Theaetetus says of the many knowledges, "all and each of them are nothing else than knowledge (146d2–3)."

This discrepancy must make our knowledge of wholes other than immediate as we necessarily oscillate between analysis and, let us say, "recognition" in the attempt to bridge this discrepancy as far as possible. In short, we must make efforts to learn regarding the beings which, in their complexity, are not available for our immediate comprehensive understanding. The need to learn suggests that without such effort our knowledge of the beings remains partial. Yet the persistent discrepancy between parts and wholes raises the further possibility that the beings are such that our knowledge of them may always be partial and thus problematic, which is a persistent source of perplexity.[53]

As a matter of sheer intellect, the idea of such wholes is available to Theaetetus as he now demonstrates by exemplifying Socrates' point with an insight from his mathematical studies.[54] However, he shows himself less willing to acknowledge their existence in areas other than mathematics. His reluctance is all the more striking given the brilliance of his mathematical insight, which we must now consider.

Theaetetus' mathematical example emerged from a conversation with his companion, young Socrates, prompted by one of Theodorus' lectures. In his lecture Theodorus demonstrated to the boys each of the numbers, from three to seventeen, for which the side of the square having this number as its area is incommensurable with the unit length (147d4–e1).[55] Thus, for example, in the case of three, the sides would be the square root of three, a never-ending, nonrepeating sum that is therefore incommensurable with any whole number. Theodorus demonstrated this to be the case for each of the relevant numbers

53 Sayre writes, "Theaetetus is the only Socratic interlocutor to provide a complex example demonstrating that he grasps Socrates' critique of examples." This fact makes all the more striking his inability to apply this insight in other areas and deepens the suspicion that this inability is not primarily intellectual. See Kenneth Sayre, *Plato's Analytic Method* (Chicago: University of Chicago Press, 1969), 57–8.

54 The connection between Theaetetus' forthcoming example and the attempt to define knowledge lies in the notion of heterogeneous wholes. See esp. Desjardins, *The Rational Enterprise*, 79, 149, 170, 189–90. Bostock sees no parallel between the two while McDowell asserts there is such a parallel without, however, spelling out its content. See Bostock, *Plato's "Theaetetus,"* 34–5 and McDowell, *Plato "Theaetetus,"* 116.

55 Fowler writes that "our first unequivocal and explicit reference to incommensurability is in Plato at 147d–148b." See D. H. Fowler, *The Mathematics of Plato's Academy: A New Reconstruction* (Oxford: Clarendon Press, 1987), 295. On the importance of incommensurability in the dialogue see Cropsey, *Plato's World*, 27–9, 34–5 and Desjardins, *The Rational Enterprise*, 38, 79, 149, 170, 189–90.

separately before stopping, for some reason, at seventeen.[56] Together, Theaetetus and young Socrates produce what Theodorus, who did not participate in the postlecture conversation, did not even attempt – specifically, a way of thinking of the infinite series of such numbers that gathers them into a unity. Theaetetus thus shows himself capable of performing the crucial act of understanding, gathering a many into a one. He does not leave these numbers a plurality as Theodorus did, or as he did with respect to the many knowledges. However, Theaetetus' act of understanding in this example is even more significant as can be seen when we appreciate the details of his insight.

His procedure has two steps.[57] First, he divides all numbers in two. One type of number he refers to as "squares" (*dunameis*), which are those produced by the multiplication of rational numbers by themselves, as for example, four, nine, and sixteen. The factors of such numbers can be conceived geometrically as a square, which as such possesses sides of equal length. The second type of number Theaetetus terms *oblong* because they are the product of unequal factors represented therefore by the figure of a polygon with unequal sides (147e9–148a5).

Theaetetus next derives two kinds of lines based on these numbers. The former type refers to lines of squares formed by the first type of number. He calls these *lengths*. The second type of line is found in squares produced by the incommensurable numbers that he terms *powers* (*dunameis*, 148a8–b3). At the beginning of his explanation of his example, Theaetetus, following the accepted usage in Greek mathematics, referred to the squares produced by the multiplication factors as *dunameis*. But here, he refers to those lines representing incommensurable numbers, which when multiplied produce squares, as *powers*. This latter usage, unusual if not unique in the mathematical context, reflects the more common, less technical understanding that connects the notion of powers with potential.[58] Plato thus alerts us to the connection of Theaetetus' efforts and the issue of potential present from the beginning of the dialogue. This connection helps explain the character of the praise Socrates lavishes on Theaetetus' example.

Certainly, with this example, as previously mentioned, Theaetetus has exercised his understanding in moving from a plurality to a unity. But Socrates' praise – "This is the best that humans can do" – is ambiguous – and intentionally so (148b4). It expresses not only admiration for an act of comprehension but also a sense of the essential limits of reason.[59] We need to understand the

[56] See Myles Burnyeat, "The Philosophic Sense of Theaetetus' Mathematics," *ISIS* 69 (1978): 503–4, 517 on why Theodorus stopped at seventeen.

[57] See the treatment of this passage as a whole by Polansky, *Philosophy and Knowledge*, 53–8. See also Burnyeat, *The "Theaetetus" of Plato*, 266n3.

[58] See Burnyeat, "The Philosophic Sense of Theaetetus' Mathematics," 495–8.

[59] Ibid., 511–12. Burnyeat confines Theaetetus' achievement to his collecting a many into one.

character of the plurality that Theaetetus unifies, especially in the context of the persistent theme of parts and wholes, to appreciate this latter point.

Theaetetus unifies a plurality of incommensurable numbers, numbers that in themselves cannot be understood in a simply rational way. Out of this multitude, he constructs a whole using a geometric image. This construction makes the incommensurables commensurable, and thus intelligible, in a way that they previously were not. The character of the "parts" of this whole determines that it cannot be grasped simply by summing them together. The whole possesses a property – commensurability – that by definition is absent from its parts. When Socrates praises Theaetetus, he is no doubt impressed by Theaetetus' ingenuity in arriving at such an understanding of a whole not evident in its parts. However, he also suggests that with respect to such objects our grasp of the whole may be insuperably distinct from our cognition of the parts. In this sense, Theaetetus' procedure is "the best humans can do."

Theaetetus' frequent and varied use of the word *dunamis* is pertinent in this regard. He uses it not only when speaking of the incommensurable lines called powers but also when he confesses his own incapacity to apply his insight to the case of knowledge (148b7, e3). In linking these instances of capacity or incapacity, his usage raises the question as to whether human powers too might require similar treatment in expressing the whole comprising them. The geometer Theodorus saw the need to generate images to represent his understanding of Theaetetus' character or, as one might say, his soul. Socrates is about to devise an elaborate image of human activity designed to enhance our understanding of it. He does so in response to Theaetetus' confession of the extent to which his own soul, being deeply divided, eludes wholeness. Theaetetus' treatment of incommensurables may be called for as well in the case of soul. But Theaetetus does not, or will not, undertake this application.

The confession Theaetetus offers concerns specifically his incapacity to apply his mathematical insight to the case of knowledge. Again, given the preceding demonstration of Theaetetus' brilliance, this incapacity cannot be simply intellectual. Accordingly, Socrates responds not simply with argument but with encouragement in the form of an appeal to Theaetetus' desire for honor. Changing his previous rhetorical tack, Socrates insists that far from being a small thing, knowing what knowledge is must be a task only for the most adept (148c2–9). He exhorts Theaetetus "to be confident about himself" and "eager in every way" to replicate his mathematical insight in this case of knowledge (142c10–d2). Theaetetus responds enthusiastically to this appeal. He swears by Zeus as he thinks about the "greats" who would be up to the task and among whom he would like to be counted (148c8). These exchanges carry forward the problematic issue now at hand insofar as Theaetetus' desire for distinction presupposes a nature that permits a vast diversity among individuals of the same kind. And the capacities for self-reflection and self-motion implied in Socrates' hortatory phrases play significant roles in widening the scope of this diversity. The question of wholes especially regarding humankind persists: in what manner is humanity, or an individual human, unified as a whole? To employ the images of the *Protagoras*, if virtue is a whole, it seems to be so in the manner of a face rather than a piece of gold, a point that later becomes explicit in the *Theaetetus*.[60]

Socrates, however, focuses not on humanity but on the whole of knowledge. He leaves ambiguous whether knowledge can be thus unified, saying that, with respect to the powers, Theaetetus "encompassed them all, many as they are, in one look (*eidei*, 148d6)."[61] Socrates asks Theaetetus to "now try to address the many knowledges with one speech (*logos*, 148d4–7)." Theaetetus did provide for one look that comprehended the powers, but he was compelled to do this precisely because he could not provide one rational account or speech for these incommensurables. With respect to knowledge, it is not clear which of these unifications is possible – or whether both must somehow play a role.

In response to this request, Theaetetus provides a rich account of his psychological struggles illustrating the elusive wholeness of his own soul. He portrays himself as caught between incapacities, able neither to find something adequate about this issue nor to cease caring about it (148e1–6). Most indicative of his dilemma is his acknowledgment that he has "heard the questions that are reported as coming from Socrates (148e2–3)." He thus knew Socrates was inquiring into questions about which he cares deeply, yet he chose only to hear about them secondhand. What counter-Socratic passion prevented him from becoming Socrates' student? Let's consider the conflict raging within Theaetetus more closely.

As I just mentioned, Theaetetus says he is incapable of persuading himself that he or anyone else speaks adequately about these issues (148e3–5). This judgment must include Theodorus whose curriculum neglects issues Theaetetus senses are most pertinent to his education. Despite his allegiance to the technical model of knowledge, he is at least partially aware that it is inadequate regarding issues that, to him, are of great concern. Theaetetus' confessed incapacity indicates that he must have tried to persuade himself that someone, whether he or others, did speak adequately about these issues. How else could he have come to realize his incapacity? This incapacity to discover anything adequate about these issues, coupled with his refusal to accept what he knows to be an incomplete answer, bespeaks a yearning to know.

But that yearning is not the only force active within him. His recognition of the need for persuasion, including self-persuasion, suggests that Theaetetus'

[60] *Protagoras* 329d4–8.

[61] This is the first use of this word in the dialogue. It is found surprisingly sparingly in the *Theaetetus*, especially given its theme. It is always used, moreover, in a nontechnical sense, i.e., in a manner unrelated to claims about separately existing, permanently enduring, unchanging intelligibles.

inquiry occurs in a context in which alternative voices contend passionately with one another. Struggling against that desire to know how things truly are, which prohibited his acceptance of inadequate answers, there must also be a voice within urging just that acceptance of something less. Thus, he refers to his other incapacity, his inability to stop caring about these issues that, again, could only have been discovered by attempting not to care (148e5–6). The struggle within him between the desire to know and the desire not to care left him a student of Socrates by hearsay alone.

Theaetetus' poignant self-analysis provides further insight as to why this conversation with him might be of such interest to Socrates. In one such as Theodorus any such psychological battle is long over. The grass covers the battlefield so thoroughly as to obscure whether a battle ever occurred on that plain. Within Theaetetus, however, the struggle rages between the passions moving him sometimes nearer to, sometimes farther from, the Socratic life.

In light of Theaetetus' forthcoming definition of knowledge, it is worth noting parenthetically that this self-portrayal reveals him as something more than mind alone. Accordingly, his cognitive life cannot be characterized, in the manner of that forthcoming definition, as a sort of pure receptivity unaffected by his being the particular person he is. Theaetetus' psychological self-portrait affirms that not only is it the case that the beings are not immediately available, but even if they were we only know them through ourselves as souls. That is, we know as embodied particulars, as beings that act and think about acting, as beings capable of self-critical judgment. As such, however, we are also capable of, and susceptible to, error and distortion. Our own complexity presents another perplexity constituting the problem of knowledge.

From Theaetetus' self-analysis, we learn that his soul is in perplexity in the face of the perplexing beings. We learn also that there must be a counter-Socratic passion that prevented him from becoming Socrates' student, prevented him from confronting these perplexities. In Theaetetus, Socrates meets an interlocutor who embodies the problem of knowledge and the resistance to confronting it. This is the situation posed by the context of the midwife image, and it is to this situation that the image responds. With that image, Socrates elucidates and responds both to the problem of knowledge that comprises the twin perplexities, on the side of the soul and of the beings, and to the obstacle to reflection on these perplexities. This response is an image of those activities of teaching and learning with which Socrates' conversation begins. It is ultimately, however, an image of his core philosophic activity, his search for wisdom.[62] That activity involves, above all, consideration of the most cherished opinions of the community. Socrates' maieutic response to the problem of knowledge proves, at its heart, to require conversation about the political things.

[62] Burnyeat writes of the midwife passage: "It is an account of a method of education which is at the same time a method of doing philosophy." See Burnyeat, *The "Theaetetus" of Plato*, 6–7.

The Midwife (148e7–151d6)

Socrates tells Theaetetus that the psychological turmoil from which he suffers is a sure sign that he is experiencing labor pains (148e7–8). To this odd observation, Theaetetus responds: "I do not know but what I've experienced I say (148e9–10)." Previously, Socrates raised the possibility of "saying nothing," of speaking on the basis of less than complete knowledge. Theaetetus' statement suggests that this is a possibility with respect to self-knowledge as well. Here too we necessarily rely on experience which does not yield perfect knowledge.

Calling Theaetetus "ridiculous," Socrates announces his qualifications to deliver Theaetetus of his pain. Not only is he the son of a midwife, he himself practices the art (149a1–2). Theaetetus has heard that Socrates' mother was a midwife – Phaenarete, "very noble and intrepid" – but he is taken aback by Socrates' bizarre claim that he too is a practitioner (149a2–3).[63] Nearing the end of his life, Socrates exercises his musical capacities to generate a novel image of his activity.[64] The image speaks not only to the particular situation, but also, with an eye to Socrates' wider audience, it expresses something essential about his own activity. For some reason Socrates chooses to be remembered as an adept of the maieutic art.

Having called Theaetetus "ridiculous" Socrates proceeds to place himself in an equally ridiculous light, underscoring one of the purposes of the image. Specifically, one of the links in the bond he aims to form with Theaetetus is a willingness to be ridiculous, to be laughed at, to be, as he later says, shameless (196d3, e11).[65] Such willingness sits uneasily with any deep concern for status or honor, that is, for the things that earn the gentleman's reputation of being "noble and good." This aspect of the image also provides an initial indication of just what it is that obstructs Theaetetus' inquiry into the human things.

The portrait Socrates proceeds to paint of himself is distinctly countercultural. Practicing the midwife's art, he explicitly follows in the footsteps of his mother rather than his father. His guide is the *goddess* of maturation, Artemis (149b9).[66] Socrates places himself far from any ideal of manliness.[67] He freely

[63] See Clay, *Platonic Questions*, 59, for a consideration of the bearing of Socrates' parents' names on his activity. Intrepidity is a quality evident in other famous midwives. See Exodus I: 15–19. I consider in Chapter 5 why midwifery and intrepidity belong together. The connection has to do, in turn, with the similarities between midwifery and politics.

[64] On whether the image is wholly unprecedented, see Myles Burnyeat, "Socratic Midwifery, Platonic Inspiration," *Bulletin of the Institute of Classical Studies* 24 (1977): 7–15. Burnyeat argues that the image is not genuinely Socratic but is rather a Platonic invention. For a counterargument to Burnyeat's see Jules Tomin, "Socratic Midwifery," *Classical Quarterly* 37 (1987): 97–102. I am interested in Theaetetus' reaction within the dialogue rather than speculation regarding the historical Socrates.

[65] I deal more extensively with the issues of shame and shamelessness in Chapter 8.

[66] On Artemis, see Howland, *The Paradox of Political Philosophy*, 84–6.

[67] See Blondell, *The Play of Character*, 267.

acknowledges that because of his odd behavior the many do regard him as *atopos* – as strange or, literally, placeless – reason enough for someone like Theaetetus to keep his distance, unsure of his place as this fatherless boy must be (149a9). Of at least equal concern, Socrates notes that his practice has also earned him the reputation of being one who induces perplexity, making others be at a loss (*aporein*, 149a9). Together, these self-characterizations led his fellow citizens to denounce him (149a6–10). We need to consider the connection between Socrates' strangeness and his reputation as a cause of perplexity.

Socrates' perplexity-causing art presupposes an initial unperplexed view, an awareness of the world that he undertakes to question. It does not presume the complete obliviousness of a blank slate.[68] As an inducer of perplexity, Socrates causes those who previously had a way to lose it, to be placed in *aporia*. Such questioning and the resultant perplexity, Socrates admits, is painful: hence, the association with labor pains. Numerous examples throughout the Platonic corpus testify to the anger that follows on such pain.[69]

Socrates' strangeness or placelessness helps us understand the character of the perplexities that cause pain and lead to his denunciation. Elsewhere, Socrates characterizes his knowledge as placeless because of its subject matter. The available knowledge of soul, of the human things, is *a-topos* because, as we have seen, it does not fit neatly into any of the categories defined by the *technai*.[70] It is especially in exploring the human things and their resistance to determinate understanding that Socrates generates perplexity.

These human things necessarily include those views of justice and nobility that constitute the political community. If one should come to question the community's view of justice and nobility, one would indeed be rendered placeless, without a home in one's homeland, as strange as an elderly Athenian man claiming to be a midwife. In causing others to question, especially the young, Socrates must arouse the ire of the community that sees its eventual demise in the alienation of its best youth from these accepted views. In urging shamelessness, a lack of concern for the opinions of one's fellow citizens, Socrates

[68] This is not, however, to invoke the doctrine of Recollection as the source of these initial opinions. The doctrine of recollection is, as I have mentioned, absent from the *Theaetetus*. That doctrine is invoked, famously, in the *Meno*. It responds to the "paradox of inquiry," the perplexity as to how we can inquire into anything insofar as such inquiry seems to require that we know the object of our search before we know it – else why must we inquire into it. The *Theaetetus* presents an alternative response to that perplexity in its examination of the context of knowing, which does not neglect the participation of the community in the genesis of our initial opinions. Nicholas White and McDowell think the *Theaetetus* bears on the "paradox of inquiry" but not in the manner indicated here. See Nicholas P. White, *Plato on Knowledge and Reality* (Indianapolis, IN: Hackett Publishing Company, 1976), 181–2 and McDowell, *Plato "Theaetetus,"* 222–3.

[69] See, e.g., *Meno* 79e7–80b7.

[70] On Socrates' strangeness in general see Pierre Hadot, *Philosophy as a Way of Life*, trans. Michael Chase (Malden, MA: Blackwell, 1995), 57, 158–70. On this relationship between Socrates strangeness and his "human wisdom" see Roochnik, *Of Art and Wisdom*, 124, 240.

threatens the very foundation of the community in undermining a powerful preservative of the community's enduring norms.[71] The point is that there is an intrinsic link between Socrates' strange knowledge and his subversiveness. No wonder they denounce him.

But why then does Socrates engage in this activity? Why, more importantly, does such activity constitute not merely an aspect but, as he indicates, the core of his philosophic activity? The most apparent sense conveyed through the midwife image is Socrates' selflessness, that he is simply devoted to others' good. The image leaves the impression that somehow it is good for others, especially the youth, to go through the pains of being perplexed. Beneficial as well is that they express themselves regarding the things about which they are perplexed.

Granting that all of this may be true, we have yet to explain *Socrates*' motivation for such activity, especially in light of those negative consequences for himself that he seems particularly eager to point out. Furthermore, the potential philosopher who reads this text might well wonder why he or she should emulate Socrates in the practice of this odd and dangerous art. More particularly, the potential philosopher might ask, can't there be serious philosophy without midwifery, without philosophic examination of others' political-ethical views? With these questions in mind let's examine Socrates' treatment of the image that he tells Theaetetus is constructed so that "you'll more easily understand what I want to say (149b4–5)."

Socrates designates those who were once fertile but are now barren as alone qualified to act as midwives (149b5–7). This is the dictate of the goddess Artemis who, as previously mentioned, Socrates invokes as his guide. Artemis oversees maturation. In this regard she is a most appropriate deity insofar as Socrates' image evokes human potential and development in all its forms. Socrates' explanation for Artemis' decision is that "human nature is too weak to grasp an art of whatever it is inexperienced (149c1–2)." Now Socrates will shortly insist that he is "sterile of wisdom" and that the god "prevented me from generating (150c4, 150c7–8)." Putting these two notions together, the possibility arises that his art does not promise to deliver others of wisdom, at least as wisdom has come to be understood in the dialogue, specifically, as identified with technical knowledge. The next step in Socrates' presentation gives us reason to question precisely the availability of wisdom so understood. It also therefore gives us further reason to wonder at the goal and thus also the motivation of Socrates' art.

The intent of this next step is perhaps signaled by the collapse of a distinction Plato elsewhere takes pains to preserve.[72] Specifically, in response to

[71] Consider Arlene Saxonhouse's insightful treatment of shame as a prerequisite of civil society. Arlene Saxonhouse, *Free Speech and Democracy in Ancient Athens* (Cambridge: Cambridge University Press, 2006), 60–82.

[72] *Laws* 656a10–b7.

Theaetetus' claim that Socrates' explanation of Artemis' activity is "likely," Socrates adds that the following is "as likely as it is necessary (149c5)." Socrates now attributes to the midwife a function that, if possible, would install necessity in a realm heretofore thought to be governed in part by the merely likely, that is, by chance.

Socrates calls the midwives "most clever go-betweens since they are all-wise when it comes to recognizing what sort of woman must be with what sort of man to give birth to the best possible children (149d7–8)." With this claim, Socrates attributes to the midwives an art far surpassing in scope what anyone else has claimed. This statement takes Theaetetus aback. He professes complete ignorance that such a task could be part of the midwives' art (149d9). Yet Socrates insists that the midwives take greater pride in this activity than in the cutting of the umbilical cord – as well they should if this art is available (149d10–e1). But is it available? Can that nuptial number be ascertained that would eliminate chance in the area of human development?[73] Socrates has indicated what those possessing such a *techne* of comprehensive eugenics would need to know. If they possess this art they would certainly deserve to be called "all-wise" for they would then know with precision and certainty how to produce what they know to be "the best possible children." They would know the meaning of human fulfillment and the means to achieve it. Unfortunately, Socrates' subsequent discussion suggests that he raises this extravagant claim only to better distinguish his own more moderate claims to know, claims reflected in his practice of midwifery.

Socrates indicates the unavailability of comprehensive eugenics in several ways. He first compares this eugenic *techne* to the art of farming, securing Theaetetus' agreement that "the care and harvesting of the fruit from the earth" is the same art as that which recognizes "what sort of plant and seed must be cast into what sort of earth (149e3–4)." He then asks, "into woman ... do you believe there's *a different art of something of this sort*, and a different one of harvesting? (149e6–7, emphasis added)." Surely, the name of the art of planting the seed in humans would be readily available if an art of such importance existed.

Perhaps, as Socrates claims, the art exists but genuine midwives refrain from its practice lest they be charged with pimping, "the unjust and artless bringing together of man and woman (150a1–2)." Yet, again, it is difficult to believe that such a grand *techne* would be laid aside out of such fears. If it were available, would not the public's demand for its practice overcome any compunction on the part of the midwives? Socrates' explanation of the midwives' reluctance seems especially dubious in view of his forthcoming admission that when confronted with students who are not pregnant in soul, "I kindly act as go-between," setting them up with other teachers, especially "wise" sophists such as Prodicus (151b6). The fear of being known as a pimp does not stop

73 *Republic* 546a1–d1.

Socrates from acting as go-between and there must be other midwives who would act in a similarly "intrepid" manner were they able to do so (149a2).

Socrates points to the source of their inability when he characterizes the defective form of eugenics as not only "artless" but "unjust." There can certainly be a question as to whether this or that use of a *techne* is just, but in the case of a *techne* of human fulfillment such a question would have to become a technical question, a question of artfulness. Yet Socrates maintains the distinction between artless and unjust. He thereby indicates that the question of justice, the question of the satisfaction of the diverse and competing human goods, cannot be treated with the precision required of a *techne*. In light of the lack of precision in the face of the multiplicity of human goods, it would seem, furthermore, that what we should mean by "the best possible children" remains a matter of controversy. On which specific good, or on which goods in what order, should the midwives orient their production of these humans? The difficulty of answering such questions suggests that the *techne* of comprehensive eugenics remains a dream. Socratic midwifery stands as the alternative to the impossible eugenics of the "all-wise."

The question raised by eugenics is not simply how to produce offspring but the "best possible children." Each community pursues this question of how to reproduce itself not just in the physical sense but also in the comprehensive psychic sense. Facing his own demise, this is no idle question for Socrates. He too is a founder, the father of a new way of philosophy. Appropriately, this metaphor of fathers and sons pervades the dialogue.[74] Thinking this practice to be good, Socrates must hope that it will persist. Moreover, Socrates' use of the word *association* evokes the institution by which old Athens aimed to reproduce itself. The equally pervasive issue of teaching and learning also asks how and to what extent Socrates can reproduce in others what is distinctive about himself.

In this regard, there is a deep connection between midwifery and political life. Both activities recognize the inadequacy of spontaneous nature alone with respect to human fulfillment. Both see the need to supplement spontaneous nature by human efforts if human life is to be possible much less to flourish. Clearly, an intrepid spirit is required to face these deficiencies of our natural home.

However, Socrates' midwifery faces these exigencies in a different manner than does the political community. The discursive community Socrates establishes with his interlocutors differs in its aim from the political community. The question remains, what exactly is that aim? Some commentators regard

[74] Dorter writes, "The parent-child relation is in fact the dominant leitmotiv of the dialogue." He cites explicit uses of the metaphor at 144c, 149, 151, 157c–d, 164, 155d, and 156a–157c. Both Dorter and Desjardins detail the extensive use of erotic and reproductive imagery in the dialogue. See Dorter, *Form and Good*, 76–9, 94–6 and Desjardins, *The Rational Enterprise*, 37–42, 52–4.

Socrates' efforts with Theaetetus as aiming to produce his philosophic heir.[75] I am dubious about this claim. If anything, Socrates' conversation with this highly talented, superbly educated boy confirms the difficulties of conveying the Socratic way. So, too, does the midwife image insofar as it places Socrates in a role other than father. As I discuss in the following text, his mention of one Aristides in this context further substantiates these difficulties. What makes the psychic reproduction of humans so difficult is the elusive nature of the soul in general and *a fortiori* any particular soul. Socrates' recognition of the complexity of soul dissipates any dream he might have had of comprehensive eugenics. And as we see in what follows, it is the soul in its perplexity that lies at the core of the wisdom that Socrates distinctively seeks.

We have yet to fully understand the aim of his midwifery. Perhaps we get a clearer picture as Socrates now explicitly distinguishes between his own midwifery and features of the usual practice. The latter delivers human offspring, easily recognizable as such. But Socrates presides at psychic births in which his students "sometimes give birth to images and sometimes to the simply true, and it's not easy to gain recognition of the difference (150a9–b2)." This difficulty to which Socrates refers is especially profound regarding those things available to us only in and through images, the images of the written and spoken word. I mean especially the human things – expressed, for example, in Theodorus' images of the soul, and in the views of justice, nobility, and good to which Socrates directs his attention. It is expressed as well in the present image of teaching and learning that, we soon see, insofar as it is an image cannot capture the complete truth of Socrates' activity. All these are "visible" to us only in speech. With respect to these especially, the distinction between the image and the truth is hard to discern. They are the focus of Socrates' art, which he now presents in an uninterrupted monologue about the centrality of the examination of such opinions, especially those of the youth, concerning the human things. It is a monologue about the necessarily conversational character of Socratic philosophy.[76]

The midwife image captures the elicitative aspect of Socrates' efforts, his coaxing students to express what is somehow already in them. Yet Socrates concludes that the midwife's function is actually "less than my own action" because not only does he elicit, but also he judges or assesses what is expressed (150a8–9).[77] In this way, he exceeds the bounds of standard midwifery. Socrates

[75] See, e.g., the reference in note 17 (in the preceding text) and the material cited therein.

[76] See Cropsey, *Plato's World*, 36.

[77] Vlastos makes a hard and fast distinction between what he terms Socrates' elenctic activity and his maieutics. See Gregory Vlastos, *Socratic Studies* (Cambridge: Cambridge University Press, 1994), 5n19. He writes also, "In the *Theaetetus* Socrates gives us a glimpse of a different much improved Socrates who has laid to rest the demon of contentiousness within him." See Gregory Vlastos, *Socrates, Ironist and Moral Philosopher* (Ithaca, NY: Cornell University Press, 1991), 155. He thus understands himself to be following Burnyeat. But Burnyeat recognizes that Socrates' most important task, and one that has no analogue in ordinary

deems this latter critical or assessment function the "greatest and most beautiful" aspect of his work (150b2). In order to capture this aspect of his work he even introduces an alternative image. Referring to the activity of mining, he designates this activity as "assaying" (150c1).[78] Socrates must elicit in order to judge, but the latter activity seems more important to him. It is what especially distinguishes his activity vis-à-vis the midwives.

Socrates' midwifery involves, most crucially, "examining their souls in giving birth (150b8–9)." It is the same activity to which he called attention at the outset of his conversation with Theodorus when he tells him, "I myself examine this on my own, to the extent I can (143d6–7)." The examination in both instances is of the young, their opinions, and their potential for growth. Socrates' practice raises several questions. Why does it proceed through questioning conversation? Why is it especially of the young? And, most significantly, as we continue to pursue the original question of his midwifery's aim, why does Socrates place such *philosophic* importance on this examination that so angered his fellow citizens?

Socrates says that he examines the "thought" of the young, access to which is through what they say, through conversation (150c2). He elicits their opinions through his famous questioning while, as he claims, he refrains from "[declaring] anything about anything (150c5–6)." But what is the purpose of these interrogations? If Socrates is in doubt regarding the meaning of human good or justice or nobility it seems he could learn more from discussions with mature intellectual equals than with the kind of sometimes tendentious exchanges evident throughout the Platonic corpus. Yet, in fact, we never see one in-depth conversation between a mature Socrates and an equally mature philosopher.[79] Instead, we see him engaging sophists, politicians, and often the youth. Some of the latter seem quite unpromising. Nevertheless, Socrates engages them well beyond the point when their philosophic potential remains in question. It is difficult to chalk up Socrates' interest in the latter to benevolence alone. He often denies, as here, that they learn anything from him, and many do seem untouched or simply annoyed by Socrates. Moreover, some distort what they take from Socrates, whether intentionally or not, for exceedingly pernicious ends with exceedingly negative consequences for Socrates.[80] Finally, Socrates' famous poverty testifies to his refusal to take pay for his

midwifery, is that of testing whether the thought-product he has delivered is genuine or a wind egg. See Burnyeat, "Socratic Midwifery, Platonic Inspiration," 8. The word Socrates uses for this activity is *elenchein* (161e7).

78 This image of assaying occurs again at 203a1.

79 See Christopher Bruell, *On the Socratic Education: An Introduction to the Shorter Platonic Dialogues* (Lanham, MD: Rowman and Littlefield Publishers, 1999), 147. My understanding of Socrates' pedagogy in general is indebted to Bruell's treatment.

80 See my "Tyranny and Self-Knowledge: Critias and Socrates in Plato's *Charmides*," *American Political Science Review* 93 (1999): 403.

services.[81] If it is neither benevolence nor material gain that fully explains Socrates' conversations with the young, how then are they explained?

In answering this question it is important to note that Socrates cites his *daimonion*'s assistance in the pursuit of these conversations (151a3–4). Judging by his references to his *daimonion* in other dialogues, this uncanny power plays an admonitory role in his life, counseling against certain activities.[82] Nevertheless, if only because every such counsel contains an implicit view of desirable action, the *daimonion* is not simply nay-saying. Rather, it protects and defends Socrates, guiding him away from those activities that would inhibit his central activity – his "terrible love" of inquiry into the good (169c1). If the *daimonion* permits his conversations with the youth, then these must contribute to the pursuit dictated by this desire. We must consider how.

We desire what we do not fully possess, what we, in some sense, lack. Throughout the *Theaetetus*, Socrates insists that he lacks wisdom (150c4, c6, 157c7–9, 161b1–5, 210c5–6). Such a lack is definitionally appropriate to the philosopher, the one who seeks, and thus does not possess, wisdom. However, Socrates' vehement denial in the present context pertains more specifically to wisdom as it has been defined in the dialogue. He has directed us to a particular version of wisdom in the present passage when he calls "all-wise" those who claim to possess the art of comprehensive eugenics. The sophists, Prodicus and Protagoras, also receive this designation (151b5–6, 152c8, 180c7–181b5). Beneath their differences they share an extravagant claim to have a kind of knowledge that eliminates chance, uncertainty, and even ambiguity.[83] It is in contrast to this claim that we should understand Socrates' insistence that he is sterile of wisdom or, more moderately, that he is "hardly wise (150d1)."[84] He is certainly bereft of that view of wisdom that earns Prodicus and Protagoras the name *wise*. Similarly, he is devoid of that capacity of the "all-wise" midwives to understand nature fully and so control it.

The hope for this kind of wisdom underlies the many's reproach of Socrates for always only asking questions instead of declaring his wisdom (150c7). But it is not only the many that harbor this hope. The view of wisdom held by Socrates' predecessors can also be connected with such an expectation. It is a hope, moreover, once shared by Socrates himself. As I noted previously, Socrates tells Cebes on his last day that he was once "wondrously desirous of

[81] *Apology* 31b5–c3.

[82] *Apology* 31c3–d6; *Phaedrus* 242b8–c3; *Theages* 128d1–130e10.

[83] Michael Davis maintains that Protagoras "claims to have an architectonic art of speech" that would "foreclose the possibility of interesting ambiguity." Michael Davis, *The Poetry of Philosophy: On Aristotle's "Poetics"* (Lanham, MD: Rowman and Littlefield Publishers, 1992), 102.

[84] Sedley, *The Midwife of Platonism*, 31n55, writes "that *ou panu ti sophos* means 'not entirely wise' not, as usually translated, 'not at all wise' was recognized by the anonymous commentator on the *Theaetetus* (55.42.5)."

that wisdom they call inquiry into nature."[85] Socrates longed for that natural science sought also by his predecessors – and not surprisingly. In answering all questions, in granting power, it is thought by nearly all to deserve the name *wisdom*. But, Socrates concludes, his search was unsuccessful. His investigation revealed that such wisdom is unavailable. And he lacks it still.

This lack provides one reason why he chooses not to converse with his fellow philosophers. They continue to adhere to this notion of wisdom. On the subject of utmost interest, therefore, they have nothing to teach him.[86] For the philosopher, the proper understanding of his or her object, that is, of wisdom, must be a decisive issue. In the Digression, the heart of the dialogue, Socrates distinguishes his notion of wisdom from that of his predecessors. The distinctive character of that notion, specifically the central object of his search for wisdom, emerges, however, with this midwife image.

An aspect of its distinctiveness is, to repeat, where Socrates seeks it: in the youth. In trying to understand why Socrates seeks wisdom there, help comes from an unexpected source. Recall Theodorus' previously mentioned comments explaining why not he but the youngsters should be participants in the forthcoming conversation. "Youth," he said, "truly is open to improvement in everything (146b5–6)." In his association with youth, Socrates spends time with those who are largely potential, those who are gestating, on the verge of giving birth to themselves. Having not yet fulfilled themselves, the character of fulfillment is more likely for them a pressing concern, an urgent question. Because they are so disposed, they are more likely to participate in that pain-inducing conversation that Theodorus rejects for himself. They would then also be more likely to share their opinions which are, and must be, the subject matter of such an investigation.

However, the reason for Socrates' focus on their opinions goes still deeper than their greater loquaciousness. In these students, Socrates confronts those seeking the good. They do come to him with an initial perception of what that good is, but not one so entrenched as to be unshakeable. It is in this regard that the young, those not fully formed, are of special interest to Socrates. What will be their reaction, he wonders, when that initial view is shaken? What are the passions engaged, the arguments mounted, as they confront the inadequacy of their view of good? These are Socrates' questions. With his midwifery Socrates aims not to learn *from* these youth, or even primarily to teach them. Rather, he aims to learn *about* them. He wants to investigate something that can best be learned from such conversations: the nature of the soul in perplexity. This is the object of Socrates' quest. It stamps Socratic philosophy with its distinctive character. He proceeds through conversation because it alone provides

[85] *Phaedo* 96a7–8.

[86] However, as we see throughout the Platonic corpus, the *Theaetetus* being no exception, Socrates is altogether familiar with his predecessors' writings. Such familiarity is a prerequisite of the self-conscious novelty of his position.

access to the conflict within the soul, a conflict more alive and more accessible in the young. And it is this investigation that brings the philosophic examination of the views of good, just, and noble to the heart of Socratic inquiry.

The *Theaetetus* shows that this aforementioned examination becomes crucial to Socratic philosophy in the face of the problem of knowledge. It becomes so, more specifically, in response to the unavailability of that wisdom that his predecessors, just as does Theaetetus, identified with knowledge. Most urgently, it is crucial to substantiate the good of inquiry. Its good must be in question insofar as Socrates, unlike the eugenicist midwives, knows that he lacks comprehensively certain knowledge of the human good. This examination remains essential, however, to guide philosophic inquiry in the light of less than comprehensive understanding. Both these considerations are present in Socrates' pedagogical activity, which he recounts at the end of the midwife passage to which I now turn.

Although Socrates frequently declares his lack of wisdom, he does nevertheless show that he is far from wholly ignorant. Among other things, he has acquired a detailed knowledge of the varieties of students with whom he is engaged. He possesses as well a deep appreciation for the character and limits of learning and teaching. This character is indicated by his frequent use of the word *association* to refer to his engagement with students. The word suggests that not everything can be conveyed by the Theodoran method of direct verbal communication. There may be lessons that can be learned but not taught, at least in any direct manner (150d2, d4, 151a2, a14, a5). Such lessons are those most particularly that involve the passions and desires of the student, which can only ultimately be dealt with by the student alone.

Socrates indicates the limits of his insight into others' souls in other ways. For example, he invokes god throughout the passage and he says that he must "guess" which teacher might benefit the student (151b4). All these indications converge on the conclusion that knowing another soul is a long, drawn-out process – hence Socrates' preference for those in close proximity because "some appear at first as even very foolish (150d3–4)." But even then it is not clear that such knowledge can be much more than a well-informed guess. When Euclides reports Socrates' prophecy regarding Theaetetus' nature, it is hedged about with qualifications (142d1–3). Neither does the glimpse of the mature Theaetetus granted by Plato confirm him as a Socratic success story. In his devotion to both Athens and mathematics he, arguably, has failed to integrate politics and his intellectual life in the manner of a true Socratic. Perhaps more significantly, he has given up this intellectual life for his city at a relatively young age.[87]

Socrates makes the character of teaching and learning especially murky, however, in his claim that these students "never learnt anything from me,

[87] Cf. *Crito* 43b10–11.

but they on their own from themselves found and gave birth to many beautiful things (150d6–8)." The image conveys the notion that Socrates as midwife is to deliver some psychic offspring that is in an important way already present, if latent, within the student. It presumes some initial awareness of that which is apparent on the part of the student, and on the part of all humans, which Socrates could not take responsibility for teaching. This notion famously appears throughout the Platonic corpus, often in mythic garb, as the doctrine of recollection. Again, Socrates chooses not to refer to this doctrine in the *Theaetetus*. But what Socrates indicates here is, I think, captured by the distinctly nonmythic statement in the *Meno* that recollection is nothing but to "bind [opinion] with causes by reasoning."[88] Recall that the distinctive activity of Socrates' midwifery is not elicitive but critical. Socrates' maieutic inducement of perplexity involves precisely this reflection on the causes or reasons for our initial opinions. Moreover, as opinions, they lack adequate grounding. The result of such reflection, therefore, must be perplexity, at least initially.

Later in the dialogue, Socrates connects this picture of our cognitive situation, explicitly and in some detail, with the issue of parts and wholes already introduced. For now, it is important to recognize that the problematic character of wholes means that our access to them occurs not all at once but in stages. For this reason, learning is possible and necessary. Socrates' use of the word *fruitful* to designate the hoped-for product of his midwifery points exactly to learning as such a progressive movement toward wholeness. He does not guarantee that ultimate wholeness but can "assay" whether what is produced is generative, leading to further development (150c3).[89]

Others can, and perhaps must, assist in this movement. Socrates too had his teachers. But Socrates also places responsibility on the student because matters of character, and not only intellect, bear on the possibility of learning. Consequently, success in learning involves tasks only accomplished by the student for him- or herself. Only Theaetetus can overcome his own reluctance to become Socrates' student. At least this is the strong indication found in Socrates' assessment of various kinds of students that he now provides. In this assessment, he recognizes the impact of passion and desire on our knowing.

[88] *Meno* 98a3–5. On the general connection between the *Meno* and the *Theaetetus* see Desjardins, *The Rational Enterprise*, 201n9, 203n21, 241n4, 244n10 and Dorter, *Form and Good*, 70–2. There is disagreement concerning the relationship between the midwife image and the doctrine of recollection. Cornford asserts their identity while McDowell, Burnyeat, and Vlastos argue against the connection, with Vlastos insisting they are separate metaphors. Sedley argues, consistent with his overall thesis, that the full-blown theory of recollection is not present in this passage but rather a notion of "learning as the realization of latent understanding" that is intended as a precursor to "the Platonic theory of recollection." I agree with all that Sedley states except, as I make clear in the text, with the claim that the notion of latent understanding is meant as a stepping stone to the theory of recollection. See Cornford, *Plato's Theory of Knowledge*, 27–8; McDowell, *Plato "Theaetetus,"* 116–17; Burnyeat, "Socratic Midwifery, Platonic Inspiration," 7–16; Vlastos, *Socratic Studies*, 5; and Sedley, *The Midwife of Platonism*, 28–30.

[89] On fruitfulness see Howland, *The Paradox of Political Philosophy*, 82–3, 89.

Perplexity-inducing complexity exists on the side of the knower as well as on the side of the beings. Both sources of perplexity are explored in detail as the dialogue proceeds.[90] Most prominent in the present context, however, is Socrates' examination of the *obstacles* to the examination of any perplexity.

Socrates' presentation makes clear that his associations are, to say the least, various in their outcome. The result is a critical typology with numerous overlapping categories of students. There are some students who make great progress in "their own opinion and *everyone else's too* (150d5–6, emphasis added)." Some of these students decide, however, to leave Socrates' tutelage. Public opinion again plays a role in this decision and in the decision of those of this group that decide to return. Those who do leave "fail to recognize" their dependence on Socrates (150e1–2). Thus, they "held themselves responsible and despised me, either on their own or *persuaded by someone else*, [they] departed earlier than they should have (150e2–4, emphasis added)." Some of these "finally got to be of the opinion (and *everyone else was too*) that they were fools" and did "amazing things" so eager were they to return (150e7–8, 151a3, emphasis added).

Those who leave do so out of an unwarranted sense of their own self-sufficiency. They leave because they are unwilling to regard themselves as dependent and thus needy beings. So loath were they to regard themselves in this way that the prodding questions and inducement of perplexity that makes them sense their neediness causes them to despise Socrates. Socrates' several references to the influence of others' views give the impression that such students are particularly susceptible to the siren song of reputation.

This is certainly true in the case of the one student Socrates mentions by name: Aristides, the son of Lysimachus (150e8–151a2). In the *Laches*, Aristides is one of two boys whose unsuccessful fathers seek to provide their sons with a good education, the kind of education they feel they did not receive due to the neglect of their own famously successful fathers.[91] They seek an education that will fit their sons for the level of success in the community that the boys' grandfathers enjoyed. Aristides' account of his experience with Socrates, reported by Socrates in the *Theages*, further substantiates this impression. When spending a great deal of time with Socrates, Aristides was able to "appear inferior to none in arguments," but once leaving Socrates he avoided such arguments out of shame.[92] Aristides' goal is victory in these arguments, and the fame attendant on that victory. He returns seeking to restore his power to achieve it.

Those who return for this reason, like those who leave altogether, are animated by the desire for power and consequent fame. They are those, more specifically, who respond to what the community thinks is the purpose of

[90] Sedley, *The Midwife of Platonism*, 33–5, also considers all that must be presupposed by Socrates strange *techne* of maieutics. My response to this issue differs from his, perhaps most significantly, in his denial that maiuetics requires a recognition of "psychic complexity."

[91] *Laches* 179c1–d2.

[92] *Theages* 130c3–6.

education, the success and honor that go with this power. The greatest thing is to possess the greatest power or control. In this light, the neediness of perplexity must appear as great weakness. The one inducing it must be despised, especially if this perplexity makes one suspect in the community. These students aspire to the condition of self-sufficiency, to be free of need, to maintain the indomitable position celebrated by the community. Driving them on is, as we will soon see, the self-concern sometimes called love of one's own.

The students so animated are not pregnant. They are those, in Socrates' words, that "don't need me (151b3)." These students Socrates passes on to "different wise and divinely-speaking men" among whom he names Prodicus, the sophist (151b5–6).[93] Socrates gives those who are not in need to the sophists, whose curriculum teaches success in public affairs through their sophistic *techne*. The sophists proudly claim the name of the wise as they provide lessons in how better to secure one's own.

The deepest fault line dividing the youth Socrates confronts runs between those who are willing to recognize their neediness and those who are not. In his association with students, Socrates sees the soul's potential arrayed along a range whose poles are, on one side, a belief in one's self-sufficiency and, on the other, an acute awareness of need. All come to Socrates seeking their good, but, as we have seen, some soon leave out of an unwarranted sense of their own self-sufficiency. Those who remain or return are willing to face their incompleteness, even, as we have also seen, recognizing themselves as fools. Of special interest to Socrates, however, are souls like that of Theaetetus, poised between mathematics and dialectic. In Theaetetus, Socrates finds a soul that oscillates between the poles of the soul's potential, desiring to address perplexity through continual inquiry while yearning not to care so deeply about it.

From his reflections on these youthful souls, Socrates learns the soul's capacity for these conflicting desires. He sees also the clash of those goods that answer to such desires. Socrates makes this clash explicit when he says that many of those he critiques "don't believe I'm doing this out of good will," but adds that he "cannot make a concession to falsehood and wipe out the truth (151c7–8, d2–3)." Many prefer their own even if it conflicts with the truth. Socrates' teaching confronts just this preference, this obstacle to further inquiry.

Of utmost importance to him, however, is what this confrontation enables him to learn regarding the soul. He learns that in light of these conflicting desires, the character of the soul's wholeness, its fulfillment, must be a question, a question powerfully illustrated by the Prologue in its juxtaposition of the

[93] Socrates does not attempt to bring these back to the old Athenian ways; he gives them over to the sophists. Although given Plato's portrayal of Prodicus in the *Protagoras*, the long-term effect of the seemingly fruitless and abstract character of his incessant distinctions is another question. See, e.g., *Protagoras* 339e3–341d8, where Socrates enlists Prodicus' distinction-making talents in a somewhat dubious way.

deaths of Theaetetus and Socrates. Spurred by interrogation regarding the human things, this clash of goods provides further evidence of the soul's elusive wholeness.

From this inducement of perplexity, and specifically from his young interlocutors' reaction to this perplexity about goods, Socrates learns something more. This uncertainty regarding the meaning of human fulfillment, expressed most vividly in the conflicts of political life, provides some substantiation for the life of inquiry as Socrates lived it. By inducing perplexity in others regarding these questions, his midwifery gives Socrates reason to believe that the choice to live this inquiring life is not simply idiosyncratic, a mere preference. Such a characterization became all too possible once Socrates realized that his predecessors' goal is unavailable, once, that is, he appreciated how problematic knowledge is. Yet, in the pain caused in students by perplexity, Socrates sees evidence that all do want to know for sure, especially regarding the good. In their reaction to this pain, he sees, moreover, that all desire reassurance concerning the goodness of their way of life because of the sense, more and less tacit, that they are not fully certain of the true human good.

This is borne out not only by those students who remain to inquire with Socrates but also even, or especially, by those who despise and flee him. In the former, he can revisit that choice taken long ago in reaction to his own disappointment.[94] But judging simply from the sheer number of the latter populating the Platonic dialogues, Socrates might have learned at least as much, or more, from those who reject his way. Perhaps this is to be expected insofar as they present the greater challenge to that way of life. Despising Socrates, these interlocutors are overcome by what he identifies as the chief obstacle to inquiry: the love of one's own. In particular, those who despise him for his critique of their views are, he says, as "angrily savage as those who give birth for the first time are about their children (151c4–5)." Comparing them to the beasts protecting their young, Socrates says his midwifery makes his interlocutors "ready to bite whenever I remove any nonsense of theirs (151c6–7)."

Contrary to the usual circumstances of midwifery, the pain of Socratic midwifery occurs in the critical rather than in the elicitive phase. Contrary, too, is Socrates goal. The Socratic version aims ultimately to assist in overcoming the attachment to, rather than in the generation of, one's own. For this drive to protect our ownmost – ourselves, our loved ones, our community, and those cherished beliefs that undergird the safety, security, and validity of our ownmost – thwarts Socratic inquiry the most.

That inquiry, in challenging these beliefs, must raise doubts precisely about the endurance of what most immediately elicits our care. In this light, it is most significant that at certain critical moments Socrates defines his own activity in

94 *Phaedo* 96a5–99d2.

terms of its stance toward death.[95] Philosophy, he says on his deathday, is nothing but preparation for death.[96] By this characterization, he refers to a willingness to face the implications of the transiency of our selves as such. We have seen, too, that Plato sets human mortality before us as he embarks on the portrayal of Socrates' last days.

Given his present and immediately forthcoming circumstances, however, Socrates is acutely aware of the difficulty and danger involved in subjecting these beliefs to scrutiny. Yet, again, it is the vehemence of the reaction against his perplexity-inducing efforts that provides the most certain assurance of the validity of his choice. For through studying the soul in its perplexity he gains assurance that his desire for what's truly good moves not only his soul but others' as well. In the subsequent examination of Theaetetus' definition of knowledge the link between the true and the good becomes ever clearer as the ground of Socratic inquiry. The reaction of his interlocutors to this inquiry is never indifference. The indignation he generates is an index of the deep desire in others to be right about the most significant concerns, and an indication that they are not sure that they are. From such conversations, Socrates gains assurance that the nature of the soul, its problematic wholeness, evident especially in its perplexity, calls for further inquiry into the good. He thereby gains assurance that such inquiry is good. In this way, the problem of knowledge makes his midwifery, his examination of the soul's perplexity about its most cherished opinions, an urgent requirement of his philosophic activity. It is urgent because it helps to determine whether this life of reason can be rationally justified.

Yet this examination of the soul's perplexity is not only an urgent requirement. Socrates preserves this conversation not only to justify the philosophic life but also to guide its practice. This need for midwifery persists because awareness of this nature of the soul must properly guide all subsequent inquiry. As my forthcoming discussion aims to confirm, the question of our good, and the question of our nature that underlies it, spurs philosophic inquiry into nature as a whole. Given this course of inquiry, it would be acutely self-contradictory to adopt a view of nature that dissolves the questionability of good and the problematic character of human nature. Continued reflection on the soul helps the Socratic philosopher avoid the self-forgetting dogmatism of Euclides and Terpsion, and the other pre-Socratics, whom they represent. The inquiry into the central question of political philosophy is an antidote to these dogmatisms that make human life inexplicable.[97] Midwifery is, finally, an image of that cognitive capacity, *phronesis*, that inquires into this question, the question of one's good, with the keenest possible awareness of the complexities surrounding such objects of knowledge.

[95] *Apology* 29a5–b6.

[96] *Phaedo* 64a4–6.

[97] The crucial importance of such political inquiry to philosophy as a whole is perhaps indicated by the fact that Plato does not regard political philosophy as a distinct branch of philosophy.

Socrates concludes the midwife passage saying to Theaetetus, "once more from the beginning, Theaetetus, try to say whatever is knowledge (151d3–4)." Socrates' own career exhibits such a return. Dictating this return is the hard-won awareness of the inadequacy of not only his predecessors and but also his own previous orientation. Concomitant with such a return, if undertaken with a clear view of its necessity, must be a deepening self-knowledge through which inquirers become more aware of their cognitive situation in relation to the world that has resisted their attempts to know. Such self-knowledge is central if we hope to make progress regarding this question of our good, a question that we cannot help but want to answer.

In presenting himself as the midwife, Socrates portrays for those who would follow him the heart of his distinctive wisdom and the obstacle to its acquisition. In so doing, he not only gains in self-knowledge, he also makes more possible the life of inquiry for those willing and able to live it. His own desire to know is in this way the prerequisite of the truly common good. Such benevolence perhaps justifies him saying of himself at the end of the passage: "no god is ill-disposed to human beings (151d1)." It is, finally, not Artemis but Socrates, the midwife of our fulfillment, who is the true god of human potential.[98]

[98] Regarding the superhuman character of Socrates' art, see Burnyeat, "Socratic Midwifery, Platonic Inspiration," 15n6 and R. G. Wengert, "The Paradox of the Midwife," *History of Philosophy Quarterly* 5 (1988), 9–10n8. As the midwife passage unfolds, Socrates shifts ever more responsibility from the god to himself, and the image comes ever closer to expressing this Socratic way of life (150c8, d8–e1, 151c8–d1).

4

The Delivery

Introduction

Socrates' exhortations in the midwife passage succeed to this extent: Theaetetus is moved to offer a definition of knowledge. "Knowledge," he maintains, "is nothing else than perception (151e2–3)." Fully one-half the dialogue's length is devoted to the formulation and examination, the delivery and assessment, of this psychic offspring. In many ways, Plato raises the suspicion that considerations beyond the initial definition's intrinsic validity dictate this lengthy treatment. The most prominent such suggestion is that it is Socrates who gives Theaetetus' offspring its ultimate form. Through Socrates' exertions, Theaetetus' initial, ambiguous definition develops into nothing less than a comprehensive view of humanity and the whole.

Socrates' guiding hand is evident not only in this magnification of the original thesis but also in its radicalization, by which I mean its thoroughgoing subversion of any trace of stability in either the beings or in us. In Myles Burnyeat's words, Socrates ultimately conjoins "Berkeley's dissolution of physical objects into a series of ideas perceived with Hume's dissolution of the self into a series of perceptions."[1] What results is an unqualified relativism in a world of universal flux. The thesis that Socrates develops ultimately denies the persistent identity of both humans and beings. Socrates achieves this outcome by linking Theaetetus' definition, Socratically interpreted, with Socratic versions of Protagoreanism and Heracleiteanism. In this mutated form, Theaetetus' newborn child must seem to him to have grown in some unforeseen ways.[2]

The dramatic claim Socrates makes when commencing the subsequent assessment phase of his midwifery guides his extension and radicalization of Theaetetus' definition. Socrates maintains that if Theaetetus' definition

[1] Burnyeat, *The "Theaetetus" of Plato*, 18.

[2] Burnyeat writes, "Thanks to Socrates' skill as a midwife of ideas, Theaetetus' original conception has proved a larger thing than he foresaw. It has grown into a whole theory of knowledge and the world." Ibid., 19.

and its supporting arguments are true then his own midwifery, his practice of conversational inquiry, must be nonsense (162a1–2). This stark alternative points to the nerve of Socrates' rationale. He amplifies and radicalizes Theaetetus' definition to articulate what he regards as the core of anti-Socratism, its theoretical premises and its animating motive.[3] In elaborating this position, Socrates depicts how the whole, including humanity, would have to be conceived so as to render his own activity *in*defensible. This depiction sets the stage for the essential purpose of this Socratic conversation. For an effective response to the most uncompromising anti-Socratism would yield Socratism's most equally compelling defense. It is an appropriate undertaking for a conversation whose audience includes all potential Socratic philosophers.

Socrates provides such a response in the assessment phase of his midwifery. However, given Socrates' radicalization of Theaetetus' offspring, that response cannot consist simply in a straightforward, logical refutation of the thesis. Such a refutation would be inadequate to a thesis that challenges the very canons of reason to which such a refutation would appeal.[4] The avoidance of such question-begging requires Socrates to address the impulse, the motive that animates the thesis. To understand his response we must then heed Socrates' numerous explorations of that motive in our consideration of Theaetetus' psychic offspring. In particular, we must not neglect the seemingly extraneous elements of the conversation that Socrates saw a need to record.

In this regard, although Socrates' elaboration of Theaetetus' thesis may exceed his young interlocutor's foresight, its trajectory accords fully with Theaetetus' original impulse. He responds to Socrates' exhortations because it would be "shameful" not to do so (151d8). Fueling the concern for honor that gives shame its power is that love of one's own, whose significance we have just seen. In honor, we perceive the power and mastery that will, we believe, grant our heart's every desire including our own perpetuation. The power of shame, honor's privation, corresponds to the sway exercised over us by the love of one's own. Despite the warnings in the midwife passage, Theaetetus continues to be moved by the great obstacle to inquiry. His definition springs from this same source. In its elaboration, Socrates simply unfolds the picture of the whole that this motive demands.[5] Such is this passion's power that even the brilliant young mathematician willingly accepts the massive contradiction that

[3] Benardete and Polansky recognize the anti-Socratic character of the thesis. Benardete, *Being of the Beautiful*, I.103; Polansky, *Philosophy and Knowledge*, 71.

[4] Burnyeat may be right that Socrates presents this view as an extended *reductio ad absurdum*, but given the issue in question, that is not sufficient to dispose of it. Burnyeat, *The "Theaetetus" of Plato*, 46.

[5] Sedley recognizes that Socrates is unfolding a view of what the whole must be if knowledge is perception. Socrates also, however, means to respond to the motive that would lead Theaetetus to articulate this view of knowledge. Sedley, *The Midwife of Platonism*, 44.

stands at its heart: his thesis, formulated out of love of one's own, culminates in the utter annihilation of the self. With this startling outcome, Socrates' delivery of Theaetetus' offspring directs his readers' attention to the character of the motive underlying this argument. And, again, it is to this motive that, in the all-important critical or assessment phase of his midwifery, he means, ultimately, to respond.

From Perception to Protagoras (151d7–152c7)

Theaetetus states, "So it seems (*dokei*) to me that one who knows anything perceives that which he knows, and as it appears (*phainetai*) to me now at least, knowledge is nothing other than perception (151e1–3)." With this statement, Theaetetus moves from an initial observation based on his experience to a hard and fast definition. The impetus this mathematical prodigy would have for fastening on to this particular definition does stem from his own cognitive experience and aspirations. Specifically, the experience of "getting it," of saying "I see," would be characteristic of such a brilliant mathematical mind. Such an experience, moreover, has the immediacy of all perception, both intellectual and sensible. What is grasped in this way has the "feel" of being known fully and at once. Knowledge so understood has an all-or-nothing quality that Socrates later exploits fully: one either "gets it" completely or not at all. The definition bears the marks of that concern for certainty, for the elimination of controversy, evident in Theaetetus' initial statement regarding knowledge. That statement, we recall, amounted to a list of "whatever one might learn from Theodorus" – namely, the various *technai* (146c7–d3). Perhaps for this reason Socrates suggests that Theaetetus' present definition has about it an element of self-disclosure (151e4–5). It fits well with his desire to avoid the shame of making a mistake.

Yet although Theaetetus identifies knowledge with perception, nothing he has said would identify it only with *sense*-perception. That identification is Socrates' move.[6] We need to inspect Theaetetus' definition more closely to appreciate all that this move entails. I would add parenthetically that in so doing we are taking advantage of the numerous and inevitable opportunities Plato provides to treat the question reflexively, to ask whether the knowledge-claims the participants make about knowledge reflect what they claim knowledge is. Let's now examine Theaetetus' definition through this reflexive lens.

[6] I agree with Polansky that it is Socrates rather than Theaetetus who specifies *aisthesis* as sense-perception alone. Polansky, *Philosophy and Knowledge*, 67. See also Michael Frede's discussion of perception in which he finds in Plato a narrow sense of perception, one that understands it as a "passive affection of the mind." It is in the *Theaetetus* that Frede finds the notion of sense-perception developed. See Michael Frede, "Observations on Perception in Plato's Later Dialogues," in *Essays in Ancient Philosophy* (Minneapolis: University of Minnesota Press, 1987), 5. For Theaetetus, perception might well include intellectual perception. As I suggest in the text, it is immediacy that matters to Theaetetus.

In his stabs at a definition, Theaetetus, quite naturally, uses such phrases as, "in my opinion" or "it appears." Speaking of how a thing appears suggests the possibility of the thing only *appearing* but not actually *being* in this way. The fulfillment of this possibility requires, in turn, an intellect capable of noting and judging this difference between what we take the world to be and what it is. This self-critical activity of soul depends on its capacity for reflection (the capacity that I have just claimed Plato encourages us to employ). I point out this otherwise perfectly unremarkable use of language simply because within a few lines Socrates denies the intellect this reflective possibility. And soon thereafter he also denies the capacity of the beings to both seem and be. Whether either denial rests on adequate grounds remains to be seen. What exactly these denials entail about our understanding in general and our self-understanding in particular also remains in question. Clarity about these considerations enables us to determine better the significance of the power of reflection for the meaning of knowledge.

In accordance with the midwife image, Socrates proposes that they examine Theaetetus' definition in common to see whether it is fruitful or a wind egg (151e5–6). In the course of this proposal he repeats, or rather modifies, Theaetetus' definition: "perception, you say, is knowledge (151e6)." Socrates' reformulation gives the impression that it is perception rather than knowledge being defined. Moreover, Socrates' formulation leaves open the possibility that although perception is knowledge, other things could be knowledge as well. Yet opening this door only makes it more evident when he slams it shut. On the basis of little actual argument, Socrates confines perception to sense perception alone and insists that perception so understood is the whole of knowledge. All this is accomplished with little resistance from Theaetetus who calmly accedes to Socrates' putting a reversed formulation in his mouth. Nor does Socrates encounter resistance when he links Theaetetus' thesis about perception and knowledge to the thought of Protagoras, or at least to Socrates' version of his thought.[7]

[7] Cornford rightly warns us not to expect historical accuracy in Socrates' presentation of Protagoras. Cornford, *Plato's Theory of Knowledge*, 31. Although, as Sedley points out, because much of the understanding of Protagoras is taken from this dialogue it is not easy to get a read on Protagoras' actual views. Sedley, *The Midwife of Platonism*, 50. It does, however, seem to be the case that Protagoras was not primarily concerned with theoretical questions of epistemology nor was he necessarily as radical a relativist as Socrates portrays him. On these latter points see Laszlo Versenyi, "Protagoras' Man-Measure Fragment," *The American Journal of Philology* 83 (1962):178–84; Joseph P. Maguire, "Protagoras – or Plato?," *Phronesis* 18 (1973): 121, 127n24; and Cynthia Farrar, *The Origins of Democratic Thinking: The Invention of Politics in Classical Athens* (Cambridge: Cambridge University Press, 1988), 48n13, 49–50, 77. Farrar is especially intent on distinguishing the historical Protagoras from Plato's presentation. Her goal is to rescue the democratic premises, which she finds, e.g., in Protagoras' "Great Speech" of the *Protagoras*, from the purportedly antidemocratic Plato. For a response to Farrar, see Saxonhouse, *Free Speech and Democracy*, 63–4. As will become more evident in the subsequent chapter, I share Saxonhouse's view that Protagoras' democratic

Socrates knows of, or strongly suspects, Theaetetus' affinity for Protagoras' work. Referring to Protagoras' book, he asks Theaetetus, "Presumably, you've read it? (152a4)." Theaetetus has, "many times (152a5)." Socrates' awareness of Theodorus' friendship with the dead sophist lets him make this link with confidence. But underlying this friendship is the substantive connection between Theaetetus' definition and Protagorean thought. This connection clarifies why there may be such an affinity not only between these individuals but also more generally between mathematicians and sophistic thought. In his delivery of Theaetetus' opinion Socrates wants especially to elicit the ground of this latter affinity. Comparing Protagoras' dictum with Theaetetus' definition, Socrates says of the former that it says "these same things in a somewhat different way (152a1–2)."[8] We begin the examination of this connection with the ideas that Socrates attributes to Protagoras.

Socrates reports Protagoras' famous dictum, *homo mensura*: "of all things (a) human being is the measure, of the things which are, that they are, and of the things which are not, that they are not (152a2–4)."[9] The way in which Socrates resolves the numerous ambiguities in this famous statement, again with little or no argument, provides insight into his purpose. For example, in the initial rendition of Protagoras' statement the locus of measure is ambiguous. It could refer either to an individual or to humanity as such.[10] If it refers to humanity, then the meaning might be that humans as such must be the ones who judge rather than the gods.[11] And, as Protagoras was inclined to maintain, we do just that in and through our political communities.[12] However, Socrates now offers a second rendition of the formula, which resolves any ambiguity by stamping an individualistic and ultimately idiosyncratic interpretation on Protagoras'

inclinations are not the deepest strand of his thought. My present point concerns the ends to which Socrates uses Protagoras in the *Theaetetus*.

8 Socrates moves here to connect Theaetetus' original definition with Protagoras' thought. Subsequently, he connects Protagoras with Heracleitus. These moves raise the question of the connections between the three legs of the thesis that is unfolding. Burnyeat writes, "having defined knowledge as perception, [Theaetetus] is faced with the question, What has to be true of perception and of the world for the definition to hold good? The answer suggested is that he will have to adopt a Protagorean epistemology, and that in turn will commit him to a Heracleitean account of the world." Burnyeat, *The "Theaetetus" of Plato*, 9. Although this description is accurate, I would add two further points. First, it is Socrates who at every turn makes the thesis more radically antiphilosophic. Second, Socrates' activity in this regard demands that we consider his purpose in doing so.

9 This saying is also found quoted in *Cratylus* 386a1–3 and Diogenes Laertius. IX. 51; Sextus Empiricus provides an interpretation of the saying. See Sextus Empiricus, *Outlines of Pyrrhonism*, trans. R. G. Bury (Cambridge, MA: Harvard University Press, 1933), I. 216–19.

10 On the ambiguity of Protagoras' formula, see Versenyi, "Protagoras' Man-Measure Fragment, 180–4; Maguire, "Protagoras – or Plato?," 120, 120n10; and Polansky, *Philosophy and Knowledge*, 78.

11 Clay makes this point in *Platonic Questions*, 221.

12 On this point, see Maguire, "Protagoras – or Plato?," 127; Farrar, *Origins of Democratic Thinking*, 45–6.

saying. Insisting that this is "somehow what he means," Socrates provides this gloss of his initial statement of Protagoras' dictum: "of whatever sort things appear to me each by each, that's the sort they are for me, and of whatever sort they appear to you that in turn is the sort they are for you (152a6, 152a6–8)."[13]

With this paraphrase, Socrates brings the issue of conflicting appearances to the fore. Given Theaetetus' desire to be indisputably correct, the issue deserves his concern. One basis of the disputatiousness that Theaetetus fears must be that things appear differently to different individuals.[14] Socrates maintains that the criterion or measure of such appearances can only be the individual human being. Thus, he adds to the preceding statement this gloss: "and you and I are human being (152a8)." This awkward phrase, assimilating humanity and individuals, again highlights the initial ambiguity in the locus of measure while also showing Socrates' exertions to push the argument in the direction of the idiosyncrasy of apprehension. The direction of these exertions gives an indication of what Socrates believes motivates Theaetetus' definition. For such idiosyncrasy, perhaps paradoxically, responds to the desire for incontrovertibility. If each is the judge of the beings then there can be no ground on which others can even dispute one's judgment.

It is the notion of immediacy that forges the link between perception and Protagoreanism and establishes this incontrovertibility of judgment.[15] If we have immediate apprehension of what is, then there can be no question of striving or struggling to know how things *really* are, insofar as that struggle depends on the possibility that they might somehow be different from what appears. The case for immediacy, however, requires two additional Socratic machinations. Socrates must characterize all apprehension as a matter of sense-perception, and then he must collapse appearance into sense-perception.[16]

In pursuit of the first requirement Socrates applies this notion only to "hot things and everything of the sort," focusing on matters of sense-perception alone rather than opinion (152c1–2).[17] Socrates asks how we feel in response

[13] It is not perfectly clear whether this line is a further quote or a gloss on the original quote, but I incline toward those who regard it as a gloss. On this issue, see McDowell, *Plato "Theaetetus,"* 119 and Gail Fine, "Conflicting Appearances" in *Form and Argument in Late Plato*, Christopher Gill and Mary Margaret McCabe (Oxford: Clarendon Press, 1996), 106n2.

[14] Concerning the issue of conflicting appearances see Burnyeat, *The "Theaetetus" of Plato*, 14 and Fine, "Conflicting Appearances," passim.

[15] Both Burnyeat and Polansky recognize that the goal is to provide certainty, to make error impossible. Burnyeat, *The "Theaetetus of Plato,"* 14; Polansky, *Philosophy and Knowledge*, 70.

[16] On this collapse of appearance into perception, see McDowell, *Plato "Theaetetus,"* 119; Benardete, *Being of the Beautiful*, I.104; and Allan Silverman, "Flux and Language in the *Theaetetus*" in *Oxford Studies in Ancient Philosophy, vol. XVIII*, ed. David Sedley (Oxford: Oxford University Press, 2000), 129–30.

[17] Fine makes a distinction between narrow and broad Protagoreanism depending on whether the thesis is taken to include opinion or is limited to sense-perception alone, "Conflicting Appearances," 107. I follow Maguire in thinking that this distinction between perception

to "the same wind": Isn't it sometimes the case that "one person shivers with cold and another doesn't? (152b2–3)." But Socrates does not let Theaetetus answer this all-or-nothing question, a question that might very well receive a negative response. Instead, he immediately asks a question posing a more plausible scenario: "or one does so slightly and another violently? (152b3–4)." Such a difference of degree is more likely to be within Theaetetus' realm of experience.

Socrates' manipulative efforts are also evident as he asks Theaetetus still another question that he does not let him answer: "Well, shall we say that at such a time the wind itself is cold or not cold? (152b6–7)." Discussing this question might have led to a discussion of whether there are beings with stable characteristics in themselves – "the wind itself" – at least preserving the possibility of judging our perception against some external criterion. Instead, Socrates has Theaetetus respond to an alternative question: "Or shall we be persuaded by Protagoras that it's cold for the one who's shivering but not for the one who isn't? (152b7–8)." By replacing the former question with this one Socrates indicates that Protagoras' view enables them to avoid the difficult question of being and seeming; there is no need to investigate what the wind *really* is.[18] The question shifts the focus to the perceiver and the idiosyncrasy of each while abstaining, for now, from making a judgment on the persistent character of the beings.[19] The move to the radical flux of Heracleiteanism will soon enough dispense with the possibility of such persistence. In so doing, it dispenses not only with the need for the aforementioned investigation but also with its possibility.[20] Socrates thus plants the seeds of the radical view. He makes this commonplace of our experience, that each has sense-perception as an individual, bloom into an entire view of the cosmos through such questionable argumentation.

Idiosyncrasy, however, is not sufficient to provide incontrovertibility. One's own perceptions might still be of what merely appears rather than what is. Socrates must therefore take the required second step that casts our knowing not only as idiosyncratic but also as immediate. This step requires the collapse of the distinction between "appear" and "perceive." He initiates this collapse by first asking whether it does not "appear thus to each of the two?" and then

and opinion is "unmistakably Platonic," "Protagoras – or Plato?," 116–17. The disanalogy between perception and opinion proves to be an important element in Socrates' critique of Protagoras and Socrates' other predecessors. Theaetetus' "discovery" of opinion as a realm distinct from perception constitutes what is taken as the refutation of his initial definition of knowledge. In this light, the recognition of the distinctiveness of opinion is central to Socrates' endeavor, the failure to recognize it crucial to the anti-Socratic thesis.

18 As McDowell says, "Protagoras refuses to make sense of questions about what the wind is like in itself, as distinct from questions about what it is like for one person or another." See McDowell, *Plato "Theaetetus,"* 119. For a similar reading, see also Bostock, *Plato's "Theaetetus,"* 43–4.

19 On the requirement of idiosyncrasy see McDowell, *Plato "Theaetetus,"* 119; and Chappell, *Reading Plato's "Theaetetus,"* 60.

20 Regarding this move see, esp., Maguire, "Protagoras – or Plato?," 121, 121n14, 138.

adding, "but this 'appear' is 'perceive' (152b10, b12)." With Theaetetus' assent to this identification, Socrates transforms the knower into a passive receptor, incapable of reflection. He eliminates the possibility of recognizing the difference between how things appear and how they actually are, a distinction that belongs to the notion of appearance.

Again, this distinction presupposes the intellect's self-critical activity which in turn requires the power of reflection. And, again, the intellect possessing this power must be thought to be complex, somehow existing in "parts" such that one part can survey the other. Concomitant with this power, however, there exists also the possibility of falsehood, that what is in one's mind does not square with how things are. Thus, as Socrates makes abundantly clear later in the dialogue, any view designed to make ambiguity, uncertainty, even falsehood impossible must also deny the soul's capacity for reflection and with it the internal complexity that enables self-awareness.

With the collapse of this distinction Socrates is well on his way to showing Theaetetus what the world would be like if his deepest hopes were fulfilled. For Socrates' summary statement leaves no doubt that the elimination of falsehood is his goal: "Therefore, perception is always of what is, and, being knowledge, is without falsity (152c5–6)." The problem with this much-vexed sentence lies in its claim that what is perceived, "being knowledge, is without falsity," that it is because it is knowledge it is without falsity.[21] The argument would seem rather to require the opposite claim: that because it is without falsity it is knowledge. But this reversed order reflects Socrates' general procedure in the delivery of Theaetetus' offspring. He begins with a view of knowledge that he takes Theaetetus to desire, and then formulates a view of the whole that answers to this desire – a view of the whole in which falsity cannot exist.

Socrates, however, does not completely cover his tracks. He enables us to see those considerations that, if reflected on, would belie the truth of the unfolding doctrine. He says, for example, that "whatever each sort of things each perceives them as, they also run a risk of being of that sort for each person (150c2–3)." There is at least a hint here of the possibility of one's perception being wrong; if there is a "risk" on one side there must also be a risk on the other side. Such counterindications are evident as well at the beginning of Socrates' discussion of Protagoras. For example, if our knowledge is immediate it is unclear why Theaetetus, or anyone, would have to read a book more than once to understand it. Moreover, what could (any) reading provide beyond the perception of the letters? How could numerous readings be any more informative than a glance?

Socrates' locution also preserves the distinction between how things appear and what they really are. He refers to Protagoras saying the same thing as Theaetetus' definition "but in a *somewhat* different way (152a1–2, emphasis

[21] Thus, e.g., McDowell differs from Cornford on whether the phrase "being knowledge" is a premise or a conclusion. McDowell, *Plato "Theaetetus,"* 120–1; Cornford, *Plato's Theory of Knowledge*, 32.

added)." He also speaks of this being "*somehow* what he means (152a6, emphasis added)." Both these phrases point to the possibility that the meaning, the truth of something, must be grasped by looking beyond the immediate, beyond the surface. This distinction of appearance and being exists also in Socrates' distinguishing throughout this passage between a thing and the sort of thing it is. This latter distinction suggests that insofar as a thing is not only this particular but also this *kind* of thing, our immediate perception of it may not provide what it wholly is.

This assemblage of details makes the point that a picture of the prerequisites of the alternative to the flux doctrine runs right alongside it as its companion. The shadow of Socratic inquiry accompanies its denial. The alternative becomes most evident in the assessment phase of Socrates' midwifery. There he returns to Protagoras – not Protagoras the theorist of knowledge, a creature largely of Socrates' making, but the sophist who teaches the keys to success in the community. But the present, far less familiar, characterization of Protagoras reflects Socrates' efforts to radicalize Theaetetus' thesis, preparing its link to Heracleitus. It also provides the hook to capture these theorists for the journey to the heart of Protagoras, the sophist. It would not be self-evident to them, or to other theoretically inclined readers, that the deepest strand of Socrates' theoretical defense revolves around issues most pertinent to the sophist. Socrates' "interpretation" of Protagoras is justified by his effort to make plausible to these mathematicians, or to his wider audience, that the key to the anti-Socratic thesis is the view of good that underlies that thesis.

Heracleiteanism (152c8–153d7)

Before we reach that stage of Socrates' midwifery, however, the delivery of Theaetetus' offspring requires one final push. Socrates takes the last step in the radicalization of Theaetetus' thesis with the introduction of Heracleitus. Having removed the possibility of judgment, and so of error, on the part of the knower, he now removes the possibility of error on the side of the beings. Socrates wants to ensure, as he says, that perception is "always of what is (152c5)." His goal is to do away with the possibility inherent in Theaetetus' response to Socrates' summary sentence: "So it appears (152c7)."

Turning to Heracleitus Socrates invokes what he says is a secret doctrine underlying Protagoras' view, a view of absolute flux. Although Plato does not portray the mature Socrates speaking, in any extensive way, with a similarly mature philosopher, he is thoroughly familiar with their work. Introducing this Heracleitean doctrine Socrates refers to Protagoras as "all-wise," in the manner of the comprehensive eugenicists. Clearly, the designation is one of distinction. Only a very few could deserve this title. Socrates appeals to Theaetetus' own desire for such distinction and honor when he suggests that Protagoras only spoke the truth to a chosen few students, leaving only a riddle for the rest of us, whom Socrates calls "the vast refuse-heap (152c9–10)."

Surely, Theaetetus would resist consignment to that heap, yearning as he does to be distinguished for his intellectual achievement.

Yet the thesis now being developed provides little support for even the possibility of such distinction. The notion that only a few achieve knowledge depends, as Socrates implies here, on the premise that truth is hidden, not universally available. But its hiddenness requires that the beings lack self-evidence, rehabilitating the distinction between how they appear and how they really are. Moreover, the selective availability of truth implies that human capacities are importantly unequal such that only a relatively few can ferret it out. However, it is difficult to see how such inequality could characterize the unreflective receptors that Socrates has made a requisite of Theaetetus' thesis.

In sum, Theaetetus' desire for honor depends on two distinctions that must be eradicated to answer that yearning for certainty produced by his desire for honor. No wonder Theaetetus grows dizzy. His desires have him striving for what cannot be. There cannot be a world in which both falsehood is impossible and achievements of the intellect can earn honor. This is the drama of Theaetetus, his deeper desire for distinction attracting him to a world in which such distinction is impossible. In showing this clash of desires that underlies Theaetetus' theoretical position, Plato exhibits Theaetetus' urgent need for self-knowledge if he is to clarify the object of his pursuit of knowledge.

The secret doctrine that Socrates reports eliminates any stable identity of the beings. Because "nothing is one thing itself by itself," there is no stable unity that would enable us to identify something as this thing rather than that thing (152d2–3). The slender evidence offered for this far-reaching claim is that with respect to a large thing "if you address it as large it will also appear small, if heavy, light and everything at all in this way (152d4–6)." In this way, Socrates refers to the relational character of being whereby a thing can be large or small depending on what it is being compared with. Socrates uses this relational aspect of our everyday experience to substantiate the vast metaphysical claim that there is no unity in the beings whatsoever, that they are in perpetual flux so that "nothing ever *is* but is always becoming (152e1)."

Socrates' particular interpretation of being's relationality is by no means the only one possible. Elsewhere in the Platonic corpus, this relational mode of being is used to exemplify a point very nearly the opposite of the present one. Specifically, it illustrates the inadequacy of sense-perception that calls for and spurs us to dianoetic thinking, to reasoning and the search for enduring intelligibles.[22] Moreover, in the present context, Socrates continues to employ other distinctions that should be impermissible on the basis of absolute flux: distinguishing again between the thing and the sort or kind of thing; distinguishing between different kinds, whether of motion or poetry; and maintaining that the things that are come to be from mutual mixings, which presumes that we

[22] See, e.g., *Republic* 523a1–524d5. For further explanation, consider also Klein, *Plato's "Meno,"* 116–25.

can discern stable differences that can then be understood as mixed (152c2, 152d7, 152e4–5). Socrates' persistent use of these distinctions suggests he is well aware of the flimsiness of his argument here for absolute flux.

However, perhaps what I am characterizing as violations of the doctrine of flux exemplify artificial distinctions into which we are drawn by our use of speech – merely matters of "grammatical habit" as Nietzsche would say.[23] Perhaps, speech, at least as we now use it, is misleading and in need of drastic revision. Socrates introduces this possibility when, referring to the beings, he says, "we say they 'are', not addressing them correctly (152d8–e1)." By raising this possibility (which I explore further in the following text), Socrates' Heracleitean turn makes clear that along with the question of the character of the knower and known, the thoroughgoing articulation of the anti-Socratic thesis brings the character of speech into question – not surprisingly, insofar as speech provides the nexus between knower and known.

With so much at stake regarding how we view ourselves and the world, it is of the utmost importance to determine the adequacy of the ground for the present thesis. To this end, Socrates assures Theaetetus that there is remarkably broad agreement on the flux thesis. Exempting Parmenides alone, he detects its presence not only in Heracleitus but also in Protagoras, Empedocles, and even the leading poets, Epicharmus of comedy and Homer of tragedy (152e2–5).[24] Offering a line from Homer to show the poet's advocacy of the doctrine, Socrates asks, "Doesn't it seem to you that this is what he means? (152e8–9)."

This is the second text Socrates has relied on in his elaboration of the "Knowledge Is Perception" thesis. In the spirit of the dialogue's reflexive character, I want to pause to consider the meaning of such reliance. As was the case with that first quote from Protagoras' book, we have here a text quoted inside another text, inside still another: the quote from Homer resides in the conversation recorded by Euclides that resides in the text authored by Plato. Each of these quotes requires interpretation, certainly a cognitive act different from sense-perception. This, at least, is the weight of Socrates' complicated question – "Doesn't it seem to you that this is what he means? (152e8–9)" – that presumes that we can err regarding the meaning of these words, that they do not disclose their meaning at a glance.

The need for interpretation arises when we apprehend that we do not fully understand, when we somehow become aware of a lack in this regard. Socrates' question presumes that this state, this awareness of need, more truly

[23] Friedrich Nietzsche, *Beyond Good and Evil*, trans. Walter Kaufmann (New York: Vintage Books, 1989), 24.

[24] On the connection between Epicharmus and Plato, see Jill Gordon, *Turning Toward Philosophy: Literary Device and Dramatic Structure in Plato's Dialogues* (University Park: The Pennsylvania State University Press, 1999), 68–70, 72–3. One might suggest that Plato's mention of Epicharmus alerts the reader to the particularly "comic" character of the present passage. But, as Gordon recognizes, this character by no means makes the passage less serious. See the following note.

constitutes our situation than does that sufficiency promised in the radicalization of Theaetetus' thesis. To answer Socrates' question we would have to engage in the deed of interpretation we have been practicing all along, starting from the abrupt beginning of this conversation. We would have to consider the quote in its context, that is, understand it as a part of a whole, the meaning of which depends on the meaning of the parts and vice versa. Furthermore, given that this quote resides in a text nested within a still larger text, we would then have to consider this initial whole as a part of a greater whole. We would have to engage in that use of dianoetic thinking that proceeds by such comparison and contrast. All this is involved in the act of reading, of which Plato reminds us in this context. Euclides aimed to eliminate all deeds from the dialogue. Plato, however, preserves them by providing such opportunities as this for the self-awareness that is inseparable from our nature as beings that think and act.

To return to the substance of this quote, its interpretation requires thinking it together with a second Homeric quote that Socrates uses to mark off a crucial passage. In this passage, surrounded by these two quotes, he discusses why anyone should accept the doctrine of universal flux.[25] Postponing the interpretation of these quotes until we have considered this passage, I now note only that both quotes occur in the *Iliad*, the first where Hera defies Zeus' threat against any god who would interfere with human affairs, the second quotation expresses that threat.

This density of Homeric quotes is especially appropriate because Socrates designates Homer as the "general" of the army of fluxists (153a2). This designation helps explain how he could have included such a heterogeneous group of figures marching under the banner of universal flux. What unites this assembly of philosophers, poets, and sophists under Homer's generalship is less a theoretical than a practical standpoint. They share a notion of good of which Homer is the ultimate source, a notion, more specifically, that the human good resides in the power to supply ourselves with whatever we might happen to desire. Accordingly, if, as Socrates maintains, he is presently articulating the anti-Socratic position, then its deepest strand is found neither in Protagoras nor Heracleitus, neither as an "epistemological" nor as a metaphysical view. It is found rather in the ethical stance expressed, for the Greeks, decisively and authoritatively in Homer. Socrates aims to lead Theaetetus, who is so

[25] McDowell writes, "I suspect that in fact the whole of 152e2–153d5 is not intended very seriously." Bostock maintains that the link between Homer and flux is not meant as "sober history." Chappell finds the passage "an exercise in parody" that aims to make the flux doctrine "look guilty by association" because of the "outrageously bad arguments" supplied for its support. Granting Chappell's characterization of the arguments, to the extent that they are arguments at all, the question that must be asked is why Plato portrays these interlocutors as both very intelligent and entranced by this flux doctrine. This passage provides some insight into that crucial question of motive and for this reason must not be dismissed as "merely comic." I.e., its comic character should be taken seriously. See McDowell, *Plato "Theaetetus,"* 130; Bostock, *Plato's "Theaetetus,"* 44; and Chappell, *Reading Plato's "Theaetetus,"* 66.

very inclined to think that the most abstract is somehow the deepest, to this alternative insight regarding the decisiveness of the ethical and political. As the argument moves toward the Digression, Socrates seeks, in addition, to steel Theaetetus to the ridicule risked by someone who would oppose such a widespread and imposing consensus (153a1–3).

Socrates now begins to make the case for this doctrine of universal flux, "evidence" for which consists not in arguments but rather in what he calls "sufficient *signs* for the account (153a5–6, emphasis added)." These "signs" prove to be the various goods that flux supplies. The passage this statement introduces deepens the impression that the flux doctrine is what we would call ideological, that Theaetetus is to accept the theory not because it is true but because it satisfies and responds to a particular unexamined view of good. Thus, Socrates' argument has the following hypothetical form: "if you think of the good in this way, then you should accept this theoretical argument advocating universal motion which (so he claims) substantiates this view of good."

The first of these "adequate signs" is that motion supplies "what seems to be, that is, what becomes, while stillness produces non-being and perishing (153a6)." Note that neither rest nor motion supplies being, which has dropped out as a consideration. Socrates proceeds to associate all good things with motion. It produces heat or fire that not only generates but "is the guardian of everything else (153a8–9)." Motion thus serves not only as the source of good, which could be conceived in an impersonal way, but it also governs all. In Socrates' portrayal it has a god-like providence. The importance of such a being to Theaetetus emerges soon enough.

The celebration of the gifts provided by motion continues. It brings about the generation of the genus of animal; it preserves the condition of bodies while "stillness and inactivity" destroy them (153b5–6). Theaetetus might find such a claim particularly persuasive having recently come from exercising in the palaestra, although it might be less convincing to him later in his life as he lays dying, owing in part to his dysentery. Socrates then asks of "the condition that holds in the soul" and attributes to motion the soul's mastery of learnable things (153b9). Through learning and studying, which are deemed motions, it "gets saved and becomes better (153b11)."

Unlike Euclides, Socrates recognizes here that the flux of particulars requires our efforts to achieve the stability characteristic of that which we call knowledge. On the basis of universal flux, however, such stability has no place. How would we judge a better from a worse condition of one's knowledge? How could these lessons "get saved," a phrase that seems to suggest endurance in their being? How, more generally, can Socrates make the distinction he uses in this context between soul and body? Many such questions are raised by Socrates' paean to motion, but such questions do not trouble Theaetetus who accedes to Socrates' point. Perhaps, as a student, he would approve of anything that supports learning but this observation simply reinforces the point that Socrates is tailoring this notion of good to all of Theaetetus' predilections.

The subsequent paragraph goes to the heart of these predilections. In this passage it becomes clear that motion is good, above all, because it saves us in the most basic sense. Socrates places the highest value on sheer preservation, on getting to shore safely (153c7–8). He connects motion to that deity by whose action "all things are and are kept safe both among gods and human beings (153d2–3)."

This last phrase refers to the second quote from Homer, which marks off the present passage. We are now ready to consider the role these quotes play in the present passage. Given Homer's decisive role in establishing the Greek view of good, it is appropriate that Socrates uses him to demarcate this passage because it articulates the view of good underlying the theoretical doctrine that links perception, relativism, and flux. Yet the two quotes that frame the passage cast a dubious shadow over the validity of its claims. In the *Iliad*, the first quote actually occurs subsequent to the second. This second quote (in the *Theaetetus*) occurs when Zeus (not mentioned by name in our text perhaps to avoid alienating these sophisticated theoreticians) asserts his omnipotence even over the other gods.[26] He threatens them should they defy his prohibition against interfering with human affairs. In particular, he threatens to punish the other gods by bringing all things to a standstill. Contrary to Socrates' suggestion, Zeus does not here aim to maintain things in motion with a beneficial intent. If we engage in the act of interpretation called for by Socrates' literary allusion we see that this allusion contributes to the numerous contradictions of the theoretical premise in this passage. It also thus contributes to the sense that this theoretical premise is less decisive than the view of good animating it.

The first quote in this passage of the *Theaetetus* speaks to that good. It addresses a guarantee by an omnipotent being that all will be preserved in safety – clearly, one of Theaetetus' deepest desires.[27] As I said, this quote occurs in the *Iliad* subsequent to Zeus' claim of omnipotence. However, it serves exactly to make that omnipotence dubious insofar as it involves Hera's eminently successful plot to defy Zeus' prohibition. Zeus' claim of omnipotence is revealed as an unfounded boast.

Though offered as if they were theoretical statements regarding universal flux, what these Homeric statements show is that the gods themselves fight over the proper course of action to take.[28] Apparently, "among the gods too . . . some believe some things just, and noble and shameful and good and bad, others believe others."[29] Through these quotes, subsequent readers of the text, if not Theaetetus, might be led to wonder whether the view of good animating these

[26] Homer *Iliad* viii. 18–27.

[27] Ibid., xiv. 201.

[28] Given Homer's generalship of the fluxists, he could hardly complain that Socrates' use of his text distorts its "true" meaning.

[29] *Euthyphro* 7e1–3.

theoretical reflections – the hoped-for guarantee of security for all one cares about – is available in any venue including among the gods.

Socrates now does bring Heracleitus to bear on perception. However, prior to considering this next step it is important to be clear about the meaning of the previous passage. It bears importantly on Socrates' motive for generating from Theaetetus' definition the comprehensive three-part thesis. Through his dubious literary allusions, his deployment of "signs" rather than arguments, Socrates has highlighted the need to consider the possibility that something other than ironclad logic connects the links in this tri-partite thesis.

Gail Fine summarizes one widely held view of the links in this way: "Plato argues that Theaetetus' claim that knowledge is perception commits him to a Protagorean epistemology which, in turn, commits him to a Heracleitean ontology. He also argues that Theaetetus' definition is best supported by a Protagorean epistemology which in turn is best supported by a Heracleitean ontology."[30] Yet, as Fine adds, "strict implication is not in view here."[31] As I have characterized the connection, there is latitude at the nexus of each of these doctrines. Socrates exploits this latitude, often in a tendentious manner, to push the argument in a certain direction. To recapitulate, beginning with Theaetetus' initial definition: perception need not have been considered the whole of knowledge; if it is the whole of knowledge, it need not have been regarded as sense-perception alone to the exclusion of intellectual perception; if it is sense-perception, it need not have collapsed appearance into perception; Protagoras' dictum need not have entailed radical idiosyncrasy of perception; and finally, as we see in what follows, the phenomenalism that results from the introduction of Heracleiteanism need not be taken to deny enduring characteristics of knower and known. It is Socrates' exploitation of the latitude between the connection of the three theses that compels us to ask what moves the argument if it is not, in Fine's phrase, "strict implication."

I have argued that the argument has an ideological character by which I mean that it is constructed to respond to a preexisting, and in Theaetetus' case, unexamined view of good. In the passage just considered, Socrates makes this ideological character explicit in his "signs" showing that good and motion are inseparable. It is powerfully present, too, in the generalship of Homer whose texts Socrates employs to plant a seed of doubt about this good. Appreciation of this ideological character is absolutely crucial for grasping the subsequent development of the dialogue because it points to the ground on which Socrates believes the anti-Socratic theoretical position rests. Only on this basis can we

[30] Fine, "Conflicting Appearances," 108. See also Myles Burnyeat, "Idealism and Greek Philosophy: What Descartes Saw and Berkeley Missed," *Philosophical Review* 90 (1982): 5–7 and Burnyeat, *The "Theaetetus of Plato,"* 7–19. Sayre sees that what joins at least the first two legs of the thesis is Socrates' aim to provide for infallibility. *Plato's Analytic Method*, 61–3.

[31] Fine, "Conflicting Appearances," 108n9.

understand the otherwise paradoxical outcome of the inquiry into knowledge: that an examination of good becomes central to Socrates' examination of the meaning of knowledge.

Back to Perception (153d8–154b6)

Socrates elaborates the theory of perception that follows on the introduction of universal flux.[32] He begins with this injunction: "Form a conception then . . . in this way (153d8)." In the view he propounds, perception is a function of an interaction, specifically, a collision, between two participants. Socrates says Theaetetus must therefore believe, for example, that the color white is not "any other thing outside your eyes (153d9–10)." For this reason, it is not accurate to speak of the participants as if these were something in themselves. Rather, to refer once again to color, it is "neither the thing bumping nor the thing bumped into, but some in-between thing that comes about *privately* for each (154a1–3, emphasis added)." Why must Theaetetus believe this? He must simply believe because if this were not the case, "then it would presumably already be in an ordered arrangement and enduring, and would not become in becoming (153d9–e2)." The ideological character of Socrates' reasoning persists.

Up to this point, Socrates' account need not entail the radical idiosyncrasy of perception. We, as humans, could possess the same perceptive capacities that react the same way to the same stimuli. But Socrates now asks a series of questions that dictates the insurmountably private character of perception. Theaetetus does not seem fully aware of what is transpiring.

Socrates asks, "would you strongly swear that the way each color appears to you is the way it also appears to a dog or to other animals? (154a3–4)." Theaetetus responds emphatically in the negative, even uttering an oath, as he pridefully distinguishes his human mode of perception from an animal's (154a5). Socrates' question replicates the ambiguity, evident in his initial treatment of Protagoras' dictum, as to whether the measure is humankind or each individual human. It is not clear, therefore, whether Theaetetus is answering for himself or on behalf of humanity over against the animal kingdom. What is clear is that as long as this ambiguity exists, there need not be anything radically idiosyncratic about the account of perception Socrates has given.

This ambiguity survives only until Socrates' next question: "does anything whatever appear alike to another human being and to you? (154a6–7)." With this question, Socrates takes a large step toward the privacy of perception. Perhaps, however, he takes too large a step. It is not so evident that this radical divergence of individual perception does form part of our experience. On the contrary, much of life depends on things appearing similarly to different people – think, for example, of driving in a large city – else how would community of any sort be possible? Accordingly, Socrates quickly asks an

[32] For a helpful sketch of this view of perception, see Burnyeat, *The "Theaetetus" of Plato*, 16.

alternative question: "or is it much more the case that it's not the same thing for you yourself, since you yourself are never holding on in a condition just like yourself? (154a7–8)."

Socrates' questions do not permit Theaetetus to pursue the idea that humans as such share a common perception of the world. Instead, he moves from the implication of a divergence between human and nonhuman to a divergence among humans to, finally, a divergence within Theaetetus. To this last question, Theaetetus responds, "The latter seems to me more the case than the former (154a9)." Note that the two options Socrates has provided for Theaetetus might both entail relativism. But Theaetetus has not selected the option most directly expressive of relativism. As an adolescent boy in some degree of psychological conflict, the feeling that he is in a state of flux is probably readily available to Theaetetus. Less familiar is the notion that the views of each human are radically idiosyncratic. This latter notion is Socrates' ultimate destination, but he must reach it by a more circuitous route. Through such "arguments" as these, Socrates moves Theaetetus toward a theoretical view that undermines all identity.

Socrates now extends the reach of his theory from color to qualities such as large or hot. At least in the case of hotness it is much less clear that it is relative to the perceiver. It is more than plausible that there is an enduring and universal perspective on, say, the hotness of this flame. Socrates' strongest "argument" for his position at this point is that if such stable qualities existed we could not explain either how we perceive differently or how the things are perceived differently unless they are nothing in themselves (154b1–6). He rules out explanations that permit both stability and flux, unity and variety. That is, these are ruled out until Socrates raises an objection to the theory being formulated.

The Wonder-Inducing Dice (154b6–155d5)

Socrates' inclusion of largeness in his list opens the door to this objection. As Lewis Campbell states, "I cannot think of any magnitude or number as great or small except in relation to some other magnitude or number."[33] The existence of such relative qualities, and especially change in these relative qualities, presents a problem for the doctrine of absolute flux (or for that matter, for a doctrine of absolute stability) insofar as its explanation requires that beings somehow be capable of stability and flux at once. Socrates explores this apparently paradoxical requirement through an example involving the comparison of dice. With this example he articulates the difference between change that produces a wholly new being and change that only produces alteration relative to another being, that is, between absolute and relative change.

33 Campbell, *The "Theaetetus" of Plato*, 44n12.

Socrates introduces the objection by saying that Protagoras and all who would agree with him would regard themselves as compelled to say "wondrous and ridiculous" things, if they were to maintain the distinction between absolute and relative change (154b6–7). A crucial distinction between these Protagoreans and Socrates proves to rest on their divergent assessments of the worth of wonder and the perplexities that generate it. The wonder that Protagoras finds ridiculous, Socrates soon deems the origin of philosophy.

What then are the things Protagoras would find "wondrous and ridiculous"? On the basis of a "small example," Socrates tells Theaetetus, "you'll know everything I want (154c1–2)." The example is small but telling: "six dice if you bring four near to them are more than the four, half again as many, while if you bring twelve, they are less, half as many (154c2–4)."[34] What is paradoxical here, and a matter of wonder, is that the six have become less without apparently changing. Somehow, they exhibit both stability and flux.

Before we consider his further examination of the example, we should note that the numbers chosen by Socrates are significant. Six is the harmonic mean between four and twelve, that is, the proportion between the difference of twelve and six and between six and four is the same as that between twelve and four so that 12:4::(12–6):(6–4). Socrates could have chosen any number to illustrate greater and lesser, but he chose three numbers whose absolute values are significant.[35] An aspect of the comparison would be lost were they not what they are in themselves. If the claim is made that this change represents an absolute change in the numbers, then that would be to deny this relationship of the harmonic mean that depends on the numbers being *both* what they are in themselves *and* how they stand in relationship with one another. This fact makes the example even more challenging to the flux doctrine than it otherwise would be. More challenging too is his use of dice and not just numbers. Viewing this example, even in his mind's eye, Theaetetus would be aware that the dice, these tangible objects, do not change when, to use Socrates' image, they are brought near to one another.[36]

Socrates says that "no other way of speaking can be upheld" than that stated in his example, and he challenges Theaetetus: "Or will you uphold any?

[34] As Cornford, among others, recognizes, this passage is a digression. In a sense it deals with the same issue as the later, more famous digression but from a different, more abstract standpoint (*Plato's Theory of Knowledge*, 41). Desjardins regards it as bearing on the core concern of the dialogue, which she terms *emergent generation*. By this term, she refers to those wholes that are more than the sum of their parts (*The Rational Enterprise*, 186).

[35] On the harmonic mean, see E. S. Haring, "Socratic Duplicity: *Theaetetus* 154b1–156a3," *Review of Metaphysics* 45 (1992): 527–8, 534.

[36] Haring suggests further that the reference to dice intends to preserve the intersubjective character of these comparisons. Games that use dice are dependent on agreement about individuals' perception of them. "Socratic Duplicity," 527, 532.

(154c5).” With this question, he places Theaetetus in an atmosphere of contention, challenging him as would the sophistic controversialists. Continuing in the same vein, Socrates springs this question: “Protagoras or anyone else” would ask, “is there a way that anything becomes greater or more, other than by increase? (154c7–9).” The question asks whether all change of any kind must be absolute, a change in the being, which leaves no enduring character to the being so changed. If so, then a thing’s undergoing any kind of alteration or modification whatsoever entails the production of some wholly new thing. And because things as such are subject to coming into being and passing away, that is, because all things necessarily alter, there can be no persistent identity for any one thing. If there is only absolute change, then all things are in constant flux.

Socrates makes Theaetetus answer this question, and Theaetetus responds in a most thoughtful manner. He is acutely aware of the two competing theses in play. They present a conundrum that has vexed him before, perhaps because it goes to the heart of his worries over being refuted. The distinction in play is frequently exploited by the disputatious. This distinction expresses the character of the beings such that they are capable of being ambiguous, and so generative of disputation.

“If,” Theaetetus says, “I’m going to answer what seems the case for the thing that’s in question now, I’ll say that there is no way, but for the thing in question before, being on guard against saying opposite things, I’ll say that there is (154c10–d2).” The former option refers to the Protagorean view that, to preserve the doctrine of absolute flux, must deny that anything becomes bigger or more in a different way than by increase. The latter option refers to the lesson of the dice example that, in the implied distinction between absolute and relative change, indicates that something can become bigger without undergoing increase in some absolute way.[37] As Theaetetus’ response makes clear, Socrates has, and not for the last time, brought Theaetetus’ desires, as expressed in his allegiance to Protagoreanism, into tension with his experience. This tension provides solid ground for a step on the ascending path to dialectics.

Socrates praises Theaetetus’ response, punctuating it with an oath to Hera, that goddess whose duplicity enabled her to defy the ordering power of her supposedly omnipotent husband (154d3). In thus praising Theaetetus’ recognition of perplexity, Socrates perhaps means also to point to a connection between that supreme political virtue of manliness and the desire to grasp the one right answer to all questions, a connection that becomes more explicit in the Digression. If this is so, then his oath to Hera would continue the self-consciously countercultural gist of his thought evident also in his image of midwifery.

37 Haring rightly notes that the dice example introduces issues that are “quite critical of Protagoras.” “Socratic Duplicity,” 525. In this judgment she differs from Cornford, 41–5; McDowell, *Plato “Theaetetus,”* 131–7; and Waterfield, *Plato “Theaetetus,”* 151–4.

Socrates' praise precedes his portrayal of the fearful situation they would face should they insist on the distinction between absolute and relative change. The existence of relative change, as distinguishable from absolute, requires that the beings are complex. Distinctly relative change depends on beings being comparable with one another, and as such necessarily other than simple. It requires that a being *is* not only as this particular individual but also as possessing these various characteristics, as this kind of thing, and so on. Only thus can a being be something that it *is not* when taken by itself but be something that it *is* when considered together with other beings. However, if a being is thus capable, then a single characterization of it might not therefore suffice to comprehend wholly any particular being. This capacity to *be* in diverse ways, in sum, renders the beings potentially ambiguous. Any single characterization might therefore be subject to refutation. But why should refutation be a source of fear?

In a public setting, where verbal facility is valued, there certainly exists the threat of humiliation. Anyone concerned to avoid shame and preserve honor would want to avoid such a situation. Yet, furthermore, a related, and perhaps more profound fear, would attend even a private refutation (if any of Socrates' conversations can be considered simply private). I refer to the fear that what one thought one knew may be refuted. Such refutation may generate fear, and this fear may provoke anger at the source of that refutation, especially if the knowledge in question provides the orientation for one's life. One would then have to face the disturbing prospect that the world may not be arranged as one might have hoped. Given Socrates' previous reflections on the pervasive and powerful influence of the love of one's own in our lives, this would most likely mean that the assurance derived from views supportive of this love may be shaken. Addressing our deepest individual concerns, the possibility of this outcome might well generate fear. Here stands the connection between Socrates' abstract "small example" and Theaetetus' fears. If Socrates' interlocutors accept the possibility expressed by the dice example, that something can become bigger without increase, then they might have to accept the prospect not merely of ongoing dispute regarding this issue but also the persistence of dispute regarding that which is nearest and dearest to them.

What good might be so valuable as to outweigh the potential pain of such dispute? This question returns in Socrates' subsequent jousting with Theodorus. But Socrates makes plain its enormous importance in the present context as well. He designates their respective willingness to live with ambiguity as nothing less than the key difference between himself and the sophists.

If, according to Socrates, we were to follow the way of these controversialists, we would believe that we "have closely examined all the things in our minds (154d9)." Then, like those whom Socrates calls "terribly clever and wise," we would compete in order to "test each other . . . out of our superior abundance and joining sophistically in that sort of battle, we would bang arguments against arguments with one another (154d8, 154d9–e3)." The sophists' belief in their self-transparency underlies their agonistic behavior. They have no doubts, nothing that calls for further inquiry. What Socrates considers a chief source of doubt, the mystery of the soul, they regard as an open book.[38] Perhaps for this reason, when referring to their internal lives, Socrates does not refer to their souls, a locution that, as the present context shows, he reserves as a designation for internal conflict or at least difference (154d9). With all serious questions settled, with no inquiry required, they can turn to competitive disputation. Rather than focusing on truth, they can strive to attain victory, with honor as its reward.

Socrates removes himself from this arena, saying that because he is among the "private people" he pursues inquiry (154e3).[39] His layman's stance seems equally opposed both to the public and to the expert character of the sophist. Socrates makes the distinction between himself and the sophists rest on their disagreement regarding human self-transparency. It depends on his view that we are best understood as souls whose complexity eludes full self-awareness rather than as wholly transparent minds. Socrates is significantly less sanguine than are the sophists regarding the extent of our self-knowledge. In Chapter 8 I argue that this stance is due to his greater awareness of the implications for such knowledge of the soul's very power of self-scrutiny. For now, it is important simply to note that by locating this distinction on these particular grounds Socrates intimates that his novel philosophic path depends, above all, on this insight into the human constitution.

This insight guides the argument as Socrates now invites Theaetetus, in the spirit of midwifery, to "look back over things again" (154e8). Specifically, they assess what he calls the "apparitions" in our minds that, as apparitions, we must not have yet fully scrutinized (155a2). Contrary to the sophists' belief, there remain views, indeed errors, which, when recognized as such, require reexamination.

In relating these apparitions, Socrates makes clearer the goal of his dice example. By this example, he means specifically to show that – and why – the doctrine of radical flux requires that relative change collapse into absolute change, that – and why – the former kind of change cannot consist with the flux doctrine. In so doing, he cannot help but also reveal the prerequisites involved in the apprehension of relative change – namely, that the beings be comparable with one another and that there exists an intellect capable of making this comparison. If relative change should prove an ineradicable possibility, these prerequisites and their attendant perplexities would have to be accounted for in any adequate account of ourselves and the world. For this reason, it is helpful to remind ourselves once more of the implications of these prerequisites. I begin with the knower.

[38] Cf. *Phaedrus* 279e4–230a6.

[39] I do not mean to suggest that Socrates refrains wholly from competition; he seems to be competing with Theodorus in this dialogue. But his ultimate purpose is not simply victory.

To use Socrates' initial example, were the intellect capable only of perception, the comparison of the dice could not take place; we do not perceive such relations but only perceive the particulars. On the basis of perception alone Theodorus could not judge, for example, that Theaetetus is the one in the middle (144c1). We can see this die and that die but the connection between them requires a further cognitive act, one that demands an intellect capable of stepping back and reflecting on the perceptions, which are as such discrete. This fact proves later to be crucial in Theaetetus' discovery of the distinctive power of the soul. On the side of the intellect, the comprehension of relative change requires the complexity that is inherent in reflection, in what Socrates calls *dianoia* or thought. To eliminate such complexity is, as we have seen, one goal of the radicalization of Theaetetus' thesis.

Complexity is also required on the side of the known. Jacob Klein writes of that situation when we confront something like six dice capable of being both bigger and smaller: "the very fact that we feel perplexed about such perceptions manifests the presence of *dianoia* 'in' them."[40] The beings are such as to call for thought, thought that relates, that compares. As I pointed out in the preceding text, for one being to be comparable with one another, it must not only be this particular but also this kind of thing such that it can share characteristics with other beings and thus be comparable. It can, while remaining itself, be in a different way when compared with, when taken together with, other beings. Even if the comparison reveals the difference between the beings, they nevertheless must be sufficiently similar so as to make possible the comparison that reveals the difference. Thus, for example, the dice are particulars but also intelligible as a certain number comparable with other numbers. But this means that the beings as thinkable in this way must *be* in heterogeneous ways. This is what I mean by designating them as complex. Such complexity too, therefore, must be eliminated to substantiate the anti-Socratic thesis. If this is the case, then the response to this thesis, or the theoretical justification of Socratic philosophy, depends precisely on the existence of this complexity and that of the soul.

Such complexity, as we have seen from the beginning of the dialogue, may elude our understanding as we struggle to explain fully how these senses of being can cohere in a unity or how the soul comprises its "parts." The Megarians' reaction to the problem of change is one possible reaction to the ensuing perplexity: deny the very possibility of such change. However, in the present context, too, the doctrine of radical flux demands the denial of the existence of relative change. Underlying this "necessity" is the desire to avoid the "battle in our soul," evident in Theaetetus, that Socrates now discusses (155b5–6).

In particular, Socrates adduces three apparitions that we believe must be true but that the possibility of relative change belies: "nothing could ever become greater or less, either in bulk or in number, as long as it is equal to

[40] See Klein, *Plato's "Meno,"* 116.

itself"; "what is neither added to nor subtracted from could never increase nor decrease, but would always be equal"; and "it's impossible for that which was not before to be afterward without having come to be and becoming (155a3–5, 155a7–9, 155b1–3)." Each of these, as Ronald Polansky has shown, is contradicted by the notion of relative change, exhibited not merely in Socrates' example but also experienced by each of us constantly.[41] In each case, relative change permits the possibility that an entity can be equal to itself and not wholly change while also becoming greater or less, increasing or decreasing, being what it was not before. Each of these is possible if we conceive of the entity in relation to other entities. Thus Socrates remains Socrates but is larger or smaller depending on whom he is compared with. Or, Theaetetus remains Theaetetus while also becoming what he was not before, specifically, a mature adult.

If we do experience these possibilities constantly, why then are we so powerfully drawn to these apparitions, these principles of change that, contrary to our experience, deny the possibility of relative change? It is not because they substantiate our lives as we live them. Their failure to do so accounts for the "battle" in our souls as, like Theaetetus, we realize that what we wish to be true cannot be true. It is rather related to that possibility of refutability just discussed, a possibility these apparitions seek to remove. They do so by answering the desire that each thing be wholly what it is, and that each be so in a simple way. These apparitions eliminate the possibility that a thing can be not only this but also something else when thought of in relation with another thing.

But this observation returns us to the issue raised above: why should we desire so fervently that this very abstract consideration hold true? It is because such an affirmation bears on the considerably less abstract consideration also mentioned there. This consideration, of utmost interest to Theaetetus, and to us, is trust – trust in our life-orienting ideas. We are all in the same boat as the fatherless boy when it comes to the desire to trust in those things, those wholes, that we look to for guidance, that serve as standards for judgment. With respect to these, we are understandably reluctant to concede that there is nothing that is wholly and only what it is, nothing, for example, that can be shown to be wholly good, through and through, everywhere and always. Our reluctance is most intransigent just at this point, when it comes to that which provides or grounds the good. It can be so intransigent as to result in such outlandish stances as the Megarians' denial of change.

Equally outlandish is the present assertion that all change is absolute. The consequent world of unceasing flux paradoxically serves the same purpose as the Megarians' denial. It likewise eliminates that complexity which makes possible ambiguity in us and in the beings. Like radical stasis, its extreme opposite, radical flux, does away with the need to undertake the potentially troubling inquiry into the good. Through his examination of Theaetetus' thesis,

41 Polansky, *Philosophy and Knowledge*, 94–5. See also R. H. Hackforth, "Notes on Plato's *Theaetetus*," *Mnemosyne* 10 (1957): 130–1.

leading as it does to the embrace of an experience-denying stance, Socrates might induce his interlocutors and readers to entertain the theoretical viability of the apparently paradoxical middle ground between the extremes of stability and flux. More importantly, he also enables these theorists to appreciate how such abstract concerns might bear on how they live their lives.

Socrates' subsequent example affirms this bearing of the abstract issue of change on practical concerns.[42] He speaks not of dice but of himself and Theaetetus. Specifically, Socrates notes that he, "being of such an age that I neither grow nor undergo anything in the opposite direction am in the course of a year bigger than you, who are now young, and afterward smaller, when nothing has been taken away from my bulk but yours has grown (155b8–c1)." In this example, Theaetetus has undergone absolute change, but the change of Socrates is relative. More importantly, we know, and when Socrates edits this conversation he knows as well, that "in the course of a year" he will undergo a most significant change – he will be dead. The point is that these issues of change, relative and absolute, bear directly on the pressing existential question of human identity. We must wonder, what is it about ourselves and others that changes absolutely, what is it that changes relatively? Is each one of us sufficient in him- or herself? Or is one's identity, one's wholeness, significantly dependent on relationships, whether to other humans, to ideas, or to the cosmos, among other possibilities?

Socrates understands that these questions trouble Theaetetus, as they might any thoughtful person. But this may especially be true for a young person concerned with the question of his or her identity or concerned as Theaetetus is, with the attainment of distinction that necessarily involves comparison. Theaetetus now confesses that he is "in a state of wonder at what in the world these things are" even to the point that "when I look into them I whirl around in the dark (155c9–10)."

Theaetetus' wonder is warranted. For one wishing to avoid the wonder-producing perplexity of change, the alternative is either the Megarians or the fluxists: either nothing changes whatsoever or all changes ceaselessly. Neither can account for the world as we experience it. Yet if an adequate account must somehow lie between these, it too gives rise to paradoxes: beings must both endure and change; beings have characteristics that exist only in relation to other beings; and the grasp of such relations requires a self-critical capacity that makes the soul's wholeness elusive. The upshot is that we are such and the world is such as to generate perplexity.[43] Theaetetus' wonder is indeed warranted.

Socrates tells Theaetetus that "this experience, wondering, belongs very much to the philosopher (155d2–3)." Invoking the Muses in his account of the source of philosophy, he asserts that there is "no other source of philosophy

42 Consider on this issue Roochnik, "Self-Recognition," 39.

43 See Benardete on this point. *Being of the Beautiful*, I. 99.

than [wonder] (155d3–4)." The world does generate perplexity and, in so doing, calls for philosophy. Inquiry is not undertaken arbitrarily.

Socrates proceeds to provide a mythic genealogy of wonder, maintaining that "Iris is the offspring of Thaumas (155d4)." Socrates' choice of Thaumas no doubt stems from the fact that the god's name sounds like the Greek word for wonder. But what commends Iris to be the deified form of philosophy? Several commentators note Iris' association with the rainbow and her occupation as messenger of the gods.[44] Accordingly, like the rainbow, Iris mediates between gods and the earth or perhaps, as the image of philosophy, she mediates between the human and the divine.

Also pertinent to Socrates' use of Iris, however, may be a specific message that the gods entrust this goddess to deliver. Hesiod reports that Iris has the power to render her fellow gods speechless if they should be caught in a lie. Offenders are, moreover, removed from the gods' councils of deliberation.[45] In this capacity, Iris is the goddess that protects and enforces the link between truth and speech. Appropriately, in the *Cratylus*, Socrates provides an etymology connecting the goddess's name to the word for speech.[46] In generating philosophy, wonder generates also the need for speech connected to truth, to the way things are. I point this out because within a few pages Socrates will designate as the hallmark of Protagoreanism its advocacy of speech severed from truth. In addition to its other connotations, Socrates' use of Iris to represent philosophy might be a warning against the speechlessness, the incapacity for deliberative conversation, evident in the original talking head: the posthumous Protagoras (171d1–3).

Back to Perception, Again (155d5–157b1)

Having "digressed" concerning the wonder-generating perplexities of relative change, Socrates again takes up the main thread of his presentation, the formulation of the view that eradicates such perplexities. Yet the alternative view persists in the penumbra of his exposition. Thus, as he had done earlier, prior to further unfolding the argument he characterizes their inquiry as a sort of initiation into mysteries (156a3). In this way, he fuels the hope that they will become renowned like those who understand the "hidden-away truth (155d10–e1)." But more generally, his comments once again nod toward that alternative, complex view of nature that must be acknowledged if we wish to maintain that humans are variously capable of piercing the veil of seeming in their efforts to grasp being.

44 Although both Benardete and Polansky recognize this point, neither gives the interpretation in the preceding text. Benardete, *Being of the Beautiful*, I.107; Polansky, *Philosophy and Knowledge*, 96.

45 Hesiod, *Theogeny* 781–810.

46 *Cratylus* 408b3–4. (The sentence is bracketed in Hicken.)

In this context, Socrates rejects a group he calls "the uninitiated," by which he seems to refer to the materialists.[47] We might have thought that the materialists – Democritus and his atomist followers – would be active members in the coalition of the fluxists. As Sedley points out, however, the atomists' view that there are real physical entities underlying change provides one reason to preclude them from the cadre of truly serious fluxists.[48]

There may be an additional reason for their exclusion. In rejecting the atomists as uninitiated, Socrates refers to their being "without the Muses (156a2)." Having employed the Muses in his fanciful genealogy, he again relies on them in now providing what he explicitly refers to as a myth (156c4). Socrates' willingness to use myth distinguishes him from his characterization of the materialists. Perhaps the atomists' neglect of the Muses reflects the view that the laws of nature apply throughout the whole. That is, the same laws, which are wholly accessible, apply to human and nonhuman. Were this true, there would be no need to rely on a mythic account. There would be no abiding question regarding the integration of the human and the whole that would cause Socrates to rely on the Muses when providing such a comprehensive account.[49] To the extent that the relationship between the soul and the whole, the human and the cosmic, remains a question, the Muses provide indispensable aid. At least this is the suggestion in what follows, for only Socrates' explicitly mythic presentation includes aspects of life familiar to our experience.

Plato has Theaetetus express this issue of the relationship between cosmic and human things in his response to Socrates' formulation of the view of the uninitiated. In it, Theaetetus applies the atomists' view of the world to their own demeanor: "It's of stiff and repellent beings that you speak (155e8–156a1)." Socrates' intent to consider the bearing of theoretical doctrines on human existence is evident in the very reference to "the uninitiated" with its implication that not every person should hear every theoretical account. Theaetetus may not realize the full weight of his critique of the uninitiated, but his inclination to ponder theoretical perplexities to the point of making himself dizzy also reflects a tacit awareness of this link between theory and practice. In any case, by referring to "the uninitiated," Socrates suggests the eventual criterion for assessing what follows: whether these theoretical doctrines can account for our own experiences.

Having dispensed with the "uninitiated," Socrates now relates a more detailed account of the fluxists' view especially as it bears on perception. He does so in two distinct stages. The first, which he labels a myth, differs in significant ways from the second demythologized version. Let's consider the details of this two-step presentation.

47 See Campbell's argument that Socrates refers here to Democritus. *The "Theaetetus" of Plato*, xli–v.

48 Sedley, *The Midwife of Platonism*, 45–6.

49 On Plato's use of myth, see Griswold, *Plato's "Phaedrus,"* 138–51.

Socrates' tale lays out the theory of nature that brings together universal flux and knowledge as perception. It rests on the view that "all is always motion and there's nothing else besides this (156a4–5)." Yet it also finds two forms (*eidei*) of motion each having a different power, one to act and the other to be acted on (156a5–7). Apparently, these forms are not themselves subject to flux. The distinction between them must be maintained because "from the intercourse of these and their rubbing against each other there come to be their offspring": a perceived and also a perceiving (156a7–8).

Socrates names these perceptions "seeings and hearings and smellings and coolings and burnings (156b3–4)." Yet in this mythic presentation he also adds "pleasures and pains and fears (156b4–5)" to the list. Those named in the latter group are not so clearly matters of perception alone. Fear, especially, is a passion experienced on the basis of a reaction to, or even judgments about, that which is perceived. As is true of the *eidei* of motion, these latter possibilities do not fit comfortably with the theory. They are not fully explicable if our mental apparatus must be completely explained by the occurrence of necessarily one-time-only collisions of agent and patient motions, for they presume a persistent self that assesses these collisions.[50]

In the next stage of his presentation, Socrates translates the foregoing myth into *logos*. He asks, what "does this story (*mythos*) mean for us? (156c3–4, c7–8)." Missing from this nonmythic presentation are the *eidei* and the existence of pleasure, pain, and fear, those elements discordant with the theory. Again, both of these elements, present in the mythic presentation, suggest stability beyond flux, whether in the persistence of kinds or of a self that can fear for its endurance. No such stability survives the present account of perception.

In this account, there are four types of motion: active and passive slow motions, which correspond to something that perceives and something that can be perceived; and active and passive fast motions, which correspond to an act of perception and a percept. When something that perceives conjoins with a perceivable, the result is a perceiving and a percept. Each of these occasions is an entirely idiosyncratic, one-time only, event. The result is that "out of all these things, there is the very thing we were saying from the beginning, that there is no one thing itself by itself, but always a becoming for someone (157a7–b1)."

In this demythologized *logos* we see the result of the work of the "uninitiated," the theoretician unaided by the Muses. Such a theorist sees no need to consider his theory's bearing on human life. Perhaps only in such a Muse-less presentation is it possible to fulfill the ambition of the theorist to have the comprehensive account. The result of the failure to recognize the resistance of

[50] Burnyeat compares this passage to Berkeleyan idealism, but, as Polansky notes, the view differs from idealism in that it cannot assume a stable consciousness. Burnyeat, "Idealism and Greek Philosophy," 4, 11; Burnyeat, *The "Theaetetus" of Plato*, 12–14; Polansky, *Philosophy and Knowledge*, 99.

the human to perfect integration with the whole is self-annihilation, the impossibility of an enduring self. But to perfect this project of theoretical overreach, the theorist must deal with one further obstacle to this comprehensive account: the limitations inherent in our reliance on speech.

Speech and Opinion (157b1–c1)

Throughout the demythologized section, Socrates insists that nothing is itself by itself, that nothing has a stable identity. Facilitating this claim is his focus on qualities such as white, stiff, and hot rather than on the things that come to possess these qualities. However, he does also implicate the stability of the beings themselves. This outcome leads to a renewal and extension of his previous suggestion that an overhaul of our speech is necessary to bring it into accord with this new view of nature (157b5–8).

For a number of reasons, it is worth dwelling on Socrates' remarks about speech. In his intellectual autobiography, delivered in the last hours of his life, Socrates characterizes his famous redirection of philosophy as a turn to the speeches.[51] Moreover, lest there be any doubt about the importance that speech plays in his philosophizing, later in the *Theaetetus* he identifies thinking with speaking. Any attempt to discern the distinctive character of Socratic philosophy must pay close attention to his remarks on speech. It should not be surprising then that the present, decisively anti-Socratic thesis requires a wholesale rejection of the validity of common speech.

Referring to our use of "being" in speech, Socrates says that "being must be rooted out from all quarters, despite the fact that we have been forced many times, and just now, by custom and our lack of knowledge, to use it (157b1–3)." The corrective program Socrates recommends is that of the pure theorists. Everyone's activity must be revised on the basis of the theorists' insight into nature as a whole. In particular, we must alter our self-understanding, including our specific capacity for speech, in light of this more comprehensive view. Given what we have seen in the dialogue thus far, however, the source of this admonition is troubling. The call to eliminate *logos*, or revise it to the point that it is unusable, is "according to the statement (*logos*) of the wise men" (157b3–4). These by-now familiar "wise men," insist that one "make no concessions," that one must be theoretically pure and perfectly consistent (157b4). Accordingly, they "eliminate being," the consequence of which is that they refuse to recognize "a something or a someone or a mine or a this or a that or with any other name that makes anything stand still (157b4–5)." Their theory, in which nothing is itself by itself, eliminates both "be" and "me." Motivated by love of one's own, the theory destroys the possibility of speaking of one's self.[52]

[51] *Phaedo* 99d4–100a7.

[52] Roochnik makes this point in "Self-Recognition," 39.

Perhaps Socrates' theorists are correct. Perhaps speech is through and through conventional, not connected with "what is." Perhaps speech is simply a matter of habituation, something we use in oblivious ignorance. If this were true, we would have to find a way to live with this fact. We ought to formulate a new form of speech more consistent with nature, as difficult as it might be to conceive what that might be. Failing this, we could nevertheless live with the realization that our usual, and perhaps unavoidable, use of names wholly contradicts nature.[53] Both these options presume that the basic premise is accurate, that speech is wholly conventional. Still, the seriousness Socrates elsewhere accords speech might lead us to hesitate before swallowing this premise whole. The present context offers further evidence of the dubiousness of this premise.

One expression of the problem of knowledge is found in the discrepancy between word and deed; our speech about the world is not itself the world. The Protagorean response to this discrepancy, I will argue, regards speech as constituting an independent, autonomous world unconnected to nature. On this view, speech obeys its own perfectly coherent laws. The discrepancy between speech and deed is thus "overcome" through ignoring deeds, ignoring the world of particulars it is supposed to express.[54] The present passage works in the opposite direction, overcoming this discrepancy by revising speech "in accordance with nature," to which we supposedly have access independently of speech (157b5). Such a revision again collapses this discrepancy but does so now by having speech mirror the purportedly incessant flux of the deeds. In this sense, the discrepancy is "overcome" by acknowledging *only* deeds or particulars. We should note that behind this latter response stands the demand that speech be more not less accurate, that it perfectly reflect the way things are. Both reactions to the discrepancy of speech and deed, including paradoxically the doctrine of absolute flux, harbor a demand for certainty more stringent than is evident in Socrates' turn to the speeches.

Yet, again, we should hesitate before taking up this demand if only because of the rationale animating it. Socrates states, "if anyone makes anything stand still by his speech, the one who does this is easily refuted (157b7–8)." The fear of refutation remains the engine driving this theory. My point here, however, is not only to reiterate the ideological character of the argument. It is also to suggest that this very possibility of refutation militates against the judgment that speech does not reflect "what is" in any way. Rather, the possibility of refutation, which this fear acknowledges, reflects something of the nature of things. Otherwise stated, we have had reason to conclude that the possibility of refutation is not simply a function of the merely customary and ignorant use

53 This view differs from Socrates' idea that our knowledge, as expressed in speech, is partial rather than wholly misguided.

54 At least ostensibly – I will also argue that motivating this view is the very particular desire of the sophist for his own good.

of language. Socrates nods toward the possibility (discussed in greater detail in Chapter 8) that the very nature of the beings makes this refutability possible. For although Socrates here urges that we speak of beings as aggregates rather than wholes, he then says, "one needs to speak this way both part by part and about many things gathered together, on any which gathering people place as a name 'human being' or 'stone' or each animal and form (*eidos*, 157b8–c1)."[55] The phrase "part by part" cannot help but imply that the aggregates must be regarded somehow as wholes inasmuch as parts are only intelligible as such in light of the whole to which they contribute. Socrates' use of the word, *eidos*, signals a capitulation to this fact. The beings understood as parts and wholes rather than as aggregates express that complexity which proves to make refutability an enduring possibility.

It may be that Socrates has not yet found a way to speak in accordance with the flux doctrine's view of nature. But the alternative I am suggesting is that the beings as such require us to speak in this way. In this latter case, it would be exactly in maintaining the possibility of refutability that speech accords best with nature. Hence, the importance of speech in Socratic inquiry, an importance that grows in the conversation as we see that speech or opinion by its very nature resists the extremes of absolute flux and absolute stasis.

In this light, it is important to note that although calling for this novel use of speech, Socrates has not yet explained how opinion is to be treated within the flux doctrine.[56] Yet it is opinion rather than perception that goes to the heart of Theaetetus' worries regarding refutation. It is not conflicting perceptions of hot and dry that trouble him. Rather he frets about the "good and beautiful," to which Socrates now refers (157d8). Such concerns are expressible only in speech. By including these topics among "all the things we were going through just now," Socrates calls attention to the fact that they have not yet explicitly treated such opinions (157d8–9). He now undertakes to do so.

This forthcoming treatment of opinion completes Socrates' delivery of Theaetetus' psychic offspring.[57] It also completes the radicalization of Theaetetus' thesis, showing him in the most dramatic way what the world must be like if it is structured in response to his desire. One point of this exercise, I have suggested, is to demonstrate the power of good in shaping how we see the world. Appreciating this power, we see also the importance of examining the view of good to which any such theoretical view answers. The more radically Socrates pushes the implications of Theaetetus' thesis, the more undeniable is that power. With this in mind, let's turn to the last section of the delivery.

55 For a treatment of some of the difficulties in regarding beings as aggregates or collections, consider McDowell, *Plato "Theaetetus,"* 144–5. For a further appreciation of how radically subversive of unity the whole presentation is, see Myles Burnyeat, "Plato on the Grammar of Perceiving," *The Classical Quarterly* N.S. 26 (1976): 31–2.

56 The dialogue first mentions opinions at 158b2. Here it refers to false opinions.

57 See Maguire's comments on the move from appearance to opinion in the dialogue. Maguire, "Protagoras – or Plato?," 116n6.

Dreams, Disease, and Insanity: The Annihilation of the Self (157c1–160e2)

Socrates asks Theaetetus his opinion of the discussion thus far: "So, Theaetetus, do these things seem pleasing to you, and would they be satisfying to your taste? (157c1–3)." His question requires Theaetetus to engage in cognitive acts whose possibility the theory denies. The possibility of judgment, not to mention the metaphorical use of sense-perception, would be very difficult to explain on the basis of the theory of knowledge being formulated. This discordance between the theory and their reflections on the theory continues in Theaetetus' response. He confesses that he does not know, nor can he even be sure of Socrates' intention. He wonders whether Socrates is testing him or stating his own opinions (157c4–6). Socrates' intention is invisible to Theaetetus, or to anyone. It thus leads to doubt, and sometimes error, about what that intention might be. Clearly, sense-perception alone does not suffice to provide knowledge of this object of intense concern.

In further recognition of this discordance, Socrates reiterates his role as midwife. He thereby reminds us that the deed of examining Theaetetus' opinion stands in stark contrast to the content of that opinion. For, as Socrates points out, midwifery presumes the ever-present possibility that what one believes may be wholly misguided, that it is a wind egg rather than something fruitful (157c7–d3). Socrates exhorts Theaetetus: "be confident and persistent and in good and manly fashion answer what appears to you about what I ask (157d3–5)." However, this exhortation makes sense only if knowledge is not gained simply by opening one's eyes.

Nevertheless, the exhortation does underscore the central conflict in the culmination of Theaetetus' thesis. For it presumes the possibility of taking a stand with respect to oneself. That is, it presumes self-awareness. More basically, it presumes the possibility of a persistent, identifiable self. Such a self stands as the final target for the radicalizing Socrates. The sources of doubt and error, human inwardness, must be eradicated if there is to be a world without the possibility of falsehood. This deed of maieutics provides a counterweight to the denial of identity that follows in Socrates' treatment of opinion. Through this reminder of his midwifery Socrates once again foils Euclides' intention.

Socrates brings up what he says is "left out" from what they have so far discussed: "what has to do with dreams and diseases, both other sorts and insanity (157e1, e2–3)." He wants to explore these in connection with "mis-hearing or mis-seeing, or any other sort of misperceiving," that is, with the possibility of error and falsehood (157e3–4). Socrates says that "you know that in all of these cases, by general agreement, the account we're going through right now is held to be refuted, on the grounds that in them more than anything, false perceptions come about for us, and those things that appear to each person are far from being so, but altogether to the contrary, nothing of what appears is so (157e4–158a3)." With respect to the perceptions of those who are dreaming, ill, or mad, if anywhere, it is universally acknowledged that appearance and being might diverge. Socrates' work is cut out for him.

For his part, Theaetetus responds, "I wouldn't have the power to dispute that those who are insane or dreaming are holding false opinions whenever they suppose themselves to be gods or think in their sleep that they have wings and are flying (158a9–b4)." Socrates has once again struck a nerve in Theaetetus. But he's not alone in his desire to refute the fantastic possibilities raised by the insane or to distinguish dreaming and waking. After all, Socrates refers to a "dispute (*amphisbatama*)" regarding these matters, by which he means a long-standing and well-known argument about just these issues (158b5). That such a disputation exists tells us there really seems to be a problem here, that there is powerful evidence on both sides of the issue: hence, a dispute. Moreover, the familiarity of the dispute indicates that it is of persistent concern to many. And the debate endures because many have a stake in a determination of which side is right.

Why should so many be persistently concerned with those who are insane or ill or dreaming? Theaetetus' initial example provides a clue. He notes that the deranged or dreaming sometimes "suppose themselves to be gods (158b2–3)." Here is the nerve of Theaetetus' concern. He cares whether some view has a more than human warrant for its truth. And, again, his concern is perfectly understandable when that view bears on issues of utmost concern and especially when there is uncertainty regarding just these issues. Theaetetus, and not only Theaetetus, cares about this dispute because he wishes to know how to live, and he is aware of his less than comprehensive understanding. Seeking guidance in this regard, many wish desperately to know whether they hear the true prophet or the false. In the face of similarly comprehensive and decisive claims regarding the weightiest issues, thinkers nearer our own time also asked of the distinction between waking and dreaming, and also of the distinction between true and false prophets.[58] They sought exactly what Theaetetus seeks: a certain measurement of belief, an indubitable criterion of truth.[59]

Socrates thus asks Theaetetus about this issue, which he knows he has "heard many times": "what distinguishing mark anyone could have to demonstrate if someone were to ask now, like this at present, whether we're asleep and dreaming all the things we're thinking or whether we're awake and having a waking conversation with each other (158b8–c2)." The issue of dreaming and waking elicits from Theaetetus a desire for demonstrable evidence that he knows what he knows. He desires epistemology, a science of how we know what

58 On dreaming and waking see, e.g., Rene Descartes, "Meditations on First Philosophy," in *Selected Philosophical Writings*, 77–8, 110, 114, 122. On prophecy see Thomas Hobbes, *Leviathan*, ed. Michael Oakeshott (New York: Collier Books, 1962), 95–7 and Benedict Spinoza, *Theological-Political Treatise*, trans. Samuel Shirley (Indianapolis, IN: Hackett Publishing Company, 1998), 5, 9–35.

59 In the Third Set of Objections to Descartes's *Meditations*, Hobbes traces the question of whether one is dreaming to Plato. See *Descartes, Selected Philosophic Writings*, 125.

we know. Such a science might provide irrefutable knowledge of knowledge, an unassailable warrant for its veracity. The desire for such an Archimedean point, immune from doubt, has not abated in our own time because the uncertainty generating this desire persists. Socrates' response to Theaetetus' yearning still merits our attention.

Socrates' question places Theaetetus where he least wants to be: on the receiving end, perhaps in public, of a question from the disputers. And Socrates' maneuvers educe from Theaetetus one of his longer speeches in the dialogue. In it he elaborates on the feelings generated by this situation and confesses that "the likeness of the latter [our dreams] and the former [a waking conversation] to those is unsettling (158c7–8)." This unsettling similarity makes him wonder, how, if we cannot even tell whether we are dreaming or awake, can we know anything for sure. Socrates traces this inevitable dispute to the soul, the locus of all such conflict. When awake and when dreaming "our soul contends combatively that the seemings that are present to it at every time are true more than anything (158d3–4)."

In its persistence the dispute concerning dreaming and waking suggests, contrary to the sophists, that we do not or cannot scrutinize fully all the things of our minds. Appropriately, in this context, just prior to the obliteration of human identity, Socrates limns aspects of our mental life that underlie this distinction, especially our capacity for self-scrutiny. Were we the passive, non-judging receivers required by the three-legged thesis – "knowledge is perception," "man is the measure," and "all is flux" – such self-scrutiny would be impossible. Yet, as indicated not only by Theaetetus' own internal conflict, but also by the kind of disputes presently under examination, this very power betokens a limit on the comprehensiveness of such scrutiny. As knower and known, we cannot attain the self-subsistent standpoint for such a comprehensive view.

Perhaps it could not be otherwise for a cognitive life that involves the activity of an embodied mind. But each of the conditions Socrates presents in this context – dreaming-waking, illness-health, and sanity-madness – testifies to the bearing of embodiedness on our cognitive life. Providing further testimony is the vehemence, the passion, with which we "[contend] combatively" about this dispute. Soul is the name given to the immensely complex inner life of incomplete self-scrutiny, rent by passionate conflict. I call particular attention to these details because all of this disappears in what follows.

To return to Theaetetus' concern, what then can serve as the criterion? Can it simply be the amount of time we insist on each being true (158d11–12)? This is dismissed as ridiculous although on the basis of Protagoras' view it could be defended.[60] In any case, Socrates pushes Theaetetus to provide an unequivocal standard: "do you have any other clear marker at all to show which sorts of these opinions are true? (158e2–3)." Theaetetus is at a loss. In response, however, Socrates does not supply such a "clear marker," such an

[60] See Polansky, *Philosophy and Knowledge*, 104n53.

unassailable criterion of truth. He offers instead a further radicalization of the Protagorean position, one that denies the very existence of what Socrates has just said is not difficult to see – namely, the possibility of dispute (158c9). Absolute certainty being unavailable, Socrates offers the alternative extreme: absolute skepticism.

Now this alternative does provide a kind of certainty, or at least irrefutability, such as is sought in absolute proof. In its way, it does answer to Theaetetus' desire. However, Socrates' lurching from one extreme to the other raises the question as to whether there is a way between these extremes. In the subsequent critical phase of his midwifery, Socrates maps that way. There he travels a middle path, maintaining that opinions can be judged, but such judgment proceeds without appeal to an absolutely certain measure. The possibility and prerequisites of this Socratic alternative become more intelligible once we consider how in the present passage he eradicates the very possibility of dispute, a possibility his own approach, in its reflection of widespread experience, preserves.

Socrates' first step involves, once again, denying the relational character of being. He collapses unlikeness into absolute difference. Theaetetus, he insists, must answer regarding what Socrates calls the "wholly different" rather than that which "is in some way the same but in another way different (158e10, e9–10)." From this unargued-for mandate follows the impossibility of anything being in any way the same as that with respect to which it is "wholly different." With this acknowledgment in hand, Socrates makes the further dubious move of maintaining that "such a thing" [the wholly different] "is unlike (159a3–4)." Thus, that which is unlike is wholly "other." The notion of likeness or similarity (and dissimilarity) is eliminated not only between two things but also with respect to the same thing at different times, that is, even with respect to "itself (159a7)." Therefore, what we might take as change or development of a thing having a stable identity must now be seen as a series of unrelated quantum leaps of one thing into a wholly other thing.

To know a being means at least to consider that it is and what it is, which means to see what it shares with others of its kind and what distinguishes it as this kind of thing. To be knowable in this way requires that the beings be comparable. Socrates does away with the possibility of disputation, of differences regarding how the beings should be understood, by doing away with this possibility of their being comparable, and thus knowable in the foregoing sense. Without the distinction between unlikeness and difference, there can be no grounds for comparison; there is only "the wholly other" understood as absolute difference. Because this applies as well to the same thing taken at two different times, no being has a stable identity. The world is reduced to that same atomicity that results from the Megarian standpoint regarding change.

Socrates does not limit the scope of this view only to the beings. To make sure the result hits home, he also urges Theaetetus to "talk about me and you and everything else in accordance with the same account (159b2–3)." Socrates uses himself to exemplify the consequent lack of persistent identity. "Socrates healthy" and "Socrates sick" are wholly other than one another (159b3–4). Theaetetus clarifies Socrates' premise for himself by asking, "Now this 'Socrates getting sick', do you mean this as a whole in relation to that whole 'Socrates keeping healthy'? (159b6–7)." To Theaetetus' realization that these two wholes have nothing in common, Socrates responds, "you conceive it beautifully (159b8)." Beings are wholly, homogeneously what they are. They do not partake of a distinction between the being itself and its qualities, between parts and wholes, that would enable them to be compared. All beings, humans included, are regarded as unique at each spatiotemporal moment. Thus, there is no possibility of distinguishing between appearance and being, no possibility of judging inferior the views of the insane, ill, or dreaming. Nothing abides, neither a self nor a being, that would permit such a judgment.

Socrates' provides a summarizing question that is worth quoting in full because it directs us to those difficulties in his radicalization of Theaetetus' initial thesis that might serve to prompt Theaetetus' second thoughts. He asks, "how then if I am without falsehood and do not stumble in my thought, would I not be a knower of the things which are or become of which I'm the perceiver? (160d1–3)." They have shown themselves to be knowers of that which they are the perceivers. The result is Theaetetus' goal of a life "without falsehood." Yet what we are said to know are "the things which are or become." This, however, is obscure. How can we know, what can we claim to know, when the object of our knowing is constantly changing? Socrates leads us farther into the dark with his qualifying addendum: "and do not *stumble* in my thought (*dianoia*) (160d1, emphasis added)." But the ground of dianoetic thinking or reasoning and its concomitant possibility of falsehood have been eliminated. Still, it is not rigorous demonstration that has eliminated these possibilities. This lack of argument pertains especially to the status of opinion. Despite the promised treatment of opinion in the flux thesis, which this section was supposed to supply, none has been forthcoming. It remains to be seen as to whether radical flux can cohere at all with opinion. At present, the key point is that all these possibilities have simply evaporated, dependent as they are on prerequisites inconsistent with that thesis. Nevertheless, Socrates persists in using these terms. In so doing, he does Theaetetus, and subsequent readers, the service of highlighting these lacunae.

From Delivery to Assessment

Socrates' elaboration of Theaetetus' definition transforms it into an anti-Socratic creed. Through articulating this most radical rejection of his own view, Socrates has provided his potential successors, if they do prove truly to be Socratic, with a key to the theoretical prerequisites of Socratic inquiry. Moreover, in conveying his teaching through what amounts to a thoroughgoing attack on his own, Socrates' deed exemplifies the character required for his brand of inquiry.

These theoretical prerequisites are evident in the thesis's culmination in the denial of identity to the beings and to humans. That denial is accomplished through the rejection of complexity for both the soul and the beings, knower and known. These two complexities are crucial to the substantiation of Socratic inquiry. For they are the sources of the partiality of our knowledge and also of falsehood, of error and deception. Without such partiality, there would be neither the possibility nor the need for inquiry. What need could there be if we cannot err? How could it be possible if we cannot advance from a state of partial to less partial knowledge? This intrinsic link between the complexity of being and inquiry is made dramatically clear when Socrates shows in his dice example that the very existence of such being generates Theaetetus' perplexity and his wonder. And it is this wonder that Socrates designates as the source of philosophy.

The question left by the delivery is whether Theaetetus' thesis is true. With this question, Socrates moves to the assessment phase of his midwifery. Here, however, a problem arises: undertaking such judgment would seem egregiously question-begging insofar as what's in question is the very possibility of such judgment. To avoid this characterization, Socrates' approach must therefore also indicate how such judging is possible and why it is unavoidable.

Socrates' maieutics responds to the radical challenge of the three-legged thesis by examining the motive animating it. Prior to considering this examination, let me suggest how this tack might successfully avoid the charge of question-begging. As I have argued, Socrates points repeatedly to the ideological character of Theaetetus' definition. He characterizes the view as formulated in response to a prior, unexamined view of good. The abstract, metaphysical and epistemological doctrines undermining the notion of relative change, undermining the part-whole structure of all beings, undermining all identity, respond ultimately to the desires of Theaetetus' soul. They serve, in particular, his desire for the certainty that would grant him the power and mastery to avoid refutation regarding those things of utmost importance to him. Socrates has traced the source of this constellation of desires to the love of one's own, the desire to secure oneself and all that one cares about as an embodied being. The delivery of Theaetetus' thesis provides a theoretical picture of the whole formulated to respond to this desire.

We have seen the numerous contradictions to which the thesis leads. Yet Socrates has made the thesis under consideration so radical as to question those canons of reason that make contradictoriness by itself dispositive. For this reason, in responding to this challenge it is important to recognize that the contradictions emerging from the delivery are not simply matters of logical incoherency, of simultaneously affirming P and not-P. They are rather preeminently *self*-contradictions, contradictions that bear on the discrepancy between action and speech. To recall just a few of the many available examples:

although motivated by Theaetetus' desire for distinction, the theory posits a radically egalitarian view; and, although the theory depends on thought and speech for its formulation, it makes such speech inexplicable. Most striking of all, a thesis rooted in the love of one's own denies the very possibility of personal identity. The contradiction lies in the conflict between the theory and those troublesome deeds, in its inability to account for the behavior of the one propounding it. Recognizing this fact enables us to see that the question of its truth is not merely a theoretical issue but an existential one of intense practical import. Can our words and deeds harmonize? Can we account for ourselves? Most specifically, do we know what is truly good for ourselves?

In pursuit of answers to these questions Socrates' approach is, and must be, explicitly *ad hominem*. Only in this way can he avoid begging the question because the issue that he confronts pertains to, and can only be answered by, each one of us for ourselves. For, in asking the question of good it necessarily regards us not as theoreticians in the Theodoran sense but as embodied individuals each seeking to live a good life. Socrates' insight, exhibited in the movement, the deed of the dialogue, is that every thesis, no matter how radical, is propounded with a view to seeking the good for oneself. The question at hand is whether the good animating the anti-Socratic thesis can be good for beings such as we are, beings capable of self-contradiction because we are beings that both act and think.

Because such questions as these are decisive for his assessment, Socrates begins in the next stage with Protagoras rather than with either perception or Heracleitean flux. These latter aspects of the thesis are not forgotten but they are subordinated to the Protagoreanism that provides the framework for the discussion. Moreover, the Protagoras of the assessment phase is a more familiar figure than the "epistemological" Protagoras of the delivery stage. Here we confront the Protagoras who dispenses practical advice regarding how to live – Protagoras, the sophist. Socrates directs his attention to Protagoras because the ultimate ground of his judgment concerns exactly how one ought to live. It concerns the view of good underlying this thesis.

5

The Assessment: Part I

Introduction

Socrates' *ad hominem* challenge to Protagoras confronts this central contradiction in the sophist's thought: the egalitarianism of Protagoras' doctrine is at odds with the inegalitarian implication of his own expertise.[1] Through this confrontation, which moves the argument toward the dialogue's central passage, Socrates shows that Protagoras' theory, his view of the character of knowledge, is instrumental to his notion of good. Protagoras expresses this notion in a particular understanding of advantage, of what's "good for" oneself. The heart of the dialogue faces the question as to whether Protagoras and his adherents, Theodorus and Theaetetus, have rightly understood human good. In particular, it explores whether advantage understood in Protagorean terms can be *the* good for him, or for any of us, insofar as we are beings capable of self-contradiction, beings whose heterogeneous nature generates such conflicts as that regarding equality, which are inherent in political life.

The "delivery" already made evident the connection between one's view of good, on the one hand, and what knowledge is taken to be, on the other. This connection makes the adequacy of Protagoras' understanding of good bear on the explicit theme of the dialogue. Doubts about the adequacy of that understanding raise the question as to whether, like Protagoras, we should regard the knowledge we seek as the most certain means to a universally accepted good. Or, in light of the questionability of good, should we rather seek *phronesis*, the wisdom concerning how we ought to live? Does *techne* or *phronesis* stand as the object of the philosophic search?

Socrates begins the assessment phase of his midwifery by introducing *phronesis* into the conversation. So begins in earnest the examination of the distinction between wisdom and knowledge. It is an examination that will be

[1] See Chappell, *Reading Plato's "Theaetetus,"* 88.

"interrupted" by the Digression, to be completed on the basis of considerations derived from that central passage of the dialogue.

Self-Sufficiency in *Phronesis*: Socrates' "Different Way" (160e2–162a1)

Socrates makes the *ad hominem* character of his approach evident in his post-delivery comments to Theaetetus. Raising the specter of the anti-Socratic passion, he challenges Theaetetus regarding his psychic offspring: "do you think that just because it's yours it ought to be reared in any case and not put away (161a1–2)"? Almost taunting him, Socrates wonders if Theaetetus "[W]ill . . . bear up under seeing it cross-examined" or be "violently angry like a woman with her first-born" if it is taken from him (162a2–3). The assessment promises to be more painful than the delivery. Exposure looms as a challenge to Theaetetus' love of his own. Clearly, there is something much more than the disinterested weighing of arguments that figures into this examination.

Socrates' aggressive approach reflects the premises of his earlier discussion of midwifery. He understands that intertwining of passions with beliefs that dictates that beliefs belong to each one of us as individuals. Only each on his or her own can ultimately untie such a knot. The present point, however, is that because beliefs are not simply reducible to abstract theses, any adequate examination of them must address such passion if only to diminish its influence on such an inquiry. The examination must speak to the individual character of the one examined. For this reason, too, it must be *ad hominem*.[2]

Theodorus fails to appreciate this requirement. He thinks he can vouch for what is in Theaetetus' heart, assuring Socrates that "Theaetetus will bear up under it (161a5)." Theodorus' action exhibits exactly that excessive abstractness which neglects the individual character of belief. Socrates underscores this defect in his treatment of Theodorus' further comments.

Urging Socrates to say how "it's not in this way," Theodorus apparently calls for a refutation of Theaetetus' thesis (161a6). In response, Socrates accuses Theodorus of regarding him as "some bag of arguments" from which he can simply pluck one contending view after another (161a8). He implies that Theodorus wishes to hear alternative arguments merely for the sake of hearing arguments. These speeches do not really touch Theodorus who is himself, like a grab bag, indiscriminate regarding the content of these speeches. Socrates refers to Theodorus as a *philologos* rather than a *philosophos* to emphasize precisely that his concern is for the speeches as speeches rather than for their bearing on the urgently practical question of how to live his life (161a7).

We get a taste of Socrates' approach in this seemingly inconsequential banter. Because it has its sights set on modifying a disposition, it does not proceed by argument alone. For this reason, I refer to Socrates' "approach" rather than, say, his "method." The latter word suggests something too technical

[2] The other reason is, again, to avoid begging the entire question.

for his conversational inquiry. More significant in any case is the one aim that underlies it: to forge a link between knowledge and self-knowledge. Such a link might counter the Theodoran influence on Theaetetus and enable him to have a clearer view of his good.

Although not properly regarded as a technical method, Socratic inquiry does, however, possess defining features.[3] Socrates repeatedly calls these to our attention in his frequent reflections on the form of his approach, an important example of which occurs in the present context. I refer to Socrates' insistence on his approach's refutative character. This refutative or, as it is sometimes called, elenctic character of Socratic inquiry has been the focus of much scholarship of the last several decades in the wake of Gregory Vlastos's work on the subject.[4] Most of this scholarship concerns what some scholars designate as the "early" dialogues, but Socrates' use of the term here shows its occurrence outside the dialogues usually included in that category. Of more substantive interest, however, is why, in the present context, this inquiry should be refutative or, more specifically, what role this refutative activity plays in forging that link between knowledge and self-knowledge. To answer this question we need to look in detail at Socrates' description of his characteristic activity.

Socrates understands the aim of his approach to be "to examine the appearances and opinions that belong to one another and try to refute them (161e7–8)." From this description it is clear that the approach is to be conversational; the examined opinions belong to "one another." Such inquiry, proceeding jointly, will most likely occur through asking and answering questions. Moreover, this conversation, although friendly, will nevertheless be challenging. Each attempts "to refute" the other's beliefs.

The substance of this refutation in other dialogues, as many commentators note, pertains not simply to the truth of the beliefs in question but to the consistency of a set of beliefs held by the particular interlocutor. It concerns those beliefs that "belong" to an individual.[5] And consistency does not only mean the coherence of beliefs between and among one another but also, and more pointedly, between beliefs and deeds. Through this approach Socrates means to put the individual as such on the line, as a person acting on his beliefs.

The etymological root of *elenchein* is pertinent here, referring as it does to a notion of honor and shame.[6] Socrates attempts to induce shame at inconsistency, shame in the face of the unmet challenge to one's consistency. Given the conversational context of midwifery, this challenge is made at least by one

[3] Earlier Socrates (e.g., 149a4) refers to his maiuetics as a *techne*, but this designation highlights the difference between it and genuine *techne*.

[4] Gregory Vlastos, "The Socratic Elenchus: Method Is All," in *Socratic Studies*, ed. Myles Burnyeat (Cambridge: Cambridge University Press, 1994), passim.

[5] Ibid., 9–10.

[6] See James H. Lesher, "Parmenidean *Elenchos*," in *Does Socrates Have a Method?*, ed. Gary Alan Scott (University Park: The Pennsylvania State University Press, 2002), 20–8.

other, and so is to this extent not wholly private. More broadly, there is an attempt, inherent in the approach, to challenge the interlocutor to give an account, a *logos*, of his life. Such an account, if successful, would make speech and deed coincide. Because Theodorus wishes so avidly to avoid it, few feel the challenge to provide such an account as more annoying than does he.

Socrates gears his approach especially to confronting the love of one's own. For it, more than anything, generates divergence in speech and deed. Under its sway, we adopt beliefs inconsistent with our deeds because we embrace those beliefs for the sake of consolation or reassurance or a variety of reasons other than truth. Only equally passionate efforts can overcome this passion-driven practice. It requires powerful rhetoric, not just argument, to overcome the potential for self-deception inherent in this passion. Nothing less than the spirited thrust of *refutative* rhetoric will do, nothing less than the threat of shame at revealed inconsistency.

As Socrates reports in his account of his midwifery, such challenging speech can embolden the interlocutor to overcome such self-deception, to achieve the self-knowledge that will permit undistorted inquiry. Or, and unfortunately more frequently, it can give offense, causing the interlocutor to flee. With the possible attainment of self-knowledge in view, each of us, Socrates included, may benefit from someone else's judgment of the validity of his or her opinions. Whether such judging is possible does remain a question. The present point, however, is that in linking knowledge and self-knowledge, Socrates' approach, his midwifery, shapes how we think of the goal of such inquiry. Pertaining to each of us as an embodied individual, it is best understood as wisdom, as *phronesis*.[7] Midwifery is, again, the image of *phronesis*, the attempt to understand the particulars of one's own life in the light of a notion of human good.

In the present context Socrates leaves no doubt that the key issue dividing him from the anti-Socratics is exactly the character of wisdom. It is, as I have indicated, just because Socrates takes wisdom to be *phronesis* that Protagoras becomes the central figure in his response to his opponents. It is also for this reason that Socrates attempts throughout this portion of the dialogue to engage Theodorus as his interlocutor. By repeatedly associating Theodorus with Protagoras as an acquaintance, Socrates aims to elicit from Theodorus a sense of personal obligation to Protagoras whom Theodorus does acknowledge as a friend (162a4). In pursuing this aim, it is unlikely that Socrates expects he can at this late date mold Theodorus into a Socratic dialectician. Theodorus has shown no inclinations in this direction – just the opposite (146b3–4). Socrates means rather to explore the grounds of Theodorus' affinity with Protagoras to provide a beneficial display for Theaetetus, and for subsequent readers. He

[7] See Polansky's comments on this first appearance of *phronesis* in the dialogue. Polansky, *Philosophy and Knowledge*, 109. Burnyeat questions the relevance of *phronesis* because he accepts the identification of it with expertise. He does not see that what is at stake is the difference between two very different meanings of wisdom. *The "Theaetetus" of Plato*, 19–21.

thus exhibits the outcome of the separation of knowledge from self-knowledge, of engaging in arguments without reflecting on their meaning for one's life. In Theodorus we see the unattractive spectacle of a life spent avoiding the issues that call for *phronesis*.

Beginning his assessment, Socrates tells Theodorus that what pleases him about Protagoras' speech is his view "that what seems to each person also is that (161bc3–4)." Socrates does understand and appreciate the particularity that is an element of each opinion. Nevertheless, unlike Protagoras, Socrates does not maintain that we are mired, wholly and forever, in our particularity, that we can never judge objectively our own opinions and the opinions of others. Socrates holds to the possibility of distinguishing knowledge from opinion.

With Protagoras having effaced this distinction, Socrates proclaims himself at a loss as to why Protagoras "when he began the Truth, he didn't say 'a pig is the measure of all things' or a dog-faced baboon' – or some other outlandish thing that has perception (161c3–6)."[8] Without the possibility of distinguishing knowledge and opinion, Socrates complains that even though we are supposed to admire Protagoras "as at a god for his wisdom, he happens, after all, to be no better off in *phronesis* than a little round frog, not to mention any other human being (161c8–d1)."[9] In what follows, Socrates shrewdly develops this notion of *phronesis* by using as a case study the tension between Protagoras' views and Protagoras' own activity, between his speech and his deeds.

Socrates maintains that if Protagoras is right then the view of each is true, and no one can judge the experience of someone else better than another. But then, Socrates asks, "how in the world, companion, was Protagoras wise, so as to consider himself worthy of being a teacher of others, justly charging high fees, while we were more lacking in understanding and had to go to school to him, though each one is himself the measure of his own wisdom? (161d7–e3)." Socrates wants most to highlight just this self-contradiction. Protagoras' theory demands equality as regards the possession of wisdom – no one can claim to be wiser and thus fit to be teacher of another – but his deed, providing education for a steep tuition, implies decisive inequality.[10]

In judging Protagoras by the standard of self-consistency, Socrates does not shrink from applying the same criterion to himself. If Protagoras is right, he asserts, then his own "art of midwifery" and "the whole serious practice of conversation" deserves ridicule (161e4–7). The stakes could not be clearer:

[8] Given Theaetetus' earlier (154a5) prideful assertion of his difference from animals with respect to perception, Socrates' examples may be directed toward enlisting Theaetetus' pride as an ally against the Protagorean view.

[9] Note Socrates' acknowledgment of Protagoras' vanity in *Protagoras* 317c6–d1.

[10] Compare *Cratylus* 385e4–386d2. As I noted in Chapter 4, n. 7, some scholars find in Protagoras a sincere democrat, especially as based on his "Great Speech" in the Protagoras. For a view that finds Protagoras' democratic leanings disingenuous, see Roslyn Weiss, *The Socratic Paradox and Its Enemies* (Chicago: University of Chicago Press, 2006), 35–8.

"to examine the appearance and opinions that belong to one another and try to refute them, when what belongs to each person is correct – isn't that a long and immense piece of nonsense if the *Truth* of Protagoras is true? (161e7–162a1)." What is in question in Socrates' contest with Protagoras is nothing less than the justification of their respective ways of life. With so much at stake, we can understand why Socrates spends half of the dialogue engaged in this contest.

Their explicitly differing views on the need for such justifications most clearly distinguish Socrates and Protagoras.[11] Unlike Protagoras, Socrates expresses a need to make his deeds and words conform, to make his judgment of good harmonize with his notion of that which is true. Socrates' version of Protagoras' thought clarifies why such harmony should be desirable. He makes clear as well that this harmony provides his criterion of judgment. Just prior to the present passage Socrates says: "I know nothing more than a trifling amount, enough to get an account out of someone else who's wise and to accept it in a measured way (161b3–5)." The criterion for Socrates' "measured acceptance," the standard for judging the truth of opinions, one's own and others, is the degree to which they make the reconciliation of speech and deed possible. This criterion, as we have seen, shapes Socrates' approach, dictating its *ad hominem* character in its attention to the connection between one's views and one's actions. What remains to be seen is how this constitutes the Socratic alternative to absolute certainty on the one hand, and radical skepticism, on the other.

At present, my point is that this criterion accounts not only for Socrates' focus on Protagoras but also for his unusual approach to the sophist. As the core of that approach, Plato has Socrates compose what might be regarded as a miniature Platonic dialogue featuring a character called "Protagoras." In so doing, Plato reveals something of the rationale for his own distinctive philosophic form. As is true of every Platonic dialogue, by using this form Socrates affords the deceased Protagoras the powers of speech and action. He thus makes it possible to examine him by the speech-and-deed measure. The dialogue form bespeaks the decisiveness of this measure as through its portrayal of such *ad hominem* inquiries Plato tests his characters and his readers by the same criterion.

In this way, Socrates confronts an individual rather than an argument. By this means, he (and Plato) can avoid the necessarily question-begging consequence of judging by laws of reason a view whose essence is the denial of those very laws. Writing this dialogue enables Socrates to confront not simply Protagoreanism but also its propounder, an individual with desires, passions, and,

[11] This accounts, I will argue, for Protagoras' aversion to theoretical considerations (as well as his agnosticism regarding the gods). On the former see A. T. Cole, "The Apology of Protagoras," *Yale Classical Studies* 19 (1966): 19–21; and Maguire, "Protagoras – or Plato?," 135n37.

above all, a view of his own good.[12] The question raised then is not whether Protagoras' doctrine violates the principles of reason. On that level question-begging is unavoidable. It is, rather, whether this individual, Protagoras, can live his own life in accord with his own doctrine. Again, the point here is not simply to suggest that one of his views contradicts another. If it were, Protagoras could simply say he has no wish to be self-consistent. He could refuse to participate in the giving of reasons. The point is rather that his doctrine comes into conflict with his good, that he is *self*-contradictory, but that, finally, he prefers his good. Protagoras' view of good is the decisive strand of his thought, and of his life. As such, it is deeper than that doctrine that renders rational argument untenable. Therefore, he is just to that extent involved in a contestable claim about his good. And, most importantly, it is a contest he would very much like to win. Protagoras, too, would like to know, or at least have persuasive reasons to think, that he is oriented on the true good. By his deeds he, therefore, eventually subjects himself to those very laws of reason his theory denies. Working individual by individual, Socratic inquiry can thus show its relevance to those who would deny its very premise.

We can now better appreciate what recommends Socrates' *ad hominem* approach.[13] It recognizes that recourse to a demonstration of the doctrine's contradictoriness would itself be dogmatically rational and so ultimately not rational at all. Yet it recognizes, in addition, that skepticism of the kind employed by Protagoras can also be dogmatic. This stance, too, can be maintained for reasons other than its validity. And these reasons underlie claims that might themselves be open to rational scrutiny. It is in its avoidance of these twin dogmatisms that Socratic inquiry, as expressed through the drama of the Platonic dialogue, provides a viable alternative approach to inquiry.[14]

As I indicated, Socrates' dialogue locates the heart of Protagoras' position in its separation of that which is good from that which is true. Insisting on this separation, Protagorean wisdom must essentially differ from *phronesis*,

[12] Edward Lee recognizes the dialogic characteristics of the passage. See Edward N. Lee, "'Hoist with His Own Petard'": Ironic and Comic Elements in Plato's Critique of Protagoras (Tht. 161–171)," in *Exegesis and Argument*, eds. Edward N. Lee, A. Mourelatos, and Richard Rorty (Assen: Van Gorcum, 1973), 226, 227n3, 233. Both Sayre and Lee also call attention to the passage's comic elements. See Sayre, *Plato's Analytic Method*, 80 and Lee, "Hoist with His Own Petard," 255–6. The dialogic and comic characters are related, connected by Socrates' *ad hominem* approach. This approach requires Socrates to engage the person as an individual and thus his idiosyncrasies, passions, etc., much of which may seem comic in a philosophic argument.

[13] On the connection between such *ad hominem* approaches and the response to skepticism in Plato see Julia Annas, "Plato the Sceptic," in *Oxford Studies in Ancient Philosophy*, suppl. vol., eds. James C. Klagge and Nicholas D. Smith (Oxford: Clarendon Press, 1992), 44–61. See also Bostock, *Plato's "Theaetetus,"* 85.

[14] Plato's use of the dialogue form raises the more general question as to whether there is an unavoidably *ad hominem* character of all arguments, as to whether all have their basis in or are connected with an individual's view of his or her good.

insofar as *phronesis* seeks to discover that which is truly good, to discern the knowledge that will enable one to live as a human being ought so that, as far as possible, one might achieve fulfillment. In separating the good and true, Protagoras' *theory* denies the need to inquire into the good because, it holds, knowledge of it is impossible. As we will see, however, Protagoras' *deeds* tell a somewhat different story. They indicate that such inquiry is, for Protagoras, not so much impossible as it is unnecessary. We can dispense with inquiry into the good because all, including Protagoras, agree on what the good is. In this sense, the elitist expert is perhaps a democrat after all. In what follows, Socrates first examines the claimed impossibility as a way of revealing the second claim that such inquiry is unnecessary. He thus has his Protagoras provide the opportunity to consider whether the good and the true can and should be severed.

Selecting an Interlocutor (162a1–d4)

Socrates says that his approach involves refuting "appearances and opinions" rather than the perceptions on which heretofore the discussion has focused. In Protagoras' case too, Socrates considers his opinions rather than his perceptions. This rehabilitation of opinion, rescuing it from its disappearance in the last stage of the delivery, connects with a claim Socrates must make for his midwifery, especially in its critical function. Socrates must, in particular, reject the position he attributes to Protagoras that "no one else will discern another person's experience any better than he, nor will anyone be more authoritative in examining the opinion than anyone else (161d3–5)." Only if appearance and opinion are distinguishable from perception can another be authoritative when it comes to one's own experience. For only these involve that mediacy that opens up the possibility of error, and especially error caused by one's own passions. And only these enable the commonality of understanding that allows one to understand the experience of another. Socrates does judge Protagoras' view. He confronts the question of its truth, saying that Protagoras' view holds only "if the *Truth* of Protagoras is true and he wasn't playing with us when he made his utterances from the inner sanctum of the book (162a1–3)." In taking this step Socrates explicitly violates the requirements of Protagoras' theory. It thus provides a specific example of something that might leave Socrates open to the aforementioned charge of question-begging. For this reason, his tactic in this instance is worth considering more carefully.

In his response Socrates goes out of his way to point to a specific deed of Protagoras, his authorship of a book bearing a particularly imposing title.[15] By this *act* Protagoras has placed himself in what we might call the situation of truth and falsehood. We occupy this situation whenever, for example, we attempt to discern the teaching of an authoritative book by reading it many times, or try to determine the intention of those to whom we look for guidance

[15] Socrates mentions this title at 161c4, 162c2, 170e9, 171b6, and 171c6.

(152a5, 157c4–6). These acts, both explicitly undertaken by Theaetetus, tacitly recognize the possibility that our opinions can be either true or false, that we care which they are, and that another's view may be more informative in this regard than our own. Protagoras' authorship of this specific book suggests further that truth emerges from the background of the false, that it becomes an issue only when we have already put into question, or refused simply to accept, the phenomena. It becomes an issue after we have experienced untruth. Otherwise, Protagoras would not have had to write a book, called *Truth*, to lead his readers from their present situation of untruth. In addition, neither should we neglect that the form of the book runs athwart Protagoras' doctrine. Socrates' suggestion that the book has an esoteric character, an "inner sanctum," argues against the equal capacity of each to understand (162a2). Finally, and most generally, the goal of Protagoras' art only makes sense if one can authoritatively judge another's experience.

Every single one of the preceding presuppositions, affirmed by Protagoras' deeds, is vehemently denied by his doctrine. As he raises the question of the truth of Protagoras' views, Socrates thus invokes behavior that shows the failure of Protagoras' theory to account for Protagoras' own practice. This goal explains the flavor of this passage with its jests, provocations, and bits of what seem mere gossip. All these aim to reveal the behavior of the individual called Protagoras.

They aim as well to provoke Theodorus to come to the aid of his now-dead acquaintance. Theodorus does acknowledge the personal link between Protagoras and himself. He even strengthens it, calling Protagoras not merely an "acquaintance," as Socrates had done, but a "friend (161b9, 162a4)." Yet Theodorus remains reluctant to participate. Theodorus' subsequent comment provides insight regarding what, in his view, are the requirements of friendship. Socrates' activity certainly does not qualify. Theodorus says, "I wouldn't take kindly to Protagoras' being refuted... (162a5–6)." The geometer sees in Socrates' refutative approach not the fulfillment of the office of friendship but the act of an enemy bent on victory. Given his wonder at Theaetetus' combination of great intelligence and gentleness, Theodorus' reaction should not be surprising. He is at one with "the wise" who consider the purpose of argument as victory rather than enlightenment.[16] It is of a piece with his preference for the fluidic, resistance-less student. Socrates' alternative perspective, from which refutation can be regarded as an act of a benevolent friend, becomes clearer in what follows.

Theodorus digs in his heels against Socrates' attempts and urges him to take Theaetetus as his interlocutor. Socrates persists, asking Theodorus, "if you went to Sparta, Theodorus, to the wrestling-gym, would you think you had the right to look at the other people naked, some of them in bad shape, and not

[16] See Lee on Protagoras' similar conception of the purpose of speech. "Hoist with His Own Petard," 237.

strip down yourself to display your form in return? (162b1–4)." Theodorus might be more inclined to engage in this sort of stripping than that which Socrates has in mind. He understands all too clearly that Socrates wants him to disrobe in an even more revealing, and potentially embarrassing, way than simply removing his clothes.[17] He wants him to strip the vestments covering his soul. Such stripping of one's own inclinations and of the conventions of one's community requires the powerful force of Socrates' *ad hominem* rhetoric.

Not surprisingly, Theodorus still prefers to "look" than to strip and wrestle. He refuses still to let the arguments touch him. Overestimating the power of speech, Theodorus believes he could persuade even the Spartans to permit him to violate their customs. Socrates lets him off the hook, temporarily, with an old saying referring to his regard for that which is Theodorus' own (162b10–c1). But the persuasive power of Theodorus' speech will soon falter before Socrates' determination to counter the anti-Socratic love of one's own. Theodorus *will* give a *logos* of his life, however unwittingly. For the moment, however, Socrates once again engages "the wise Theaetetus," an appellation we have learned to suspect (162c2). The present context is no exception.

Taking up Theaetetus as his interlocutor, Socrates induces him to provide a glimpse of his dominant motive that, arguably, applies to "the wise" more generally. He asks Theaetetus about an implication of Protagoras' egalitarian view of wisdom: "are you too in a state of wonder when you're brought to light so suddenly as being no worse in wisdom than any human being or even any god? (162c3–5)." Socrates' identification of humans and gods with respect to wisdom so shocks Theaetetus that he rejects at once the entire thesis. Uttering an oath, he confesses that his assessment of the thesis "has instantly fallen over to the opposite way (162c7, 162d2)." To elicit such a dramatic, instantaneous reversal Socrates must have hit a sensitive point very near the heart of Theaetetus' attraction to his thesis.

Yet why should he react so precipitously, and so negatively, to the notion that humans and the gods are equally wise? It has to do with his own sudden elevation regarding wisdom. Recall that Theaetetus' otherwise odd attraction to Protagoreanism reflects his desire for a kind of certainty, for freedom from error. Desiring such freedom, he must suspect that he cannot guarantee this outcome on his own but rather must rely on beings superior to himself. Moreover, for someone oriented on knowledge, conceived as he does, "superior" must mean "more knowledgeable" in the sense of being error-free. If, however, Theaetetus' thesis shows these superior beings to be no better than a mistake-ridden human such as himself, Theaetetus must reject it at once. Theaetetus' reversal, then, reflects his yearning for the existence of beings that exceed humans in every respect, beings that perfect our inadequacies especially as regards wisdom. Such beings can represent, and guarantee, the existence of

[17] On the connection between nakedness and truth telling, consider Saxonhouse, *Free Speech and Democracy*, 112–13.

the perfect knowledge that will provide him the certainty he desires, the security for his life.[18] Whatever theoretical view fails to support this outcome can be, must be, jettisoned. This applies especially to a view such as the "Knowledge Is Perception" thesis that was formulated precisely out of this desire.

This explanation of Theaetetus' reversal means, however, that his instant rejection of Protagoreanism does not constitute a rejection of what animates that view. It only reflects his disappointment at its failure to live up to its promise. Theaetetus' rejection, therefore, does not mean he is ready to undertake the search for *phronesis*. That undertaking acts on the need to inquire into the good that, for Theaetetus, has not yet come into question.

This moment also illuminates Socrates' intention. His goal cannot simply be to disabuse Theaetetus of the "Knowledge Is Perception" thesis. If it were, the dialogue could now conclude. Rather, his continued efforts seek to move Theaetetus, or those now listening, to the necessity of that inquiry just mentioned. That, at least, is where the movement of the argument carries us in its progress to the Digression.

The necessity of such inquiry also connects more immediately to Socrates' consideration of the formal characteristics of the argument. As I have said, he punctuates the entire undertaking with commentaries on his approach. Socrates' present manipulation of Theaetetus' yearnings prompts one such commentary. Adopting a self-critical stance, he accuses himself of practicing demagoguery in these comments regarding the gods (162d3). Such demagogic speech appeals to passions to procure the good of the speaker rather than of his addressees. Demagogic speech does not aim to secure a good truly common to the participants, an outcome achievable only by speech at its best. This self-criticism spurs Socrates to relate what "Protagoras, or someone else on his behalf, will say in response to these things (162d4–5)." Thus begins his initial impersonation of Protagoras.

Approaching Protagoras: The Ethics of Inquiry (162d4–165e7)

Although Socrates' poetry does not quite produce a Protagoras made young and beautiful, it does produce one reanimated and apparently more just.[19] Specifically, Socrates' Protagoras is devoted to fairness or justice in speech (and more generally) in a way not evident in Protagoras' other main appearance in the Platonic corpus.[20] In response to his anti-Socratic position, Socrates exhibits a remarkable evenhandedness, even to the point of having Protagoras

18 In the *Euthyphro*, the dialogue immediately succeeding the *Theaetetus*, dramatically speaking (i.e., succeeding the conversation reported in the *Theaetetus*), Socrates focuses on piety. He speaks with Euthyphro, another interlocutor who invokes the gods to validate his desires. In Euthyphro's case, it is to validate a certain notion of justice.

19 *Second Letter* 314c4.

20 See, e.g., *Protagoras* 323a5–c2. See also Lee on the irony of Socrates' Protagoras calling for the just treatment of arguments. "Hoist with His Own Petard," 237.

level several charges against Socrates. Socrates' Protagoras makes three such charges. He finds Socrates' practice questionable insofar as it brings gods into the argument; appeals to the many; and relies on that which is likely rather than on demonstrations and necessity to make its case (162d5–163a1).

Elaborating on the first charge, Socrates' Protagoras notes that he specifically abjures discussion of the gods (162d6–e2).[21] Although he gives no reason for such reticence, on the one hand, we can readily understand that an itinerant sophist might want to avoid the issue out of self-preservation, although apparently Protagoras' agnosticism did not prevent the destruction of his writings by the Athenians.[22] Yet, on the other hand, it takes little imagination to appreciate the bearing of his thesis on the gods' status. As Socrates has just made evident to Theaetetus, it most obviously makes humans (or even dog-faced baboons) equal to the gods as the measure of all things. Protagoras' professed agnosticism thus makes us wonder whether his self-restriction follows from the theoretical substance of his position or from more practical considerations. More generally, it raises the question as to whether he intends his view as a comprehensive account of the way things are, or rather as instrumental to other, more circumscribed goals.

Protagoras next explains his charge of demagoguery. He maintains that Socrates simply appeals to the many, saying things "that most people would approve of hearing," such as, "that it's a terrible thing if each human being isn't going to be any different in wisdom from any sort of livestock (162e3–5)." This second charge connects with the first in its circumscription of Protagoras' view. Just as he abjures consideration of the gods, of that which transcends humans, so does Protagoras criticize the comparison of the human and subhuman. Unlike Socrates, this Protagoras sees no need to locate the human in relationship to the sub- and the transhuman, a fact Socrates underscores with his earlier invocation of pigs, baboons, and frogs. Perhaps this is so because he, again unlike Socrates, sees no need to examine the kind of being we are in order to determine our good.[23]

Because of the publicly egalitarian thrust of his theory, Protagoras is even reluctant to explore differences within the category of humanity, a reluctance that underlies the third of his charges. The charge concerns Socrates' reliance on likelihoods. A mode of reasoning based on likelihood would, he claims,

[21] The historical Protagoras makes clear his agnosticism in one of the preserved fragments of his work. See Hermann Diels and Walther Kranz eds., *Die Fragmente der Vorsokratiker* (Berlin: Weidmannsche, 1954), B4. In the *Protagoras*, Plato does have Protagoras discuss the gods in his "Great Speech (320c8–328d2)." Protagoras does pay lip service in these circumstances to the divine rule of Zeus but that rule is not evidently philanthropic. Moreover, it leaves great latitude to the practitioners of the many *technai* if human life is to be at all commodious. In short, Plato has Protagoras deliver what he calls a myth about the gods that, as in the *Theaetetus*, subserves Protagoras' advantage.

[22] Cf. Diogenes Laertius *Lives* IX. 51–2.

[23] On Protagoras' unwillingness to inquire into whether there is that which is specifically human, see Lee, "Hoist with His Own Petard," 240, 253.

never be used "by Theodorus or anyone else of the geometers (162e6–7)." Socrates has his Protagoras associate himself with the geometer on the paradoxical ground that the sophist and the geometer share devotion to "demonstration and necessity" rather than to the "likely" (162e5, e6). One might have thought that the sophist most readily appeals to the latter. But with this charge Socrates deepens our understanding of the affinity between the sophists and the mathematicians.

Earlier I mentioned that Protagoras aimed to formulate an architectonic art of speech.[24] On this understanding, speech is guided by its own internally coherent set of rules and need not be sullied by contact with anything external to it. Omnipotent within this domain, speech can ignore what falls outside it. Protagoras' forthcoming distinction between good and true reflects just this possibility. He thus shares with Theodorus an overestimation of the power of reason, maintaining the possibility of demonstration where perhaps only the likely is possible. In this, too, they are both more sanguine than Socrates regarding the power of reason. Protagoras preserves this sanguinity, however, only by that just-mentioned circumscription of the topics under examination.

Above all, Protagoras avoids the question central to Socratic inquiry, the question of human good. This question, insofar as it is a question, demands that we seek to know the nature of humanity. However, the issue Socrates raises and Protagoras obscures – namely, the relationship, the similarity and dissimilarity, between the human and both the trans- and subhuman – illustrates the difficulty of that quest. Such comparisons as these are required because of the elusiveness of the human things. In light of that elusiveness, the investigation often proceeds through arguments of likelihood rather than demonstrations. Both Protagoras and Theaetetus wish to regard the question of human good as essentially noncontroversial because it is resolved by necessity. Throughout this assessment phase of his midwifery, Socrates aims to raise the question as to whether the good is as noncontroversial as these parties believe. If such a question exists then Socrates' brand of inquiry cannot be dismissed so easily as nonsense.

One result of Protagoras' charges against Socrates and, specifically, of his plea for greater seriousness on Socrates part, is Theaetetus' agreement that justice is a pertinent criterion for judging arguments. Yet Socrates does not, in the name of justice, provide "demonstration and necessity" regarding the issues at hand. Instead, he says "it has to be examined in a different way (163a4)." This different way involves exactly that juxtaposition of the theoretical position with the deeds of the one propounding the theory. Still, this does not mean that justice disappears as a consideration, for by this approach Socrates seeks to be truly just, to give to each according to his or her nature.[25]

[24] On this point see Michael Davis, *The Poetry of Philosophy: On Aristotle's "Poetics,"* (1992; repr., South Bend, IN: St. Augustine's Press, 1999), 101–2.

[25] I owe this point to Leonard Sorenson.

To initiate the response to Protagoras' charges, Socrates offers Theaetetus three different anti-Protagorean arguments, each of which refers to an activity Socrates knows Theaetetus has experienced. Their sophistical air ultimately prompts Socrates to engage once again in an extravagant display of self-dissatisfaction. Commentators have rightly wondered at the function these arguments serve in the dialogue.[26] In my view, they do raise serious objections to the thesis under examination, objections considered more thoroughly later in the dialogue. Yet more pertinent at present, Socrates' self-critical demeanor invites us to follow his lead in now considering the form of the arguments and the spirit in which they are offered. Through these arguments we can derive an even clearer picture of the contours of Socrates' "different way." Following the movement of the dialogue, I first consider the substance of the first two arguments, second, Socrates' comments on his sophistic approach, and finally the third argument.

Especially in the first two arguments, Socrates means to make a distinction between perceiving and understanding. In the first, he discusses the fact that we can hear a foreign language or see letters as shapes without in either case understanding the meaning conveyed. Theaetetus, who we know has often read Protagoras' book, is aware of this distinction. He has had to engage in the act of interpretation seeking the meaning of an obscure text. Theaetetus knows too that the expertise in which he trusts depends on this distinction: "what the reading teachers and language interpreters teach about them, we should say that we neither perceive by sight or hearing nor know (163c1–4)." Socrates praises Theaetetus' answer but acknowledges at once that Theaetetus still has room to grow and so expresses doubt that Theaetetus has really understood the distinction he is pursuing (163c6).[27]

Socrates alerts Theaetetus to another argument that is, as he says, "coming at us," on the attack (163c6–7). This one concerns Theaetetus' thesis's devaluation of memory. It is an argument that again hits close to this student's home, for it confronts him with the possibility that once having learned something he cannot claim to know it when he simply remembers it. Theaetetus is nonplussed by this possibility, calling it "a monstrosity," a characterization later

[26] Cornford, ultimately refers to these arguments as "essays in sophistical disputations." McDowell, referring to the last argument, sees it as exemplifying the use of "logic chopping"... "to derive spurious contradiction." This he does because "he feels constrained to offer a different reading just because otherwise the argument would indeed be a powerful one, which Plato should not so lightly brush aside!" Cornford, *Plato's Theory of Knowledge*, 68; McDowell, *Plato "Theaetetus,"* 164. Among those who recognize the seriousness of the arguments are Lee, "Hoist with His Own Petard," 221–30, 232n15; Burnyeat, *The "Theaetetus" of Plato*, 29n22; and Polansky, *Philosophy and Knowledge*, 114–18.

[27] McDowell sees this distinction between knowing and perception, between simply seeing letters and knowing their meaning. Cornford also says that it is implicit here but adds that Plato does not want to make it explicit because this would involve discussion of the Forms. McDowell, *Plato "Theaetetus,"* 160; Cornford, *Plato's Theory of Knowledge*, 62n2.

picked up by Socrates (163d6). The monstrosity resides in the incongruity between Theaetetus' experience and his thesis about knowledge. Socrates further heightens this discord by sharpening the conflict between what is required to "save the speech" and Theaetetus' own experience. He does so to such an extent that Theaetetus utters an oath at the tension between the speech and his experience (164a3).

Together, Socrates and Theaetetus reach the unacceptable conclusion that memory does not constitute knowledge because one can remember without immediately perceiving which, *ex hypothesi*, is alone knowledge (164b4–5). Socrates helpfully reminds Theaetetus that this is "the very thing we were saying would be a monstrosity if it were to come about (164b5–6)." In other words, "something impossible appears to result (164b8)." In light of this outcome, Socrates concludes, again, that they must begin again from the beginning (164c1–2).

With this conclusion, Socrates once more opens the floodgates of self-reproach. The ensuing torrent makes the character of his approach thematic. The two preceding arguments bear on whether the speech, the theory, can substantiate what he and Theaetetus experience themselves as saying and doing. The word *monstrosity*, used first by Theaetetus and then by Socrates to characterize an unacceptable theoretical position, most clearly points to the implicit criterion of Socrates' approach: whether the speech accounts for the deed. And in this case, the tension between the theory and their experience, between speech and deed, produces a monstrosity, an impossible being. We are led to make "impossible" claims, impossible in the sense that they violate rather than explain our experience.

Yet not only do these arguments elicit this criterion, but they also exhibit another feature of Socratic inquiry. Specifically, although they deem the result of these arguments a monstrosity, Socrates gives the impression that there is, nevertheless, profit in this outcome. Such profit lies, paradoxically, in the realization that the main question, the nature of knowledge, has not been resolved by this thesis. It is this realization that produces the awareness "that one must say that again from the beginning (164c1–2)." Returning to the beginning with such awareness is not to begin *de novo*. Precisely because the call is to begin *again*, such a beginning is a self-conscious act. As such, it can include awareness of those theoretical paths that culminate only in monstrosities. Returning to the beginning with such self-awareness must also involve reflection on what that beginning should involve. Especially in light of the criterion just invoked, this new beginning must incline toward theories that express considerably more sensitivity to our experience. Deepened self-knowledge governs the new beginning.

That return, however, does not occur immediately. Rather, Socrates "interrupts" himself to exhibit still another aspect of his approach, one that is intrinsically related to those elements just discussed. He pauses to reflect on the spirit of their activity, on the motives animating their inquiry. The awareness of the view of the good that makes the juxtaposition of speech and deed decisive is another essential aspect of Socrates' approach. Precisely because it involves this juxtaposition, and attempted reconciliation, of speech and deed, Socrates' approach must also inquire into the motive for such inquiry. Socrates' focus on what we can call the "ethics of inquiry" follows from the theoretical reflections related to his notion of the proper criterion of knowledge.[28] It is the explicitly hypothetical character of his inquiry that demands such ethical inquiry. This point is of great significance for my interpretation of the dialogue. It requires further explanation.

I begin from the observation that the deeds are not self-explanatory. Knowledge is a problem precisely because there is a discrepancy between that which is available to experience and our account thereof. The arguments offered in the present context, as inadequate as some have found them, make the distinction, crucial in this regard, between perceiving and understanding. On the basis of this distinction interpretation is possible and necessary. Accordingly, explanations or hypotheses regarding the deeds must be generated. Even if a hypothesis maintains the immediate intelligibility of the deeds it still indicates that there is a question to be answered. But these hypotheses must be tested against the deeds to prevent their being "monstrous." The process requires constant readjustment and frequent returns to the beginning. Testing these hypotheses often moves in the realm of "the likely" rather than arriving at a demonstration. Insofar as "the likely" is its usual medium, there is space for the influence of motives other than truth to skew inquiry. As Socrates acknowledges in the midwife passage, constant attention must be given to the possibility that inquiry will respond to other powerful desires and passions, especially the love of one's own. For this reason, an ethics of inquiry becomes an enduring requirement.[29] In sum, given the persistence of the problem of knowledge, assessment of the motives for inquiry must accompany all inquiry.

The culmination of such an ethics is a full-scale examination of the good that ought to guide our inquiry and our understanding of knowledge. Socrates' "interruptions" of the argument, with his self-critical reflections on motive, exemplify such an ethics. Yet these "interruptions" are minor tremors that presage the major eruption of the Digression. There, Socrates examines most deeply this question of good in its relation to inquiry.

This sketch of Socrates' "different way" should not then be taken to suggest that experience alone is sufficient, that it is not in need of explanation. If this were the case, there would be no need to continually begin again. It is rather to insist that the hypotheses we generate to clarify what is perplexing in our experience must not deny that experience. That this is an ever-present

[28] See Cropsey, *Plato's World*, 109–10 and Francois Renaud, "Humbling as Upbringing: The Ethical Dimension of the Elenchus in the *Lysis*," in *Does Socrates Have a Method?*, ed. Gary Alan Scott (University Park: The Pennsylvania State University Press, 2002), 192–8.

[29] On this point see Stanley Rosen, "Socrates' Dream," *Theoria* 42 (1976): 183.

possibility accounts for Socrates' insistence on, and his enactment of, an acutely self-critical awareness of what it is that motivates us to clarify our experience. Only by virtue of such awareness can we ensure that this inquiry does result in greater clarity and not in an ultimately self-denying rationalization of that experience. With such awareness, when we do begin again, we can see further, if still not fully, as to what our hypotheses must account for.

In his self-dissatisfaction, Socrates says he and Theaetetus are "crowing like a badly begotten rooster before it's won a fight (164c5–6)." They are, in addition, acting in a "spirit of contradiction" and "without being aware of it," "doing the same thing as those terrible men," who strive for victory rather than clarity (164c8, 164d1, 164d1–2). This last distinction clearly pertains to the motive that spurs inquiry. With it, as Socrates now indicates, we move closer to the key difference between the ethical and the unethical approach, which lies at the heart of the distinction between the philosopher and the sophist.

Socrates says that the stories or "myths" of both Protagoras and Theaetetus were destroyed by the argument regarding memory (164d8–9). At least with respect to Protagoras this would not have happened "if the father of the other myth were alive, but he would be fighting off the danger in many ways," going to the aid of his offspring, his own (164e2–3). In continuing his characterization of the situation, Socrates refers to the argument as an orphan and chides its "guardians" for their neglect: the "father of the myth" being dead, Socrates and Theaetetus are "flinging mud on the orphan itself, and not even the guardians whom Protagoras left behind, of whom Theodorus here is one, want to come to its aid (164e3–6)." According to Socrates, they themselves must do it "for the sake of the just (164e6–7)."

If Socrates' powerful rhetorical ploy were to succeed, Theaetetus would provide aid to the arguments in a way that his "guardians" had failed to provide for him (144d2). He would treat the arguments justly. Any definition of just treatment would have to include a willingness to give what is deserved to each without distortion by consideration of one's own. Socrates exhibits such just treatment in speaking up for an argument that is most definitely not his own. Not only is he not the argument's father, this argument aims to refute Socrates' own argument. Recall that if Theaetetus' thesis is true, Socrates' life's work is "nonsense."

But why treat arguments justly? Would it be so objectionable to be the celebrated, victorious sophist rather than the private inquirer? Socrates refers to these positions as myths or, as we might call them, hypotheses generated in the attempt to explain our perplexing experience. Insisting on this hypothetical status, Socrates reminds us of the lack of that criterion that would resolve once and for all these most profound questions about how we ought to live. Lacking such a criterion, the just treatment of arguments, even or especially those that contravene one's chosen way of life, can only redound to one's good. How else can we respond to the question that drives Socrates' midwifery: which of the many possible ways of life is truly choiceworthy? Such willingness to be just can guard against the harm of the Theodoran life so well illustrated in Theodorus' subsequent response to Socrates' comments.

Following his usual practice, Theodorus tries to duck his obligation. He insists that not he but Callias is the guardian of Protagoras' things, adding, "Ourself, for some reason or other, turned away sooner from bare words to geometry (165a1–3)." Theodorus' comment is striking. The choice of this his lifelong profession, perhaps the decisive choice of his life, was made on the basis of less than certain reasons: "for some reason or another (165a1)." It is doubtful that Theodorus has ever provided, even to himself, that *logos* of his life which Socrates soon urges him to provide. Judging by Theodorus' comment, he sees before him only two alternatives: either abstract speeches, which fail to touch his life, or the notation of geometry. He has long ago ceded authority to Protagoras concerning any examination of his conception of good. Or, more accurately, he has in this way justified avoidance of such an examination. His self-concern, exhibited especially in his fear of disgrace, has prevented him from taking such speeches seriously (165b1).

Socrates makes Theodorus more prominent exactly because he illustrates the key difference underlying that ethical distinction between the seeker of victory and the philosopher. The philosopher's stance is not simply a selfless obligation mandating justice toward arguments for its own sake. Rather, such justice paves the way to a very great good and precludes a very great harm. For it provides the opportunity of ascertaining that which is truly good for oneself while precluding the Theodoran spectacle of a life based on a whim, a guess, an unreflective urge. Inquiry rather than victory becomes the end when the inherently controversial character of the good is made clear. Awareness of this controversy, and willingness to act accordingly, ultimately distinguishes the sophist and the philosopher.[30] It is this awareness that underlies the ethics of inquiry as well. Socrates tells Theodorus that he speaks "beautifully," perhaps because he has expressed so clearly, if unwittingly, the most objectionable consequence of his avoidance of self-knowledge. In this sense, Socrates' practice reflects his greater seriousness about his good than is evident in his sophistic competition.[31]

With Theodorus resisting Socrates' efforts, Socrates temporarily accedes to his attempts to volunteer Theaetetus for the job. With Theaetetus once again his chief interlocutor Socrates asks a question that he deems the most terrifying question. It is a question that bears directly on the incomplete knowledge of the good just discussed: "is it possible for the same person, while knowing

[30] As we saw earlier, the sophists are unwilling to face their lack of self-transparency. In other words, they won't face the implications of the ambiguity on which their art depends.

[31] As comes to light in the *Protagoras*, Socrates is more serious about attaining the true good than is the sophist. Although Protagoras understands himself as oriented on gaining his own advantage, the only sensible thing to do from his perspective, he still admires the sacrifice of that advantage in acts of courage (359e1–4). He will not adhere to the premises of his own view. See Bartlett, *Plato "Protagoras" and "Meno,"* 86–9 for an elaboration of this point.

something not to know the thing that he knows (165b2–3)"? Theaetetus' answer is an example of that which it denies – "Presumably that's not in his power, I suppose" – for it indicates the partiality of his own knowledge. Theaetetus can presume or suppose something to be so without knowing for sure (165b6).

In response, Socrates offers his third argument, one that is almost universally held to be unserious owing to its highly sophistic tenor. Socrates portrays a scene in which Theaetetus is compelled to say whether he sees someone's cloak while one of his eyes is covered (165b7–c2). Affirming that he sees it with one eye but not the other, he is led by Socrates to conclude that if knowledge is perception, this simultaneous seeing and not seeing must likewise also be simultaneous knowing and not knowing (165d1). The result is a complete reversal with Theaetetus concluding the opposite of what he had just maintained (165d1).

For the now-whirling Theaetetus, Socrates conjures the specter of a horde of such arguments by which he could be attacked. Following this argument, the sophist "would now have kept on refuting, attacking, and not letting up until, wondering at his much prayed-for wisdom you were tied up hand and foot by him, and when he had gotten the better of you and chained you up, from then on it would be about ransom (165e1–3)."[32] The student would want to pay the sophist tuition to extricate himself from the sophistically imposed fetters.

Yet, despite their sophistic tone, each of the arguments, even this third argument, does make a serious point regarding the "Knowledge Is Perception" thesis. The first two arguments suggest that although sense-perception is involved in knowing, it is not the whole of knowing. Only the absolute identification of knowledge with sense-perception narrowly construed, which leads to monstrous outcomes, could sustain the alternative view. On a broader understanding of perception, it evaporates, along with Theaetetus' thesis as construed by Socrates. And as inadequate as it seems, the third argument also raises, or at least points to, the consideration that will eventually be regarded as decisive for the rejection of the "Knowledge Is Perception" thesis – namely that, as will be claimed, we do not see with the eyes but through them to the soul that processes our perception. So that, again, sense-perception can only be part of what we mean by knowing. In sum, from these arguments we learn that cognitive possibilities exist that depend on, but are not limited to, what we see.

Yet, if these arguments possess serious content, why does Socrates present them in this sophistic vein? I take the point of this exercise to be that serious arguments, arguments expressing Socrates' own perspective, can easily be stated sophistically. The refutative function of midwifery, meant to be beneficial, can in response to other motives, easily be mounted as a refutative attack (165e1). It is for this reason that Socrates sharpens the point that his inquiry

32 See *Protagoras* 328b5–c2.

differs from the sophists on the basis of an ethical stance rather than simply following from an epistemological insight. He wishes to place special emphasis on *how* one acts in the face of that attack. His inquiry depends on, or at least responds to, the same situation of cognitive ambiguity that makes possible the attack of the sophists. The point of the passage leading up to Protagoras' "Apology" is this: the content of these sophistic-sounding arguments points to the source of the cognitive ambiguity that both makes sophistry possible and its antidote, Socratic inquiry, necessary.

That approach to inquiry is, as I have said, explicitly *ad hominem*. It invokes the speech-and-deed criterion as it seeks to avoid "monstrosities," those theories that make human life inexplicable. It prepares us for the need to return to the beginning, to attain an even greater awareness of the character of the experience we seek to explain. In light of the necessarily hypothetical character of the endeavor, this approach insists on a self-critical monitoring of those motives that always threaten to distort such inquiry. Moreover, we are to engage in such activity ultimately not out of some selfless concern for justice but owing to the concern we have for our own good. As Socrates' examination of Protagoras intensifies, this conclusion becomes ever clearer: we inquire in this manner because of the seriousness each has about his or her good and the awareness, more or less tacit, that the true good eludes us. With this in mind, we now turn to the crux of Socrates' treatment of Protagoras, his presentation of Protagoras' "Apology."

Socrates' Protagoras' "Apology" (165e8–168c5)

Protagoras' "Apology," his longest speech, falls into three parts. After a brief response to the argumentative mercenaries, he first answers Socrates' "memory" argument through an appeal to the doctrine of radical flux. The appeal denies again the existence of identity, questioning the very grounds of rational discourse. In the second part, formally and substantively the heart of the speech, Protagoras responds to Socrates' central concern, the meaning of wisdom. Here Protagoras is most serious because he discusses the concerns that guide his deeds. In this central section, Protagoras maintains that wisdom is possible. This claim rests, however, on the divorce of the good from the true and so repudiates Socrates' view of wisdom as *phronesis*.[33] The final portion of Protagoras' speech returns to the question of the approach to argument. Here he extols rational discourse, assigning it powers well in excess of those acknowledged by Socrates. The task of interpreting this lengthy speech requires that we understand the meaning of each of these heterogeneous parts – the polar

33 As Polansky notes, Protagoras makes wisdom strictly practical in this portion of his speech. But Cole and Burnyeat provide good reasons to reject any attempt to read Protagoras as a pragmatist. Their common objection regards that attempt's failure to appreciate Protagoras' abstention from the question of truth. Polansky, *Philosophy and Knowledge*, 121–2; Cole, "The Apology of Protagoras," 36; Burnyeat, *The "Theaetetus" of Plato*, 24.

stances on rational discourse being the most dramatically divergent – and also discern what binds it together as a whole. Having achieved such an understanding, we must then consider how the speech stands in relationship to its author(s).

In the first portion of his defense, Protagoras aggressively chides Socrates for exploiting a child's fears to refute his position (166a2–3). He insists moreover that unless a refutation of his position uses exactly his terms, it is merely a refutation of some other, probably defective, version of his thought (166a6–b2). Having administered these lessons, Protagoras proceeds to deal with the argument regarding memory, ignoring the first and third of Socrates' previous arguments.[34]

Protagoras distinguishes between a memory and the experience that the memory records. Now, it must be granted that a memory as such must be different from that experience of which it is the memory. But one must also grant that as a memory of this experience it must not be wholly different.[35] Yet, such gradations of likeness and difference are not to Protagoras' point. Instead, he summons the atomistic world, previously laid out, in which any difference amounts to complete otherness. He then applies this vision to memory and experience in order to deny memory its characteristic nature. He even extends this atomism to the person remembering. The result is that this person lacks any identity persisting from the time of the initial experience to the memory thereof. Only reluctantly, as Protagoras indicates, do we use the word *be* in such a world (166c6). Moreover, the person occupying this world is not rightly called a "him" but a "them, with these becoming infinite (166b7–9)." It would be difficult to say how in such a world we could heed his earlier mandate to use "just the sort of terms that I would answer" or even participate in discourse at all (166a8).

Yet such consistency of argument is not the goal of Protagoras' defense. Protagoras' selective response to Socrates' objections reveal his true goal. He does not respond to Socrates' argument regarding reading although, or because, he himself wrote a book. He knows his book can be misconstrued and even warns Socrates against speaking against his writings (166c8–9). These acts presume the distinction between perception and understanding, the very distinction evident in the first and third arguments, which his doctrine denies. Protagoras does, however, respond to Socrates' wonder at his privileging of human perception as the measure. He takes seriously the objection that might cost him high-paying students. Protagoras' desire to secure his own good shapes his speech.[36]

[34] McDowell recognizes, contrary to Cornford, that Socrates focuses solely on this argument concerning memory. McDowell, *Plato "Theaetetus,"* 165; Cornford, *Plato's Theory of Knowledge*, 69–70.

[35] For an elaboration of this point, see Lee, "Hoist with His Own Petard," 235–6.

[36] See Saxonhouse's comments on the way in which Protagoras' concern for his security shapes his conduct. *Free Speech and Democracy*, 184–7. For further elaboration regarding the merely individualistic character of Protagoras' view of good, see Weiss, *Socratic Paradox*, 48–9.

Protagoras specifically ridicules Socrates' provocative objection to his privileging of human perception. He says, "so when you talk about a pig or a swine and dog-faced baboons not only are you being pig-ignorant yourself, you also carry over the people who hear you to act this way toward my writings (166c7–9)." Such name calling is not an argument. Still, his epithets do provide further insight into Protagoras' view.

In calling Socrates a swine, Protagoras seems to lose the distinction between the metaphorical and nonmetaphorical use of the word. Yet this distinction would be difficult to maintain in the world just sketched, a world in which there is no being, nothing nonmetaphorical for language even to approximate. I mention this point because it prepares us for the next stage of Protagoras' speech. There he completely severs the question of good from any connection to the truth of things. In light of this move, there is no choice but to regard the "theoretical" considerations of this first part not as true but as practically instrumental to his goal. For this reason, Protagoras' contradictions between speech and deed, which could be endlessly adduced, simply do not matter in terms of theoretical consistency. For Protagoras, speech is not related to what is. Rather, speech is liberated, free to aim at whatever good the speaker, the manipulator of words, might seek. In accord with this view, Protagoras defines wisdom as power to effectuate change. It certainly does not involve the discovery of truth (166d5–7). More specifically, wisdom and its tool, reason, are instrumental, mere servants of one's notion of good. As such, they need not be used to determine what that good might be.

We can now see better why Protagoras does not respond to Socrates' desire to distinguish the human and the subhuman with anything but ridicule. We see, too, why Protagoras does not consider the bearing of his view on the gods. He avoids both issues because he has no need to define our humanity insofar as our good is not in question. Where Socrates' strange and perplexing inquiry seeks the truth about the good for a being such as we are, Protagoras' endeavors evince the utmost respect for the conventional boundaries.[37] He can and, given his personal good, must accept what Socrates cannot: the widely shared consensus concerning the nature of human good. That is, even, or especially, if Protagoras in pursuit of his own success simply pretends to accept what the many think, the very motive for this pretense shows that he does endorse the many's view of good.

Driven by the desire to succeed, to gain the security and prestige bestowed by the community, Protagoras, like his friend Theodorus, bows before convention. Accordingly, he finally answers Socrates' query concerning the constitution of our humanity with an appeal to politeness. Socrates should act "in a way more suited to a well-born man," that is, in a more well-mannered way (166c3). With this admonition, Protagoras embarks on the central portion of his speech in which he relates his definition of wisdom.

[37] On the roots of Protagoras' conventionalism, see Saxonhouse, *Free Speech and Democracy*, 191–2.

Protagoras says that the "very person is wise who, for anyone of us to whom bad things appear and are, makes them change over into appearing and being good things (166d5–7)." Although Protagoras does recognize this distinction between good and bad, he adamantly denies that this change should also be understood as one from false opinions to true: "One does not, however, make someone who's been having some false opinion afterward have some true opinion (167a6–7)." We should note that in his movement from the first to the second portion of his speech Protagoras replaces appearance with opinion, and only when he speaks of opinion does he raise the issue of good. To the extent that it involves comparison of alternatives, the issue of good can only be addressed in and through speech. In this way, Protagoras, despite himself, does tacitly recognize the difference between human and nonhuman in the capacity of the former to ask of the good insofar as humans alone speak.

Having previously insisted on following his views to the letter, Protagoras now recommends a certain looseness of terminology (166d7–e1). Perhaps he means to prepare us for the looseness in the argument that follows. The heart of Protagoras' view, his notion of wisdom, may not withstand careful scrutiny. As indicated in the preceding text, this notion holds that wisdom aims to effect a change in the listener rather than to ascertain the truth. For, according to Protagoras, "there is no power to have as opinions either things that are not, *or* other things besides those one experiences, and the latter are always true (167a7–8, emphasis added)." The first limit on opinion points to an external objective standard that prevents us from opining falsehood. The latter insists that whatever we opine must be true because "what is" is a function of each individual's idiosyncratic experience. Protagoras' use of these competing rationales illustrates, again, the freedom of his "argument" from any connection to "what is." But further, by placing both these rationales in Protagoras' mouth, the former recalling Parmenides' dictum, Socrates also suggests something potentially troubling: these apparently opposing views amount to the same thing. Neither a doctrine of radical flux nor one of radical stability can connect good and true.[38]

Protagoras proceeds to elaborate his conception of wisdom as an expertise, mastered by few. Contrary to Theaetetus' stated view, it is, as such, distinguished from knowledge, which is now nothing else but the perception of each. Lest this be thought to place Protagoras in Socrates' camp, let me hasten to add that Protagoras shares with Theaetetus the wish to preserve wisdom as technical expertise alone. Socrates' Protagoras makes Theaetetus see the lengths to which he must go to fulfill this wish. Pertinent in this regard are the analogies Protagoras now employs to substantiate his notion of wisdom. These raise the question whether the separation of good from true, on which his definition of wisdom depends, can be maintained.

Socrates' Protagoras first draws an analogy between the physician and the sophist. The former "produces a change by drugs, a sophist does so with

[38] I consider this point more fully in Chapter 7.

speeches (167a5–6)." He further likens the wise to technicians, saying "when [the wise] have to do with bodies I call them doctors and when they have to do with plants I call them farmers; for I claim that the latter induce in plants, in place of burdensome perceptions, whenever any of them are sickly, serviceable and healthy perceptions and truths, and that wise and good rhetoricians make serviceable things, instead of burdensome ones seem to cities to be just (167b6–c3)." Perhaps we would be more willing to accept the analogy if we could conceive of plants holding certain views as truths.[39] To be more specific, the ground of the disanalogy is Protagoras' desire to regard the object of the sophist's art – his subjects and the changes he hopes to effectuate in them – as equally unproblematic as either the physicians' attempt to bring health to the body or the farmers' inducement of bountiful crops from plants.[40] Protagoras finds himself mired in the same dilemma as the "all-wise" comprehensive eugenicists.

However, Protagoras' own references to the sophist's object make this analogy dubious. When explaining the realm in which the sophist works, Protagoras refers to the "just and beautiful," and how these appear to the city (167c5). And it is exactly here that we see most clearly that the just and beautiful are controversial in a way that health and bounty are not. All easily recognize the latter. They thus fit well with the model of expertise that Protagoras uses as his paradigm for wisdom. We can readily understand wisdom as a means to these universally recognized and accepted goods. Yet this is not so clearly the case with the just and beautiful whose very meaning, Protagoras points out, fluctuates dependent on fluctuating opinions: "whatever sorts of things seem just and beautiful to a city are those things for it so long as it considers (*nomizdei*) them so (167c4–6)." These are, for him, matters of law or convention, and the law can change. This changeability is central to the sophist's activity. The task of the "wise and good rhetoricians" is exactly to "make serviceable things instead of burdensome ones, seem to cities to be just (167c2–4)."[41]

Protagoras determines the meaning of good as "serviceable," that is, as useful or advantageous. "Good" means "good for" someone or some group rather than good in itself. Of utmost importance now is what exactly Protagoras thinks qualifies for this designation. Fortunately, Protagoras' own behavior reflects and specifies what he means. He concludes this portion of the speech saying, "the sophist who has the power to train in this way those who are being educated is both wise and deserving of a lot of money from those who

39 I am not persuaded by Burnyeat's reference to *Timaeus* (77b) to show that Plato believes plants can perceive. See Burnyeat, *The "Theaetetus" of Plato*, 26.

40 On the difficulties of the analogy between medicine and sophistry see Cole, "The Apology of Protagoras," 110–12; McDowell, *Plato "Theaetetus,"* 167; and Maguire, "Protagoras – or Plato?," 126–30.

41 One notable difference between the outcomes for plants versus cities is that the perceptions of the former change, while for cities the *objects* of their perception change to things that actually are serviceable or useful. This difference may prefigure the forthcoming "modified Protagoreanism" in which there are things with an enduring being.

get educated (167c8–d2)." Here we have the goal of Protagoras' theoretical formulations. To maintain the prestige of his art – wisdom as the power to effectuate an unquestioned good – Protagoras must obscure the potentially controversial character of good. He must render meaningless the question of whether or not something is truly good. Were this acknowledged as a serious question, it would be much more difficult to understand wisdom as power, as instrumental to some acknowledged good. Instead, it would mandate what Protagoras *in the name of his own good* seeks to avoid – namely, an inquiry into good, more akin to the *phronesis* that Socrates seeks. As many of Socrates' former students recognize, such an inquiry provides no guarantee of success in the community. To echo the complaint heard from ancient Athens until the present day, it's not clear what one can "do" with such an education. Such concerns do not trouble Protagoras' school. And this makes clear the nature of the reconciliation of Protagoras' theory of knowledge and his art. Protagoras' theory supports the definition of wisdom that defines his practice. His epistemic commitments are formulated to promote his good.

Socrates soon terms this good "advantage." In Protagoras' case, as we will see, advantage is understood as having its roots in what would later be termed "self-interest" without being limited thereto. It comprehends as well the honor and prestige often useful for the security of one's own.[42] Yet, as we will also see, Protagoras' claims about those other political things, the just and beautiful, make dubious that advantage is thus rightly understood. In its forthcoming pages, the dialogue makes us wonder, for example, whether the foregoing notion of advantage is appropriate to a being whose beauty can be expressed in such diverse ways, from physical beauty to the beautiful speeches of an ugly youth. Moreover, the contradiction between Protagoras' egalitarianism and his inegalitarianism raises the question as to whether this view of good pertains both to what we all share in common and to the fulfillment of those capacities that enable some to be regarded as gods to other humans (151d1, 170a11). In thus pointing to the problem of justice, Protagoras' contradiction itself makes dubious the univocal good of such a being.[43]

These differences regarding the just and the beautiful, between and within cities, are, we recall, the source of that conflict with which the dialogue begins. The allusion to the deaths of Theaetetus and Socrates presages Socrates' central challenge to Protagoras: is it possible to abstract from the truth of what we regard as good? This abstraction could be possible were the good to be a matter of indubitable, universal consensus founded on demonstrable proof – or, if we simply did not care very deeply about it. But the drama of the dialogue

[42] Lee ("Hoist with His Own Petard," 238) recognizes that Protagoras' concern, above all, is for his own. See also n. 35 in the preceding text.

[43] Cole notes the importance of the distinction between just and beautiful versus beneficial, the latter understood in what Cole makes clear is a narrowly utilitarian way. "The Apology of Protagoras," 111–13. Compare Maguire, "Protagoras – or Plato," 127–9.

indicates that its meaning is profoundly controversial and that we care about nothing so much as the good. Hence, both Theaetetus and Socrates stake their lives on political conflicts brought on by this controversy.

Those to whom these goods of justice and beauty apply are not as clearly knowable as the bodies or plants on which the physician and farmer respectively act. Contrary to Protagoras' eccentric view, plants do not possess truths regarding their own well-being that may be altered by another. They lack those qualities of mind that Protagoras attributes to them. As Protagoras' reference to education in this context reminds us, those beings capable of, and in need of, education – capable of, and in need, of political order – are for that reason less clearly knowable regarding their being (167c8–d1). The *agon* between Socrates and Protagoras – and ultimately between Socrates and the generalship of Homer – concerns exactly whether the human good is essentially controversial and thus properly the object of inquiry. In this central portion of Protagoras' "Apology," Socrates makes clear that the ground on which that contest is waged is the meaning of the conflicts intrinsic to political life.

In the third portion of his speech Protagoras returns to methodological concerns, offering advice on how to approach these issues. In this way, Socrates links the foregoing issue of the character of the good with a certain view of inquiry. Protagoras' advice initially sounds very Socratic until, that is, it exceeds even Socrates' hopes for the power of reason. Protagoras' soaring ambitions in this regard continue to be fueled by an acute sense of his own advantage. The consequent corruption of reason makes ever clearer the ground that divides the Socratic philosopher and the sophist.

Protagoras begins by insisting again on being just in the use of speeches. He defines justice in light of the Socratic distinction between competition and conversation (167e4, e5). His rationale for maintaining this distinction, however, differs markedly from Socrates'. Whereas Socrates embraces the possibility of a common benefit from challenging conversation, Protagoras focuses on the greater popularity and higher wages accruing to the leader of such discussion. Specifically, he portrays such just behavior as a way to make one's interlocutors "hold themselves responsible for their own confusion and perplexity and not you (168a2–3)." The hoped-for result is that "they'll pursue you and love you (168a2–4)." He calls proceeding in a less just manner "a big-time irrationality (167e3)." And so it must be, if reason is only an instrument for the satisfaction of the teacher's desire to be greatly admired and compensated accordingly.

Protagoras' advice obviously pertains to Socrates. He has told us that his midwifery led him to be denounced by many in his community who blamed him for their perplexity. We know too, however, that Socrates offers the present advice to himself. It is his fictitious Protagoras speaking these words. There can be no doubt that Socrates is aware of these Protagorean hopes for reason. Yet his assessment of his situation in the midwife section, not to mention the events that begin with the culmination of the present conversation, indicate that he does not share these hopes. In particular, through having Protagoras express such extravagant hopes, Socrates enables us to see his own awareness of the limits of reason, the recalcitrance of nature to transformation through speech. Such awareness was evident in his maieutic practice. It is what calls for this practice. In what follows, Plato widens the gulf between Socrates and Protagoras in this regard.

Socrates' Protagoras promises that if this just practice is maintained, one's interlocutors will "run away from themselves to philosophy, in order to become different people and be set free from what they were before (168a4–6)." The midwife section depicted a significantly less optimistic picture of the possibility of philosophic education. There, such progress as occurred was achieved only by a relatively few students. Moreover, the vehicle of progress was not simply rational but involved *association*, a term whose capaciousness well expresses Socrates' uncertainties surrounding the development of human potential. But, for Protagoras, such is the transformative power of speech that it can easily alter human beings in significant ways, make them *be* different. Above all, it can set them free. In Protagoras' world, which is also the world of Theodorus' hopes, speech rightly used can overcome what Socrates regards as ineluctable necessities. It can free us from those perplexities, the focus on which generates such animosity toward Socrates.

At the end of his speech, Protagoras does mention perplexities. However, contrary to Socrates' view, he does not hold that they are inherent in the nature of things. Rather, they exist only because of the "customary phrases and words, which most people, when they drag them around any which way at random, hold out as all sorts of insoluble perplexities for one another (168b8–c2)." It is the many's misuse of words that produces perplexities. Presumably, an art of speech, which Protagoras would happily supply for a fee, could remedy this defect. Nature does not enter in to Protagoras' world of words, a world in which he is in perfect control, governed only by the perfectly coherent rules of grammar.[44] Protagoras' world is constituted by convention and, for that reason, is wholly manipulable by art.

Socrates' rendition of Protagoreanism brims over with hope. Yet in its midst he does not fail at least to allude to the reasons for the more restrained account of the midwife passage. In a statement summarizing Protagoras' position he has him say: "you'll truly examine what we mean when we declare . . . that whatever seems so also is that way, both for each private person and for each city (168b4–6)." In the concluding phrase, Socrates glances at the complexities of political life that cast doubt on Protagoras' hopes. Both we and Socrates know that the "private person," as Socrates has referred to himself, potentially has a view of good significantly at odds with that of the city. Moreover, both Socrates and the community will care deeply about being right, neither being inclined to the epistemological laissez-faire of Protagorean relativism. Socrates' own circumstances, of which he is acutely aware, makes dubious that speech alone

44 See Diogenes Laertius *Lives* IX. 52–4; and Davis, *Poetics of Philosophy*, 101–2.

is sufficient to alter this care. In the political conflict between the individual and the political community Socrates discovers an enduring, a natural, perplexity that reason cannot simply resolve.

The extremes of Protagoras' position arise then because he severs the connection of reason or speech to nature. Without this connection he proceeds, seemingly oblivious to any natural concern for the truth about our good. He sees no obstacles impeding reason's way. Reason has no standard beyond itself. But Socrates' Protagoras reveals that this effort to dispatch nature does not succeed. Reason is regarded as autonomous but ultimately only to act in an instrumental capacity. It is so regarded precisely to serve that most-powerful natural desire, the love of one's own. In Protagoras' case, much like cases occurring nearer our own time, if reason is not focused on the truth of things, seeking to ascend to more comprehensive understanding, it will be driven by lower desires. It then becomes a tool answering to the desire of the one that manipulates it. As Hobbes puts it, in this case, thoughts become "scouts and spies" for the desires, where these are understood as those eminently natural desires oriented on the body.[45]

The sophists portray reason as omnipotent, undaunted by insoluble difficulties. For them, contrary to Socrates' earlier indication, every issue is fully translatable into *logos*.[46] Although they may use myth as it suits them, they see no necessity to rely on myth as expressive of the limits of knowing.[47] In this soaring dream, reason grants to the sophist a sense of freedom from bondage by any necessity. Both Theodorus and the Philosophers of the forthcoming Digression share the aspiration for such freedom. Yet Protagoras' violation of rational consistency to enhance his prestige, and thus secure his livelihood, enables us to see that such freedom masks the most abject enslavement. It is all the more abject for being a product of self-deception.

In the forthcoming passages of the dialogue Socrates intensifies his probe into the adequacy of this Protagorean freedom. Becoming ever more prominent in this investigation are those "political things" that provide an acute sense of the difficulty of knowing the true human good. It soon becomes evident that the blinders of Protagoreanism, the refusal to inquire into the truth about our nature, cannot withstand the natural desire to know our good. As Socrates' dialogic undertaking gives us to see, it is a desire evident even, or especially, in Protagoras.

Protagoras' Egalitarianism and Inegalitarianism (168c6–171d3)

The significant difference between Socrates' and Theodorus' views of good becomes even more explicit as Socrates urges Theodorus to give an account

45 Hobbes, *Leviathan*, 62.

46 *Protagoras* 320c2–4.

47 Although he is willing to use myth for the sake of persuasion, Protagoras sees no difference between it and logos. See *Protagoras*. 320c3–4. See also Davis, *Poetics of Philosophy*, 169n104.

of his life. Theodorus likens Socratic inquiry to a wrestling contest and to the activity of great mythic criminals whose aim is to murder their victims (169a9–b4).[48] Both images portray domination as Socrates' goal. Preparatory to this wrestling contest, Theodorus believes that Socrates makes him strip, puts him in a position of vulnerability, so that Socrates can achieve victory over him. Theodorus sees humiliation on the horizon. Even if the outcome were reversed, however, the significant point is that Theodorus regards this conversation as a zero-sum game. Whatever good comes out of it can only be enjoyed by an individual as such, not by both in common.

Socrates disagrees. He notes that he has not always emerged from his conversations unscathed and victorious. Many who are "strong in their speaking, have met up with me and bashed me good and well (169b7–8)." Still, Socrates persists, not out of some insatiably competitive spirit, but because he, unlike Theodorus, does not regard conversation as competition. Driven rather by the "terrible love" of such conversation, he considers even, or especially, being bested in speech as a good (169c1). Thus, he exhorts Theodorus: "So don't you begrudge a drubbing and a benefit of yourself and me at once (169c2–3)." For Socrates it is possible that this conversation, whatever its outcome, can result in a good shareable by both, that he can receive "a drubbing and a benefit . . . at once." Such truly common goods are not diminished but enhanced by others' participation in them, a possibility evident in Socrates' midwifery. Perhaps because he does not acknowledge the possibility of true sharing, true friendship, Theodorus does not distinguish, as Socrates had, between an acquaintance and a friend (161b9, 162a4).

This distinction between Socrates and Theodorus regarding the potential commonality of good is evident, more generally, in the difference between Socrates and the "serious" men of the community, the "*spoudaioi*." This issue of seriousness, of what one should be serious about, is emphasized throughout the passage. Socrates' Protagoras urges Socrates to conduct the discussion in a serious rather than childish manner (168d3–5, 167e5–8). Socrates also appeals to Theodorus' seriousness – his age and lack of playfulness – in his effort to enlist Theodorus' aid for his friend, Protagoras (168d4–e3). The *spoudaioi* are those men of status in the community that take seriously the things of the community, which certainly include security and well-being. Yet Socrates has referred to himself as a layman, a private person (154e3). In addition, he has juxtaposed his own playfulness with Theodorus' humorlessness (145b10–c2). The pursuit of the serious men of the community is by contrast sober and even grim. Perhaps because it has its roots in the love of one's own, this grimness reflects the inevitable failure to secure one's own in the most important regard. In any case, Socrates does not seem serious about the same things as these serious men.[49]

48 On these wrestling metaphors see Herrmann, "Wrestling Metaphors," 92–109.

49 Consider Lee's point that there can be a higher kind of seriousness related to the refutative art. "Hoist with His Own Petard," 235.

This fundamental divide concerning the good bears also on the issue at hand, the proper meaning of wisdom. Protagoras deems wisdom as power to ascertain the best available means to certain, universally accepted goods. But, as I have suggested, if the meaning of the good should itself prove controversial it would then seem that wisdom must also include inquiry into the nature of good not merely into the means thereto. Socrates now broaches precisely this question: is wisdom oriented on means or also on ends? Accordingly, Socrates asks his interlocutors to get hold again of the issue he raised just after the delivery of Theaetetus' offspring. He asks, is "each person self-sufficient in *phronesis* (169a4–6)"?

For each to be self-sufficient in *phronesis* would mean that each knows fully his or her own good and the means to it. Lacking such self-sufficiency, we would be lacking in this regard. Notably, with this question Socrates connects the question of our neediness to the character of wisdom. Socrates explores the implications of this connection through examining Protagoras' simultaneous affirmation and denial of this neediness. This examination reveals, in turn, the tension between the egalitarian and inegalitarian sides of Protagoras' view.

Protagoras' egalitarianism follows from his theoretical stance that we are each self-sufficient with respect to knowledge. Socrates here expresses this position in terms of opinion rather than perception: "what seems so to each human being also is that way for the one to whom it seems that way (170a3–4)." Opinion is shareable in a way that perception is not. Addressing opinion enables Socrates to juxtapose the claimed idiosyncrasy of the opinion of each with a universally shared content of opinion, a content that denies such idiosyncrasy. This opinion "of all human beings" is that "no one at all does not consider himself wiser than others in some respects and other people wiser than himself in other respects (170a7, 170a8–9)." Contrary to Protagoras' theoretical position, everyone recognizes human inequality with respect to knowing. In this respect, everyone recognizes that, in some manner, each is needy.

For Socrates, the crucial manner concerns the pursuit by each of his or her good. He states, "in the greatest dangers, at least whenever people are in distress in military campaigns or diseases, or at sea, they have the same relation to those who rule them in each situation as to gods, expecting them to be their saviors (170a9–b1)." We are needy with respect to the security of our good. We are also aware of that neediness. Such awareness is responsible for the fact that "all human things are filled with people seeking teachers and rulers for themselves ... and in turn with people who suppose themselves to be competent to teach and competent to rule (170b2–5)." Sensing our inadequacy we, like the students in Socrates' initial speech, seek those we think can remedy it.

Socrates thus claims there is universal recognition of what Protagoras' theory denies: inequality with respect to knowledge, even to the point that some are regarded as saviors and gods to the rest of humankind. What drives humankind to this recognition – and Socrates reiterates that it is humans in general about which he speaks – is the desire, contra Protagoras, to connect the good and the true (170a7, b2, b6). Being serious about their good, they want that which is truly good. Consequently, being aware that they lack the requisite knowledge, they seek it. With good reason did Socrates begin his conversation with Theodorus stressing this critical fact. "In all these situations," Socrates asks, "what else are we going to say but that human beings themselves consider there to be wisdom and lack of understanding among them (170b5–7)"? And not only this but also "they consider wisdom true thinking and lack of understanding false opinion (170b9–10)." When it comes to our good, our deeds testify that truth matters. The seriousness of each for his or her good, coupled with awareness of the neediness regarding how to attain it, makes us seekers of *phronesis*. It makes us unwilling to sever the good from the true.

Socrates' characterization of Protagoras' reaction to this universally held opinion suggests that this same seriousness drives Protagoras too, at least in his deeds. This universally held opinion places Protagoras in a serious bind. If he affirms the content of the opinion, the *homo mensura* thesis is refuted because the opinion maintains that each is not equally the measure. However, if he denies it, the thesis is refuted by the implication that some opinions, notably his own, are superior to others. In this case, once again, each is not equally the measure. Protagoras could challenge the opinion's universality. However, this would ultimately require him to support the claim that no one believes that anyone is wiser than someone else (170c5–d2). This claim not only flies in the face of what all have experienced, but it also undermines Protagoras' chief goal – the marketing of his services to high-paying clients.

As many commentators have pointed out, there does remain one option for Protagoras. He could adhere to the self-consistent version of his doctrine that Socrates here neglects to provide. With such adherence, the contradiction, so evident in the version presented, could have been avoided by strict fidelity to the claim that all opinions, including Protagoras' own, are true only for each individual.[50] Socrates' neglect prompts us to ask whether Protagoras would favor this option. His deeds suggest he would not.

[50] This argument is usually referred to as the self-refutation argument, a name derived from Sextus Empiricus *Adversus Mathematicos* vii. 389. The argument has generated considerable commentary largely focused on the omission of the qualifier "for Protagoras" at certain crucial points. The issue is that the inclusion of these qualifiers would have made Protagoras' position self-consistently relativistic and thus less susceptible to Socrates' refutation. Among those who hold that the omission of the qualifiers simply undermines Socrates' argument are Sayre, *Plato's Analytic Method*, 87–90; McDowell, *Plato "Theaetetus,"* 169–72; Bostock, Plato's "*Theaetetus*," 89–92; and Waterfield, *Plato "Theaetetus,"* 172–6. The question then is why they are omitted. Burnyeat offers three possibilities: inadvertence, irony, and perverse dishonesty. See Myles Burnyeat, "Protagoras and Self-Refutation in Plato's *Theaetetus*," 85 *Philosophical Review* (1976): 174–7. Gregory Vlastos opts for the first in *Plato "Protagoras"* (Indianapolis, IN: Bobbs-Merrill, 1956), xivn29. Lee explores the second. Rejecting both explanations, Burnyeat attempts to defend Plato from the final charge by essentially arguing that it doesn't matter if the qualifiers are omitted. But Fine shows that Burnyeat's argument

Socrates maintains that the living, breathing Protagoras would be a much more vigorous defender of "his own things" than would Socrates (168c5). Moreover, Protagoras would "disparage our attempt while solemnly upholding his view (168c4–5, d2–4)." Furthermore, when Socrates has the deceased "Protagoras" pop out of the ground, the late sophist asserts the superiority of his own view and so once again contradicts the radical relativism that Socrates has attributed to him (171d1–3). When it comes to his good, Protagoras is anything but indifferent. After all, as Socrates again reminds us in this context, Protagoras was the author of a book entitled *Truth* (171c5–6). Equipped with this title, his aim in authoring the book must be to provide a general, nonrelative teaching about the way things are, a teaching so promulgated as to win him a broader clientele (171c6). With such deeds, it is clear that, as in his earlier speech, Protagoras sacrifices consistency for the same reason that all human beings seek those who are wiser: seriousness about his good, a good he would defend.

It is this seriousness that involves Protagoras – and Theodorus and Theaetetus – in self-contradiction. In Protagoras' case, as we have seen, the self-contradiction lies in his effort to maintain a view of humanity in general that cannot apply to himself as the individual expressing the view. He attempts to exempt himself from the limits of his individual existence, forgetting or neglecting that he speaks as an embodied individual concerned, as such, with his own good. We have seen such cases of self-contradiction throughout the dialogue: the Megarians of the Prologue, adherents of a philosophical school that denies the reality of potential, discuss whether Theaetetus fulfilled his potential; mathematicians adopt the view that all knowledge is perception with its consequent denial of any stable entities; a teacher and a student adhere to a view that makes impossible an account of learning. We are in the midst of an assessment of a thesis formulated out of self-love that culminates in the denial of the self. This self-contradictoriness may seem paradoxical in light of my earlier claim that seriousness about the good leads us to connect the true and the good. Yet what we want is *to be convinced* that what we take to be good is truly so, however that might be achieved. What our seriousness will not permit is genuine indifference to the question.

depends on not taking Protagoras' relativism seriously enough. See Gail Fine, "Relativism and Self-Refutation: Plato, Protagoras, and Burnyeat," in *Method in Ancient Philosophy*, ed. Jyl Gentzler (Oxford: Clarendon Press, 1998), 148–9, 152–3, 159, 161. In particular, she argues that Burnyeat permits himself an unwarranted move from what is true in someone's world in a relativistic sense to what is true of the world objectively. The result is that Burnyeat's argument is either question-begging, if the qualifiers are put back in, or invalid, if they are omitted. Lee makes a similar point in response to much the same argument. He attributes the omission to irony, but the purpose of such irony (if that is the correct term) must be spelled out. Lee does capture the dilemma into which Protagoras is placed: he can either adhere to his doctrine or he can maintain his career. Lee, "Hoist with His Own Petard," 245–6 and 253n37, 248–9.

We have seen this seriousness about the good powerfully evident in the words and deeds of Socrates' interlocutors that express their attraction to Protagoreanism. Induced by his teacher and by his own inclinations, Theaetetus has joined his mathematical education with an affinity for Protagorean relativism (152a5). The great desire of this bright, eager student is to find the correct answer, to avoid making a mistake (146c6). Apparently antithetical, both mathematics and Protagoreanism speak to Theaetetus' desire in their shared insistence that unassailable knowledge is immediately available, whether in the rational necessity of mathematics or in the absolute idiosyncrasy of Protagoreanism. Both provide immunity from doubt. Both, in particular, reject the notion that our knowledge must be gained mediately, through ascent from the particular to the general. Or, to use the language of the Digression, they reject the need for the *ascent* from "the things nearby" to "the nature of each whole of the things that are (174a1–2)." On the basis of this rejection, Theaetetus can set aside such phenomena as error, falsehood, and opinion, each of which exists because of the incomplete character of that ascent. But in rejecting this ascent from opinion he must also reject that possibility essential to the activity of the teacher and the student, the possibility of learning (145d5–9). This he is willing to do in order to secure his desire that knowledge be unassailable. In avoiding the realm of opinion, Theaetetus especially wishes to avoid the realm in which he might confront perplexing questions of good, questions that might shake the solidity of his beliefs. Thus, although he was aware of Socrates' investigations, he avoided Socrates and the dizziness induced by the perplexities of Socratic inquiry (148e2–3). Precisely in his embrace of the apparent indifference of Protagoreanism we can see his fervent desire that he possess the true good.

The same can be said regarding his teacher's exertions in this regard. Subsequent to the speech of Protagoras Socrates makes Theodorus, the senior mathematician, his interlocutor. Theodorus has previously shown great reluctance to join in Socrates' dialectical mode of investigating through question and answer. Seeking to overcome this reluctance, Socrates throws down this challenge to Theodorus: should Theodorus accept Protagoras' doctrine he would also have to accept that everyone is as competent as himself in geometry, astronomy, "and everything else in which you are charged with excelling (169a4–5)." This Theodorus is unwilling to do. He is provoked and charges Socrates with compelling him to "give a *logos*," a defense of his way of life (169a7). Now, again, it is clear that Socrates does not press Theodorus so hard because he harbors some hope of converting him to Socratic philosophy (146b3–4). Rather, Theaetetus and Socrates are the intended beneficiaries of this conversation. For both, the benefit derives from Socrates' examination of Theodorus' own Protagoreanism.

It may seem odd that a mathematician, oriented as such on permanent invisible objects, should be drawn to the unceasing flux underlying Protagoreanism. It is hard to see how any objective claims could be made on such a basis.

Yet Theodorus' reluctance to give a *logos*, to examine the underpinnings of his deepest choices, helps explain the affinity Theodorus feels for Protagoras (161b8, 162a4, 168c3, 168e7, 171c8). As with his student, Protagorean relativism enables the mathematician Theodorus to dismiss the realm of moral and political choice as one of endless and thus fruitless contention, exemplified precisely by the ceaseless questioning of Socrates. Theodorus can use Protagoreanism to carve out a realm of certainty free of the controversies generated by such questions.[51]

The source of Theodorus' concern for certainty becomes evident in the dilemma Socrates sets before him. Throughout the passage Socrates pummels Theodorus with the aforementioned point: Protagorean relativism goes too far to serve Theodorus' purpose; it cannot be prevented from infecting all of knowledge. Theodorus cannot adopt a doctrine that renders his view invincible *because all views are equal* and maintain the superiority of his own knowledge in its pristine certainty. In this way, Socrates captures Theodorus in the web of Protagoras' central contradiction between equality and inequality. It becomes clear that what moves Theodorus to adopt this untenable position is not so much his devotion to Protagoras' theory as it is his self-concern – and a concomitant desire for mastery. Accordingly, in response to Socrates' question – "don't thousands battle you on each occasion with counteropinions, convinced that you judge and believe what is false"? – Theodorus swears, "By Zeus, Socrates, that's right, many thousands, as Homer says, and they're the ones who cause the troubles I have with human beings (170d8–e3)."[52] Theodorus too wishes knowledge to be unassailable so that he can silence those "thousands" who would challenge his view and so dominate his world. So deep is this desire for dominance, that he is willing to purchase unassailability at the cost of rendering his own theoretical pursuits indefensible. Socrates' interrogation of Theodorus exhibits the fact that, like Protagoras, Theodorus' epistemic allegiances are shaped by an understanding of his good. It is this understanding that determines what, in his view, counts as knowledge. This willingness to be self-contradictory is then itself an index of the seriousness about their good. Such is its power that it moves even these highly intelligent individuals to embrace any view that might rebut the challenge to the notion that their good *is* good.

Like those that leave Socrates' maieutic practice, both Theodorus and Theaetetus aim to preserve a sense of self-sufficiency as regards *phronesis*. They wish to obscure their neediness in this respect. Crucial to this end is the denial that the character of the good itself, not merely the means to the good,

[51] On this point, see Hemmenway, "Philosophical Apology," 341–2.

[52] See Homer, *Odyssey* xvi. 1212; xvii. 422, xix. 78. Theodorus' reference to Homer (prompted by Socrates) to characterize his feeling of being besieged suggests that what may lie at the root of the heroic: a desire to have the world comply with one's all too frequently thwarted desires. See n. 55 in the following text and my discussion of Homer in Chapter 6.

is in question and needs to be sought. Yet their own deeds, like those of Protagoras, have made this denial dubious. Their very attraction to Protagoreanism, miring them as it does in self-contradiction, bespeaks a desire to conceal from themselves their doubts about their grasp of the problematic good. What their Protagoreanism accomplishes for them suggests that they doubt not merely the firmness of their grasp on the good but whether they know with confidence what it is. Especially in Theaetetus' case, Socrates tests the limits of his capacity for self-deception by bringing his theoretical views into conflict with his experience. In this context, it is worth noting Theodorus' unwonted insight in likening Socrates to Sciron and Antaeus, both of whom were killed by turning their own tactics, their own deeds, against themselves.

Socrates hones in on the source of the good's elusiveness. He states that Protagoras would have had to concede "neither a dog nor any random human being is a measure about any single thing that he doesn't learn (171c1–3)." He would have to acknowledge "that one person is wiser than another and also that one is more lacking in understanding than another (171d6–7)." He would have to see, in sum, that there are significant, nonreducible differences not only between the human and nonhuman but also within humankind. The good for such a potentially diverse being must be a question.

Wringing this acknowledgment from Protagoras elicits from Theodorus the worry that they are "running down my companion too much (171c8–9)." In a remarkable response, Socrates conjures a Protagoras who pops out of the ground "just up to his neck (171d1–2)." He lingers just long enough to rebuke Socrates for his nonsense and Theodorus for agreeing with it (171d2–3). Then he's off and running once again (171d1–3).

This striking image displays the ingenuity of Socrates' imaginative power. It is, however, only the culmination of the poetic exercise in which he is now engaged, composing a dialogue starring the deceased Protagoras. Through his poetic activity, Socrates brings Protagoras (partially) back to life. Moreover, by calling attention to Socrates' activity in this regard Plato gives us a glimpse of his own art as the enlivening source for both Protagoras and Socrates – and for himself. It is worth considering why Plato selects just this moment to advertise his philosophy's employment of poetry.

It is especially useful insofar as we are on the verge of the Digression's picture of philosophy as nonpoetic, akin to the Muse-less materialists. Not knowing (or caring) if his neighbor is a human being or some different nursling, the Philosopher of the Digression sees no need to employ poetic skills to address him (174b1–4).[53] One reason that poetry becomes useful for philosophy is if, as with Socratic maieutics or the Platonic dialogue, there is a need to speak to individuals, to proceed in an *ad hominem* manner. The philosopher can then employ the resources of poetry to engage other individuals' passions. As we

53 I capitalize Philosopher when referring to the figure described by Socrates in the Digression to distinguish him from the Socratic philosopher.

have seen in the context of Socrates' dual presentation of perception, poetry becomes useful as well when the philosopher portrays humanity's place in the cosmos insofar as such a portrayal exceeds the scope of discursive analysis. In sum, when philosophy confronts the human things it enlists poetry as an ally.

Yet the Socratic philosopher's use of poetry does not entail assimilation of poetry and philosophy. Forthcoming too in the Digression is Socrates' confrontation with the poet Homer. This esteemed general of the fluxist army is, in Socrates' view, the source of anti-Socratism. The decisive difference between Homer and Plato concerns the good each has in view. Their poetry differs along these same lines. For some, poetry is required to construct a humanly inhabitable world in the face of cosmic indifference or even maleficence. Only through poetry, it is believed, can we overcome that ceaseless flux that carries each of us away in death. Yet Socrates', and thus Plato's, use of poetry does recognize the limits of our natural home. It does recognize the need for poetry when reason requires supplementation, whether to articulate a mythic account of humanity's place in the whole or to address individuals' passions. Plato thus uses poetry not for consolation, not to respond to the love of one's own, but for understanding.

This is evident in the present context and helps explain the passage's spotlight on poetic activity. The need for poetry may lead some to conclude that what order exists is humanly devised (and thus not really an order). Nevertheless, for Plato it is possible and necessary to ask what we are and what nature is such that poetry is possible. More generally, it is possible and necessary to ask about the order that permits and requires such human creativity. Plato directs us to this question by the distinction he now introduces, the distinction between nature and convention. As with poetry, we must also ask with respect to this distinction central to philosophic inquiry into politics, what we are, and what nature is, such that the latitude of convention is available to us. With this question Socrates holds out the possibility of a natural order, however complex, that might guide human life. Unlike Protagoras, therefore, he does not speak his merely self-serving piece and run away. Socrates persists in the necessarily shared human inquiry into this possibility.[54]

Nature and Convention (171d3–172c1)

In dealing with the distinction between nature and convention, we must heed Socrates' dictum: "it's a necessity for us to deal with ourselves as the sort we

[54] This point bears on the issue of how, on the basis of his relativism, Protagoras can so easily glide from the individual to the community as the measure. See Cole, "The Apology of Protagoras," 126n22. It is an issue related to the disanalogy between perception and opinion that I discuss in the text. Several commentators take Protagoras' hasty exit as an indication of his inability to engage in a common inquiry. See, e.g., Burnyeat, "Protagoras and Self-Refutation in Plato's *Theaetetus*," 191–2 and 192n23.

are (171d3–4)." To this end, prior to considering the introduction of this crucial theme of the dialogue, let's consider where we stand.

Socrates has determined that the issue concerns the proper meaning of wisdom. He has, furthermore, directed us to the question as to whether we require knowledge of means alone or also of the ends. If means alone are in question then we can more readily equate technical understanding and wisdom. In this case, we then should seek knowledge of the precise way to achieve the fully comprehensible and universally accepted good or goods. Certainty will be the touchstone of such knowledge as it grants the power to obtain this good. But the discussion has led us to see that the character of the good itself, the character of the end and not just the means, is in question. To the extent that this is the case, wisdom cannot simply amount to *techne*. Through the long road of this argument, Socrates has brought us to see that Theaetetus should have taken advantage of the opportunities Socrates provided at the outset to rethink the identity between knowledge as *techne* and wisdom.

By moving the discussion in this way, Socrates shows the deep connection between, on the one hand, a consideration of the nature of good and, on the other, the meaning of knowledge. In his portrayal of Protagoras he has shown, in particular, that how we conceive of good shapes how we conceive of knowledge. And through his elucidation of the mathematicians' adherence to Protagoreanism, that is, to beliefs that make impossible an account of their own mathematical activity – or even of their lives as humans – Socrates has also exhibited the power of the desire for good as it exerts its pull even on those passionately devoted to knowledge. Awareness of this power assists him in assessing the truth of those views that cast doubt on his own "terrible love" for speeches about the human good. He can better judge whether his way of life is defensible, an outcome that can benefit not only the young Theaetetus but also Socrates. However, most pertinent to the present point, this forthcoming defense cannot therefore involve an abstraction from the orientation on one's own good. To adopt, or even to seek, some view liberated from the question of good would be to repeat the same self-forgetting mistake of his interlocutors. It would be, once again, to forget or neglect, in the manner of Protagoras' theory what his deeds affirm: that we speak as embodied individuals, concerned as such with our own good. It would be to neglect the human context of theoretical inquiry.

Socrates' point is not simply that one's view of good can affect and even distort one's epistemic commitments. The manifest devotion of his interlocutors to the acquisition of knowledge tells a broader story. The influence of the view of good on those who most assiduously attempt to avoid it – on one who in the case of Theaetetus is indisputably brilliant – suggests that such a view is inalienable. We cannot help but consider the world through a lens of good. For exactly this reason, a careful examination of views of good in relation to knowledge becomes necessary. This, at least, is the indication of Socrates' own forthcoming deeds. Far from undertaking a "value-free" analysis of the meaning and possibility of knowledge, he now examines precisely that view of good that motivates the identification of knowledge with *techne*. The character of Socrates' examination makes clear that the question of good provides the pretheoretical framework within which we seek knowledge and therefore accounts for what we take knowledge to be. Socrates now also makes clear that this question is best considered through the medium of politics. It is there that it shows itself most clearly.

Admittedly, it is not immediately clear how Socrates' examination of the more comprehensive issue of good might resolve all difficulties. After all, this issue assumes importance precisely because of the elusiveness of comprehensive certainty. The evaluative perspective from which we view the world can wield such influence because of the uncertainty of our knowledge. But if, as Theodorus and Theaetetus suspect, it proves impossible to acquire certain knowledge of these views of good, then all claims to knowledge will be dubious.

Socrates responds to this concern, but he does so by interrogating the *expectation* of such certain knowledge rather than by directly providing a comprehensive and certain account of the good. In particular, he examines the view of good on which this criterion of certainty is based. The deepest strand of this examination involves asking whether this could be the good for a being such as we are. The vehicle through which Socrates asks this question is an examination of the human things, the "political things." In Socrates' forthcoming presentation these divide between advantage, on the one hand, and beauty, justice, and piety, on the other. The discussion focuses especially on the former – namely, a specific understanding of advantage, the reason people initially seek knowledge (170a9–11). We are now ready to consider further the rationale behind Socrates' explicit introduction of the political things.

Socrates maintains that although Protagoras' *homo mensura* is appropriate in the realm of taste, when it comes to a good such as health even Protagoras would want to recognize the existence of superior knowledge (171e4–5). Moreover, according to Socrates, as it is with an individual and health, so it is with a political community and its advantage (171a5–b2). By "advantage" Socrates means that which is useful or profitable, in a sense distinguishable from any notion of beauty, justice, and piety. One sign that this is his intended meaning is that there can be little doubt as to whether the steps a community has taken to secure the good in this basic sense have been successful. It is not difficult to determine whether or not the community endures and achieves material well-being. Accordingly, with respect to advantage so understood, even Protagoras would "hardly have the daring to say that *whatever* a city sets down as advantageous for itself, supposing it to be so, is also what will be advantageous to it beyond any question (171a8–b2, emphasis added)."

With this statement, Socrates easily transforms radical Protagoreanism into a modified version that does recognize a good not simply dependent on the view of each person.[55] If it were Socrates' goal only to respond to radical Protagoreanism, he could once again end the discussion with this conclusion. He continues, however, because he is more deeply concerned with the view of good that underlies both radical and modified Protagoreanism, the good of advantage as it has been defined.

Advantage, so understood, renders the community a means to secure that which we enjoy as individuals, the good of our own. Like health, the goods of security and material gain answer to needs we have as embodied, individuated beings. Again, it is good so understood, as answering to our most basic needs, that first calls forth our desire for knowledge (170a9–11). It calls forth as well the recognition of the decisive inequality with respect to knowing. We do not want to be misguided regarding our survival. Error is well-nigh intolerable when it concerns our very existence. This notion of good is oriented on what we might now call power, a broad category that, in response to the requirements of this goal, expands to include not only dominance over nature but also over other humans in the form of political power and the glory that can confer such power. What is sought are the means to the satisfaction of those desires each feels as an individual. In the Athenian Stranger's summary statement, it is "to have things happen in accordance with the commands of one's own soul."[56]

This hope, to satisfy our heart's every desire, links knowledge with certainty. Such certain knowledge might provide the kind of control, the kind of power, that enables us to overcome any obstacle. It might ultimately free us of need. Thus do the beliefs that the good is advantage so understood and that the touchstone of knowledge is unassailable certainty go hand in hand. Theodorus and Theaetetus, as well as Protagoras, desire to have, or be seen as having, the knowledge that will let them either master the uncertain future or be free of these nagging uncertainties. Their notion of good provides the framework within which they seek knowledge and so accounts for what they believe knowledge to be. Yet this means that if our view of good should change so must the sought-after object of knowledge. In particular, if our good is not properly thought of as advantage, in the sense just defined, then we must also question whether unassailable certainty is properly thought to be the touchstone of knowledge.

But it is difficult to question advantage so understood. Its solidity stands in marked contrast with the variability of those other constituents of the political things: beauty, justice, and piety. With reference to the variability of the latter, "people are willing to insist strongly that there are not any such things by

[55] On modified Protagoreanism see David Bradshaw, "The Argument of the Digression in the *Theaetetus*," 18 *Ancient Philosophy* (1998): 63–5.

[56] *Laws* 687c5–7. On the notion of freedom to which this view leads see Stephen Salkever, *Finding the Mean: Theory and Practice in Aristotelian Political Philosophy* (Princeton: Princeton University Press, 1990), 29–30, 221–25.

nature, having their own being (172b4–5)." In short, they are merely conventional. This conclusion is widely held. In view of the widespread agreement that such advantage is the human good, this consensus should not be surprising. If our understanding is expected to provide the certain means to this good, then whatever partakes of the sort of fluctuations evident in the meanings of beauty, justice, and piety must be ruled out as part of the natural human good.

Given this broad consensus, it is clear that the sophist Protagoras is not alone in drawing this conclusion. Nor is Protagorean relativism necessarily required for this outcome. With his introduction of modified Protagoreanism Socrates confirms that Protagoras' relativism is a tool wielded in pursuit of the same view of good underlying conventionalism.[57] Others oriented on wisdom, others who need not wholly share Protagoras' orientation, also reach this conclusion. As Socrates remarks, "even those who would not completely say what Protagoras says regard wisdom in some sort of way like this (172b7–8)."[58] The Digression makes clear that these others include Socrates' philosophic predecessors who do share the view of good that leads to this conclusion.

Yet this near-universal consensus takes insufficient account of the vast diversity of humankind and of the way this diversity bears on the conception of good. In particular, it does not adequately appreciate the implications for the meaning of human good of the distinction, characteristic of political philosophy, that Socrates now introduces, the distinction between nature and convention.

Socrates maintains that Protagoras' speech generally holds true regarding "things that are hot, dry, sweet and everything of that type (171e2–3)." The case for the absolutely private and idiosyncratic character of our cognition is best made – perhaps only made – when the focus is on perception alone, at least if perception is understood as sealed off from any capacity for reflection and judgment. Socrates then draws an analogy to the political things saying of

57 Various commentators have arrived at this point although expressed in diverse ways. Cole sees that there is a distinction in Protagoras' thought between what Cole calls "subjectivism" and "utilitarianism," with the latter taking precedence. Lee states that Protagoras' "epistemology and politics are logically independent." Those who do not see this point also have trouble deciding just who might be included among those that regard wisdom in the same way as does Protagoras without adopting all his views. Cole, "The Apology of Protagoras," 114; Lee, "Hoist with His Own Petard," 256n3. This point may be helpful in trying to understand the widespread relativism of our own time.

58 On the translation of this sentence see Burnyeat, *The "Theaetetus" of Plato*, 33n41. Cornford and Polansky believe that Socrates is referring to some who exceed Protagoras in their denial of any natural basis for the city, including advantage so defined. Burnyeat and McDowell maintain that it refers to some who are less extreme in their relativism than Protagoras, applying it only to justice. My view is closer to the latter but differs in holding that Socrates is ultimately more interested in conventionalism than in relativism because the former reveals the view of good to which relativism (of whatever degree) is instrumental. His ultimate concern is for this understanding of good that is shared by his philosophic predecessors. Cornford, *Plato's Theory of Knowledge*, 81–3; Polansky, *Philosophy and Knowledge*, 133n86; Burnyeat, *The "Theaetetus" of Plato*, 32–3; McDowell, *Plato "Theaetetus,"* 172–3.

them that "whatever sorts of things each city supposes are beautiful or ugly, just and unjust, holy and not holy, and sets down as lawful for itself, these also are that way in truth for each (172a1–4)." It is here that the distinction between nature and convention comes into play: advantage, as it has been defined, is "by nature," the other components of the political are merely "lawful" (172b4, 172c3).

It is the philosophers rather than the practitioners of politics who make this distinction. Appropriately, Socrates uses the language of philosophy to introduce it. He speaks of "things by nature" and of things "having their own being (172b4–5). He considers the phenomena of political life from a philosophic perspective. And he does so in the context of addressing an issue, the meaning of knowledge, which is likewise explicitly philosophic rather than political. Concerned as we are to understand the political character of Socratic inquiry, we must be struck by the fact that his purpose in examining politics is not primarily to give direction to political life. It is, rather, to respond to a philosophic perplexity, albeit one, as we have seen, of great practical import.

Prior to considering how Socrates' consideration of this distinction assists Socrates in responding to this perplexity, we should note that in the course of presenting this distinction, Socrates once again makes the same questionable assimilation of perception and opinion as he did in Protagoras' "Apology." There I argued that this move, not based on strict Protagorean grounds, enabled Protagoras to address the question of good insofar as this question depends on a comparison of alternative possibilities, which speech alone makes possible. This disanalogy thus only serves to highlight the difference between perception and opinion, which is appropriate in introducing the distinction between nature and convention. For our distinctive capacity for opinion and, more generally, for speech and reason proves to be crucial to this distinction. We need to consider this point in more detail.

As just mentioned, Socrates includes among what he calls the "political things" advantage, on the one hand, and the beautiful, just, and holy, on the other. The former is by nature, but with respect to the latter, "what seems so to people in common becomes true at that time, whenever it seems so and for as long as it seems so (172b5–6)." Again, these are by convention. Contrary to the inclination of Socrates' predecessors, however, this status does not mean that they can simply be dismissed. "Each city" has its view of these things, and with respect to these, each "sets down as lawful for itself" its particular views (172a2, a3). Although the content of convention may vary, the human need and capacity for it does not. This fact is central to Socrates' introduction of the political things. He is interested, above all, in what the need and possibility of law, and of politics more generally, reveal about our nature, especially about its complexity. As I suggested with reference to Socrates' poetry, although he recognizes the distinction between nature and convention, as did his predecessors, Socrates wants also to investigate a further question: what is the natural basis of convention, that is, what must we be such that we are capable and in need of convention? An answer to this question about our nature must profoundly affect the conception of human good. To get a glimpse of what the distinction between nature and convention might entail about our nature we need to recur to the distinction between perception and opinion.

It is the capacity for speech or opinion that makes the distinction between nature and convention possible. We are capable of lawgiving because the power of reflection enables us to step outside the flow of particulars to recognize kinds, to employ nouns. It enables us to note patterns and establish principles. Accordingly, Socrates later connects this power of lawgiving with the notion of the future. This power of reflection, and the attendant notion of the future, must decisively affect our lives. Possessing this notion, we can consider our lives as wholes rather than being driven by a series of momentary instincts. Because of the possession of this capacity, we *must* so consider our lives if they are to be in any way human. The power that makes us capable of law also dictates our vital need for it.[59] Our reason grants us latitude in determining the direction of our lives. This capacity entails that we not only act but also reflect on our action. In this capacity rests our freedom. But this freedom carries with it a great burden. Freed up in a significant way from biological determinants, we must take a hand in ordering our lives. We must ask and answer the question of how we ought to live. Through law and convention – and through poetry – we supply what our biological inheritance does not. The affinity between the legislator and the poetizing midwife extends at least this far: both recognize the need for human efforts to sustain human life in the face of an imperfectly ordering nature.[60]

These efforts can be informed by transhuman sources. Socrates is in the course of investigating what nature, imperfect though it may be, can tell us about how to live. Yet it is up to humans to establish the guidelines that reflect the direction given them by such a source. For communities, these are the conventions or laws by which political communities organize themselves. As Socrates indicates, these answers are diverse and variable, for individuals and communities. They can be wildly misguided, to the point, as we have seen, of making human life inexplicable. Nevertheless, being what we are, we cannot avoid the need for convention. These conventions, and political orders more generally, may not then be simply natural, at least in the sense of being generated spontaneously. But, arguably, such conventions have a natural basis in our nature, in its complexity. We can thus better understand why Socrates insists that "each city" possesses them.

However, because of this variability – especially of the beautiful, just, and holy – many, including Socrates' philosophic predecessors, dismissed the political realm as lacking in philosophic interest, as a matter of mere convention.

[59] For a discussion of this point, see Salkever, *Finding the Mean*, 74–7.

[60] Cropsey's treatment of the philosophic and political trial of Socrates makes the appropriate human approach to an imperfect nature a key theme of the saga.

Instead, they sought only "that which is." Animated by the intense desire to know how things are, they sought that which is stable, that which abides, because it is more knowable, more explanatory than that which varies. Clearly, the "things by nature" answer to this desire in a way that the fluctuating meanings of just, beautiful, and so on do not – especially when the latter seem to fluctuate because of human whim. Whether this disdain for the variable should be identified with a concern for truth remains a question. To answer it is the purpose of Socrates' philosophic consideration of politics.

Unlike his predecessors, Socrates finds political life of intense philosophic interest as he examines the notion of good that animates their reflections. In his examination of this view of good, Socrates assesses whether their judgment regarding the conventional status of beauty, justice, and piety does not already presuppose a specific conception of the good, a conception belied by the very distinction between nature and convention his philosophic predecessors used to dismiss the political things. Socrates considers whether these constituents of the political things, even, or especially, in their variability, could be as expressive of our nature and of our good as is this particular notion of advantage. Reflection on political life raises this possibility as it reveals the heterogeneity of our nature expressed in the characteristic conflicts of political life.

In approaching this question of good through a consideration of the political things, Socrates means not merely to critique Protagoras. Rather, he aims ultimately to understand more clearly than did his own predecessors, the character of that knowledge that is the ultimate goal of inquiry. Socrates' modification of the object of knowledge would then follow from a view of good distinct from that held by philosophers before him, one contrary to that which designates certainty as the criterion of knowledge. In exploring this deepest strand of the dialogue through what appears as a digression, Socrates has the *form* of the conversation pose the connection between the problem of knowledge and the philosophic centrality of political life *as a question*. Responding to this digressive form, Socrates' interlocutors and subsequent readers can permit his consideration of political life to remain disconnected from the dialogue. Or we can heed his words to Theodorus as the passage begins: "a greater speech . . . from a lesser speech is overtaking us (172c1)."

6

The Digression

Introduction

The Digression begins with Theodorus reminding Socrates that they are at leisure, to which Socrates replies, "we *appear* to be (172c3, emphasis added)." Socrates knows he is on the threshold of a very unleisurely epoch in his life. At the center of the upcoming turmoil, and of this dialogue, is the conflict between the philosophic and political lives that Socrates now explores.[1] His examination of this issue elaborates, in particular, on those necessities of political life that intrude on the Theodoran hope for a life of leisurely freedom. We have already seen Theodorus' desire to be free of those harsh necessities, but it intensifies in the Digression (172e2, d1–2, d4, d5, d8, e1–5, 173a4–5, 173b6). Fueling this hope, a hope evident also in Protagoras' outlook, is the possibility that speech can secure one's freedom from these necessities, that it can provide the leisure to do whatever one pleases.

Much to Theodorus' delight, Socrates does juxtapose the freely flying Philosophers to the slavish participants in political life. Socrates' exaltation of the philosophic life enflames Theodorus' desire to such a degree that he envisions on the horizon the possibility that Socrates' speech could bring about "more peace and fewer evils among human beings (176a3–4)." Yet, just as this reign of perpetual peace is about to dawn, Socrates brings Theodorus smack against a most profound necessity. Evil, Socrates asserts, is a necessary concomitant of good and, as such, can never perish. Evil is ineradicable.

[1] The connection between Socrates' trial and the central passage of the *Theaetetus* is made most clearly by Scott Hemmenway and Rachel Rue. They also provide the most sustained discussions of the Digression as a critique of pre-Socratic philosophy. See Hemmenway, "Philosophical Apology," 331–6; and Rue, "The Philosopher in Flight," 71–100. Harry Berger Jr. and Mark Waymack make the same general point but without the same degree of detail. See Harry Berger Jr., "Plato's Flying Philosopher," *Philosophical Forum* 13 (1982): 400 and Mark H. Waymack, "The *Theaetetus* 172c–177c: A Reading of the Philosopher in Court," *Southern Journal of Philosophy* 23 (1985): 483.

The abstract notion of the relational character of being has come home to roost in the center of our most urgent practical concerns. This distinguishing insight precedes the dialogue's deepest portrayal of Socratic philosophy. In this portrayal, Socrates provides the grounds on which we must reject the notion that the good can be advantage as previously defined. That near-universal consensus, a consensus comprising not only Socrates' political opponents but also his philosophic predecessors, must be mistaken. Accordingly, this altered notion of good must also result in an altered notion of the knowledge we ought to seek. This altered notion demands the replacement of the apolitical or antipolitical Thalesian philosopher with the Socratic seeker of *phronesis*.

The Philosopher's Neglect of Politics (172c2–176a1)

The Digression considers the question of good through a comparison of two ways of life, the life of the Philosopher and that of the orator-politician. Yet, as several commentators have recently shown, in this comparison, Socrates not only roundly demeans the orator-politicians, but also the Philosopher comes in for a share of criticism. Specifically, in opposition to his own philosophic concern for that which is good, beautiful, and just, Socrates portrays the Philosopher as other-worldly and apolitical, ignorant, or neglectful of the transitory, particular, and so, trivial affairs of humans.[2] In light of this criticism,

[2] The distinction between Socrates and the Philosopher he portrays in the Digression is widely noticed. See, e.g., Cornford, *Plato's Theory of Knowledge*, 88–9; Burnyeat, *The "Theaetetus" of Plato*, 34–6; and Sedley, *The Midwife of Platonism*, 66–7. For a list of the differences between Socrates and the Philosopher that are expressed within the dialogue see Eugenio Benitez and Livia Guimaraes, "Philosophy as Performed in Plato's *Theaetetus*," *Review of Metaphysics* 47 (1993): 300–1. The question is what to make of this difference. I agree with those commentators who argue that Plato intends to point to the superiority of Socratic philosophy that takes seriously the human realm as opposed to the otherworldly abstractions of the Philosopher. What remains to be specified, however, are what problem compelled Socrates to take human affairs seriously and how Socrates' focus on human affairs constitutes a response to this problem. See Hemmenway, "Philosophical Apology," 331–6; Rue, "The Philosopher in Flight," 78–82; and Howland, *The Paradox of Political Philosophy*, 63–4.

Chappell and Sedley draw the opposite conclusion. To use Sedley's phrase, they see Socrates as a step on the way to the "idealized philosopher," represented by what I refer to as the Philosopher. This position is fleshed out in greater detail in Sedley's book whose theme is precisely that the *Theaetetus* as a whole "midwifes" Platonism. I.e., it shows the way in which Socrates' thought made possible and necessary Platonism, the latter understood as based on Plato's "discovery of the transcendent moral forms." The meaning and status of the Forms in the Digression (or the lack thereof) enter in to commentators' judgments on the relative rank of Socrates and the Philosopher. Both Sedley and Chappell, following Cornford, understand the text to be alluding to the Forms in several places in the Digression. Like Cornford, Sedley takes the Digression as intended to recall, in Cornford's words, "the whole argument of the *Republic*, with its doctrine of the divine, intelligible region of the Forms, the true objects of knowledge." See Cornford, *Plato's Theory of Knowledge*, 88–9; Chappell, *Reading Plato's "Theaetetus,"* 127–8; and Sedley, *The Midwife of Platonism*, 66–74. For arguments that Plato does not intend to point in these passages to the Forms, see McDowell, *Plato "Theaetetus,"* 177

we must count again the ways of life examined here. There are not two but three human possibilities under scrutiny in the Digression: the political life, the (non-Socratic) Philosophic life, and, providing the criteria for the critique of the Philosophic life, the Socratic life. Ultimately, these three possibilities collapse again into two but not exactly as one might have predicted. Paradoxically, in light of the most explicit thrust of the passage, the political and Philosophic lives prove to share the same notion of good. For this reason, they join hands in opposing the Socratic way of life.

Now, it is true that Socrates presents the Philosophic life in the Digression as the most extreme antithesis of the political life. Yet Socrates' self-portrait and (despite the efforts of Euclides) his deeds in the dialogue combine to drive an unmistakable wedge between his life and that of the Philosophers he now portrays. To see how Socrates creates this distance between the Philosophers and himself we need first to consider his juxtaposition of the Philosophic and the political life.

Those leading the Philosophic and political lives diverge to such an extent that they even interpret the exact same phenomena in opposite ways; that which the orators believe possesses the utmost importance, the Philosopher thinks is "little or nothing (173e4)." This radical divergence in perspectives conduces not only to ridicule but also to contempt issuing from both sides (172c8–d2).[3] Socrates' initial distinction between the Philosopher's speech and courtroom oratory underscores this opposition. He remarks to Theodorus that the Philosophers "always have available that which you said – leisure" to speak at whatever length they desire (172d4–5). But the orators who embody the Protagorean doctrine, being swept along in the Heracleitean flow of time, "are always talking in an unleisured way, since flowing water is sweeping them along, and there's no room for making speeches about whatever they desire (172d9–e2)."[4]

Socrates is at some length about the deleterious effect such activity has on the orators' souls. As a result of having to argue out of self-interest, rather than orienting their speech on "that which is" as do the Philosophers, the orators "become sharp and shrewd . . . small and not upright in their souls (172d9, 173a1–3)." Furthermore, "the slavery they've been in since youth has taken away their growth, straightness, and freedom, forcing them to do crooked things by piling great dangers and fears on their still tender souls (173a4–7)." Ultimately, these orators suppose of themselves that "they've become dreadfully clever and wise," though they "have nothing healthy in their thinking

and Burnyeat, *The "Theaetetus" of Plato*, 37–9. My disagreement with the Cornford-Sedley interpretation rests on an alternative view of the intention of the dialogue as a whole.

3 See the discussion of this point in Rue, "The Philosopher in Flight," 84.

4 As Benardete notes, a water clock measured the speaker's allotted time in the courtroom. See Benardete, *Being of the Beautiful*, I.187n44.

(173b2, 173b1)." Socrates' condemnation of the orators also provides an insight regarding his present treatment of the soul. His image conveys a picture of the soul as living and dynamic, shaped by its possessor's activity.

Socrates asks Theodorus if he should now discuss the Philosophers, whom he refers to as "our choral group (173b3–4)." But the fear that he might thus abuse "what we were just now talking about, our freedom" makes Socrates hesitate (173b5–6). Theodorus' feelings are emphatically to the contrary. He cannot conceive of an abuse of freedom for those who wield the tool of speech. Theodorus takes Socrates' point to be that "we who belong in this kind of chorus are not subordinate to the arguments but instead the arguments are like servants of ours, and each of them waits on us, to be finished whenever that seems good to us (173c1–4)." It is a point much to his liking because it permits Theodorus to affirm the disconnection between reason and nature. He can regard reason as but an instrument of our good; however that good might seem to us. Theodorus provides insight into his conception of what that good is as he concludes, "since no judge is set up over us . . . to criticize us and govern us (173c4–5)." His good involves responding to the desires of his soul to have what he wants when he wants it, unfettered by any external restraint, whether it issues from his fellow humans or nature itself. He yearns to be master of his world.

Socrates does now examine the chorus of Philosophers, but the focus of this examination differs from his scrutiny of the politicians. Specifically, when he responds to Theodorus' desire for absolute freedom, Socrates addresses the Philosopher's neglect of politics. There is, therefore, a distinct asymmetry between his analyses of the two "choruses." Socrates has just spoken of the effect the politician's activity has on his soul. We should have expected Socrates now to speak of the way the deeds of the Philosopher shape *his* soul for upright growth. But this alternative topic replaces this discussion of the Philosopher's soul. As I said, Socrates turns instead to the Philosopher's treatment, or rather neglect, of political life.

This asymmetry heralds the gulf between Socrates and his philosophic brethren. For he makes emphatically clear that he regards the Philosopher's neglect of politics as a grave error. Socrates levels against the Philosopher his most serious charge: the Philosopher does not know that he does not know these things (173e1). Socrates thus judges the Philosopher as deficient in exactly the kind of knowledge essential to Socratic philosophy – namely, self-knowledge. If we possessed no other evidence, this charge would by itself alert us to the profound difference between the forthcoming portrayal of the Philosopher and Socrates' own activity.

Given the connection I have drawn between political life and the complexities of the soul, it is most appropriate that this lack of self-knowledge, the Philosopher's lack of insight into his own soul, should be indicated by replacing an examination of his soul with an examination of his neglect of political life. To discern all that the Philosopher has missed in his dismissal of politics we must consider just what it is that the Philosopher ignores. Socrates provides a lengthy list. The Philosophers, Socrates states,

> don't know the way to the marketplace, or where the courthouse or council chamber is, or any other place of public assembly of the city, and laws and things voted on, spoken or written, they neither see nor hear, and as for the zealous efforts of political parties for offices, and their meetings and dinners and celebrations with flute girls, not even in their dreams does it occur to them to have anything to do with them. And whether anyone in the city has been born well or badly, or has any taint that has come from his ancestors on either the paternal or maternal side, is something he no more notices than the proverbial drafts of water in the sea (173c8–e1).

Before considering this catalogue of neglect, it is worth reminding ourselves of Socrates' editorial oversight of the transcript of the conversation (143a3–4). The items in the forgoing list reflect this care in that each helps display an additional characteristic of political life.

The marketplace, of which Socrates speaks first, exists, most basically, because of our mutual dependence in the satisfaction of our corporeal needs. These are more efficiently met through the division of labor that, in turn, necessitates trade. Yet this mutual dependence does not prevent conflicts arising in the satisfaction of these needs. Limited resources and unlimited desires contribute to these conflicts, making individuals unwilling to reconcile the satisfaction of their needs with the needs of others. The need for government, with its council chambers, courts, and other public assemblies, thus arises.

In recognition of the persistence of these individual differences, governmental institutions rely not merely on the rulers' decrees but on the rule of law that aims to endure beyond the reign of a single individual. Moreover, as an amalgam of reason and coercion, law implies that these differences can be controlled or minimized but not dissolved in the medium of reason alone. The political community is thus always characterized by a conflict among parties. In the pursuit of their divergent interests these parties seek offices and power within the community.

Yet these divisions emerge not only from the clashing of those needs we have as embodied beings but also, and perhaps more insistently, from our psychic needs. We want not only to eat but also to engage in "dinners and celebrations with flute girls."[5] We have psychic capacities and needs that find fulfillment in friendship and conversation. The political community attempts to respond to these higher aspirations, producing further distinctions among its citizens with regard to their nobility, which it often understands in terms of being well or badly born (173d4–5). However, as seen in Socrates' plight, these needs may lead beyond what the community believes it can tolerate.

[5] *Symposium* 212d6.

In this unusually extended and informed encapsulation of political life, Socrates highlights those elements that portray it as a scene of persistent, buzzing conflict. Given that political life exists as a response to human need, these conflicts must be regarded as reflective of tensions between and among these needs. Again, the persistence of these tensions makes law, courts, and vying for office characteristic institutions of political life. The ongoing existence of these institutions suggests that the conflicts among humans and their needs may be only imperfectly reconcilable. The saga of Socrates' trial indicates just how imperfectly. Even if all corporeal needs could be perfectly satisfied, there would still be the desire for the kinds of activities portrayed, for example, in the *Symposium* – that is, the desire to satisfy psychic needs for friendship, conversation, and for beauty that can threaten the common good.

Socrates introduces the Digression with the *question* of the natural status of justice, beauty, and holiness precisely because this questionable status, suggested by the variety of definitions of each, reflects an important fact about our natural constitution.[6] More specifically, by including these among the political things, he recognizes that political communities attempt to respond to the whole range of our needs, including our psychic needs. But by raising the question of their natural status, Socrates points to the essential controversy surrounding these virtues and the source of that controversy. He points to the complexity of human needs that can give rise to variety, and thus difference, regarding notions of human fulfillment or happiness. From the variety of needs emerges a vast range of human potentials such that, as is tacitly recognized in Protagoras' central contradiction, individuals can differ radically from one another while still being human. The problem of justice lies in determining what notion of good, if any, could satisfy such diversity. The problem of beauty poses the question how a beautiful appearance and a beautiful soul can both deserve this designation.

The point is that this complexity of needs makes the meaning of human fulfillment or wholeness a problem. Socrates focuses on political life and its persistent conflicts to shed light on exactly this problematic character of the human whole. This purpose becomes ever more evident in what follows. For Socrates shows that in neglecting politics, this problematic character is just what the Philosopher misses. He also traces this neglect to the founder of the philosophic tradition, Thales, and shows that its cost is the lack of self-knowledge mentioned in the preceding text.

Socrates describes the incident in which Thales, gazing aloft, fell into a well. His fall prompts a witty Thracian slave-girl to say that "he was eager to know

[6] His goal here is not, then, to demonstrate that one particular definition of any one of these has a natural rather than a merely conventional warrant. It is the case that inferences about the criteria for a more just regime are possible on the basis of Socrates' argument. But these are not presently his focus nor, more importantly, does he initiate philosophical inquiry into political life with the primary aim of providing such guidance.

the things in the heavens but couldn't notice what was in front of him right at his feet (174a6–8)."[7] This comment, according to Socrates, is applicable to "all those who spend their lives in philosophy (174a4–b1)." However, Socrates maintains that the Philosopher appears laughable not only in public, as he had previously stated, but also "in private" whenever he must speak about the particulars "in a courtroom *or anyplace else* (174c1–2, emphasis added)." The Philosopher's thought explores "in every way the nature of each and every one of the beings as a whole (173e6–174a1)." In "not lowering itself at all to any of the things nearby," however, the Philosopher's thought appears laughable to Socrates and to everyone else (174a1–2).[8]

Among the particulars, "the things nearby," that the Philosopher finds difficult to discuss are his neighbors. "For in his very being, such a person is unaware of his next-door neighbor, not only unaware of what he's doing but little short of unaware of whether he's a human being or some different nursling; but what a human being is, and what's appropriate for such a nature, as distinct from the rest, to do or have done to it, he inquires into and keeps up his efforts to investigate (174b1–6)."

The Philosopher bypasses his neighbor, the individual human, and attends instead to human nature as a whole. Yet it is just this procedure that precludes him from accurately grasping the human whole in all its complexity. In particular, he fails to see what Socrates' attention to political life reveals: the perplexing diversity of human needs and the vast range of human possibilities that this diversity produces.

The lack of self-knowledge, manifest by his own words, makes this failure evident. For example, he finds trivial the possession of a great deal of land, "accustomed as he is to look at the entire earth (174e4–5)." Yet although the Philosopher's mind may conceive of the entire earth, he, like all other humans, must occupy one small portion of this earth and derive from it his sustenance. Furthermore, when he hears praise of wealthy ancestry, "he's convinced the praise is from those whose sight is altogether dim and limited, who are incapable, by lack of education, of looking over all eternity (174e7–175a1)." But although he can reflect on eternity, he too is generated, born into a family on which he was dependent for, among other things, his education.

The Philosopher's neglect of human diversity is particularly on display when he does briefly address political life. Politics, for him, certainly does not involve the give and take among citizens necessary for the rule of law. Akin to the view found in the *Statesman*, he regards rule as a form of herding.[9] The Philosopher banishes the ruled from humankind altogether. Humans are "different

[7] This reliance on a slave-girl's judgment is itself a powerful suggestion of Socrates' ability to see the conventional as such.

[8] I follow Rue in thinking that *ta engus* means the "particulars" and "the things nearby." "The Philosopher in Flight," 80.

[9] See *Statesman* 295e4–296a2.

nursling[s]" (174b3). Yet, in the course of speaking in this way, Socrates has the Philosopher call the one ruled "a more conspiratorial animal (174d6–7)." But to conspire is to speak, to plan, to deliberate – the province of humans alone (174e4–5, 175a1). Such beings are properly ruled not by herding but by law (*nomos*) that, as an amalgam of reason and coercion, responds to both those aspects of our being expressed in the phrase "conspiratorial animals" (174d4, d7, e1).[10]

This understanding of humanity, reflected in the rule of law, is also evident, if unwittingly, in the Philosopher's very ridicule of the politicians. This ridicule best reveals the impact of his ignorance of "the political things" on his self-understanding.[11] The Philosopher's ridicule would be ridiculous if those he criticized were not fellow humans. Seldom do we ridicule herd animals for their inability to follow abstract arguments. However, this ridicule also tacitly acknowledges the perception of deep distinctions between different ways of life. The Philosopher believes he recognizes in the politician, and vice versa, the existence of a significantly different conception of the human good. Thus, the ridicule is comprehensive, touching on every aspect of life. But the mutual ridicule between the adherents of the two ways of life also shows that the followers of both want to be assured that they have chosen the right way, that their way of life will secure the good. The inability of both the Philosophers and the politicians to let an alternative way of life go unremarked, regarding it instead as an object of ridicule or a threat, expresses exactly this need for reassurance. It expresses a deep sense of uncertainty about what that good is that fulfills our humanity. Yet this is just where the Philosopher's self-understanding is deficient. He does not adequately appreciate that his own ridicule implies the questionability of the good. His obsession with the wholes has obscured the source of this question – namely, the problematic character of the human whole.

Admittedly, given the vast range of human potential, our capacity to be in so many diverse and conflicting ways, everyone finds difficulty in considering what human fulfillment or maturity should mean for oneself as an individual. So great is this range that to predict accurately an individual's future can be regarded as a wondrous bit of prophecy (142c4–5). Moreover, in the Prologue, Plato puts this perplexity of human wholeness before the reader in a variety of ways: by the remarkable device of providing a "snapshot" of the mature Theaetetus prior to recounting the story of the young Theaetetus; by having Euclides and Terpsion hold both Theaetetus and Socrates up as models, even though the one dies for the city that executes the other; and by having Euclides

[10] We are reminded of this connection by a frequent use of words in this context that have the *nom*-stem.

[11] The terms he uses are similar to those used to describe Socrates in Aristophanes' *Clouds*. On the echoes of the *Clouds* in this passage, see Howland, *The Paradox of Political Philosophy*, 59–62.

refer to Theaetetus as "beautiful and good," a phrase that evokes the vexed issue of the unity of human excellence (142b7). Nevertheless, the Socratic philosopher can least of all afford to neglect the problematic human whole, for it is also the initial cause of that wonder which Socrates designates as the beginning of philosophy (155d2–5).

The name that Socrates gives to this problematic human whole is *soul*. In the Digression, soul refers to a living, growing thing capable of a variety of levels of development as dictated by one's education and way of life.[12] As I mentioned in the preceding text, the image is of the growth of a tree that through improper care can be deprived of "growth" and "straightness" to become "bent and stunted (173a3–4, b1)." What Socrates means by soul in this context is perhaps best understood as the assemblage of potentials, more and less fulfilled, that must find their realization in body. Socrates makes clear that because soul does involve this kind of realization we are capable of a vast array of possibilities. We certainly do not automatically achieve our full humanity. Midwifery is required.

In seeing the need for philosophic inquiry into political life, Socrates directly contravenes his predecessors' orientation. For, unlike Socrates, who certainly knows the way to the marketplace and the ancestry of his fellow citizens, the Philosopher dismisses the political things as "small and nothing (144c5–8, 173e4)." It is appropriate that the discussion of the Philosopher's neglect of politics replaces an account of his soul. For in neglecting politics, in thinking that "his body alone is situated in the city," while his "thought" explores "everywhere every nature of each whole," the Philosopher neglects the soul (173e2–174a2). He thereby reveals something of his own soul, specifically, his reluctance to encounter that which resists the certainty of quantification much as do the innumerable "proverbial drafts of water in the sea (173d8–9)."[13] He focuses instead on the "things in heaven," the wholes that he can believe are permanent and unchanging, that are uniformly what they are without complexity. Turning his attention aloft, he misses the point revealed by Socrates' own examination of politics: that our wholeness, the character of our fulfillment is a question and so then must be our good. As we see in what follows, it is this understanding of humanity, revealed by reflection on political life, that makes particularly doubtful that advantage, as previously understood, can be the ultimate human good.

The Imperishability of Evils (176a2–8)

When, earlier in the dialogue, Socrates shifted the discussion to the problem of knowledge it may have seemed that he acceded to Theaetetus' desire to avert his eyes from the perplexity surrounding the question of the goodness

[12] The first use of *soul* in the passage at 172e7 refers to an individual's life.

[13] On this phrase, see Benardete, *Being of the Beautiful*, I. 87n46.

of his soul (145b1–9). Yet because this question asks the extent to which a particular individual fulfills his or her humanity, it is formally analogous to the problem of knowledge. Both concern the connection between the parts and the wholes. Both the Philosophers and the Protagoreans wish to deny any tension between the parts and the whole, with the former wanting to see only abstract wholes and the latter only elements or particulars rather than parts, only discrete instances of perception. The dialogue provides evidence that belies both views. The dubious character of the Protagorean claim is evident in its inevitable generation of self-contradiction. But, as we have just seen, the aspiration of the Philosopher to concern himself only with wholes is just as dubious leading as it does to species-confusion or error regarding his own neighbor. It is with respect to this question of wholes as applied to the good that Socrates provides the deepest insight concerning our nature and our good.

He makes the key point in response to Theodorus who, much taken with Socrates' account of the Philosopher, expresses the hope that if all could be persuaded by it "there would be more peace and fewer evils among human beings (176a4)." For Theodorus, the opposite of evil is peace. Such peace prevails when all agree with him. He longs for a world in which all differences are absorbed into generalities, in which the rational necessity of mathematics compels the assent of all. In the resulting peace, none would contest him. Responding to Theodorus' vision, Socrates expresses one of the most far-reaching statements in the Platonic corpus about the nature of humanity and the world we inhabit: "But it's not possible for the evils to perish, Theodorus, since it's *necessary* that there always be something contrary to what's good, nor is it possible for evils to be established among the gods, but of *necessity* they haunt *mortal* nature and this region here (176a5–8, emphasis added)." This statement provides the animating thought of the dialogue as a whole. Appropriately located at its heart, it is the place into which and out of which the diverse issues of the *Theaetetus* flow. We need to consider the statement as carefully as possible, beginning with the two announced necessities.

The first necessity holds that evils cannot perish because there must always be something contrary to the good. If this is the case, then the existence of that which is good in itself must be dubious. Rather, that which is good is so only in relation to something else, specifically, in relation to evil. Without evil, good does not exist. With this claim, in this central portion of the dialogue, Socrates conjoins the apparently disjointed strands of the dialogue: the "epistemological" and the political-ethical. For he makes clear that the abstract question of wholes, of the wholeness of wholes, which engenders the problem of knowledge, is most salient with respect to our good.

The desire to see only wholes, wholes of perfect uniformity, evident in the mathematicians and the Philosopher, derives from the desire to accept only an unadulterated good, a good that is so in its parts and as a whole. It is ultimately the love of one's own that fuels this desire. We cannot be perfectly assured regarding the things we care about most deeply unless we have pure knowledge of the pure good. This motive is strong in the young orphan's soul. The link between this motive and the notion of knowledge now under examination explains what would otherwise be baffling – namely, how Socrates' elaboration of Theaetetus' thesis, devoted to the eradication of the relational character of being, can at the same time be an examination of Theaetetus' particular soul. Perhaps the dubious implications of this eradication might spur in Theaetetus or subsequent readers the need to entertain the possibility of the necessarily impure character of good. Especially for those devoted to the pursuit of knowledge, what provokes the belief in the purity of the object appears as *the* obstacle to inquiry. Socrates drives home the importance of this obstacle by locating it in its most disturbing form in the center of the dialogue. He shows that the path to its overcoming depends ultimately on individual effort by labeling that central passage a digression – easily dismissible by those who find its presence out of place.

The one who would face this obstacle, however, might well ask: why should we accept the relational character of good as true? Why must good only exist in relation to evil? The second necessity helps answer this question in defining what is meant by evil. Evils are said to be a necessary aspect of *mortal* nature. They are thus linked to our finitude, to our lack of that perfect self-sufficiency assigned to the immortal gods. For this reason, evils are said to haunt "this region here" rather than the home of the gods (176a7–8). Death exemplifies this lack, but it is simply the most prominent example of the general condition of deficiency or neediness that characterizes us insofar as we are mortal. Socrates' association of evils with mortality therefore also connects evils with this neediness.

To understand fully the imperishability of evils, however, the character of this neediness requires further specification. All living things are mortal and thus needy. Yet, in associating the notions of good and evil with this neediness, Socrates and his interlocutors have in mind specifically human neediness. Theodorus' hopes pertain to the evils "among human beings"; Socrates' response provides advice relevant only to us (176a4, 176a8–b2).[14]

Although all living things are mortal, the character of specifically human neediness is perhaps most evident with respect to mortality. What distinguishes human mortality is that it includes not only the brute fact of our demise but also awareness of that fact. Plato frames the saga of Socrates' trial and execution with this awareness, beginning with the dying Theaetetus being carried homeward and culminating with Socrates' discussion of immortality on his own deathday (142a6–b1). This most dramatic example of our neediness provides further insight into what Socrates means by evils. For humans, evils are not only the needs but also our awareness of these needs. Evil is a condition

[14] Perhaps this is why Cornford and McDowell translate the phrase, *thnata phusin* as "our mortal nature." Cornford, Plato's Theory of Knowledge, 87; McDowell, *Plato "Theaetetus,"* 53. Levett (in Burnyeat, *The "Theaetetus" of Plato*, 304) translates it as "human life."

known as such, a condition that, therefore, can be conceived to be otherwise. Accordingly, we can also conceive that it might be remedied or at least ameliorated. What remedies or ameliorates this condition, this evil, we call good. In sum, evil is neediness of which we are aware, and good is that which we judge might answer to this condition of neediness. Insofar as evil is the condition to which good is the remedy, what is good is so only in relation to evil. There is not the good in itself. For this reason, Socrates maintains that where there is good there must also be evil.

Socrates' far-reaching statement might well puncture the hopes of his interlocutors for the pure good. But they, and we, might still ask why, to use Socrates' language of necessity, must evils be imperishable? Why is the existence of evil inherent in the nature of things? Could it not be possible for neediness to be fully satisfied and thus evil eliminated?

The most obvious answer to the foregoing question is that our most basic neediness, our mortality, is an unovercomeable fact. Yet this answer is not altogether satisfying especially in light of later philosophers' reaction to this fact. In the face of mortality such philosophers as Descartes urged that we devote our intellectual resources to ameliorating, if not eradicating, this condition, in order to prolong life as far as possible with no prejudgment of any necessary limits on such efforts.[15] They publicly called for the reorientation of the goal of philosophy from fruitless contemplation to the development of effective responses to this most basic condition of neediness. Moreover, if my account of Socrates' treatment of *techne* is accurate then Socrates knew at least of *techne*'s aspiration, and of that love of one's own that fuels this aspiration. With this in mind, it is not clear that the evil of our mortality alone justifies Socrates' conclusion regarding evil's necessary imperishability.

I want to suggest another possibility. Although it may be that good consists in the satisfaction of neediness, it may also be that it is not possible to satisfy all needs simultaneously, at least, that is, if we are to be human. We have already seen the considerations that lead to this conclusion. They derive from those heterogeneous needs that dictate the character of political life. Precisely because we are capable of being aware of our neediness, precisely because therefore the very notion of good can become an issue for us, we necessarily have permanently conflicting and irreconcilable needs. Even if we could go very far in satisfying our corporeal needs, it is not clear that these efforts would provide the comprehensive satisfaction that is happiness. Such efforts can inhibit, or even preclude altogether, the satisfaction of psychic needs. Socrates' preceding description of political life indicates that the psychic capacities that enable such awareness generate needs whose requirements are not perfectly compatible with corporeal needs.

This description resides in a transcript edited while the philosopher awaited execution for pursuing the satisfaction of his psychic needs. The drama of

[15] Descartes, *Discourse on Method*, 47.

Socrates' trial and execution is the most poignant reminder of exactly this conflict, of the notion that exactly insofar as we are capable of asking the question of good, our nature is such that all our needs cannot be perfectly satisfied. Plato rightly makes this trial the centerpiece of his work because it is most revelatory of this nature.

Socrates' use of the language of necessity is appropriate then because inherent in the capacity that defines us, the capacity to ask of the good, is the existence of ineradicable need or imperishable evils. It is, finally, this existence of need, of evil, and thus of good, that distinguishes the human region from the divine (176a6–7). Where there are humans there will be evil and also good.

Given that the specific character of political life in general, and Socrates' trial in particular, elucidate the irreconcilable character of human needs, it is appropriate that Socrates makes the claim about the imperishability of evils in response to Theodorus' desire for freedom from political life. Socrates, Theodorus hopes, might "persuade everyone" to go beyond "'What injustice am I doing to you or you to me?' and to an examination of justice and injustice themselves (175c1–3)." Peace would be more widespread if Theodorus' desire to comprehend all particulars within wholes resulted in a transcendence of all individual claims by justice itself (176a4). In Theodorus' dream, reason would have the power to answer all needs and thus bring about the perfect harmony of all individual goods in one common good. Theodorus' dream of freedom from politics connects with his extravagant hopes for the power of reason or speech; he believes his words could be effective even in Sparta (162b4–7). These hopes reflect that desire for mastery promised by sophistry with its ability to manipulate words and images to attain its ends.

Yet political life, with its characteristic institutions of law and the courts, persists. Its very existence testifies to the imperfect resolution of these particular goods, with respect to one another and to the common good. Reason, it seems, is incapable of overcoming fully that self-concern rooted in our individuated existence that is, after all, the source of Theodorus' dream (170e1–3).

No one could be more fully aware of these limits than Socrates whose lifelong pursuit of *phronesis* will soon result in his execution. Such awareness stands in stark contrast to the Philosopher who, sharing Theodorus' dreams of freedom, longs to be more than human (172c8–d2). However, the fulfillment of these dreams of freedom – from politics, from ambiguous words, from the body, from necessity in general – so reminiscent of the Enlightenment hopes that persist in our own time, proves elusive. These dreams founder on the necessities that Socrates has adduced: the imperishability of evils, the ineradicable neediness attendant on our mortal and complex nature. Socrates adduces these necessities through his philosophic inquiry into politics. And through such inquiry he not only examines the good of his own activity but also finds a monitory guide for inquiry as a whole.

But how then do these necessities bear on the central question of the Digression, the question of our good? That which is good, we have learned, is so in relationship to some need. There is no good in itself. Rather, by "good" we should mean "good for" someone, good for that person whose need is satisfied. Good is advantage in this sense. However, the question then becomes, how should we conceive of advantage? Especially if our needs, and thus their satisfaction, are irredeemably heterogeneous, we must assess which of them deserves priority, in what circumstances, and to what degree.

Precisely the dubiousness of Theodorus' dreams suggests that the good for us cannot be advantage as understood by Theodorus, Theaetetus, and Protagoras. It cannot be that notion of advantage, animated by love of one's own, which is oriented on mastery, or providing security for all that one cares deeply about. It cannot because this notion of advantage is oriented exactly on achieving complete freedom from need. This is not to say that everyone who strives for advantage so understood has this end in mind. But it is to maintain that this end shapes the trajectory of such striving. It is also to maintain, more importantly, that if our humanity is inseparable from both good and evil, if this tension defines our nature, it is to strive for that which denies our humanity. To live in the hope of flying must necessarily distort the kind of being we are.

Here is the central point. Given the connection we have established between the good, on the one hand, and knowledge, on the other, if advantage so understood cannot rightly be regarded as the ultimate human good, then the knowledge we seek in pursuit of our good cannot be oriented solely on the certainty that would supply this advantage. This is not to say that such knowledge cannot be *a* good. Whenever "in the greatest dangers . . . in distress in military campaigns or diseases or at sea," people seek rulers and teachers who "are no different from themselves by any other thing than by knowing (170b1)." There can be no doubt that the knowledge that answers to our urgent needs – to know with certainty, for example, which of the many objects in the world might heal or protect us – is good.[16] However, such knowledge cannot be the ultimate goal of inquiry precisely because Socrates has maintained that evils are imperishable, that, insofar as we can ask the question of our good, not all needs can be fully answered. The knowledge that might stand as the ultimate goal of inquiry would have to acknowledge this truth. It would, in particular, have to acknowledge this persistently needy condition and the complex nature that underlies this neediness.

In this light, it is at least as important that we seek the knowledge that helps discern which of the many conflicting goods we ought to pursue. The knowledge sought should be that *phronesis* in which Socrates doubts we are self-sufficient (169d5). Such knowledge could not be oriented on the "wholes" alone because if evils are ineradicable for all, then matters that reflect this condition, matters thought dismissible by the Philosopher, have crucial importance. The Philosopher, too, pursues his own good and insofar as that good is the good of an embodied being, he cannot afford to focus only on unchanging

[16] *Apology* 22c9–d4.

intelligibles. He would have to study those evils of which Socrates says the Philosopher is ignorant (174c7–8). He would have to consider as well "things at his feet and things before his eyes," which would include the political things – justice, beauty, piety – dismissed by Socrates' predecessors (174c2–3). These too define the ground on which he stands. No object of inquiry, practical or theoretical, could be precluded beforehand as unworthy of investigation. In particular, only such a being would appreciate the need to understand the *problem* of knowledge as it is examined in the *Theaetetus*, the problem of relating wholes and parts. Such a being would, in sum, seek the knowledge of all things.[17]

Taking his bearings from the criterion of certainty about the whole, the Philosopher shares with the political community the same view of good: to have the good in perpetuity, to disregard his mortality, to be free of necessity as he "takes flight . . . 'above the heavens' (173e5–6)." He gazes at the stars instead of reflecting on himself and his neighbor, instead, that is, of considering political life. The Thalesian Philosopher thereby misses the problematic wholeness of humanity. In thus failing to take politics seriously, Socrates' predecessors avoided confronting the necessarily questionable meaning of good.

Because of their failure to reflect fully on the good, they are left unable to defend the good of their own way of life, even to themselves. For this reason, Socrates ends his comparison of the two ways of life saying that what distinguishes the Philosopher from the politicians is merely that he knows "how to throw his cloak over his right shoulder like a free man (175e7)." The distinction between these ways of life becomes wholly conventional. Failing to consider the realm of opinion, the Philosopher remains mired in it. Yet on this basis there is no possibility of a reasoned defense of the life of reason. This one, Socrates tells Theodorus, "nurtured in his very being in freedom and leisure, [is] the one whom *you* call a philosopher (175e1–2, emphasis added)." In what immediately follows, Socrates paints a very different picture of the one he would call a philosopher.

Socratic Philosophy (176a8–177b7)

At this point, there occurs the long-awaited confrontation with the general of the army of fluxists rather than with his lieutenants. Because of the primacy of the question of the good, the articulation of Socratic philosophy must ultimately involve a confrontation with the poet, Homer, rather than with the philosophical flux theorists. It is Homer who provides the Greeks with their paradigmatic portrayal of the good life, in part through his depiction of the Olympian gods.[18] Accordingly, the initial focus of Socrates' formulation concerns the philosopher's relationship with divinity.

[17] My discussion of "evils" and their bearing on philosophy is indebted to David Bolotin, *Plato's Dialogue on Friendship* (Ithaca, NY: Cornell University Press, 1989), 172–3.

[18] See Herodotus *Histories* II. 53.

Socrates begins specifically with the advice that the philosopher should flee our region of evils for the divine region (176a8–b1). Given Socrates' earlier statement regarding the relationship of evils and good, such a flight would also leave behind the notion of human good. It would fulfill the Philosopher's dream of being more than human.[19] Appropriately enough, Socrates states that "flight is becoming like a god (176a9–b1)." However, he adds, this significant qualification: "as far as is in one's power (176b1)." This qualification prepares us for the fact that Socrates' advice, so reflective of the Philosopher's yearnings, quickly undergoes modification. Socrates does not maintain the notion of actually going somewhere (176b1–3). Furthermore, he alters the meaning of flight. Initially, "flight" means "becoming like a god," but subsequently it is taken to mean "becoming just and holy with *phronesis*."[20] Socrates equates this latter destination with the flight from wickedness, the opposite of the pursuit of virtue (176b1–5). What began sounding distinctly otherworldly becomes ever more terrestrialized.

The qualities sought by the fugitive philosopher are, to say the least, not usually attributed to gods.[21] Each involves an awareness of human limits and dependency. Justice, singularly lacking in many of the Greek pantheon, reflects humans' dependence on one another. Holiness, the possession of which by gods would be contradictory, involves an acknowledgment of subordination to that which transcends humanity.

Finally, there is *phronesis*. This intellectual capacity replaces beauty in the trio of virtues mentioned prior to the Digression. As we have seen, Socrates refers to *phronesis* in contexts that bear directly on the special problem of knowing how one should live and thus on the problem of knowing the character of human fulfillment or wholeness. As such, it is a capacity unnecessary for an eternally self-sufficient being such as a god. It is appropriate then that in this account of his own philosophic activity *phronesis* replaces beauty,

19 On this passage, see Plotinus *Enneads* I. 2. Julia Annas states that this "unworldly strand" has its afterlife in religion. She associates its unworldliness with the definition of philosophy offered in the *Phaedo*. There it is said that philosophy is preparation for death. See Julia Annas, *Platonic Ethics, Old and New* (Ithaca, NY: Cornell University Press, 1999), 64. But this definition can be understood in a wholly this-worldly manner. The same is true of Socrates' advice in the *Theaetetus*. On this phrase in the *Phaedo*, see Ronna Burger, *The Phaedo: A Platonic Labyrinth* (New Haven, CT: Yale University Press), 6–7, 13, 121; my *Socratic Rationalism and Political Philosophy: An Interpretation of Plato's "Phaedo"* (Albany: State University of New York Press, 1993), 174–8; and Peter J. Ahrensdorf, *The Death of Socrates and the Life of Philosophy* (Albany: State University of New York Press, 1995), 199–201.

20 As Sedley notes, the phrase "with *phronesis*" suggests that even the former qualities are not virtues unless under the guidance of *phronesis*. See Sedley, *The Midwife of Platonism*, 75–6 and Campbell, *The "Theaetetus" of Plato*, 112–13. On *phronesis* in the *Theaetetus* more generally see Polansky, *Philosophy and Knowledge*, 142–8.

21 On this point see Hemmenway, "Philosophical Apology," 335; Rue, "The Philosopher in Flight," 89; and Sedley, *The Midwife of Platonism*, 84n51. The absurdity of attributing these virtues to the gods was recognized by Plotinus.

that quality which throughout the dialogue expresses the problem of human wholeness.

Socrates constructs this new version of the philosophic life in light of the necessities that have just been announced, and the Socratic philosopher is imbued with a sense of the limits these necessities impose. Just as the "god" to whom Socrates advises assimilation is not quite like any recognizable member of the Greek pantheon, neither does this portrayal of the Socratic philosopher resemble the Philosopher previously encountered in the Digression. Accordingly, this new orientation of philosophy requires a redefinition of the essential distinction between the philosopher and all others. Socrates provides such a definition through a critique of his opponents' rationale for practicing virtue and avoiding vice. This critique turns into a consideration of their view of wisdom.

Socrates holds that the many and the sophists maintain that one practices virtue and avoids vice in order to *seem* to be good (176b6).[22] Because they conceive of all goods, other than their particular notion of advantage, as merely conventional, Protagoras' followers are driven to this conclusion; any claims to the good other than such advantage must be mere seeming. However, Socrates proceeds to cast his net even wider. He attributes this view also to those that engage in "the practice of political power ... and the arts (176c6–d1)." The many, the sophists and politicians, and the practitioners of the arts are now included among those who share this view. What unites them is the desire for what the arts aim to provide: freedom from need. Still more significant for the present point, as long as philosophy takes its bearings by the criterion of certainty about the whole, it too must be held to share this same motive and orientation. Socrates' philosophic predecessors must therefore also find common ground with this group.

There is, however, an alternative to the preceding view of virtue. It is, specifically, the *recognition* that trying to become as just as possible is true virtue. *Ignorance* of this view is vice (176c5). Because virtue, for Socrates, is therefore a cognitive matter, he identifies virtue with wisdom (176c4–5, 176b3–7). And he distinguishes this wisdom from what he calls "vulgar" and "common" wisdom (176c7, 176d1). He elaborates on this latter non-Socratic view of wisdom with a pointed description of one of its adherents' self-understanding. This one thinks himself "clever in his criminal willingness to stop at nothing for they glory in the reproach and believe they're hearing that they're not lightweights, *useless burdens on the earth*, but men of the sort one needs to be to stay safe in a city (176d2–5, emphasis added)."

Achilles utters the emphasized phrase in grief over the death of his friend, Patroclus.[23] Socrates' allusion to Homer's *Iliad* leads to the heart of the distinction between the two views of wisdom. His gloss on the allusion suggests

[22] See *Protagoras* 323b5–7.

[23] Homer *Iliad* xviii. 104; see also *Odyssey* xx. 379.

Achilles' view is oriented on the axis, death-safety. As such, it is oriented in particular on the provision and security of one's own – one's own friends, family, and life – the ruling conception of advantage. Believing that this is the good, those who hold this view conclude that wisdom, and human excellence in general, consists in directing all of our power toward securing this end. As we have seen, wisdom thus becomes identified with cleverness, the capacity to calculate the most efficacious means to this predetermined end of advantage so understood.

This identification follows from the example of Homer's heroes, Achilles and Odysseus, through which he portrays death as the greatest threat to human good, as the greatest evil.[24] This Homeric conception spurs us to overcome those limits on our mortality, "to stop at nothing," in the hope that evils are not imperishable, that we might possess the perfectly good forever (177a8). Following the Homeric hero's example, these efforts should be aimed at the acquisition of that power and mastery, as signified by glory, which will grant us our heart's every desire, including above all our own perpetuation.[25]

But as was the case for Achilles, and is so for each one of us, these efforts must ultimately fail. From this thwarted hope one might conclude that the world is a scene of instability, of senseless and ceaseless change, wholly inhospitable to human good. This nearly intolerable conclusion conduces to a belief in beings greater than ourselves, beings such as the Olympian gods, that care for us, reward and punish, altering what might otherwise be considered as unchangeable necessities. Plato portrays this psychology in Theaetetus' instantaneous willingness to jettison the flux doctrine, with which he had identified himself, when hearing of its negative impact on the authority of the gods (162c7–d2). However, underlying both his acceptance and rejection of this thesis is that single concern for his own. This common concern explains the otherwise paradoxical claim that Homer can be not only the authoritative source regarding the gods but also, as Socrates deems him, the general of the army of fluxists. The poet articulates the view of good that underlies both.

To oppose this view is to strike at the very heart of the accepted notion of piety.[26] Yet Socrates does just that by rejecting the claim that the reward for living virtuously is some sanction apart from this life. Of those who do believe this claim, Socrates states, "they're ignorant of the penalty for injustice that they ought least to ignore. It's not what it seems to them to be, beatings

24 Homer *Odyssey* xi. 489–91. This phrase is expunged in Socrates' purification of poetry in *Republic* 386c3–7. On this view of the Homeric hero see Jean-Pierre Vernant, "Death with Two Faces," in *Reading the "Odyssey": Selected Interpretive Essays*, ed. Seth L. Schein (Princeton, NJ: Princeton University Press, 1996), 58.

25 See ibid. 61.

26 In the dramatically subsequent *Euthyphro*, Socrates discusses piety with Euthyphro. The version of piety with which Socrates leaves Euthyphro is not as serviceable as was his initial view to the purpose of invoking the gods' aid for the satisfaction of our individual passions. See *Euthyphro* 11e2–16a3.

and executions, which people who do no injustice sometimes suffer (176d7–e1)." Those who are concerned, above all, with their own, those for whom safety is preeminent, might well think that beatings and executions are the true punishments for the evil life. Yet this is to ignore what Socrates makes explicit: that it is often the just that are punished. It is the unwillingness to accept this fact that moves people to fill the world with gods that can provide the sort of order that the world evidently does not. Socrates resists the nearly irresistible desire to subscribe to this belief. Steeling his resistance, and underlying his civic impiety, stands his view that the city's gods reflect the Homeric conception of the human good that he considers dubious.[27]

Piety does remain a virtue for Socrates. There still is that to which he looks up. Yet, for him, the object of piety is the paradigm of the "divine as most happy" life (176e4). The ultimate reward for living according to this paradigm, as opposed to the paradigm of the "godless as most miserable" life, is not, however, some extraneous sanction (176e4). As was said of the orator's soul, each becomes more like these contrary "paradigms" through his own actions (176e3). The reward is the life that is lived (176e3–4).

The ultimate penalty, too, is "this worldly." It is, in particular, to live life without seeing the true end, without seeing how things truly are. Socrates insists that the miserable life is followed not out of some evil inclination but from a failure to see clearly the alternatives. Those who follow the godless and miserable paradigm do so by "folly and utter senselessness" and act "unaware" (176e4–177a1).[28] Its adherents are those clever men who are self-deceived. Socrates refers here, I think, to the "all-wise," those who are "the sort of people they think they're not, all the more so because they think they're not (176d5–6)." These clever students of Homer, including not only the sophists but also Socrates' philosophic predecessors, cannot help but be self-deceived. The belief that the goal is advantage as outlined in the preceding text must involve self-deception insofar as it defies the necessities that define our existence.

Socrates' criticism of the clever implies that what is truly good is, instead, the avoidance of self-deception. It is clarity. The reward in this light is to see our situation clearly, to see and accept that we do not inhabit a world that answers to all needs. The virtues of this life – justice, holiness, and *phronesis* – are those that reflect our limits: our dependence on others and on that which transcends us, and above all our persistent need for guidance regarding how to live our lives.

But why believe that this is our ultimate need, that the good lies in seeing how things truly are, especially when so few desire this end? Why think that

[27] An alternative view of Socrates' heterodoxy can be found in Sedley, *The Midwife of Platonism*, 85.

[28] For a reading that sees in these paradigms reference to the Forms, see Sedley, *The Midwife of Platonism*, 78, 78n39.

by nature humans would rather live according to the way things really are, especially when so few do live in pursuit of clarity? Socrates suggests an answer when he maintains that following the wrong way is a matter of error rather than evil, that all do really desire the same thing but just do not see clearly enough. The Digression supports this claim precisely in its portrayal of the ridicule to which the conflict between the two ways of life leads.

As I have maintained, this mutual ridicule shows that both desire reassurance concerning the goodness of their way of life, moved by the sense, more or less tacit, that they are not fully sure of the true human good. In speaking of the orators at the end of the Digression, Socrates points to one symptom of this desire: the self-dissatisfaction they experience when they cannot "give an account (*logos*) and get one back about the things they object to (177b1–7)." The desire for assurance is evident not only in the orators. It is also manifest in the reluctance of those who, like Theodorus and Theaetetus, avoid giving "an account (*logos*)" because they fear an outcome similar to that of the orator. It is present as well in the widespread adherence to beliefs, such as those provided by Homer, that offer such assurance at the cost of obscuring a clear view of our own nature. And, finally, it is exhibited in the Philosopher's contemptuous dismissal of political life (169a7). Each of these is a reaction to doubt, and a concomitant desire for reassurance, that one's good is truly good. Each of these deeds reflects the fact that running alongside the powerful desire to secure the good so conceived is the desire to be assured that it is truly good. It expresses the human desire to be right about our most significant concerns.

Through his conversation with Theaetetus and Theodorus, Socrates perceives that these powerful desires can drive even these extremely intelligent interlocutors to adopt self-contradictory views. Yet, most importantly, such maieutic conversations throughout the Platonic corpus provide Socrates with some assurance that his desire to *know* what is truly good is not idiosyncratic. Whether in the intricate, but often indefensible, beliefs devised by his interlocutors to substantiate their view of good, or in their indignant rejection of Socrates' probing, he sees evidence of profound concern to know the good as such. Socrates' "terrible love" of speeches can benefit the young Theaetetus in pointing toward this surer, if more arduous, path to the good (169c1). But his conversations also benefit himself, in making possible a reasoned defense of his chosen way of life. On the basis of the universal desire for that which is truly good, and on the basis of the equally universal sense, more or less tacit, that certainty regarding the good eludes us, Socrates can legitimately claim that his way of life at least brings him closer to what humans by nature want.

Socrates' self-dissatisfaction or, stated positively, his "terrible love of speeches" drove him to confront the question his predecessors had left unanswered: whether the philosophic life is good. Failing or neglecting to subject this question to rational scrutiny, these philosophers left the entire philosophic endeavor unfounded. In this, they were the most self-deceived in pursuing the life of reason without directing their inquiries to themselves.

Responding to this defect, Socrates undertook the philosophic scrutiny of political life because it provides the window through which he could best view the complexity of the soul and thus understand our nature and our good. Socrates' achievement, exhibited in the Digression, ensures that the distinction between his way of life and that of others is not simply conventional. On the basis of Socrates' discovery, a reasoned assessment of ways of life becomes possible. Socrates initiates political philosophy to substantiate the good of his own way of life.

7

The Assessment: Part II

Introduction

Socrates' continued assessment of Theaetetus' offspring subsequent to the Digression brings to bear the lessons learned in that crucial passage. As reflected in the order of topics and the treatment of each topic, Socrates begins his inquiry with facts about political life. He does deal once again with the three-legged thesis, generated with his guidance, but not in the order originally presented. Rather, he takes up once more the treatment of Protagoras that immediately preceded the Digression. Only subsequently does he turn to the Heracleiteans' notion of being and finally to Theaetetus' original definition.

In his continued treatment of Protagoras' thought Socrates connects an examination of political life, and especially the rule of law, to those limits of our knowing that follow from the elusiveness of the human good. The one who appreciates these limits, and their source, emerges as the true measure. Socrates, "the nonknower," replaces the "wise" possessor of a *techne* with the seeker of *phronesis*, the one who acknowledges the need to seek the good.

Socrates' examination of law explicitly postpones the previously announced need to consider being. By this deed, he shows that political life provides a less distorting access to our nature and nature as a whole than the direct confrontation with being. That direct confrontation might well obscure what being must be insofar as law is possible and necessary. When Socrates does turn to being, he notes this danger by characterizing the proponents of competing views of being in frankly political terms. The advocates of rest and of motion, the fluxists and the stabilists, appear as political partisans, perhaps an inevitable outcome for those theorists who neglect the Socratic path that travels through political life to being.

Socrates' treatment of being considers, then, not only the Heracleiteans but also the Parmenideans. He orients himself on the question of being by locating himself between Heracleitus and Parmenides, his two eminent and opposing philosophic predecessors. Socrates aligns himself instead with the common sense of the shoemaker who believes that motion and rest must *somehow* both characterize being. The prerequisites of knowing, grasped through reflection on the shoemaker's, or anybody's, cognitive experiences, dictate Socrates' position on being. His response to the Heracleiteans involves a reconsideration of the possibility of everyday speech in the face of the radical flux advocated by that doctrine. Persisting with his *ad hominem* approach, Socrates questions how on the basis of radical flux there can be Heracleiteans, that is, how their doctrine accounts for the establishment and maintenance of the shared understanding required for this or any other philosophical school. Such an understanding would seem to have determinativeness or rest as a prerequisite.

Yet Socrates' allegiance with the shoemaker requires him also to distinguish himself from the venerable Parmenides. This he does, if less conspicuously, in the final stage of the assessment where he returns to Theaetetus' original definition. It is the recognition of the distinctive power of soul that finally disposes of the definition. Along with this recognition, however, Socrates makes clear that the exercise of this power, the power of "gathering up" the perceptions that makes possible speech or reason, cannot be understood wholly divorced from motion.

The Digression thus shapes the final stage in Socrates' assessment of Theaetetus' original definition. It directs us to the ground on which Socrates examines and rejects each leg of the three-legged thesis. Beginning with an examination of political life, it proceeds through a consideration of speech and, finally, to the soul, the power of which was neglected by his predecessors. But through this final assessment Socrates provides something more than refutation. He also adds illuminating details to his self-portrait. He comes into focus more clearly as the "nonknower," the colleague of the shoemaker, and, above all, the psychologist investigating the soul.

Linking these themes is the soul's power of reflection, which makes possible law and speech. Both depend on that power by which we lift ourselves from the flow of particulars. Still, contrary to the pretensions of the Philosopher, that ascent remains incomplete. Accordingly, Socrates' assessment culminates in the discovery of the realm of opinion. Far from any dogmatic assertion of reason's comprehensive power, the subsequent treatment of knowledge examines the perplexities left by this partial loosening of our bonds, the perplexities created by the distinctive power of reflection.

Socrates as "Nonknower" (177b7–179d1)

Socrates designates the previous discussion as a digression or "side-issue" and asks Theodorus to return to their earlier discussion "if that seems good to you (177b8, 177c2)." The quoted phrase can also be translated, "if it is so resolved," the phrase used in passing laws in the assembly. Socrates undertakes to legislate for their little community. After reiterating his preference for long speeches, and appealing once again to his age, Theodorus agrees, saying, "if it seems good, let's go back (177c4–5)." Theodorus subordinates his good to that of the community. He thereby makes possible the common good of philosophic conversation. Theodorus acts justly.

Yet the agreement proves to be only temporary, lasting no more than a few pages. The goods of Theodorus and of Socrates soon diverge. This little legislative drama occurs, appropriately, in a passage whose theme is the necessarily imperfect attempt of law to establish the good for a community. Beginning with this discussion of the distinction between common and individual good, Socrates suggests that law's unavoidable inadequacy has to do with those same considerations that make the agreement between Socrates and Theodorus only temporary. The forthcoming argument elucidates those considerations.

The political beginning makes a further point, one that bears repeating. It pertains to the premise of Socrates' approach. Socrates initially states they must return to a discussion of being, specifically to the flux doctrine and thus to "the people who claim that the being that's carried along also *is* (177c7)." Yet what immediately ensues seems far from an examination of being. The aforementioned discussion of the inadequacy of law explicitly replaces this examination. Only after this discussion does Socrates return to being. This replacement shows Socrates' adherence to one of the key lessons of the Philosopher's neglect of politics in the Digression: political life provides the crucial means of access to our understanding of the world in general. It does so, at least if we hope to understand the world as free as possible from political distortion. As I have suggested, the subsequent discussion of being illustrates the consequences of the failure to inquire, in as clear-eyed a way as possible, into the conditions of our experience.

Socrates returns to the distinction between the conventional character of justice and the natural character of advantage, at issue prior to the Digression. In the course of reiterating this distinction, he makes explicit another distinction, one that expresses the problem of knowledge. Socrates acknowledges that one could *call* something that's disadvantageous its opposite. One could "just give it that name (177d5–6)." But, he insists, "it's not the name that one needs to talk about, but the thing named that one needs to look into (177e1–2)." To do otherwise, Socrates says "would surely be a jest in light of what we're saying (177d6)." As I discussed in Chapter 3, the serious meaning of jests bears on the distinction Socrates here raises between our words and deeds, between our understanding and the particulars we aim to understand. Raising this distinction again, Socrates reminds us that it is eminently possible for us to misunderstand, to mischaracterize the way things are, whether intentionally or not. How this discrepancy is possible is the question of the foundation of the problem of knowledge. We have had reason to doubt that the discrepancy can be overcome by disregarding words and proceeding directly to the deeds or the particulars, as Socrates' language suggests we do: "whatever this is the name of... (177e4)." The problem persists.

Socrates' subsequent discussion indicates that he begins with this look at political life because the problem of knowledge is most acute, or at least most urgently felt, in our attempt to pass laws providing for our future advantage. That problem asserts itself because this attempt necessarily often fails to find exactly the right words that can capture the deeds, the appropriate principles that might provide for the multitude of particulars. Socrates examines the cause of this failure in order to get closer to the source of the problem of knowledge.

Socrates begins by calling attention to the fact of the community's less than perfectly successful legal efforts. The city, he says, "aims" at the advantageous in its lawmaking but what we aim at we do not always hit (178e4–5). Moreover, it makes all its laws not simply advantageous but "as advantageous as possible to itself (177e5–6)." It does so not out of full knowledge but only "to the extent it supposes them to be so" and "has the power" to do so (177e6, 177e5–6). Socrates paints a picture of a community striving for, but falling short of, its goal. Making the laws as advantageous "as possible" suggests there is a limit to this endeavor. That limit resides first in the clarity of the city's conception of advantage. It may "suppose" something is advantageous that is not. Nevertheless, even assuming such clarity, providing what's advantageous may be beyond its "power."

However, we need not rely solely on these suggestions of the law's frequent inadequacy. Socrates makes it explicit. He asks, "does it always hit what it aims at, or does each city also often completely miss its target? (178a2–3)." Within a page, Socrates makes an even stronger claim: "everyone would agree that it's *necessary* when making laws for a city often to fail to attain what's most advantageous (179a5–7, emphasis added)." The frequent failure of law is not only possible but also necessary. Political communities necessarily fail to attain what they all seek.

Consider the implications of this claim. Through law political communities attempt to account in a general manner for the many particulars, to find those principles, those words, to comprehend the particulars. As I noted in the preceding text, so conceived, the legislative art constitutes one of our most significant and most urgent attempts to know, to say how things are in an enduring manner. In its generality and stability, law possesses the character of what deserves to be called knowledge. But, Socrates says, law necessarily often fails to achieve its aim. It certainly cannot be for lack of effort. Nearly every community seeks through law to instantiate the understanding of itself and the world that will enable it to endure. No, these efforts must founder on some obstacle inherent in the nature of things. What substantiates this far-reaching claim? Let's consider how Socrates moves from the possibility to the necessity of frequent failure.

Socrates takes the first step toward necessity by placing the goal of law, the advantageous, in the *eidos* of the future (178a6–8). "Whenever we engage in lawmaking," it is the future with which we are concerned (178a8).[1] Lawmaking and the future also connect in a still deeper way. What enables us to have the notion of the future also enables and requires us to make laws. Through the power of reflection, we step outside the moment-to-moment flow to note patterns, to recognize that what exists now also existed in some way previously and thus is part of a pattern that will persist. The latitude gained means also, however, that our lives are formed less by determinative forces and thus require human ordering. Because we can see the need for law, we require law.

Part of this recognized pattern, part of what we recognize as persisting, is our own existence. With the awareness granted by reason we see the need to secure ourselves, our existence, and our well-being on into the future of which we are now aware. Law represents one of the most important such steps aimed at providing for our future advantage. But, again, Socrates is heading toward the conclusion that these efforts *necessarily* often meet with less than complete success.[2] What proves to be the case is that the very possibility of law's providing for the future contains within it the seeds of its own limitations. The rationale for this conclusion emerges from Socrates' juxtaposition of Protagoras' *techne* with the other arts to which he now turns.

Socrates maintains that all believe that some views of the future are superior to others. To substantiate this claim he adduces several areas of technical competence in which all would prefer the expert's view of what the future holds (178b9–179a3). This, after all, is what a *techne* claims to provide: a set of general principles that make intelligible, and therefore predictable, the particulars in some area of inquiry. With such knowledge, we can also manipulate these particulars for our good. Socrates offers a variety of examples of such *technai*. Their very possibility would seem to cut in the opposite direction of law's necessarily frequent failure. Such, however, is not so clearly the case for Protagoras' *techne* with which Socrates' overlong list of examples culminates. As a more detailed examination of this list shows, with the distinctive

[1] Many commentators have regarded the argument concerning the future as particularly strong. Sayre calls it "conclusive." Chappell deems it "the best argument Plato produces against Protagoras." The reason is nicely expressed by Burnyeat: "The very notion of the future makes us submit to objectivity. So then, does action. That is to say, life itself." Despite its strength, as Burnyeat notes, few commentators have spent much time analyzing the argument. Sayre, *Plato's Analytic Method*, 90; Chappell, *Reading Plato's "Theaetetus,"* 131; Burnyeat, *The "Theaetetus" of Plato*, 42, 246. For a brief use of the argument with reference to the later consideration of the soul in itself, see John M. Cooper, "Plato on Sense-Perception and Knowledge (*Theaetetus* 184–186)," *Phronesis* 15 (1970): 141–2. There is even less consideration of the role of law in the argument. As I indicate in the following text, although the argument may well be decisive regarding Protagoras, Socrates is at least as intent on explaining his own way of life as he is on refuting Protagoreanism. For this reason, our incapacity to know the future with perfect clarity becomes of great importance.

[2] Plato thus does more than give a "hint" about skepticism regarding knowledge of the future. Cf. Bostock, *Plato's "Theaetetus,"* 97.

character of this final example, Socrates takes another step along his path to law's necessarily frequent failure.

Socrates' examples include the doctor's knowledge of health, the grower's knowledge of wine, the musician's knowledge of music, and the gourmet cook's knowledge about the pleasures of eating. In each case, the question concerns who is the better judge of what is going to occur. In each case, the laymen can judge for themselves when actually experiencing some particular instance of illness, sweetness, disharmony, or tasty food. Yet it falls to the expert to predict the future in each of these cases because there are principles that govern the particulars, and he alone grasps these principles. The expertise that constitutes these *technai* is based on the grasp of those principles whose intelligibility provides for predictability. But it is not possible to square this predictability with Protagoreanism's denial of the existence of such enduring principles and of minds that might grasp them. With this conclusion we have again reached a point where if the refutation of Protagoreanism were Socrates' sole goal the conversation could have ended. It continues. We need to see what further, and possibly more significant, point Socrates wishes to make.

The *technai* mentioned pertain to our corporeality, to the goods of health and bodily pleasure. With respect to such *technai*, judgments of success and failure can perhaps be made with more assurance. In now introducing Protagoras' *techne*, however, Socrates introduces a distinction that takes us into the realm of opinion and opens the door to uncertainty. He asks, "About the pleasure there already is for each person, or that there already has been, let's not yet do battle with the account, but about how things will *seem* and how they're going to *be* for each person in the future, is he himself the best judge? (178d10–e3, emphasis added)." Socrates hones in further on Protagoras as he asks about "what's going to be persuasive to each of us in speeches in a courtroom? (178e4–5)." This is the crux of Protagoras' *techne*, the art of defending one's interest through speech (178e7–8). As Socrates puts it, and as Theodorus agrees, Protagoras claims that "no prophet or anyone else could judge better than he what was going to be and to seem to be so in the future (179a1–3)." It is immediately following this statement that Socrates affirms the necessity that laws aiming at advantage necessarily often fail. There must then be something specific to Socrates' discussion of Protagoras' *techne* that justifies this claim.

We can begin to understand what that might be by considering the distinction between seeming and being, twice employed by Socrates in this context. Notably, he uses it to characterize Protagoras' *techne*, and only Protagoras' *techne*. The very existence of this distinction reflects the resistance of the particulars to being captured fully by a single understanding. One index of the relative fulfillment of a *techne* is the degree to which it overcomes this distinction, the degree to which it sees beyond mere appearance to the underlying determinative principles, grasping which it can make predictions. For the more developed *technai*, general principles can be grasped under which the particulars are all but wholly subsumable. Socrates' repetition of this distinction, however, makes it an intimate and permanent aspect of Protagoras' claimed *techne*. Protagoras' art tells us not only "what was going to be" but what is going "to seem to be (179a2)." The distinction is part and parcel of his art. Given that its aim is to persuade in doubtful cases, to use words to shape perceptions of reality, its whole existence presumes the distinction between seeming and being. And its goal is not simply to replace seeming with being, appearance with reality, but to manipulate what seems.[3] The subject matter of Protagoras' art makes his *techne* peculiar in this regard. Protagoras aims to persuade jurors in the courtroom, to convince them that this particular act is or is not just. However, the distinction between seeming and being pervades the realm of justice to a degree not true of other fields of inquiry. His field involves the insuperably complex question of human good: "the just and the unjust, and noble and shameful, and good and bad."[4] Persuasion is pertinent to these issues because they are always shadowed by the distinction of seeming and being. Moreover, the objects of judgment in Protagoras' field are not matters of perception at all but hearsay and opinion, where doubt and mere likelihood are pervasive (178e2–4).

In sum, the distinction between seeming and being is inseparable from Protagoras' *techne* because it involves judgment about human good which, as is made evident in the Digression, is persistently complex. Because of this difficulty, Socrates compares Protagoras' powers of judgment to that of the prophet, "echoing" Euclides' characterization of Socrates' assessment of Theaetetus' future (179a2). It is the appropriate image when speaking about the human future. The subject matter lacks the determinacy to make it susceptible to perfectly predictive principles.

This observation lies at the heart of Socrates' claim that law necessarily often fails. Law aims precisely to establish principles of justice under which the particulars can be subsumed and so provide perfectly for the future human good. However, as the character of Protagoras' own *techne* testifies, these particulars, human souls, are not subsumable with precision and certainty under general principles.

With this argument, Socrates makes the point about the limits of law made more famously by the Eleatic Stranger in the *Statesman*.[5] The indeterminacy of human being, the vast diversity among humans, makes unattainable the kind of account of the soul that would make possible that *techne* of the soul that would yield perfectly predictive laws. And so the Eleatic Stranger maintains

3 Cf. *Protagoras* 323a5–c2.

4 *Euthyphro* 7d.

5 *Statesman* 294a10–b6. I treat this passage more fully in "The Rule of Wisdom and the Rule of Law in Plato's *Statesman*," *American Political Science Review* 91 (1997): 264–76.

that the rule of law must always be at least supplemented by the rule of wisdom.[6]

Law's inadequacy is a poignant and daily reminder of how the problem of knowledge infects our lives. For example, through the "law" establishing the community of this conversation the participants can say that they are united, but their words cannot control the future. In fact, they do prove ineffective in the face of Theodorus' inclinations that cause him to turn his back on his agreement (183c4–d5). Those complex and irreconcilable needs, explored in the Digression, generate the desire for likewise irreconcilable goods. Law, which aims to answer fully to these needs, necessarily founders on this irreconcilability. In this light, law is the most prominent expression of that partial knowledge that we call opinion. Its partiality reflects the complexity of the soul to whose needs it attempts to respond. As we now see, the soul's *techne*-eluding complexity dictates a revision of Protagoras' notion of the locus of measure.[7]

Socrates defines his philosophic inquiry in light of this limit of knowing revealed through his reflection on law and politics. Earlier he had said that in his inquiry his aim is "to get an account out of someone else who's wise and to accept it in a measured way (161b3–5, 179a10–b1)." We now begin to get a better idea of where this measure resides. He says of Protagoras,

> it's necessary for him to agree both that one person is wiser than another and that such a person is a measure, while for me, the non-knower, to become a measure is not necessary in any whatever, as the argument on his behalf was forcing me to be, whether I wanted to or not (179b1–5).

Socrates is not *compelled* to be a measure, as he and everyone else would be on Protagoras' view. But he can *choose* to be a measure. Socrates' self-designation as "the nonknower" points to the qualification for this position (179b3). Assigning this designation to himself, Socrates' nonknowing cannot be identified with ignorance. He knows himself as the nonknower. In what sense then is he a nonknower? To know himself as a nonknower he must know what he lacks. Based on the preceding analysis, he must be aware that he lacks specifically a *techne* of the human things. His embrace of the "*techne*" of maieutics is only an apparent exception that proves the rule. Socrates is aware, moreover, of the reasons for that lack. It is this awareness that qualifies him as the measure, especially of the human things.

Near the center of this awareness is the point that Socrates says Protagoras must agree to and that disqualifies Protagoras' notion of the measure: the

6 For another recognition of the natural limits on law see John Locke, "The Second Treatise of Government," in *Two Treatises of Government*, ed. Peter Laslett (Cambridge: Cambridge University Press, 1988), 371 (para. 156), 374–80 ("Of Prerogative").

7 Sedley rightly notes that Socrates' argument involves showing Protagoras to be practicing a pseudoexpertise. However, his endorsement of legislation as an unproblematic example of an "authentic expertise" indicates that his reasons for thinking Protagoras' art is questionable differ from the ones I have laid out. See Sedley, *Midwife of Platonism*, 87–8.

existence of decisive human inequality that follows from our capacity to reason.[8] As recognized by the Eleatic Stranger, this human diversity, having its source in the complexity of the human whole, makes judgment of the human things necessarily nontechnical, a matter for "the nonknower."

Echoing a formulation made in my treatment of the Digression, the point might be put this way: because we can and must "lay down the good for ourselves," that is, because we can and must make laws, no law can perfectly capture our good. The power of reflection that gives us the ability to make laws generates needs not fully compatible with those needs oriented on advantage narrowly understood. Judgment of the human things must rather be a matter of *phronesis* insofar as the human soul resists determinative understanding. It must be a matter, more specifically, of that capacity that undertakes to judge the particular acutely aware that they are only imperfectly subsumable under general principles. Such is the character of Socrates' nonknowing. It is the wisdom of the midwife.

In light of Socrates' conclusions regarding law, we can conclude that the nature of the human being cannot simply be deduced from the being of the whole. There is, instead, irreducible heterogeneity because of the presence of humanity in the whole. "Law," as he says in the *Minos*, "aims at being," but for that reason it is not to be identified with being.[9] Only with this insight in view, drawn from reflection on politics, is Socrates ready to take up the postponed consideration of being.

As he had done with Protagoras, Socrates now employs Heracleitus (and Parmenides) to fill in the details of his self-portrait. Given what he has learned in his reflection on law, any subsequent account of being as unitary, whether as universal flux or universal stability, must be suspect. We move toward being through reflection on human experience of the political.

The Shoemaker and the Partisans of Being (179d2–183c3)

Failing to consider the bearing of politics on his life, particularly the implications of its existence for the partiality of his understanding, the philosopher risks infecting his most abstract reflections with the unreflective partiality of politics. When the philosopher neglects the pretheoretical context, what results is not philosophy but ideology. Socrates depicts this danger in the scene he now describes. Referring to the Heracleitean view of being, Socrates says "a battle has come up about it, no low-level one and among no few people (179d4–5)."

Before considering that battle, we should recognize that the view of being under consideration bears not only on perception but also on opinion insofar as the latter can be distinguished from the former. On the basis of considerations

[8] I do not mean to suggest that Protagoras is an egalitarian but rather that Protagoras does not appreciate the bearing of this inequality on his own claims to expertise. See Chapter 5, n.10.

[9] *Minos* 315a2–3.

in the previous section it would seem that such a distinction is necessary. We do not perceive the future; we have an opinion about it. This greater prominence of opinion continues as Socrates introduces his treatment of the Heracleiteans by referring to "perceptions and the opinions resulting from them (179c3–4)."[10] The long-promised treatment of opinion, especially in its complex relationship with perception, actually occurs in this second phase of the midwife's assessment. It becomes ever more explicit until, in the very last stage, the possibility of opinion itself emerges as the ground on which the entire thesis is rejected.

Acutely aware of the battle over being, Theodorus responds to Socrates' mention of it with one of his longest speeches in the dialogue, second only to his account of Theaetetus' character. Like that speech, this one is especially revealing of Theodorus' character, in particular, of his monumental self-forgetfulness. For Theodorus, the battle is about what he calls "these Heracleitean things, or as *you* say, Homeric and still more ancient (179e3–5, emphasis added)." Theodorus does not quite accept Socrates' genealogical analysis of the flux view because he does not accept that it has its roots in a view of good. Failing to see these roots, neither does he appreciate the extent to which the critique he levels at the Heracleiteans also bears on himself.

In his critique, Theodorus directly connects the theoretical doctrines of these men and their characters. He says that "they are simply carried away, just like the things they write about (179e7–8)." Theodorus never finds them "standing still for an argument or for a question and calmly asking and answering in turn (179e9–180a1)." In fact, "there's not even a little bit of calmness that's to be found in these men (180a2–3)." They "allow nothing to be stable, neither in speech nor in their own souls," existing as they do "in a state of total war" against stability (180a8–b1)."

The man who so adamantly resists the give-and-take of Socratic conversation now criticizes others for their reluctance to converse. Moreover, he traces that reluctance to a view of being that, at least in Socrates' hands, is intimately linked to the view that Theodorus himself employs to avoid discussion. He fails to notice that the link he draws between theoretical doctrines and character might also apply to himself. One cannot help but admire Plato's artistry in portraying this paragon of self-forgetfulness. By having Theodorus introduce the examination of being with this speech, Plato underscores the need to approach this examination through the experience, the deeds, of those who articulate these views of being. This approach shapes the subsequent inquiry.

In response to Theodorus' complaints, Socrates stages a mild defense of the fluxists. He claims that when among themselves they are at peace, especially with respect to students "whom they want to make like themselves (180c7–8)." Theodorus won't hear of it. His anger rising, he vehemently disputes Socrates' favorable characterization. Unrelentingly, he heaps scorn on the

[10] On this distinction see Burnyeat, The "*Theaetetus*" of Plato, 42.

Heracleiteans. But Socrates' defense merits further consideration. In addition to being another example of his calm and impartial assessment of opposing views, it helps us understand his own forthcoming remarks on being.

We see in these remarks Socrates' continued use of his *ad hominem* approach as he considers not simply the fluxists' doctrines but also the deeds of the doctrines' proponents.[11] These deeds manifestly contravene their doctrines. In particular, their desire to teach carries with it certain implications that incline these fluxists willy-nilly in the direction of stability. Socrates speaks of them, as I noted, "when they're at peace" and "at leisure," when, that is, they engage with their disciples "whom they want to make like themselves (180b5, 180b6–7)." To make students "like themselves" clearly requires that the Heracleiteans possess some stable self-conception. It requires, more specifically, that they possess some determinate doctrine that they then aim to convey through speech. Even these most avid partisans of motion thus evince in their deeds the need for rest.

Socrates' comments do not mollify Theodorus. Continuing in high dudgeon, and reaching new peaks of unreflectiveness, he complains about his opponents' unwillingness to give "an account" of themselves (180c4). His anger belies his previous self-satisfied judgment that there exists only the opposition between the "chorus" of political types and "our chorus," the philosophers (173c1–2). Disagreement, and even "battle," characterizes philosophy too, a characterization Socrates details as the passage proceeds. The partiality of knowledge, even tacitly recognized as such, can generate the kind of spirited defense of one's position that makes it indistinguishable from political conflict. Partiality begets partisanship.

However, the Socratic exploration of this partiality is not for Theodorus. Rather, he wishes to retreat from this messy conflict, suggesting instead that they "investigate it like a geometrical proposition (180c5–6)." Socrates acknowledges that this is a "measured response," but he does not follow Theodorus in his retreat into geometric abstraction (180c7). Unlike Theodorus and his predecessors who, as depicted in the Digression, fly to the whole,

[11] This approach results in the kind of "comic" aspect to the passage we saw in Socrates' *ad hominem* approach to Protagoras. For this reason, McDowell regards the passage as the "less serious" part of the argument, and Bostock sees it as Plato "[poking] some fun" at the Heracleiteans. McDowell, *Plato "Theaetetus,"* 179; Bostock, *Plato's "Theaetetus,"* 99. Burnyeat suggests that by the "comic" aspect Plato intends to suggest the present treatment of the Heracleiteans is an "inconsequential addition" to the earlier treatment. Burnyeat, *The "Theaetetus" of Plato*, 47. These judgments miss the importance of the *ad hominem* approach and its reliance on the speech-and-deed measure evident in Socrates' earlier treatment of Protagoras. This neglect has an important consequence in the present context insofar as it bears on exactly what about the Heracleiteans is refuted. As emerges in the text, I share the view of Silverman and Sedley that what's shown is not so much the collapse of all language but that the Heracleiteans cannot formulate a kind of language that enables them to do what they wish to do – namely teach others their views. See Allan Silverman, "Flux and Language in the *Theaetetus*," in *Oxford Studies in Ancient Philosophy, vol. XVIII*, ed. David Sedley (Oxford: Oxford University Press, 2000), 151; and Sedley, *Midwife of Platonism*, 97–8.

Socrates ascends toward being along the mundane path of human experience of the human.[12]

In his subsequent analysis, Socrates makes two related distinctions. First, speaking of the proponents of comprehensive flux, he distinguishes the "ancients" that held this flux view from "the latter-day people (180c8, 180d3)." But, second, after he completes his examination of these two groups of flux-ists, Socrates broadens the scope of his inquiry to include not only the flux theorists but also those who "proclaim things opposite to what these say," the proponents of rest (180d8–9). We need to consider these distinctions and their connection with one another.

The chief distinction between the ancient and more recent proponents of flux is that the former practiced esotericism as "they concealed [the doctrine of flux] from most people with poetry (180c8–d1)." Socrates' subsequent mention of the flowing streams of Ocean and Tethys suggest he is speaking here of Homer, the previously designated general of this army (180d2, 152e7).[13] Contrary to these ancients are

> the latter-day people who, because they're wiser, declared it openly, so that even shoemakers would understand their wisdom once they'd heard it and stop foolishly believing that some things stand still and others are in motion, but having learned that all things are in motion they would honor those who declared it (180d2–7).

If nothing else, the dialogue has taught us to be wary when Socrates designates some group as wise, and so it's necessary to weigh his critique of the ancients against his "praise" of the contemporaries. In this assessment, we need first to reflect on why Socrates makes such an issue of the form in which they presented their views.

One rationale for the ancients' practice of esotericism is the consideration to which Socrates points: some views ought to be "concealed from most people (180d1)." Subscribing to this belief, those who practice esotericism for this reason must presume a significant difference among humans. They must see in humankind an inequality so decisive that only some relatively few humans are equipped to hear and understand the truth about things – and act accordingly.

Those who subscribe to this rationale often rely on poetry to convey their views in an appropriately concealed manner. As I discussed in Chapter 4, Socrates' vehement denial that the atomists employed the Muses also linked the use of poetry, the reliance on the Muses, with the recognition of decisive human inequality. It is because they see no real difference between soul and body that the atomists easily reduce the former to the latter. Hence, there

[12] Benardete and Polansky maintain that Socrates does treat the issue as a "problem" in a technical sense drawn from geometry. In this sense, a problem is approached by first making an analysis of it and then putting the resultant elements together in a construction. In my view the approach is more maieutic with the rejection of the position based finally on the motives of its proponents. See Benardete, *Being of the Beautiful*, I. 136 and Polansky, *Philosophy and Knowledge*, 154, 154n110.

[13] Homer *Iliad* xiv. 201.

exist for them no serious differences among humans (nor in the whole), nor obviously therefore any need for them to take cognizance of such differences in the expression of their views.

Likewise, the latter-day fluxists see no need to tailor their writings to the varying capacities of different audiences, not even to conceal the bearing on the status of the gods when, as Socrates puts it, they "set motionless things in motion (181b1)."[14] They practice no kind of esotericism, poetic or otherwise. In this way, they are more theoretically consistent than are their ancient forbearers. In addition, they seem significantly more political in the narrow sense – as they should be; if the distinctions among humans are not real then all things can be understood to share the same goal, a desire to stay in motion, to endure. The accumulation of power facilitates the achievement of this goal. Accordingly, Socrates states that these latter-day fluxists pursue honor for the same reason as do many political actors: to enhance their power (180d7). Any notion of an essential distinction between the political life and at least this notion of the philosophic life, a distinction based on conflicting views of the orienting good, must be rejected.

The fluxists were not, however, Socrates' only predecessors. He now brings up Parmenides, portraying his introduction as something of an afterthought. We are asked to believe that Socrates, the possessor of a prodigious memory, "almost forgot" to mention his famous precursor (180d7–8). And Parmenides is no ordinary precursor. Within a few lines, Socrates praises Parmenides as he does no other philosopher. He also lets us see that his long-ago meeting with Parmenides continues to be a force in his life. Precisely Parmenides' elevated status, however, helps explain Socrates' unusual introduction. I want to suggest the possibility that, having just called attention to the practice of esotericism, Socrates' own treatment of Parmenides will be less than explicit. In this way, he can subject his predecessor to scrutiny without wholly subverting that which makes him so venerable. He can, more specifically, protect those who, unlike the fluxists, do not "set the motionless things in motion (181b1)." If Socrates' present purpose is, as I have maintained, to orient his own view of being, he cannot avoid dealing with Parmenides. He can only show the need for being to partake of both motion and rest by examining the proponents of these opposite extremes.

In the present context, the character of Socrates' treatment of Parmenides is illustrated by the significant poetic license he takes in the reproduction of Parmenides' sayings. Socrates' quote actually appears to be a saying constructed out of the end of one sentence in Parmenides' poem and the beginning of another. The source seems to be line 38 from fragment VIII of Parmenides' poem. In the poem, this line reads as follows:

> For you will not find thought without what is, in relation to which it is uttered; for there is not, nor shall be, anything else besides what is, since Fate fettered it *to be*

[14] On this phrase, see Benardete, *Being of the Beautiful*, I. 188n59.

entire and immovable. Wherefore all these are mere names which mortals laid down believing them to be true – coming into being and perishing, being and not being.[15]

The italicized words are those from which Socrates derives his "quote." Yet not only does he remove the words from their context, but also he does not even reproduce these accurately.[16] To consider Socrates' purpose in doing so, we can compare the sense of the original with Socrates' version of it.

Socrates' version runs as follows: "Since it is wholly motionless, being is the name for all (180e1)." This "quote" omits Parmenides' explicit notice of the dubious character of names. What is responsible for this dubious character is the distinction between seeming and being that enables us to believe things to be in a certain way that they are not. Such a distinction must present a problem for any monism, including Parmenides'. This is not to say that there could not be a valid Parmenidean response to this distinction, and Parmenides highlights this distinction in his poem. But just as monism would need to respond to the *appearance* that things are in motion, so also some modification, some complication, of the original monism would be required to account for the distinction of seeming and being if all is being. Such an explanation might be particularly troublesome for Parmenides who famously forbade discussions of not-being. In the face of this prohibition, the challenge lies in explaining why things are such as to appear in ways they are not. Again, theoretical defenses of the Parmenidean view may well be possible, but they would involve opening up lines of thought that may cast doubt on the stability of the stabilists' view.

Socrates' brief, pithy Parmenidean slogan makes these problems somewhat less explicit. However, the purpose of his, or any, serious esotericism is not to conceal them completely. Socrates' slogan identifies as the key issue the relationship between being and all. A question raised by his formulation is whether that by which the whole is a whole is *being*, taken as some unifying principle. Or, whether by the whole we should mean something more akin to the "all," that is, the whole as that which comprises all things. But if being and all are thus distinguishable, how can it be that all is one? There is a question as well if being is said to be the "name" for the all, for this suggests that this name is not therefore the "all" but is instead again distinguishable from it. Or, finally, if this impression of difference that permits these different names is a

[15] Parmenides B8, I.38 (emphasis added).

[16] Cornford writes, "I cannot believe that Plato concocted the verse from two halves of frag. 8, 38 . . . which belong to different sentences and have quite a different meaning." Cornford, *Plato's Theory of Knowledge*, 94n1. Woodbury writes, "Before Cornford . . . it had been universally agreed, as by Diels and Kranz, that the line is a distortion of fr. B8.38 which it closely resembles." Woodbury ultimately sides with Cornford but largely because he is reluctant to attribute to Plato a "creative" use of texts, even though he acknowledges that "Plato . . . is not always precise in his quotations." See Leonard Woodbury, "Parmenides on Naming by Mortal Men: Fr. B8.53–56," *Ancient Philosophy* 6 (1986): 5–7. For a more recent argument against Woodbury (and Cornford) see John Palmer, *Plato's Reception of Parmenides* (Oxford: Oxford University Press, 1999), 259–60.

mere seeming, then the question suggested by the extended quote arises. As he proceeds, Socrates quietly points to still further difficulties. He somewhat archly attributes the view of motionlessness to "many a Melissus and Parmenides (180e2)." Those others cannot actually be Melissus or Parmenides; they are both like and unlike them. Once again, significant differences disturb Parmenidean monism.

The overall point is that there are differences in this Parmenidean unity that make a difference. In its presumption of decisive differences among humans, Socrates' use of esotericism must trouble any serious monism. He even suggests that Parmenides himself may have engaged in the practice, that he may have been thinking one thing and saying another (184a2–3). Even the venerable Parmenides might then stand convicted of self-forgetfulness in the manner of the Philosophers of the Digression.

Socrates' portrayal of Parmenideanism presents it as unqualifiedly opposed to any form of motion. But this portrayal does not wholly conceal the difficulties with such a view. In his treatment of Parmenides, Socrates orients himself with respect to his predecessors in as philanthropic a way as possible – if, that is, the judgment that the doctrine of radical flux is, at least on its face, less life-enhancing than the Parmenidean understanding carries any weight. However, Socrates does characterize the Parmenideans too as a school. As such, it too comprises like-minded believers who form a partisan camp, holding views that they "strongly insist on in opposition to all these folks (180e2–3)."

Socrates locates himself (and Theodorus) in the middle, caught in a tug of war between "the flowing ones (*hoi reontas*)" and the "stationeries (*hoi stasiotai*)" (181a5, a8). He clearly designates both as quasipolitical parties, even using the usual word for seditionaries to designate the stable types. Caught in the middle, Socrates aligns himself with the "foolish" shoemaker who thinks that being must partake of both rest and motion (180d4–6).[17] If nothing else, the shoemaker is always aware of the presence of the ground beneath our feet.

Socrates makes clear that he withholds his endorsement from either of the warring factions. He holds out the possibility that these "ancient and thoroughly wise men," a group comprising all of his predecessors in both "parties," may "be saying nothing within measure" (181b3–4, 181b2). Despite the venerable character of his predecessors, Socrates means to apply his measure to them. And this means not only the Heracleiteans but also the Parmenideans with whom he is not yet finished. I have stated that his most far-reaching response to Parmenides is contained in the final stage of his assessment during which occurs the discovery of soul. Socrates does mean "to [go] forward into such a great danger" as is posed by the assessment of Parmenides (181b5). But his intrepid expedition leads him first to the confrontation with the Heracleiteans to which we must first turn.

[17] Cf. *Sophist* 248e7–249d4.

Socrates begins his analysis of the Heracleiteans considering what sort of thing motion is. He introduces the notion that there are two *eidei* of motion, local motion and alteration (181c4, 181c9–d3). On the basis of this distinction he proposes a discussion with the fluxists. Socrates determines that the fluxists must claim that "all things always have to be moving with all motions" if their doctrine of absolute flux is to be maintained (182a1–2)." He takes special care to point out that in their resultant view of perception the fluxists do not claim that the collision of agent and patient produces some quality (182a4–b7).

In a strikingly unusual usage, Socrates says that the thing acting "comes to be of a certain sort, though not a certain-sortness (182a8–9)." Socrates notes the oddness of his own locution, a "certain-sortness (182a9–10)." We will return to his neologism, but for now I simply want to note that his intention seems to be to distinguish between, say, being hot and the quality of hotness. More broadly, he intends to preclude the possibility that something is produced that might persist beyond the temporary meeting of agent and patient, something sufficiently enduring to be expressed as a noun. He insists as well that both kinds of change, local motion and alteration, must be in play here. If this were not the case we would be able to say "what sorts of things are in flux." Change would then happen to things whose identity is discernible and therefore stable. In such a case, where discernible things are in flux, being would be characterized not only by motion but also by rest.

Yet, according to the fluxists, this is impermissible. And at this point Socrates articulates the flux view in its most radical form. If motion includes not only local motion but also alteration, then the possibilities of change are endless. Colors must be changing into other colors, perceivables into nonperceivables, and knowledge into nonknowledge. But even this is insufficient. Colors must change into ideas, ideas into lawnmowers. There can be no persistent sorts or kinds. Bringing the implication of this whirling chaos to bear on the claim that knowledge is perception, Socrates concludes that every answer to every question is, or becomes, correct (183a3–8). Or, we could add, incorrect. Every answer is equally valid and invalid, there being nothing that *is* in any determinate way. What is decisive is that on the basis of all things being in motion, no claim can be substantiated. On this basis, there is no such thing as measure.

Socrates applies the metaphysical foundations of Theaetetus' definition to that very definition. He reminds Theaetetus that both of them stated that perception is knowledge (182e8–9). But, he goes on, "when we were asked what knowledge is, we answered no more about knowledge than about non-knowledge (182e11–12)." The upshot is, again, that "if all things are in motion, every answer, no matter what one is answering about, is equally correct in claiming it's this way or not this way (183aa4–6)." No position, including that knowledge is perception, can be substantiated more than any other.

In this way, Socrates makes explicit the point implicit throughout much of his analysis of Theaetetus' thesis: on the basis of this doctrine, we cannot account for ourselves as thinking, speaking, acting beings. We cannot explain our self-experience. It is important to note that in coming to this conclusion,

Socrates does not beg the question. As in the discussion of Protagoras, he addresses the deeds of the fluxists as well as their views. These deeds exhibit the desire to speak and to be understood, especially by "those whom they want to make like themselves (180b7–8)." Having this goal, the fluxists' use of speech carries with it prerequisites that they are not simply free to deny. Socrates points to the character of these prerequisites in this context as he revisits the incapacity of speech to be faithful to the flux doctrine.

Pertinent to this issue is Socrates' invention of the word noted earlier. This word is often translated as "quality" or "sortness." As Seth Benardete notes, it "became the standard substantive for the pronoun for 'sort'."[18] Formed by the word for "sort" with a noun suffix, the word means something like "the quality of having a certain quality." Put still another way, the word connotes *nounness*, by which I mean the existence of kinds, comprehending the particular, which are expressible in speech. Socrates explicitly dismisses this possibility. It would, as I indicated, accord stability to the collisions of perception, contra the Heracleiteans. Yet if one wishes to speak or teach, as the fluxists wish to do, it is not clear that this dismissal is possible.

These nouns are arrived at through the "gathering together" power of reason that Socrates soon discusses. Insofar as this power is available to speech or reason there cannot be comprehensive flux. Speech as such would seem to capture that which abides in our world such that the many particulars can be designated as this kind of thing, much as the *eidei* of motion comprehend the fluctuating particulars.

Socrates makes this stabilizing effect of speech thoroughly explicit. Using the example of color, he asks explicitly whether on the flux view, "is it ever possible to address it as any color so as to give it a name correctly (182d4–5)"? He asks of the possibility of the noun. Theodorus doesn't see how this could be possible if "it's always slipping out from under the one who's speaking (182d7)." As with color, so too is it the case with perception. One "must not attach the name of seeing to it... if all things are in motion in all ways (182e4–6)." The prohibition stems from the unavoidably stabilizing effect of speech. When we attach a single name to the many particulars, we "stop them in our speech (183a7–8)."[19] Socrates finds no alternative to this outcome. And he applies

[18] See Benardete, *Being of the Beautiful*, I.188, n61. It eventually becomes the English word *quality*. For further discussion, see Chappell, *Reading Plato's "Theaetetus,"* 136n113.

[19] Cornford writes, "The conclusion Plato means us to draw is this: unless we recognize some class of knowable entities exempt from the Heracleitean flux and so capable of standing as the fixed meanings of words, no definition of knowledge can be any more true than its contradictory." Thus far, I can agree. Cornford adds, however, "Plato is determined to make us feel the need of his Forms without mentioning them." Cornford, *Plato's Theory of Knowledge*, 99. Silverman too sees this passage as an invitation to the Forms. Silverman, "Flux and Language," 151–2. As I argue in more detail in Chapter 9, the object of knowledge developed in this dialogue – "the class of knowable entities" – does not express the usual notion of Forms as, I believe, Cornford and those who follow him conceive of them. This is not to say that Plato does not lead us to forms conceived in a different way.

it explicitly to the actions of "those who state this account (183b3)." "They have," he concludes, "no words for *their own hypothesis* (183b3–4, emphasis added)."

The deeds of the fluxists once more belie their doctrine. They wish to speak with a view to being understood. They have a hypothesis. They wish to teach it. And so they must have words for their hypothesis because, as Theodorus recognizes, their teaching has succeeded. A school has arisen. As evidenced by Theodorus' complaints, there is a discernible philosophic camp produced by the Heracleiteans' sharing of "their own hypothesis." This possibility, fulfilled even in the case of the fluxists, indicates that being cannot simply be in motion. The prerequisites of their own activity, specifically, their desire to employ the soul's capacity for speech, dictates what being must be. Socrates does not take the measure of the Heracleiteans through some *techne*. He remains the nonknower. Rather, he arrives at this judgment through reflection on the particulars of his, and their, activity.

This conclusion deserves emphasis. The Heracleitean view is not rejected simply because it leads to the collapse of language. Socrates grants that there might yet be a way for the Heracleiteans to express themselves consistent with their doctrine (183b4–5).[20] But they cannot so express themselves *and* teach their doctrine.[21] Socrates thus applies the speech-and-deed measure of *phronesis*.

Socrates underscores the importance of this approach as he bids good-bye to Protagoras. In the same breath in which he now finally dismisses Protagoras, Socrates states explicitly the locus of measure: "we'll no longer go along with him that every man is a measure of all things, if he's not a *phronimos* (183b8–9)." The person of judgment, with all that the need for judgment entails, becomes the measure. He does so because in all these cases what are being measured are not simply doctrines but deeds, not simply theories about life but life on the ground, as lived by the shoemaker and everyone else.

The Beautiful and the Soul (183c4–186e12)

Socrates is in the course of exhibiting how such judgment proceeds. That exhibition continues. The reflections that dictate the preeminence of the *phronimos* bear on the Parmenideans as well as the Heracleiteans. We must see why, in particular, having distanced himself from the Heracleiteans, Socrates cannot simply go the way of the Parmenideans. Having negated absolute flux, Socrates does not simply embrace absolute stability. Apparently, the stabilizing effect of speech is incomplete. Again, the character of being proves to depend on reflection on the character of the soul's power.

20 See Sedley, *Midwife of Platonism*, 98, 98n11.

21 Silverman writes, "The demise of the Heracleitean doctrine of total instability is the result of his inability to express the doctrine. Plato does not show that it is false or impossible. Rather, he 'proves' that the theory is untenable because it cannot be coherently put forward as an account of the world." Silverman, "Flux and Language," 151.

With Protagoras having been dismissed, Theodorus exercises the escape clause in his contract with Socrates (183c5–6). Theaetetus, however, wants to hear the other side of the story, urging them both to turn to an examination of the proponents of rest (183c8–d2). Although exempting himself from further conversation, Theodorus fully expects Socrates to eagerly fulfill this request. When it comes to Socrates giving arguments, Theodorus says, "Just ask and you'll hear (183d9)." Socrates, however, declines. Quoting Homer, he characterizes Parmenides as "an object of reverence to me" and at the same time "terrifying (183e6–7)." With this quote, Socrates places himself in the role of Helen viewing the aged Priam.[22] Perhaps Parmenides, the "one being" who propounded the doctrine of One Being, will not meet a fate as regrettable as Priam's, but he does not emerge from what follows unscathed (183e5).[23]

Socrates recalls for Theaetetus his long-ago meeting with the philosopher, a meeting analogous to the one Theaetetus now experiences (183e7–184a2). A question in the air at the end of the former conversation concerns the possibility that the form, the intelligible, might be both in motion and at rest. This possibility is connected to the requirements of knowing.[24] As such, it bears directly on the issue that Socrates now raises with Theaetetus. The no-longer-youthful Socrates, nearing the end of his own life, returns to the soul in this last portion of his assessment. He continues to take Parmenides' philosophic challenge with utmost seriousness. This seriousness, rather than his explicitly hands-off approach, shows Socrates' true esteem for his fellow philosopher. I note parenthetically that it is not nearly so clear that the mature Theaetetus responded similarly to Socrates' philosophic challenge.

It would be unwise, however, simply to dismiss as coy or misleading, or even as simply cautious, Socrates' reasons for his reluctance to deal with Parmenides. These reasons also *inform* us regarding Socrates' assessment of Parmenideanism. As I have argued, Socrates' practice of esotericism says something important about his regard for Parmenides' view. Yet, as I have also argued, the need for this practice stands as a substantive critique of monism. In this latter vein, Socrates' other expressions of reluctance serve the critical function of pointing to potential difficulties with the Parmenidean view.

For example, one reason that Socrates gives for his reluctance to deal with Parmenides is that they "won't understand what was said, and that we'll be left much further behind what he was thinking when he said it (184a2–3)." It is a perfectly understandable concern given the somewhat enigmatic character of Parmenides' poem. But having been taught by Plato to think reflexively, we must apply this concern to Parmenides' own doctrine. If by this characterization Socrates means to attribute the practice of esotericism to Parmenides

22 *Iliad* iii. 172.

23 See Cornford, *Plato's Theory of Knowledge*, 101n1.

24 *Parmenides* 162b9–e3. On this point see Mitchell H. Miller Jr., *Plato's "Parmenides": The Conversion of the Soul* (University Park: The State University of Pennsylvania Press, 1991), 149–55.

himself then, as I mentioned previously, the pre-Socratic stands accused of self-forgetfulness. Yet even if this is not the case, the question still arises whether Parmenideanism can account for the implied elusiveness of meaning expressed in Socrates' worry.

Socrates offers another reason for reluctance that raises further difficulties of a similar sort. He claims that time constraints, imposed by his maieutic efforts on behalf of Theaetetus, require him to stay with the question of knowledge rather than engage the proponents of rest (184a3–b1). He just doesn't have the time, therefore, to treat an issue that, he suggests, would take him in a very different direction. Yet there remains sufficient time to consider in detail two additional definitions of knowledge. Still more substantively, given the subject matter of the last argument of the *Parmenides*, it is not so clear that this examination would strike off in a new direction. Socrates' explicit reference to his maieutics in this context raises a question akin to that suggested by his first reason: can Parmenides' unitary view account for the complexities of soul and being that make meaning elusive and maieutics necessary?

The point is that in expressing the reasons for his reluctance to deal with his valued predecessor he has directed us to the source of their difference. Given his admiration for Parmenides, preeminently among all his predecessors, we can expect to find in Socrates' distinction from Parmenides something crucial regarding Socrates' distinctiveness. With this in mind, we now turn to his consideration of the power of soul in which he adds defining brush strokes to his self-portrait.

Socrates begins this final stage of the assessment making a distinction regarding the senses. When we say we perceive *through* the senses we can take them as conduits of perception, with "through" connoting the senses as mere passageways. Or, conversely, we can take the senses as the very means of perception, with "through" connoting the senses as the instruments of perception (184c5–7).[25] Socrates somewhat apologetically insists on precision in language about this matter. Understandably, he insists as well that the former understanding is correct because the latter would accord perceptions a reflectiveness Socrates has long denied them (184d1–5). Selecting the former option enables Socrates to maintain that the perceptions should ultimately be understood to "converge into some one look (*eis mian tina idean*)" and that this look should be available to some common mental apparatus

[25] For a treatment of the importance of this grammatical difference see Myles F. Burnyeat, "Plato on the Grammar of Perceiving," *The Classical Quarterly* N.S. 26 (1976): 29–36. Burnyeat writes that Plato makes this distinction "to distinguish perception and judgment in a way that effectively denies to the senses the judgemental function they had in the *Republic* and earlier in the *Theaetetus*." I agree that this is the use to which Socrates puts the distinction, but as the argument proceeds, Socrates is much less clear concerning the line between judgment and perception. This ambiguity is recognized by Cooper. I differ from Cooper in thinking this ambiguity is intentional, that it aims to elicit the interweaving of perception and judgment or opinion. Cf. Cooper, "Plato on Sense-Perception," 130, 132.

other than the senses, "whether it's the soul or whatever one ought to call it (184d3)."[26]

Socrates does not conceal his eagerness to reach this conclusion, saying, "I suppose it would be a terrible thing" if this were not the case (184d1)." He even chides himself for trying to manipulate Theaetetus' answers in a certain direction, while nevertheless persisting in his manipulations (184e3–4). Socrates' eagerness in this regard should alert us to the presence of lingering questions even once Theaetetus' momentous "discovery" of the soul has occurred. He has recently taught us to beware partisan fervor.

Socrates' argument depends on the recognition of certain limits of our senses. In particular, he has Theaetetus agree that perceptions such as hot, hard, and sweet belong to the body. This agreement prepares the way for a clear distinction between, on the one hand, the senses understood jointly as bodily apparatuses and, on the other, some cognitive apparatus, presumably nonbodily, belonging to something called soul. He maintains further that "those things you perceive through a different power are incapable of being perceived through another one (185e8–185a1)." Certainly the same object can be perceived through a variety of senses but what Socrates seems to be saying is that sight belongs to the eyes, hearing to ears, and so on. His main point is that, to the extent we think anything general about a thing, anything that involves a variety of senses, there must be some apparatus that elicits from the products of these necessarily distinct perceptive powers some common idea. And this apparatus, again, is not to be understood as a function of "the body."

At just this point Socrates asks about the connection between sound and color. Notably, in so doing, he uses language that expresses "the problem of two," the shorthand way, found throughout the Platonic corpus, of referring to the issue of heterogeneous wholes. He first inquires whether regarding sound and color Theaetetus thinks "this very thing about both, that the pair of them is (185a8–9)." He then asks, whether "each of them is other than the other and the same as itself" and "that both together are two, but each is one (185a11–12, 185b2)." Socrates' present point is that the relationality expressed in "the problem of two" is not available to the senses as such. We cannot grasp what's common to things through sight or hearing. We do not see likeness (or difference). Nor, most significantly and most generally, do we see being. It is available only through the wholly cognitive acts of comparing and relating, of reasoning.[27] Later I will consider whether the absolute separation of perception and those cognitive acts that come to be called opinion is sustainable.

Socrates now asks Theaetetus what this power is called through which we apprehend that which is common to many things. Theaetetus responds, "we

[26] For this reason, Burnyeat finds in this passage "the first unambiguous statement in the history of philosophy of the difficult but undoubtedly important idea of the unity of consciousness. See Burnyeat, "Grammar of Perceiving," 49.

[27] On the soul as in itself relational, see Heidegger, *The Essence of Truth*, 128.

perceive them with the soul (185d3)."[28] Punctuating his further response with an oath, Theaetetus proclaims "the soul itself, through itself, appears to me to observe the common things involved in all things (185d6–e2)." It is Theaetetus' discovery of the distinctive power of soul that finally puts to rest his initial thesis, at least explicitly (186e9–10). For, insofar as perception cannot touch on being, neither can it touch on truth (186e4–5). And what cannot touch on truth "has no share in knowledge either (186e7)." Therefore, perception and knowledge would not ever be the same (186e9–10)."

This is a momentous point in the dialogue, not only for Theaetetus but also for Socrates. We recall that Socrates put the validity of his own way of life at stake in the examination of this thesis: if it is true then Socrates' way must be nonsense. We have seen, too, that Socrates' central critique of his predecessors is that, neglecting politics, they did not understand the significance of the soul. Given its importance, we need to be especially clear as to how this discovery of soul bears on the substantiation of Socrates' way of life. It remains also to be seen how this discovery distinguishes Socrates from all his predecessors including especially Parmenides. Why, in particular, should we think that this notion of "the soul, itself by itself" entails that being must comprise not only rest but also motion?

Finally, however, an assessment of the passage bears on our contemporary situation. Martin Heidegger has made this passage most pertinent by designating it a crucial source of what he calls Plato's rationalism – and thus of all rationalism up to the present day.[29] In particular, Heidegger finds in this passage telling evidence for his claim that Plato's appeal to reason rests on a dogmatic assertion. This claim must also figure in to our examination of this final step in Socrates' assessment of the three-legged thesis.

I want to begin this examination from Socrates' striking response to Theaetetus' discovery. When Theaetetus hits on the soul itself by itself, Socrates showers him with praise, telling Theaetetus he has made this key discovery "[b]ecause you are beautiful, Theaetetus, and not ugly as Theodorus was saying, for one who speaks beautifully is beautiful and good (185e3–5)." Why, at this decisive moment, does Plato have Socrates explicitly evoke for Theaetetus in this most intimate way the tension within the notion of beauty, especially human beauty? We need to discern the connection between this problem of beauty, on the one hand, and the power of soul, on the other. This connection enables us to appreciate the bearing of the present moment on Socrates' philosophic way of life.

[28] Cornford maintains that these "commons" are what he terms the Forms. See Cornford, *Plato's Theory of Knowledge*, 105–6. For a detailed rebuttal of this claim see Cooper, "Plato on Sense-Perception," 126–38. I concur with the latter insofar as I maintain that the exact character of the objects of knowledge is exactly what is in question in the dialogue. And that object is ultimately problematic.

[29] See Martin Heidegger, *Introduction to Metaphysics*, trans. Gregory Fried and Richard Polt (New Haven, CT: Yale University Press, 2000), 190, 207–8.

Now, clearly, Theaetetus has not in the course of the conversation become physically more beautiful. If Theodorus were asked, he would no doubt confirm his earlier judgment that his young student is unattractive. But, significantly, Socrates here goes out of his way to remind us, and to tell Theaetetus more explicitly than he had yet done, of Theodorus' judgment. By doing so, he juxtaposes, as clearly as possible, two alternative conceptions of beauty: beauty in appearance and beauty in speech. This question of beauty, of its problematic wholeness, has been present from the beginning of the dialogue. I have argued that the issue of the problematic status of wholes in general is the abstract version of the practical and perplexing question of our own wholeness. I have also argued that the notion of beauty, which Socrates now raises, compels reflection on both the abstract issue and its human iteration. And it is with respect to the latter that it bears directly on the distinctive power of the soul. To understand this connection, we need to consider the issue of wholeness in general.

This issue concerns, to repeat, the existence of wholes having properties found in none of their parts. Hence, again, each of the units constituting two is something when both are taken together that neither is in itself. Recall Socrates' allusion to the "problem of two" in the present context (185a11–12, 185b2). The notion of beauty in general perfectly illustrates this possibility especially when beauty is understood as order or symmetry. On the basis of such an understanding, beauty exists by virtue of the arrangement, the relationship among and between the parts. Such a relationship, by definition, cannot inhere in any one of the parts, and so we must speak of a whole having characteristics found in none of its parts. A beautiful whole may, and even must, emerge out of, or at least depend on, parts that themselves may not be beautiful.

Moreover, the manner in which the parts are related to the whole must therefore also be murky. Summation of the parts does not yield the whole. That which constitutes a whole as such, given this heterogeneity, cannot itself be merely another part because precisely what requires explanation is how the parts can come to be what they were not. That which accounts for this change, that which unifies, must be on a different ontological plane if we are not to avoid an endless and, with a view to explanation, futile reference to other parts. Thus, to take the dialogue's example of a being fulfilling its potential, what constitutes that fulfillment cannot simply be another element of the being because in the actualization of that potential many, or even all, of the elements may be left behind. What guides this change must be distinct from that which is subject to change.

This discrepancy between the being of parts and wholes when applied to the human things makes the issue of intense concern, and even consternation, for those like Theaetetus who long for pure knowledge of the pure good. It must be troubling if objects for which we yearn, such as justice, good, and knowledge, are not wholly what they are – if justice in general requires particular unjust acts; if good is only intelligible in relation to evil; and if knowledge relies on the fluctuating, less knowable, particulars. Theaetetus, and many others, wish instead for wholes that are homogeneously what they are through and through. As a means of inducing reflection on this yearning by Theaetetus, or anyone else, Socrates makes the nerve of the explicit argument a denial of the relational character of being that underlies the possibility of such wholes. The lessons of the dice continue to exert their influence. By thus articulating the theoretical core of anti-Socratism, he points also to the issue that underlies the need for his inquiry.

Socrates calls attention to the issue of beauty exactly at this point because this difficulty regarding wholes is very acute, and very deeply felt, with respect to human beauty. This is especially the case if beauty is taken, as it is here, as a characteristic not only of body but also of soul. As such, beauty can be taken as a synonym for human fulfillment in general. With respect to our beauty or fulfillment, the issue is then at once of urgent practical concern and thoroughly problematic. For it is unclear how these "parts" – the varieties of excellence or virtue, physical versus psychic fulfillment – constitute that whole. But, in addition, so heterogeneous are they that it is not even clear how that whole, the human whole, should be conceived. Accordingly, radically divergent ways of life vie for preeminence within and among our communities. In the dialogue whose explicit theme is beauty, *Hippias Major*, Socrates makes clear what his present praise of Theaetetus suggests: human beauty would have to be such as to strike us as beautiful *both* through sight *and* through hearing.[30] As such, human beauty is external and internal, evident in appearance and in speech, the outward expression of inward, psychic beauty.

The crucial point is that this latter kind of beauty comes into the picture insofar as we possess the distinctive power of soul now discovered by Theaetetus. It comes into view, that is, insofar, as there is that cognitive power of reflection here attributed to something called soul that is not simply reducible to body. This power distinguishes us from among all other beings. Yet its discovery, far from being the end of the story, introduces a sea of perplexities. For the lesson of the Digression is that it is precisely our possession of this psychic power that so thoroughly complicates the meaning of human fulfillment.[31]

Socrates' reference to Theaetetus in this context as beautiful and good also recalls these difficulties, as does his praise of Theaetetus' beautiful speech. The kind of beautiful speech for which Socrates now praises Theaetetus did not redound to Socrates' good in a perfectly unqualified way. The central point of

30 *Hippias Major* 298b2–304b6.

31 Heidegger notes the importance of Socrates' reference to beauty in this passage. He does not, however, recognize fully the extent to which this notion carries with it the problems I note in the text insofar as he sees beauty in a one-sided way, as referring only to "inner beauty." Heidegger comes closer to the view of beauty presented herein when he calls beauty, "the point of departure and inner impetus to further questioning." See Heidegger, *Essence of Truth*, 234n17.

these reflections is then that although the power of soul enables understanding, including self-understanding, it brings with it profound difficulties for that self-understanding. And so, the question raised at the outset of the dialogue recurs: what is the unifying notion of human fulfillment that should guide our judgment? With this question we come closer to appreciating how Theaetetus' discovery, properly understood, might substantiate the inquiry that examines the perplexities raised by this discovery.

It is, however, not clear that Theaetetus understands his discovery in just this way. He is tempted to respond to this problem of human wholeness by looking away from it, to conceive humans as constituted by "soul itself," which stands over against "the body." The temptation arises from that desire for the pure good, free of any taint of perplexity. Yet although the concern for good may be the deepest current of Theaetetus' motivation, Socrates does not address this concern directly. As has been true throughout the dialogue, he approaches this deeper concern through Theaetetus' more explicit interest in the purity of knowledge. Specifically, Socrates considers, on the one hand, the soul's reflective power and, on the other, perception. He considers this heterogeneous pair in light of knowledge as a whole.

Because of Theaetetus' longing that knowledge be unadulterated, that it be wholly what it is, Socrates easily induces him to accept any position he thinks will yield this outcome. In the present context this entails Theaetetus' abandonment of any role for perception whatsoever in the acquisition of knowledge. "Soul itself by itself" is held to be sufficient (186a4). Theaetetus thus supports Socrates' thoroughgoing, and most explicit, rejection of perception's contribution to knowledge (186e11–12). He willingly neglects either side of this heterogeneous whole in order to preserve the homogeneous purity of it. To achieve this end, Theaetetus easily trades in his used-up definition for the more attractive notion of the autonomy of the soul.

Socrates elicits this outcome in an ostentatiously dogmatic manner. He thanks Theaetetus for bringing up the soul, a word Socrates had not used, because in doing so Theaetetus "did me a favor by sparing me a very long speech (185e5–6)." He says, moreover, that what Theaetetus has now come to accept is "what *seemed* to me about it, and I wanted it also to seem that way to you (185e8–9, emphasis added)."

Clearly, Socrates' dogmatic display does not constitute a full treatment of the issue at hand. We might even conjecture that the "very long speech" he mentions is nothing less than the subject matter of his entire *Socratic* career. Socrates' suggestion that this is something he used to believe lends further plausibility to this conjecture. In his pre-Socratic life, Socrates, like Theaetetus, did yearn for such purity and comprehensiveness of knowledge. It pleased him to think that there was a perfect harmony of the human and cosmic mind.[32] Yet perhaps prompted by the question at the conclusion of the *Parmenides*, it

[32] *Phaedo* 97b8–d4.

is no longer clear that he finds this picture adequate. Pertinent to the present point, it is not as clear that knowledge is the homogeneous whole envisioned by Theaetetus and the youthful Socrates.

Socrates' mature view depends on the acknowledgment of soul in all its distinctiveness. This discovery, which he shares with Theaetetus, does provide a more fruitful beginning point than the soul-denying outlook that knowledge is perception. It does make less plausible those self-forgetful comprehensive views in which the specifically human gets distorted and ultimately lost. Yet precisely insofar as it acknowledges the distinctiveness of the soul in the whole, Socrates' mature view depends as well on an examination of the perplexities this acknowledgment brings. In the present context he opens the door on these perplexities through the numerous locutions that call attention to the aspirational character of the soul's activity. As we now see, these locutions serve to significantly modify Socrates' more explicit presentation.

Socrates states that the soul "*tries* to judge" its appropriate objects (186b8–9, emphasis added). Moreover, the judgments concerning these objects, "being and advantageousness, come to be present with *difficulty* and over time, through many *troubles* and through *education*, to *those to whom they come to be present at all* (186c3–5, emphasis added)." These statements express the soul's aspirational character, the notion that we arrive at our judgments of being and advantageousness only through great efforts, efforts that, like the law, can often fall short of their goal or even fail utterly. Thus Socrates can ask, "Is it possible, then, for someone who doesn't even reach being to reach truth? (186c7)."

In his description of the soul's activity, Socrates suggests why knowledge is an object of aspiration rather than immediate apprehension. This activity involves what Socrates calls the "gathering up" of "those experiences that *stretch through the body to the soul* (186a11, 186c1–2, emphasis added)." With this description, Socrates casts doubt on that absolute separability of knowledge and perception on which he previously insisted. Rather, these experiences, "present by nature for both human beings and animals to perceive right from birth," are exactly our perceptions of particulars (186b11–c1). This "gathering up" constitutes the activity of reasoning about them. Thus, although "perception and knowledge could not ever be the same thing," neither can there be knowledge without these experiences (186e9–10). It would, therefore, be a misleading abstraction to insist on the absolute separation of knowledge and perception.

Socrates makes this point clear as the dialogue proceeds. For example, in the forthcoming image of the wax block, knowledge involves memory of the imprints in the "wax" of the mind. These imprints are unambiguously the products of perceptions. Moreover, Socrates retracts the always-dubious removal of judgment from perception that he had imposed on Theaetetus' definition with his collapse of "appear" into "perceive." Soon, in his forthcoming examination of false opinion, Socrates asks, "if he sees at least any one thing, he sees one of the beings? (188e8)." Socrates expects affirmation of this point. The point is that perception is not wholly separable from that power of soul called opinion insofar as our perception concerns the beings, and it is opinion that grants awareness of the beings as such.[33] Socrates expresses this insight by locating the beginning point of our knowing in opinion rather than in a notion of perception somehow shorn of opinion. The absolute separation of perception and knowledge is not then in accord with our experience, as Socrates recognizes.

Knowledge involves an ascent from these experiences, through their being gathered up, toward the truth of them. Knowledge must somehow comprise perception and reasoning – or rather, *experiences* and reasoning, for Socrates here alters the way in which he refers to the starting point of cognition (186c2). But the unity of this combination remains a question. Neither here nor in the forthcoming final definition of knowledge does Socrates deny the heterogeneity of the whole of knowledge. Most pertinent to the present point, if knowledge requires perception then, contrary to the stabilists' view, it necessarily involves motion and change.

Socrates' further description of the soul's activity in knowing provides additional evidence for this conclusion. Success in the soul's ascent to knowledge depends on "the power" of the individual. With respect to such power, there is significant inequality; only for some do these judgments of soul "come to be present at all (186c5)." In this context, Socrates refers also to the possibility of education in which the soul must be conceived of as alterable, and by its own efforts. It must be capable, in addition, of partial understanding

33 As Silverman writes, "scholarly debate about this argument divides over whether perception is here said to be a judgmental capacity or whether it is denied such a status." (For his part, Silverman argues for the latter alternative.) See Allan Silverman, Plato on Perception and 'Commons'," *The Classical Quarterly* N.S. 40 (1990): 158–75. Among those arguing the former are Cooper, "Plato on Sense-Perception," 126–38; and Bolotin, "False Opinion," 184–6. (Cooper, however, regards the undeniable ambiguity between the two possibilities as a matter of Plato's "indecision" or "inconsistency," rather than as an intentional movement of the argument. See Cooper, "Plato on Sense-Perception," 30, 132.) Deborah Modrak, following Cooper's general point, puts the issue in this way: "A simple perceptual judgment is an articulation of a state of affairs directly given in perception. It uses concepts that are implicitly given in sensuous representation." Deborah Modrak, "Perception and Judgment in the *Theaetetus*," *Phronesis* 26 (1981): 44n1. Writing on this passage Heidegger notes that "Perception is always already more than perception." Heidegger, *Essence of Truth*, 174. The issue at stake here regards the importance of opinion in our cognition. Or, as I indicate in the text, it is the recognition that our knowing is "always already" shaped by foundational opinions, that our perception is itself so shaped. If we begin our inquiries at the beginning, in the manner of Socratic midwifery, such an understanding of the role of opinion even in our most basic act of cognition is crucial. In his own work on these issues McDowell formulates a view very much like the one I am attributing to Plato. McDowell labels this position "naturalized Platonism." See John McDowell, *Mind and World* (Cambridge, MA: Harvard University Press, 1996), 77–8, 83–4, 91–5, 110, 176–8. I am arguing that "naturalized Platonism" is Plato.

such that it "reaches out for" or desires being but for that reason does not achieve it (186a4–5). Each of these observations reflects the way in which the soul is affected by its embodiedness, and thus its partaking of motion. There is, finally, no more explicit acknowledgment of this fact than the very character of Socrates' presentation in this context. For it recognizes the extent to which the acquisition of knowledge depends not only on intellectual capacity but also on the willingness to overcome those passions that obstruct its pursuit.

In the preceding paragraphs I have gathered together Socrates' qualifications of his more explicit presentation. The latter maintains that perception "has no share in knowledge," preserving the soul in pristine isolation from perception and the corporeal. If Theaetetus persists in his willful neglect of the heterogeneity of things, then this one-sided view may well be preferable to its opposite, which denies the possibility of stable intelligibles. In the soul's irreducibility he might also find a spur to rethink his reductionist orientation. But, as we have seen, Socrates does not simply obscure the path from this one-sided view. Through his qualifications of his categorical denial of a role for perception in knowledge, he marks the way that might take Theaetetus, and other readers, from where he now stands to an investigation of the perplexities that animate truly Socratic inquiry.

This path lets us see that the acquisition of knowledge is, or involves, the actualization of a power that, as such, changes, alters, develops in its use. It is the attempted fulfillment of a potential that, much to the consternation of the Eleatic-influenced Megarians, must involve both motion and rest. So understood, knowing cannot be taken as a static unity of soul itself by itself with the intelligible itself. Such a stabilist account misses the aspirational, and therefore partial, character of knowledge. In its presentation of this aspirational character, this final step of Socrates' assessment does constitute a response to Parmenides.[34] Specifically, through reflection on the prerequisites of the soul's power of reflection it substantiates the Socratic position that being must comprise motion and rest – the most comprehensive heterogeneous whole. More generally, the discovery of this power of reflection puts Theaetetus' anti-Socratic thesis to rest because this power gives rise to that human complexity that makes Socratic inquiry possible and necessary.

Heidegger and the *Theaetetus*

This aspirational character of the soul also bears on the allegedly dogmatic character of Plato's Socrates. At the outset I indicated that one goal of my interpretation of the *Theaetetus* is precisely to cast doubt on the notion that Plato is a dogmatic rationalist, indeed, held by some to be the progenitor of all such rationalism. In the context of the *Theaetetus*, this charge amounts to the

[34] *Parmenides* 162b9–e3; *Sophist* 248e7–249d4. I do not mean to claim that this is the most comprehensive response to Parmenideaism in the Platonic corpus, only that the kernel of that response can be found in the *Theaetetus*.

claim that there is no significant difference between Plato and his Theodorus. Rather, they join at the summit of self-forgetfulness in their pursuit of rational inquiry on the basis of an unfounded, and so nonrational, preference. As I noted, one profound expression of this charge occurs in the work of Martin Heidegger. Clearly, a detailed analysis of Heidegger's work, or even his comprehensive view of Plato, is beyond my present scope. Still, we can consider at least the outlines of Heidegger's charge in this context by attending to his essay on the *Theaetetus* which pays particular attention to the passage we are now examining.

Heidegger understands this passage as decisive for Plato's thought as a whole. He writes, "This (*Theaetetus* 184 to 187) is the essential and decisive section. Here also the turning point is particularly clear, where Greek thought turns away from its origin to go over into 'metaphysics', i.e. to ground thought in the doctrine of being as *idea* and truth as *homoiosis*. Only now does 'philosophy' begin."[35] Heidegger's judgment regarding the significance of this passage follows from the orientation of his own thought on the notion of being itself (hereafter, Being). The core of his reflections concerns Western philosophy's neglect of Being, its failure to distinguish it from the beings, to appreciate what is called "the ontological difference."[36] This seemingly abstract issue has dire practical results, amounting for Heidegger to a form of nihilism. Crucial to the present point, as Heidegger's preceding statement indicates, it is Plato who takes the world-historical misstep, and he does so in the present passage.

Before we consider Heidegger's view of this passage, however, it is necessary to appreciate that the word *misstep* is not quite accurate. It suggests that Plato, and Western philosophy in his train, might have done otherwise. Yet Heidegger writes of Plato's treatment of Being: "No more than Aristotle, and later Kant, did Plato find his way through this problem. The reasons for this already lie hidden at the beginning of ancient philosophy; Plato was no longer able to master them. The superior strength of what had *already* determined the direction of the understanding of being remained in force."[37] In Heidegger's view, it is Being that discloses itself as it will. We cannot dictate its character. It is ultimately "a mystery of the spirit itself."[38] Plato did not choose to regard Being as *idea*, but the fact that he did shapes all that follows.

The main reason that Heidegger finds the present passage so important is that here Plato shows that, and how, we apprehend Being so understood through the soul. That understanding takes seeing as its model, as indicated by a form of the verb *to see* in designating the meaning of Being. This is

35 Heidegger, *Essence of Truth*, 232. See also ibid., 131, 235.

36 On the ontological difference see, e.g., Martin Heidegger, *The Basic Problems of Phenomenology*, trans. Albert Hofstadter (Bloomington: Indiana University Press, 1982), 17, 319 and Heidegger, *Introduction to Metaphysics*, 33–5.

37 Ibid., 159.

38 Ibid., 227.

not to say that Heidegger takes Plato to be endorsing Theaetetus' definition. He understands that for Plato perception and knowledge are not identified, although he also maintains that for Plato they are absolutely separable. The point is rather that visibility provides the model for all knowledge, but most especially for Being.[39]

Heidegger's account of Plato's view runs along the following lines. A being presents itself to us as this or that through its look. We, in turn, have the capacity to view that look, to take this being as this or that.[40] A being is what it is, and is knowable as such, as it presents itself as this kind of thing.[41] This mode of the apprehension of beings provides the blueprint for the apprehension of Being. Being comes to light as what all beings share, the difference between Being and the beings is thus denied insofar as Being arises as merely an abstraction from the beings. Specifically, insofar as a being is such in terms of its look, as it presents itself, Being, as what all beings share, is understood as this quality of presence.[42] The soul itself by itself grasps this quality as the property shared in common by all beings.[43]

As presence, Being is itself most present, most enduring as what it is, and so most knowable. In this case, to know truly becomes a matter of ensuring that our speeches, our *logoi*, accurately reflect the being of things. Again, as Heidegger states, the criterion of truth is similarity, *homoiosis*, the correspondence of a proposition to a being or to Being. Much as Theaetetus insists, we are to aim at correctness, and on this model of Being such correctness is comprehensively achievable.

It is this notion of, in principle, comprehensive intelligibility that has such malign consequences for our lives. For with such presumed knowability comes also the belief that the beings are in our control awaiting the direction of our desires. Heidegger describes the consequences:

> Whether something "is something", whether there is "anything in it" as we say, is no longer decided by the being itself and the power with which it can immediately speak to man, but something only *is* something, or is nothing, depending on whether one *talks* about it or not. So, in both great and small things, contemporary man lives according to what is prescribed by journalism in the broadest sense.... Works of art, irrespective of their inner association with cult and ritual, no longer have their own being and effectiveness, but exist for the interest of American tourists, visitors to museums, and historians of art (who explain how art can be "appreciated"). It is the journalist who decides what "nature" is, so that e.g. a literary midget from Berlin presumes to advise us on this. When the familiarity of beings in their immediate power is uprooted to this degree, it is certainly difficult to awaken a real understanding for the unmediated perception of beings and their immediacy.[44]

39 Ibid., 129.
40 Ibid., 133.
41 Ibid., 126.
42 Ibid., 116, 146.
43 Ibid., 146.
44 Ibid., 150.

The result is a species of nihilism in which we feel reverence for nothing because nothing stands above us. We have "disposal over things," each being "stands ready for our arbitrary employment."[45] Ultimately, there is a "self-losing amidst all kinds of needs."[46]

This result should be familiar to us from the *Theaetetus*. However, it reflects the aspiration to a kind of freedom sought by Theodorus and his student rather than any goal of Plato's Socrates. It is, again, Theaetetus who is oriented on correctness. It is the two mathematicians who are attracted to certainty, hoping to find therein the control that will satisfy the love of their own. And it is Plato's Socrates who subjects the comprehensive claims of *techne*, the view of knowledge that speaks to these hopes, to critical scrutiny. Neither does Socrates regard either of the forthcoming definitions of knowledge as free of perplexity. The dialogue begins, and it ends, with knowledge understood as a problem.

Why does Heidegger, an extraordinarily careful and insightful (if at times tendentious) reader of the dialogues miss these facts? Heidegger does advise us to read the dialogues with the kind of care characteristic of "genuine auditors, i.e. co-questioners."[47] Yet he does not fully heed his own advice. For example, his treatment of the *Theaetetus* begins with a passage that occurs well over halfway through the dialogue. In a note to his essay he does call attention to the Prologue and the intricate narrative structure it creates:

> However, this conversation proper is already an account of Socrates' *recounting* of a prior conversation with *Theaetetus*.
>
> Therefore: the actual conversation, the narration of Socrates, the record of Euclid, the reading of this record, the conversational introduction to this record. For what purpose all these complicated layers and levels?[48]

Heidegger poses a question worth answering. But he does not answer it. Had he done so he may have seen that the Prologue introduces the notion that knowledge is a problem, casting doubt from the beginning on the notion that Plato held to some view of comprehensively unproblematic intelligibility.

These remarks on Heidegger's approach to the dialogue are not mere quibbles. They have philosophic import because the dialogue form has philosophic import. This form reflects the insights of Socratic midwifery regarding the importance of the conversational approach to inquiry. The awareness of our distance from "what is" makes this approach most appropriate. Given this distance, given the problematic status of knowledge, inquiry requires challenging conversation as a means of checking the influence that passions can exert in light of our ignorance. This influence is particularly acute regarding the question of greatest import, the question of our good. The dialogic approach reflects

45 Ibid., 153.
46 Ibid.
47 Ibid., 110.
48 Ibid., 232n9.

the crucial need for self-knowledge in response to the problem of knowledge. This problem demands heightened attention to the character of the knower. This is emphatically true insofar as the problem has its source in the kind of wholes exemplified by the human whole. For Plato, far from Heidegger's view of him, soul makes knowing possible and makes its perfection problematic. Perhaps for this reason this distinctively Socratic dialogue is devoted to showing the struggle to know the one soul after whom it is named.

Heidegger's judgment of Plato reveals a divergence between the two thinkers that lies at the heart of the *Theaetetus*. This divergence concerns the status of the beginning point of reflection.[49] We have seen that in his desire to ensure that inquiry proceeds as impartially as possible, Socrates' midwifery begins from political opinions. Such opinions express the conflict regarding human good born of the complex human whole. Heidegger, too, insists on the need to return to the origin of thought, to rethink the roots of our present situation. His judgment of the ultimate adequacy of that origin differs, however, from Plato's. He writes:

> It is no exaggeration to say that the possibility of Western philosophy through to Kant rests upon this short section of our dialogue, as too does the transformation made by Kant himself. To be sure, what was later built up, and arranged in disciplines, by reference to this short section of the *Theaetetus*, counts as "progress", but progress is inessential to philosophy. It is always the beginning that remains decisive. The authenticity and power of philosophical understanding can only be estimated by whether and how we measure up to the origin, by whether, if we ourselves are to begin over again, we *are able* to make anything of this origin. The prerequisite for this is that we leave aside everything which was *later* thought up, read in, and merely learnt, and that we feel, out of the most vital actuality, the origin of an elementary questioning.[50]

For Heidegger, the beginning is constituted by an event to which later thought strives to measure up. There is an original wholeness or unity that later thought seeks to recover. Plato's Socrates also directs us to the importance of the beginning. But his midwifery points us to reflection on politics precisely because that realm, with its diverse views of good, reflects the conflicts, the disunity, engendered by the distinctive power of soul.[51] Ascent beyond this beginning is possible through understanding its problematic character but, as I have argued, perfect unity remains elusive. The present point is that it is precisely because Plato's thought arises out of, and never wholly overcomes, this conflict or disunity that it avoids any dogmatic character with respect to either its need or its possibility.

[49] On the issue of the "background" of cognition, see also n. 33 in the preceding text.

[50] Heidegger, *Essence of Truth*, 131–2.

[51] On this point, see Catherine Zuckert, *Postmodern Platos* (Chicago: University of Chicago Press, 1996), 273–4 and Richard Velkley, *Being after Rousseau* (Chicago: University of Chicago Press, 2002), 7, 143–5.

The intent of the preceding observations is to suggest that the characterization of Plato's thought as dogmatic requires further scrutiny. Animating this need is not only the desire for historical accuracy. It is also the desire to open up the possibility that Plato's view might yet be philosophically viable, that is, to consider whether rational scrutiny of the good might be possible without either embracing the dogmatism against which Heidegger warns, or passively awaiting whatever the "mystery of the spirit" might grant.[52]

From Perception to Opinion

The rejection of Theaetetus' initial definition is based most explicitly on the discovery of the distinctive power of the soul. However, as I have maintained from the beginning, Socrates' treatment of this definition has a broader purpose: to explicate his life's work, to justify a particular kind of inquiry. Through the three-step treatment of this definition, three steps that he is largely responsible for constructing, Socrates emerges as the nonknower, the shoemaker's disciple, the intrepid psychologist. These characterizations, based on consideration of law, speech, and the soul, derive from the soul's power of reflection. From this power follow those perplexities that make Socratic inquiry possible and necessary. In light of their existence, Socratic midwifery is anything but nonsense.

When Socrates endorses Theaetetus' name for the result of the soul's activity – Theaetetus calls it "opinion" – he makes clear that his focus will be on the perplexities that pertain to the wholeness of the soul and its objects (187a7–8). These compel the notion that our knowledge is partial. Appropriately, Socrates makes the examination of Theaetetus' next definition of knowledge treat exactly the possibility of that partial knowledge that requires and makes possible such inquiry. However, in the course of this examination he does not fail to ask a further, characteristic question: is such partial knowledge desirable? With this question, Socrates begins to map his home base, the realm of opinion, which is preeminently the political realm.

[52] Heidegger, *Essence of Truth*, 227.

8

False Opinion

Introduction

On the basis of his discovery of the distinctive power of the soul, Theaetetus produces a new definition: knowledge is true opinion.[1] This definition seems crucial to the examination of knowledge as Socrates understands it. Throughout the Platonic corpus he approaches the meaning of knowledge by distinguishing it from opinion. The very need for Socrates' inquiries arises out of a sense of the inadequacy of opinion. Socrates does not discover the distinction between the Way of Truth and the Way of Seeming.[2] He does, however, acquire an insight regarding the imperfect separateness of the two realms. It is this insight that mandates the examination of opinion characteristic of Socratic inquiry.

Socrates' philosophizing retains a significant tie to opinion because it culminates in knowledge that is explicitly partial. Animated as it is by the incompleteness of opinion, Socratic inquiry does not fly wholly free of its bonds. The *Theaetetus* is paradigmatic in this regard, most obviously because of its culmination in explicit aporia (210b8–9). However, the dialogue as a whole

[1] The word translated as opinion, *doxa*, can also be translated as judgment or belief. I have retained the translation as opinion to preserve the sense of partial knowledge implied especially when taken in juxtaposition with knowledge. Chappell argues that this translation is misleading precisely in its resonance with the *Republic*'s distinction between knowledge and opinion, especially in light of Socrates' endorsement of Theaetetus' labeling the power of the soul, opinion. Chappell, *Reading Plato's "Theaetetus,"* 154. But Socrates endorses this label, and dwells on opinion, because the issue at hand is the possibility and desirability of partial knowledge, the knowledge that constitutes his "human wisdom." Socrates does not wish to sweep by opinion to knowledge as the theorist is wont to do. Retaining this translation highlights Socrates' unusual focus on the nature of opinion. For other reflections on the translation of *doxa* see McDowell, *Plato "Theaetetus,"* 193; Bostock, *Plato's "Theaetetus,"* 157; and Burnyeat, *The "Theaetetus" of Plato*, 69–70.

[2] The reference is to the two parts of Parmenides' poem. See G. S. Kirk and J. E. Raven, *The Presocratic Philosophers* (Cambridge: Cambridge University Press, 1957), 265–6, 278.

also illuminates the manner in which opinion exerts its influence on inquiry, shaping its concerns, and even informing what it is we take knowledge to be.

Socratic philosophy appreciates the significance of opinion because it considers most deeply the implication of the partiality of knowledge. As reflective of our self-experience, the problem of knowledge actually asks how we can know only partially. In this examination of Theaetetus' second definition of knowledge, especially in the consideration of false opinion, Socrates explores the roots of this partiality and so explores further the theoretical underpinnings of his philosophic activity.[3]

The dialogue leaves little doubt that Socrates grasps the reins of this examination securely in his own hands. Although its ostensible goal is to examine Theaetetus' definition of knowledge as true opinion, Socrates almost immediately steers their attention from true opinion toward the possibility of false opinion. And the possibility of false opinion is an issue he designates as very much his own perplexity (187d1–4).[4] When Socrates does finally deal explicitly with Theaetetus' definition he dispatches it easily, as he could have done at any point in the argument (201a4–5). We must, therefore, determine why it is to Socrates' purpose to approach the distinction between knowledge and opinion through the possibility of false opinion.

At present, I want only to note that he begins the inquiry remarking that it will have two possible outcomes: either they will "discover the thing we're advancing on, or we'll be less apt to suppose we know what we don't know at all (187b10–c2)." The latter cognitive possibility captures the result of Socratic inquiry, his famous knowledge of ignorance. Most importantly, in the forthcoming discussion he makes the possibility of false opinion hinge precisely on the possibility of the existence of such partial knowledge, going so far as to maintain that if false opinion is possible so must be partial knowledge (196c7–8). It is this claim that places such weight on the forthcoming examination as an insight into Socratic inquiry.

There is a further point to make. Socratic inquiry does not only and, perhaps, not even primarily, treat partial knowledge as a *cognitive* possibility. It also regards it as a possibility bearing on our affective life, raising ethical issues. Given these two aspects of the approach to the partiality of knowledge, when assessing Socratic inquiry we need to consider not only whether and how it might be cognitively possible. If it does prove possible, we must also determine whether such a pursuit with such an outcome is desirable. Its desirability is for many, including Theaetetus, at least as much in question as its possibility. For

[3] On the importance of partial knowledge in this section of the dialogue see Bolotin, "False Opinion," 179–93 and Polansky, *Philosophy and Knowledge*, 177–8.

[4] This is not to suggest, however, my agreement with the view, held by numerous commentators, that the Eleatic Stranger exceeds Socrates exactly in his provision of a solution to this perplexity. For a recent statement of this view, see Sedley, *Midwife of Platonism*, 134, 149. I have more to say on this issue in the following text.

this reason, in predicting what the outcome of the present inquiry might be, Socrates adds, in an understated way, that we may learn that such partial knowledge provides a "reward [that] is nothing to complain about (187c2–3)."

Bearing as it does on the possibility and desirability of his philosophic activity, this issue of the distinction between opinion and knowledge is certainly worthy of attention at any time. In framing this section with references to his trial, however, Socrates provides a sense of urgency behind the understatement. It is high time to get on record his self-understanding. He thus says, again in a restrained fashion, "it may not be inopportune (*ouk kairou*)" to consider the issue of false opinion now (187e1–2). The theme of this section provides the substantive underpinning to the connection indicated by its form. For it is the issue of the nature of opinion, especially false opinion, that provides the nexus between Socrates' activity and his fate.

From True Opinion to False

With knowledge as perception dismissed, Socrates calls for further investigation. After all, their discussion did not aim "to find out what knowledge is not, but what it is (187a2–3)." Yet their efforts have not been simply futile. In the very next breath Socrates regards the discovery that knowledge is *not* perception as progress (187a3). By his deeds, Socrates indicates that he does consider it possible to know what he does not know. He knows, specifically, that he does not yet know what knowledge is. Moreover, in considering the attainment of this knowledge as progress he must also deem it desirable (187a3, b2). The work of the present definition of knowledge bears on the substantiation of both these claims – that partial knowledge is both possible and worth having. The action almost immediately reveals that the latter claim has at least equal importance as the former.

Although he derives his new definition of knowledge from his discovery of opinion, Theaetetus realizes that all opinion cannot be knowledge. For in his unusual and reiterated phrase, it would be "out of one's power (*adunaton*)" for all opinion to be knowledge (187b4–5). He thus regards true rather than false opinion as knowledge (187b5–6). Granting only that there is a "chance" that this definition is true, he says if it proves otherwise "we'll try to say something else, just as we're doing now (187b7–8)."

Such appreciation of the searching, hypothetical character of their endeavor earns Theaetetus Socrates' ardent praise (187b9–10). Theaetetus' willingness to begin again from the beginning in the face of a demonstrably inadequate hypothesis does show the stirring of Socratic inclinations. More strikingly, his last words – "just as we're doing now" – reflect a newfound awareness of the bearing their deed might have on the conclusion of their inquiry. In such awareness lies the antidote for the self-contradiction that has so far plagued him.

Unfortunately, promising as all these signs are, Theaetetus' growing self-awareness withers in the course of the subsequent discussion. This disappointing outcome does serve to highlight the importance of the issue of the desirability of partial knowledge. It suggests, in particular, that this ultimately practical consideration remains Socrates' most formidable foe. But the general lesson taught by the Platonic dialogue's form concerning the interweaving of the theoretical and practical applies specifically to this issue of the possibility and desirability of partial knowledge. These aspects are intertwined and must be dealt with not only separately but also in connection with one another. They unite in Theaetetus' preference for the existence of absolute opposites to which Socrates appeals as he begins the examination of opinion.

As we have previously seen, much like his Eleatic intellectual ancestors, Theaetetus prefers the logical clarity of wholly separable opposites. Such hard and fast distinctions, applied to the opposition between knowledge and ignorance, pervade the forthcoming argument, at least in its explicit form. Yet, as we have also seen, it is not simply clarity that attracts Theaetetus to these absolute distinctions. Rather, he finds in them a certainty and stability seemingly unavailable once the relational character of these oppositions is admitted, once, that is, it becomes evident, that they may only be, and be intelligible, through one another. Thus, time after time, the brilliant orphan, Theaetetus, proves intellectually capable but affectively unwilling to accept such ambiguity (144d1–4). And here, once more, Theaetetus' initial openness to the partiality of knowledge soon vanishes.

Socrates notes that there is "a pair of forms (*eidei*) of opinion, one truthful and the other false," the difference between them existing "by nature" (187c3–5, e7). Theaetetus' tentative response, that this "now appears so to me," could be taken to shake the solidity Socrates attributes to this distinction. One might grant that it holds "now" but ask, what about later? Or, one might acknowledge that it "appears so" but wonder whether it is truly so (187c6). Theaetetus' response partakes of the unclarity associated with the realm of opinion as a whole in its contradistinction from knowledge. Moreover, it is possible that the distinction between true and false in that realm of opinion might well be blurred by the features of opinion as such. Socrates strengthens this possibility by now pursuing the issue of true opinion through an examination of false.

Socrates does later chide himself for traveling down this road to false opinion without first considering the meaning of knowledge (200c7–d2). For his part, Theaetetus immediately regards it as a detour from the main business of the discussion. He remarks on the leisure that allows them to pursue the arguments wherever and whenever we will (187d10–11). He thus recalls Theodorus' vivid image at the outset of the Digression where he conceives of the arguments as our servants, awaiting our direction (173c2–4). For Theodorus, they clearly do not impose themselves on our lives in any decisive way. Yet, just as in the previous instance, the substance of the Digression belied Socrates' leisureliness, so now we have reason to doubt the accuracy of Theaetetus' judgment on the digressive and leisurely character of what follows. Recall that it is, in Socrates' view, the *kairos*, the perfectly opportune time, for such a presentation.

Granting the urgency of Socrates' presentation we must still wonder why Socrates makes the argument travel down the particular road he does. Why does an examination of *false* opinion provide the best approach to his self-understanding? In considering Socrates' strategy, it is crucial to note that he is taking up the issue of false opinion *once again*. As he is at pains to point out, it had been raised earlier in the treatment of Protagoras where it was maintained that "everyone" believes there is false opinion (170b5–10). He insists, nevertheless, that the possibility of false opinion remains a perplexity (187d1–4). By this insistence Socrates prepares the distinction between "what everyone believes" and some more adequate view that at least moves toward knowledge. Stated more pointedly, the universal view that there is false opinion may well be true, but unless and until we can account for false opinion that view will be less adequate even than one that appreciates the perplexity of its existence.

This belief in, or opinion about, the existence of false opinion thus perfectly exemplifies the status of what we mean by opinion as distinguished from knowledge. But it is much more than just one example among an infinite number of such possible examples. Socrates focuses on an opinion that "everyone" believes because he wishes to address our cognitive situation more generally. Given the discrepancy between, on the one hand, this universally held belief in the existence of false opinion and, on the other, the all-but-universal inability to account for it (as seen in the perplexity regarding its existence), the conclusion can be drawn that we are all-but-universally mired in false opinion. The status of this opinion regarding false opinion characterizes our cognitive situation in general. What shapes that situation is the decisive and pervasive false opinion that we think we know what we do not know.

Socrates focuses then on the possibility of false opinion to elicit the peculiar character of our pretheoretical existence. Our need to learn means that we begin in ignorance somehow understood. Socrates wants to address the precise character of this ignorance in its cognitive and affective dimensions. That character becomes of supreme importance owing to the following consideration: insofar as knowledge remedies ignorance, it is this character that dictates what it is we take knowledge to be.

In beginning with false opinion Socrates permits an understanding of knowledge to emerge that might otherwise be dismissed without consideration. If our ignorance is understood as primarily false opinion, as believing we know when we do not, then the door is open for such ignorance to be remedied by a kind of partial knowledge. *The* cure for our ignorance could consist in knowing what it is we don't know rather than the comprehensive knowledge for which Theaetetus yearns.

Admittedly, it is the latter understanding that explicitly informs the forthcoming argument. That argument regards knowledge and ignorance as complete opposites, with the former taken as absolutely comprehensive understanding and the latter, absolute obliviousness. However, this understanding, so attractive to Theaetetus and many others, is opposed by one that takes its bearings from false opinion. And it is this latter possibility that Socrates wishes to introduce and make available for Theaetetus' and our discovery. Accordingly, Socrates links the possibility of false opinion to the possibility of partial knowledge, binding together the particular character of our ignorance with the particular kind of knowledge needed to assuage this ignorance.[5]

This rationale for Socrates' treatment of false opinion helps us understand an oft-commented on feature of the *Theaetetus* – namely, the absence in Socrates' self-portrait of his famous doctrine of Recollection.[6] Elsewhere, this doctrine is invoked to account for our initial cognitive state and our ascent beyond it. Beginning, however, from the presumed prenatal vision of all things, recollection by itself does not explain how we come to hold false opinions. Nor can it explain the partial knowledge central to the Socratic approach. The knowledge of what we do not know can only be postnatal because, according to the doctrine, prenatally we knew all things. The meliorative knowledge of what we do not know is knowledge of a condition that can only exist postnatally.[7] The orthodox doctrine of Recollection has no cognitive place in the argument.

If the endeavor can be linked to recollection in any way it must, again, be to the entirely terrestrialized version presented near the end of the *Meno* where Socrates calls recollection nothing other than to "bind [opinion] with causes by reasoning."[8] It is to reason about the causes for our opinions, precisely as Socrates does through this reflective look at false opinion. In raising the possibility of false opinion again as a perplexity, Socrates indicates the inadequacy of the opinion (as an opinion) that false opinion exists. The subsequent examination of this archetypal opinion shows how to move from opinion toward knowledge without prejudging what it is we will allow knowledge to be.

Socrates addresses a different type of interlocutor in the *Meno* than he does in the *Theaetetus*. Accordingly, the *Theaetetus* concentrates on knowledge rather than virtue. But the theorists in the *Theaetetus* are at least as in need

5 Several commentators attribute this all-or-nothing principle of knowledge to Plato himself. They do so based on the contention that Plato failed to distinguish, in McDowell's words, between "'knowledge of x' and knowledge of what x is'." On this view, knowledge is a matter of acquaintance with an object that one either has wholly or not at all. See McDowell, *Plato "Theaetetus,"* 115, 197. Gail Fine thinks this acquaintance model is in play but is recognized as defective and used to buttress Theaetetus' definition. When that definition is rejected so is this model. Gail Fine, "False Belief in the *Theaetetus*," *Phronesis* 24 (1979): 70, 70n1, 77–8. I agree that the use of the all-or-nothing principle reflects Socrates' particular goals at this dramatic stage in the dialogue. Generally speaking, those who consider this principle as held by either Socrates or Plato do not sufficiently attend to the drama of the dialogue as philosophically significant.

6 I discussed this issue in Chapter 3. For further confirmation of its absence in the present context see 197e2–3.

7 I owe this point to Bartlett, *Plato "Protagoras" and "Meno,"* 146.

8 *Meno* 98a3–5. See Chapter 3, 109 and 109n87.

of Socrates' ministrations as the young, ambitious political type with whom he engages in the *Meno* and many other dialogues – perhaps more so, for the former are the ones who should be least unaware of their ignorance. In this sense, as Socrates suggests in the Digression, they are even more self-deceived in thinking themselves superior to their fellow citizens in freedom of thought. The falsehood that has its source in self-deception is ultimately Socrates' greatest concern.

Socrates' approach places the particular source of this self-deception in jeopardy. If examining true opinion through the lens of false can bear fruit regarding both kinds of opinion then true and false opinion must not be as distinct as Theaetetus wishes deeply to believe. Socrates thus addresses the dilemma in Theaetetus' soul, a dilemma evident in those more strongly drawn to certainty than to truth. On one side of this dilemma is that which all have been seen to believe: falsehood exists. With his deep need to be correct, Theaetetus feels the weight of this belief more than most. On the other side lies precisely what his deep yearning for perfect knowledge leads him to deny – that there can be wholes, such as knowledge and ignorance, good and evil, that are not purely and distinctly what they are. In the face of this dilemma, Theaetetus must either deny the testimony of his experience or confront the desire that would compel such a denial.[9] He must choose between certainty and truth. Such a confrontation could open him up to the relational aspect of being, but such a confrontation, as I have insisted and as Socratic midwifery recognizes, has an affective and an intellectual dimension. It involves not only the capacity of our intellect but also, at least as importantly, our desires and the notion of good that answers to these desires.

In this way, Socrates addresses more broadly the characteristic temptation of the theorists: to let the allure of pure knowledge obscure their own experience. Had Socrates begun with true opinion, it may have been too easy for the theorist to regard knowledge as wholly separable from opinion, too easy to deny the possibility and worth of partial knowledge. The theoretical inquiry into the possibility of partial knowledge coheres with the drama in Theaetetus' soul, the intellectual dimension of the issue with the affective. In the forthcoming examination of false opinion Socrates has both dimensions unwaveringly in his sights.

Knowing, Being, and Other-Opining (187a1–190e4)

Socrates now announces his perplexity about false opinion. Again, although the opinion that it exists is universally asserted, Socrates confesses, "I don't have it in me to say *what* in the world this experience is that's here with us, or in what way it *comes to be present* in us (187d3–4, emphasis added)." Socrates' implied distinction between the being of false opinion and its genesis

[9] On the tension within Theaetetus, see Bolotin, "False Opinion," 183–4, 190–3.

foreshadows a significant source of the possibility of false opinion as such. Yet rather than dwelling on this point, he wonders if they should let this issue go or "examine it carefully in a different way than we did a little before," perhaps undertaking to demonstrate what previously was merely asserted (187d7–8). Socrates' question draws from Theaetetus his mention of the leisure they now enjoy. It may not be the most urgent topic for him, but they do have time on their hands, so why not? The significance of the examination eludes Theaetetus. Believing that the realm of opinion is easily transcended, Theaetetus remains wholly enmeshed in it. In particular, he evinces little appreciation of how this realm exerts its influence on philosophic inquiry. Nor does he grasp the connection of this examination with Socrates' political predicament, highlighted by the reference to the Digression. In sum, he does not now understand the philosophic need that dictates the urgency of Socrates' circumstances, the need that makes this the *kairos* for exactly the discussion that follows.

Socrates begins the examination of the hard and fast distinction between true and false opinion. And, as previously mentioned, he goes so far as to insist that opinions are true or false "by nature," an idea Theaetetus is happy to endorse (187e7–8). To Theaetetus' further delight, Socrates pronounces the principle that explicitly governs what follows: "this is what's possible as far as we're concerned in connection with all things and with them each by each, either to know or not to know (188a1–2)." Socrates immediately demonstrates the experience-denying implications of this principle by dismissing learning and forgetting because "they are nothing according to our present statement (188a4)." Were he to refrain from taking this step, the entire aporia of false opinion could have been avoided. Its existence depends on the elimination of the possibility of partial knowledge, a possibility inseparable from learning. This, however, is precisely the point. In making this extravagant claim, Socrates makes clear that learning, part of everyone's experience, depends on the rejected possibility of some middle ground between knowing and not-knowing. If the experience of learning, so central to this student's life, is to be possible, so must the existence of partial knowledge. By this claim, Socrates must increase the tension within Theaetetus' soul. Nevertheless, at this point, Theaetetus blithely accedes, joining in the view that "there's nothing left about each thing except to know it or not know it (188a5–6)." Once again, his affinity for this absolute distinction has drowned out the voice of self-awareness that might have reminded him of his own status as a learner.

In this affinity for absolutes Theaetetus reveals his own Eleatic inclinations. These inclinations, present from the beginning of the dialogue in the persons of the Megarians, dominate this section of the dialogue owing to Socrates' explicit treatment of knowing and being in terms of absolute distinctions. If, as I have claimed, this section further explicates the theoretical underpinnings of Socratic philosophy, Eleaticism's presence is most appropriate. Socrates' distinctiveness rests exactly on a denial of the Eleatics' contention that the whole, which includes the soul, is intelligible in terms of absolutes.

This denial explains the philosophic attention Socrates pays to the realm of opinion, to what I have called our pretheoretical understanding, which the Eleatics found so easy to ignore or reject. For the Eleatics, as for Socrates, the realm of opinion is a realm of half-truths and ambiguity. Unlike Socrates, however, they regard this realm as simply dispensable, as a realm in which the common sense-denying paradoxes of such as Zeno thrive. The rejection of the realm of opinion, and of common sense, as having any worth forges the bond between the Eleatics and the eristic practice of the sophists evident earlier in the dialogue in Protagoras' use of Parmenides (167a7–8). On the basis of the Eleatic understanding it can be "shown" that, contrary to our experience, no one can really move or, as here, learn. The testimony of our everyday experience can be shown to be false and ungrounded, those who adhere to it revealed as unsophisticated dupes. The Eleatics pave the way for those who can exploit in speech these perplexities of our experience and teach others to confound and dominate their more straightforward, less sophisticated countrymen.

I dwell on these connections because Socrates now uses just these Eleatic-type paradoxes in the first three of a total of five attempts to account for the possibility of false opinion. The Eleaticism is most clear in the first two attempts which depend respectively on a version of Meno's paradox and on Parmenides' paradox-generating strictures regarding being and not-being.[10] In the third (and overall, the central) attempt Socrates does for a moment shake free from paradox to suggest what seems a viable explanation, but it too is ultimately vitiated by adherence to the absolute distinction holding that one either knows wholly or not at all. In these first three considerations of false opinion Socrates thus investigates its possibility first from the standpoint of knowing, second, of being, and, third, of what he calls *allodoxia* or other-opining, which proves to combine both views.[11] Each of these maintains, at least explicitly, the cognitive all-or-nothing principle just announced. Each proves explicitly inadequate. But these inadequacies point in the direction of what an adequate account would have to maintain, chief among which is a rejection of the all-or-nothing principle. In the course of this presentation, as always, Socrates provides sufficient direction, if we heed it, of how we might think through to an alternative to these Eleatic impasses.[12] We need now to consider each of these in turn, beginning with the standpoint of knowing.

[10] Parmenides B2.7–8; *Sophist* 237a4–9.

[11] Both Cornford and Bostock regard this third attempt as a recurrence to the first. They make this judgment because they do not sufficiently appreciate Socrates' introduction of the notion of being as "other" before his retraction of it. It must be said, however, that Cornford does think that Socrates comes to the very edge of this position. See Cornford, *Plato's Theory of Knowledge*, 116–17 and Bostock, *Plato's "Theaetetus,"* 169–70.

[12] E.g., Socrates' reference in this context to "all things and with them each by each" points to the consideration that permeates the proceedings – that a thing taken together with other things may *be* in a different way than if taken each by each (188a1–2).

Based on the all-or-nothing principle, Socrates insists, to Theaetetus' approval, that "the one who has an opinion has it either *about* one of the things he knows or one he doesn't know (188a7–8, emphasis added)." Following this assertion Socrates adduces several cases in which false opinion would not be possible. Each of these is said to be out of our "power" (*adunatov*, 188b1). Prior to considering Socrates' claims I want to comment on some aspects of his terminology in these statements because they bear on the substance of his claims.

Socrates says that opinions are *about* the things. By this usage he must mean that opinions are predicative, referring to properties of things. When we speak about the beings we say "this is that"; "this tree," for example, "is an evergreen." Based on this understanding, error may consist in misdescribing the object in question by concentrating only on a single aspect of it to the neglect of others, mistaking a partial account for a comprehensive account. One of the prerequisites of such speech, along with its attendant errors, is, as I have noted and will consider again in the following text, that the beings must be complex, having parts, and so capable of being in relation with one another.

Yet, this understanding, suggested by Socrates' use of the word *about*, does not predominate in the argument that follows. Instead, Socrates uses the existential rather than the predicative meaning of the verb *to be*. He speaks of the beings as wholes, such that a being wholly is or is not. The kind of error he has in view is thus misidentification rather than misdescription, for example, mistaking Theaetetus for Socrates.[13] The all-or-nothing principle is invoked to substantiate this notion that a being wholly is or is not at all. No room is left

[13] Several commentators maintain that Plato's Socrates (and Plato) does not grasp the difference between these kinds of judgments and their corresponding errors. This conclusion joins with the view that Plato also subscribes to the all-or-nothing principle of knowledge. Allowing only misidentification makes it easier to maintain that we either know this thing as a whole or we do not. With misdescription the possibility of predicates is introduced along with the possibility of knowing a thing partially, i.e., knowing some of its predicates but not all. Among the aforementioned commentators see Cornford, *Plato's Theory of Knowledge*, 117; Sayre, 106–7; and J. L. Ackrill, "Plato on False Belief: *Theaetetus* 187–200," *The Monist* 50 (1966): 389. Ackrill does see hints of an alternative in the wax-block passage, but he ultimately decides that the relevant distinction is unavailable to Plato. Ackrill, 394, 401–2. Bostock thinks that what is in play in "the passage on other-judging" are "subject-predicate statements which are not identity statements," especially in the allodoxia section, but that Plato did not clearly distinguish the different senses of being involved in the different kinds of judgments. See Bostock, *Plato's "Theaetetus,"* 196–7. Burnyeat argues that Socrates focuses on identity judgments and offers several accounts of why this might be the case. He maintains, however, that "Plato's intention is to provoke us into looking for a faulty assumption that makes Theaetetus accept so unacceptable a conclusion." Burnyeat, *The "Theaetetus of Plato,"* 70–3. I share Fine's view that both kinds of judgments are present, that Plato is aware of the distinction, and that Plato has his Socrates concentrate on identity judgments to raise doubts in Theaetetus about the all-or-nothing notion of knowledge that underlies this second definition. See Gail Fine, "False Belief," 74, 76–8. On these points Fine is in agreement with C. J. F. Williams, "Referential Opacity and False Belief in the *Theaetetus*," *The Philosophical Quarterly* 22 (1972): 295–8. For a useful overview of scholarly commentary on the passage, see Chappell, *Reading Plato's "Theaetetus,"* 154–7.

for it to be in diverse or heterogeneous ways. Nonetheless, Socrates' language alerts us to the need to pay attention to this alternative view of the beings and the corresponding type of falsehood, both of which exist in counterpoint to the dominant view.

Socrates' frequent use of the phrase, "out of our power," dictates this same vigilance on the side of knowing. Referring to what is within or without our power evokes the notion of potential, a notion so difficult for the Megarians and not only for the Megarians. The problems presented by the idea of potential in the context of knowing provide a taste of these difficulties. When applied to knowing, the idea of potential raises the possibility that our knowledge is not wholly present or wholly absent, that it may exist in varying degrees of actualization depending on the degree to which we have actualized our latent power. As with all qualities that we might speak of in terms of potential, the possibility raised is that our knowledge can both be and not be what it is. It is to avoid just this unsettling conclusion that the Megarians and Theaetetus prefer to think of opposites only in an absolute sense: hence, the all-or-nothing principle, something wholly is or is not. I also explore this issue further in what follows. The present point, however, is that the character of our cognitive powers, the variety of their actualization and their inherent limits, may also contribute to the possibility of false opinion. Following his examination of false opinion and the beings, Socrates takes up this possibility in earnest with his two images of the mind, the wax block and the aviary, which constitute the fourth and fifth of his attempts to explain false opinion. These images, both insofar as they are images and multiple, support the notion that the specific character of our cognitive power plays a role in understanding the source of false opinion. With such indications, Socrates erects warning signs against swallowing the present argument whole without at least a bit of chewing. Properly alerted by Socrates' language we are now ready to consider the details of the argument.

Socrates has Theaetetus agree to several cases in which, based on the all-or-nothing principle, false opinion could not be possible: when someone supposes that "the things he knows are not those things but some other things that he knows"; next, when someone considers "things he doesn't know to be some other things among those he doesn't know"; and finally, "when someone supposes things he knows to be things that he doesn't know, or in turn that what he doesn't know is what he knows (188a10–c3)." In the first, if he truly knows both he would not mistake one for the other. In the second, using as his example the recognition of Socrates and Theaetetus by someone who knows neither of them, Socrates maintains that if he knew neither he would not have sufficient knowledge to mistake one for another. And finally, in a case that expresses Socrates' own claim to have knowledge of ignorance, one cannot both know and not know something.

In this way, Socrates draws together the possibility of false opinion and the key Socratic possibility of knowing what one does not know. But Theaetetus obligingly agrees to dismiss all three cases including this expression of Socratic wisdom. With Socrates insisting that "in these cases it appears there's nowhere that it's in one's power to have false opinions," the investigation reaches an impasse regarding the possibility of false opinion (188c7–8). Perhaps, he suggests, their investigation might make progress if they move from the realm of knowing to that of being.

Socrates begins this next attempt with the hopeful statement, "Maybe it's something simple (188d3)." Unfortunately, this simplicity is not borne out even in his first mention of the beings that refers again to their predicative character and so belies this claimed simplicity (188d3–5).[14] Socrates renders the promised simplicity of the beings still more dubious as he initiates the discussion by conjuring an imaginary questioner (188d7–8). We might well wonder where such an entity might fit in the forthcoming rigid distinction between being and not-being. Moreover, the words of the imaginary questioner perpetuate the ambiguity about the beings, in claiming that his question is relevant "whether it's *about* any of the beings or whether it's something itself by itself (188d9–10, emphasis added)."

Again, these seemingly insignificant details bear on the argument's substance and validity. The possibility under consideration is that false opinion consists in having an opinion about something that is not. These details, pointing to an ambiguity about being, raise the question whether in saying that it is not, we mean that the thing is not "this" or "that," or that we mean the being is not at all. Although calling attention to this difference in such a suggestive manner, Socrates again highlights only the latter sense in the subsequent argument. To sharpen this focus he now speaks not of opinion but of perception, of seeing something or seeing nothing at all (188e6). As I noted in Chapter 7, ultimately Socrates does not wholly sever perception from knowledge. However, at present it is also important to note that this reversion to perception for the sake of absolute distinction reminds us why Theaetetus gave the initial definition that he did.

Aiding this focus as well is Socrates' insistence that when we see something we see one thing that is either there or is not (188e8–9). In this argument, so redolent of Parmenideanism, Socrates concentrates on oneness. It is, however, just this Parmenidean character that makes the argument suspect. In particular, Socrates has the argument move from addressing a being's oneness to its existence as "one of the beings (188e8)." It is Parmenides who famously insists that there is at least one *one* that is decidedly not one of the beings – namely, The One.[15] Socrates alludes to this Parmenidean point by asking Theaetetus here, "or do you suppose that what's one is ever among things that are not? (188e8–9)."

[14] Bostock recognizes the complexity of the objects of belief. He maintains, however, that Plato did not have a good grasp on this complexity until the *Sophist*. Bostock, *Plato's "Theaetetus,"* 194.

[15] See *Parmenides* 138a2–b6.

In response, Theaetetus might well have recalled Parmenides' teaching and concluded that it is truly difficult to grasp how that which is truly one, and thus unique, could be designated as "one of the beings." To be knowable as "one of the beings" it would in some way have to share something with its fellow beings and so not truly be one in the sense of being unique. It is for this reason that I linked the predicative character of the beings to their complexity. To be "one of the beings" a being would need to be sufficiently complex so as to both be itself and share properties with other beings. No simple being could meet these requirements. Accordingly, it would be one only in an equivocal sense. Its being, as well as its not-being, could in this case well refer to its being (or not being) this or that, rather than not-being in the absolute sense. All this exists only implicitly in Socrates' argument whose explicit aim is to rule out this possibility of diverse or heterogeneous senses of being.

The dubiousness of Socrates' explicit argument becomes still more evident at its conclusion. Bringing the argument to bear directly on the possibility of false opinion, Socrates maintains that "someone who has an opinion about something that is not has an opinion about nothing (189a10)." From this claim he concludes that "someone who has an opinion about nothing doesn't even have an opinion at all" and so could not have even a false opinion (189a12–13). In this conclusion Socrates provides still another reason to balk at this argument for Socrates has himself just stated an opinion about nothing.

Beginning with his imprecise use of the predicational and existential senses of being, extending to the ontic status of the imaginary questioner, and finally, and most pointedly, eliciting the ambiguity regarding the meaning of not-being, Socrates has at least raised questions about the all-or-nothing principle when applied in the realm of being. In mounting a third attempt to explain the possibility of false opinion, Socrates exploits the implicit considerations that have generated these questions. The result, at least initially, is a view of not-being that is not wholly opposed to being, one that, moreover, could begin to account for false opinion.

To Socrates' claim that having false opinion differs from opining about things that are not, Theaetetus acknowledges, "It's something else (*allo*), it seems (189b6)." In his third attempt to consider the possibility of false opinion Socrates focuses exactly on what he now labels *allodoxia* or other-opining. The animating insight of this attempt is that by "not being" we need not refer to that which absolutely is not. We can rather mean that a thing is simply other than something else, that it is not *that*. False opinion in this case can result from grasping only a part of such necessarily complex beings. In the course of making this argument, Socrates finds it necessary also to provide an account of what it is he means by thinking, an account that harmonizes with this complexity of the beings. Both these aspects of this third attempt make it difficult to maintain the all-or-nothing principle of the preceding sections. Yet, at the end of this section, Socrates once again insists on that principle and, at least explicitly, rejects this alternative account. Theaetetus does not protest. We need to consider the details of this important argument, including what is the first of several disappointing course changes engineered by Socrates.

Allodoxia occurs when someone "says that one of the beings is another of the beings in turn (189c2–3)." Socrates again confines such acts to misidentification rather than misdescription, that is, to mistaking one being as a whole for another being as a whole – say Theaetetus for Socrates. He does not include mistakes made concerning some characteristic of the same being. Yet he does leave the door open a crack for misdescription in emphasizing that the being is always "a thing that is" but is simply *other* than it is thought to be.

Theaetetus is much taken by Socrates' treatment of *allodoxia* and bestows on it his highest praise calling it "most correct (189c5)." However, the example Theaetetus offers to elaborate this notion fails to employ the idea of otherness introduced by Socrates. He speaks of someone having an opinion "with ugly in place of beautiful, or beautiful in place of ugly" and so persists in regarding these opposites as absolutely distinguished from one another rather than *other* than one another (189c6).

Yet careful attention to the transcript, which Socrates makes available for our study, again pays off. Concluding his appreciative statement, Theaetetus utters a phrase that, should he reflect on it, as we are able to do, might lead him out of his impasse. He states that the person having false opinion "truly has false opinions (189c7)." Appreciating the potential of this phrase, Socrates seizes on it. He huffily accuses Theaetetus of being "contemptuous" of him, complaining that in reply to the offending phrase, "truly false," he might ask "whether it's possible to become slowly quick or heavily light or for any other opposite thing to come to be opposite to itself in accord not with its own nature but with that of its opposite (189c8, c11–d3)."[16] Now, Theaetetus might well have replied, after sufficient reflection, that each of these is a perfectly intelligible possibility if the beings exist not as homogeneous wholes but as wholes constituted by parts, characterized by diverse attributes. Yet, Theaetetus, always intent on avoiding an incorrect answer, responds to the tone of Socrates' comments and lets the opportunity slide away. For his part, Socrates says he will not press the point – not because it may not be true but rather so as not to disturb Theaetetus' confidence (189d4). The excursus into the nature of thinking that Socrates now inserts into the argument attests that the point may be true.

[16] Taking the charge of contempt (*kataphronesis*) literally, we could surmise that Theaetetus' failure to see this possibility places him in opposition to *phronesis*. He lacks judgment or, more basically, the realization of how judgment becomes the crucial cognitive capacity insofar as wholes have the heterogeneous character suggested by his offhand remark. For, this character dictates that our grasp of them may not move seamlessly between parts and whole. As Socrates' indirect approach in the present context suggests, such judgment, and the reflections that lead to its necessity, cannot be conveyed by direct instruction.

Having referred several times to our thinking (*dianoia*), Socrates asks Theaetetus whether he agrees that thinking is:

> Speech that the soul itself goes through with itself about whatever it considers. Of course it's as one who doesn't know that I'm declaring it to you. For it has this look to me, that when it's thinking the soul is doing nothing other than conversing, asking itself questions and answering them itself, and affirming and denying (189e6–190a2).

In its assimilation of thinking with speech, this definition assigns to the former the predicative character of the latter.[17] When we speak, we say "this is that" or, as Socrates says here, we speak "about" things (189e7). We affirm and deny propositions about them. If, as Socrates maintains, our thinking shares this nature with speech, then it too must, at least in part, be predicative, it too must be *about* things. It would proceed through the kind of commensuration, comparing and distinguishing, characteristic of speaking. Just as the complexity of the beings seen previously denies the all-or-nothing principle, so too does thinking, so understood. A further aspect of Socrates' definition provides support for this conclusion.

I refer to Socrates' claim that the internal conversation of thinking is characterized by the soul "asking itself questions and answering them (190a1)." The need to proceed through questioning indicates a certain elusiveness about the beings such that we can and must ask questions. Questioning becomes possible and necessary when we know enough to know that we do not know fully. In this light, too, the task of learning, already dismissed, must be an intrinsic part of thinking so conceived insofar as the purpose of questioning is to progress from more to less partial knowledge – that is, to learn. To bring this point home Socrates interjects the assertion that "of course it's as one who doesn't know that I'm declaring it to you (189e7)." The beings then must be such that we approach them only partially. Such partiality is remedied, to the extent possible, by the internal application of the same method of question and answer that Socrates uses on others.

Requiring this approach, the beings must also be inherently disputable. For this reason, Socrates notes the presence of that same rhetoric in our internal conversation as in those external conversations that bear on controversial issues. The cognitive polity of our souls bears a striking resemblance to that of the communities we inhabit at least to the extent that both experience contentious debate over pressing issues. Socrates asks whether Theaetetus "ever tried to persuade yourself" of some particular conclusion (190b5). It may seem odd to find rhetoric employed in conversations with oneself. But,

[17] Sedley writes that the passage helps confirm the notion that Socrates "viewed dialectic not just as a particularly effective method of argument, but as embodying . . . the essential processes of rational thought." Curiously, he also sees this passage as assisting in substantiation of the all-or-nothing principle while also recognizing the notion that "belief is internal discourse" as an ingredient in what he regards as the successful solution to the perplexity of false belief in the *Sophist*. Sedley, *The Midwife of Platonism*, 130–2.

we recall, this internal conversational situation involves questioning because of the partiality of our knowledge, by reason of which there must certainly be room for alternative possibilities. Such room also affords ample opportunity for one's own dispositions, fears, and desires to influence the relative volume of the contending voices. However, it can also afford opportunities to assess these influences and to let each voice be heard, much as Socrates does in his conversation with Theaetetus.

In sum, persuasive speech is at home at least as much in our internal conversations as in our external. In its awareness of this possibility, Socrates' internal conversation does not differ from his midwifery. It is precisely this possibility of rhetoric in internal conversation, the possibility of *self*-deception, which requires the challenging questions of Socrates' conversational approach to philosophy as its most effective antidote.

This notion of thinking as internal conversation bears profound implications for our self-understanding. In particular, this picture of our mental life conveys the sense that the soul is necessarily somehow divided. Otherwise, we could not engage in the conversation with ourselves that is called thinking. There are, admittedly, occasional resolutions of this dividedness, when the soul "has made a determination, whether more slowly or with a quicker leap, and it asserts the same thing from that point on and is not divided (190a2–4)." Socrates calls such determinations "opinion" (190a4). He does not call them truths. His locution perhaps acknowledges that, given the intrinsic connection between the soul's dividedness and thinking, these determinations must reflect an end to thinking. In any case, the notion of soul as homogeneous entity, conveyed by Theaetetus' reference to the soul "itself by itself," must, it seems, be revised (186a4). The wider point is that the very possibility of thinking implies the elusiveness of comprehensive self-understanding, a theme explored in Socrates' forthcoming images of our cognitive apparatus. But in the present context, Socrates' attention continues to be directed at the beings and their contribution to the possibility of false opinion.

Socrates asks Theaetetus, have you "ever tried to persuade yourself that one thing is, more than anything, some other thing (190b4–6)." He asks, in addition, whether anyone "in sleep," "healthy or insane" ever asserted these things (190b6, c1). Theaetetus swears "by Zeus" that this has never happened, forgetting the previous confession of his inability to disprove the hallucinations of the dreaming, sick, and insane (190c4). Of greatest significance, however, is that what elicits Theaetetus' oath is Socrates' final example of such an "outlandish" conclusion – namely, that the two might be one (190c3). The "problem of two" again emerges to remind us just here of the heterogeneous, relational being of the beings. In his earlier reflections on the incommensurability of the powers, and in the example of the dice, Theaetetus had articulated the possibility that a being can be in one way when taken in itself, but another way when in relation to something else. To take the former instance, he had shown how the individually incommensurable powers became commensurable when taken in relation with one another (147e9–148b3). Thus, neither of the components of "two" in itself possesses the character they have when taken in relation with one another. Yet when now confronted with this possibility he is unwilling to abide such ambiguity. His indignation moves him to solicit the help of a god to stamp it out.

This heterogeneous being of the beings, which contributes to the existence of opinion, true and false, only emerges gradually in the argument. As I have noted, pressing the argument forward, Socrates focuses explicitly first on the comparison of two wholly different things rather than the attributes of a single thing being in diverse ways. He refers to someone "forming an opinion about both of two things" and insists that this person could not have "the opinion that one thing is another (190c6–8)." Yet this latter locution, literally that "another is another," can certainly apply to a single thing being in diverse ways. It raises the possibility that in our designation of a thing as "this" it can also be *other* than "this" – just as "two" is both one ("the number two," with its distinct properties) and multiple (constituted by two elements). Socrates' further examples indicate that the beings being more than, and so other than, our characterizations of them may be not only a possibility but also a necessity.[18] If this is so, then these characterizations, these opinions, must always be less than true. Opinion as such, including true opinion, would always also be in some sense false in its partiality. It would maintain an account that could always be contravened by a more comprehensive account of any particular being.

But why must the beings be more than, and thus other than, our characterization of them? The answer can be found in Socrates' assimilation of thinking with speech that, as we have seen, makes them both be *about* the beings. As such, they pick out characteristics of the particular being that can be distinguished from its being as a whole. I have maintained that in order for the beings to be knowable in this way they must *be* in diverse or heterogeneous ways. Yet what does it mean that every being *is* in diverse ways? Isn't there any being that is just simply itself?

Consider the following: even if we focus on *what* an object is, this does not yet designate fully that particular object I now see before me. To say that this thing now before me is a desk does not yet designate it as this desk on which my foot now rests. Its "deskness" is a characteristic shared with other desks. Or, to speak more broadly, the characteristics of a being, even or especially what it is, are shared with other objects of the same kind. Each being is sufficiently complex such as to be both this particular thing and this kind of thing. Each being is itself but *is* also by virtue of existing in relation to other beings. Given this heterogeneity, whichever characteristics of a being we pick out, it seems there are more and other characteristics that equally belong to it.

What I am arguing here is that the predicative nature of speech and thinking reveals what Socrates calls the otherness of the beings, that any particular being

[18] My discussion of this point is indebted to Bolotin, "False Opinion," 186–7.

is not only this but also other than this. This otherness provides a foundation for falsehood on the side of the beings insofar as any characterization of one of them will be partial. But, furthermore, as will be detailed in Chapter 9, even at the end of this road there awaits a difficulty. That is, even with a comprehensive catalogue of the aspects, the parts, of a being, there remains that question raised earlier: how do these parts cohere as a unity?

Appropriately, in the present context, Socrates refers to the possibility of regarding "another as another" (190b5–6, c7–8). And Socrates heightens our awareness of this phrase, "another is another," by instructing Theaetetus to disregard it (190c8). Attributing this notion of otherness to Socrates, however, may seem anachronistic, as might his whole response to falsehood in this passage, because it anticipates what many regard as the distinctive innovation not of Socrates but of the Eleatic Stranger in the dramatically subsequent *Sophist*.[19] Specifically, many commentators consider the Stranger's introduction of this notion of otherness as the key that unlocks the perplexity of false opinion. Yet, first, as for its being anachronistic in terms of the drama of the dialogues, any concern along these lines would have to attend to the fact that Socrates edits the present transcript *subsequent* to hearing the conversation in the *Sophist*. Furthermore, the kernel of the Stranger's response to the perplexity of false opinion is undeniably present in this passage of the *Theaetetus*.[20]

I would go still further. Socrates' approach to this perplexity reflects a deeper understanding of the perplexity than that expressed by the Eleatic Stranger. Socrates is aware that even with the recognition of otherness as crucial to understanding this perplexity, understanding a being, or the beings comprehensively, remains a problem. For this reason, moreover, the desirability of such understanding also remains a question. Socrates thus considers the problem not only in connection with the possibility of partial knowledge but also in its bearing on the question of its desirability, that is, on the ethical-political aspect of the Socratic pursuit. In appreciating this problem as something more

[19] On this point compare Polansky, *Philosophy and Knowledge*, 181 and McDowell, *Plato "Theaetetus,"* 201.

[20] Among those who recognize the kinship between the two passages are McDowell, Williams, Fine, Polansky, and Sedley. See McDowell, *Plato "Theaetetus,"* 203; Williams, "Referential Opacity," 298; Fine, "False Belief," 74; Polansky, *Philosophy and Knowledge*, 181; and Sedley, *Midwife of Platonism*, 131–6. McDowell does so with two reservations that are, however, dealt with by Fine, "False Belief," 79n14. Sedley also hesitates to attribute all the details of the *Sophist*'s treatment to the *Theaetetus*. He maintains that Socrates could not go the whole way with the Eleatic Stranger (whom he identifies with Plato) because of his inadequate or incomplete "metaphysics." See Sedley, *Midwife of Platonism*, 133–4, 148–9. Burnyeat and Polansky see the similarities between the two dialogues but also a division of labor between them. Burnyeat regards the *Theaetetus* as posing the puzzles addressed in the *Sophist*. While Polansky sees the *Theaetetus* as focusing on the knower and the *Sophist* on the beings. See Burnyeat, *The "Theaetetus" of Plato*, 72–3, 78–80, 89–90 and Polansky, *Philosophy and Knowledge*, 176, 181.

than a technical issue, Socratic conversation has resources not available to the Stranger's diairesis.[21]

These resources are on display in what follows as Socrates refrains from spelling out for Theaetetus the full implication of this notion of otherness. He only provides indications that might lure Theaetetus into a fuller examination if he is able and, more importantly, willing to see them as such.

In one such indication, Socrates recurs to the insistence on the absolute distinction between opposites and claims that Theaetetus would never maintain that "what's unjust is just" (190b3–4). But even in the unlikely event that Theaetetus has never thus misjudged, certainly others have, including perhaps those about to participate in Socrates' upcoming trial. Nor, as Socratic also asserts, can it be that "*no one* has the opinion that what's beautiful is ugly," because we have seen it occur in the dialogue before us (190d1–2, emphasis added). Finally, Socrates strews metaphors throughout the passage ("we'll give up as though we were seasick," the argument will "walk all over us and treat us however it wants") the existence of which depend on this possibility that we can take one thing as another in a way just denied (191a4–5).

Theaetetus fails to pursue any of these indications of the heterogeneity of the beings. He accepts the notion that they are speaking about two wholly different beings, rejecting the possibility that Socrates' might here refer to one thing being in diverse ways. Furthermore, he adheres to this thread of the explicit argument and follows Socrates' advice to disregard this wording ("another is another"). He thus misses the issue as a whole.

Socrates draws the conclusion that "if anyone is going to define false opinion as having crosswise-opinion, it wouldn't have any meaning (190e1–2)." Literally, they would be "saying nothing," even though this has previously been declared impossible (190e2). But Socrates' concluding pronouncement cannot outweigh the validity of the notion of otherness he has introduced here, a notion confirmed by the testimony of our common experience that beings can be in diverse ways.

Theaetetus' Sentimental Education Continued (190e5–191a6)

Or so, at least, it would seem. Yet reason and experience can still be thwarted by the powerful desires that can muffle their voices. In its awareness of the hold such desires can have on our knowing, in its awareness of the manner in which these too constitute the lens through which we view the world, the Socratic approach surpasses any other in the Platonic corpus. Appropriately, at just this point Socrates addresses the powerful affective aspect of knowing as he interrupts the argument to reflect on its implications. These "interruptions" form an essential aspect of Socrates' approach. Their form is part of Socrates' toolkit as he tests whether his interlocutor will see for himself the link between

[21] I indicate my view of the relationship between Socrates and the Eleatic Stranger in "The Rule of Wisdom and the Rule of Law in Plato's *Statesman*," 275, 275n54.

the substance of the argument and the motives behind it, whether, that is, he will see these as something more substantial than mere interruptions. Through this approach, Socrates shows us how we must confront the issues that bear on us insofar as we think, act, and think about acting. He brings the argument to bear on Theaetetus' life by revealing how it bears on his own life.

Socrates insists again that the possibility of false opinion continues to perplex him, that, moreover, it bears on his own doings in a most serious and direct way. He laments that if they fail to demonstrate the possibility of false opinion, "we'll also be forced to agree to many strange things," things that he "would be ashamed for us to be forced . . . to agree to (190e5–6, 190e9–191a1)." It gets worse: if they find themselves "to be at a loss (*aporia*) in every way, then once we've been humiliated, I suppose we'll give up as though we were seasick for the argument to walk all over us and treat us however it wants (191a3–5)." This is no merely abstract consideration for Socrates. Here the arguments are clearly our masters, exerting compelling force as they impinge on our lives in the most dramatic and immediate way.

Yet Socrates refuses to tell Theaetetus what those "strange things" might be. His surprising reticence connects with one of Socrates' goals for this examination of false opinion. In particular, his reluctance to detail the content of these "strange things" indicates, I think, his great concern for Theaetetus' and the potential philosopher's "sentimental education." I refer to their efforts to overcome those passions that make them reluctant to sustain engagement with the strange or wondrous things, reluctant to scrutinize the perplexities to which Socrates frequently refers in this passage.

We can rather easily imagine what the content of these "strange things" might be. If false opinion is impossible then it would seem that all opinions would be equally valid (or invalid).[22] There would be no possibility of distinguishing them along the lines of validity. The Protagorean position, once pronounced dead, would then be alive and kicking, Socrates' way of life confirmed as nonsensical (161e4–162a3). Clearly, these arguments impact on him in a most personal manner.

So why not tell Theaetetus the substance of these concerns? I think it is because through his forbearance Socrates exemplifies a lesson he wishes to convey to Theaetetus, a lesson perhaps only conveyable through example. Through the explicit failure to account for false opinion, Socrates has sharpened the conflict within Theaetetus' soul. Specifically, he has exacerbated the tension between, on the one hand, Theaetetus' desire for pure knowledge and, on the other, his intimate experience of false opinion. To acknowledge his experience fully Theaetetus would have to abandon the all-or-nothing principle that has preserved pure or perfect knowledge at the cost of making his experience of learning, of falsehood and error, inexplicable. Socrates cannot take this step for Theaetetus because what impedes it is not simply intellectual but a function of Theaetetus' own passions.

[22] See Polansky, *Philosophy and Knowledge*, 184.

Socrates can do exactly as much as he does do. In refusing to relate the substance of his arguments, Socrates places the spotlight on this forbearance, on this ethical stance, rather than on the content of the arguments. He exhibits, more particularly, his refusal to endorse hypothetical arguments of the kind that respond to our desires for how we wish the world to be. Instead, he shows his willingness to follow the argument even if it overturns his whole way of life. Socrates tests Theaetetus for this kind of courage, a kind not simply identifiable with that for which Euclides and Terpsion so effusively praise him.

As part of his efforts in this regard, Socrates speaks of the shame and even ridicule that await them if they remain in aporia regarding the possibility of false opinion. Theaetetus feels acutely the dread of shame, haunted as he is by the humiliation attached to giving an incorrect answer. Socrates' reference to shame must make Theaetetus prick up his ears. But the kind of shame to which Socrates calls attention differs decisively from Theaetetus' usual worries. Already in the midwife section it became clear that Socrates does not fear the kind of shame that most fear. He freely acknowledges, without indicating any desire to change his behavior, that his strangeness made him a subject of ridicule, and even contempt, by his fellow citizens. As I noted in that context, this outcome may have been an obstacle to Theaetetus becoming Socrates' student. But in the present passage, the shame that Socrates wishes to induce is not before their fellow citizens. Socrates says that if they fail to find a way out of their aporia, the argument will "walk all over us and treat us however it wants (191a5)."[23] Rather than before his fellow citizens, it is before the argument, above all, that Theaetetus needs to feel shame.[24]

In the face of his perplexity looming ever larger, Socrates maps out a "passageway for our inquiry (191a6)." He calls attention to a mistake they have made in agreeing that "it's out of one's power for one to have the opinion that things he knows are things he doesn't know, and get them false (191a9–1)." Socrates' "passageway" involves an examination of what exactly is *in our power* cognitively speaking.[25] Socrates moves the inquiry to an examination of the soul.

23 On the "seasickness" image of which this is a part, see Burnyeat, *The "Theaetetus" of Plato*, 67.

24 Saxonhouse provides an excellent account of this transformation of shame in the context of the *Apology*. Saxonhouse, *Free Speech and Democracy*, 112–26. As we see later, Theaetetus seems to require a movement beyond shame altogether.

25 This phrase, referring to the scope of our power (*dunaton*), invokes the notion of potential around which so many of the dialogue's difficulties revolve. It is a notion intimately tied to the capacity for reflection, to the capacity to take things as such and conceive how they might be what they are now, how they then might change, but nevertheless remain in some sense what they are. It confounds attempts to treat with precision what should be the most evidently straightforward fact about a being, namely, its identity. For this reason, it is not a notion looked on favorably by those who would banish ambiguity from human life. Accordingly, much of the explicit argument of the dialogue has attempted to abstract from this notion of potential beginning with the Megarians in the Prologue who are famous for little else than their denial of it. But the notion has, if anything, become more prominent because of the

Socrates' discovery of the "otherness" of the beings has made this move necessary. The deepest strand of the preceding examination points to this otherness as a source of false opinion and, hence, of partial knowledge. Otherness is a term of relation that is therefore only available to that which can apprehend such relations. Both Theaetetus and Socrates agreed that this power constituted the distinctive power of soul. The soul is no mere passive receptor in this relationship of knower and known. Any comprehensive examination of false opinion, and its allied notion of partial knowledge, must include a consideration of the soul's contribution. This consideration is all the more necessary if it is not within the soul's power to overcome the beings' intrinsically partial availability. In this case, examination of the full range of psychic activities, not only cognition but also desires and passions, becomes critically important. For, in this case, the latitude afforded by the beings' complexity can give rein to desires other than the desire to know; thus, the need for passages like the one presently under consideration.

Socrates' examination of the soul proceeds through two quite distinct images of our cognitive activity, neither of which ultimately disposes of the problematic character of false opinion. In considering their inadequacy, we must attend to the images' form and to their content. The former, too, illuminates what is "in our power" by inducing reflection on the very need to rely on such diverse images and the need to rely on images at all. This reliance raises the question whether a nonimagistic, strictly discursive, account of our knowing is unavailable. If we knew that, and why, such an account might be "out of our power," we would know much more about the partial character of our knowledge. Such knowledge of the possibility of partial knowledge is the necessary prelude to Socrates' other task – namely, to show that this knowledge is also desirable.

The Wax Block (191a7–195b5)

Theaetetus agrees with Socrates that they have made a mistake in dismissing the possibility that "one can have the opinion that things he knows are things he doesn't know and get them false (191a9–b1)." Socrates exemplifies such an error by an instance of misidentification: seeing someone from far away and mistaking him for Socrates. This failure of recognition provides the agenda for the discussion and image that follow.[26] It also dictates its inevitable inadequacy

extremity of these exertions. The forthcoming passage is no exception as the idea of potential comes into and then recedes from view. However, insofar as the central consideration of what follows is the soul's distinctive capacity for reflection, the idea of potential must always be on Socrates' mind.

[26] Some commentators think that the wax-block image considers misidentification and misdescription. Among these are Ackrill, "Plato on False Belief," 394–5; McDowell, *Plato "Theaetetus,"* 214–16, 217–18; Bostock, *Plato's "Theaetetus,"* 177–8, 181–2, 264; and Sedley, *Midwife of Platonism*, 136. Burnyeat, with whom I agree, holds that the image is meant to

which lies in its being limited only to the kind of knowing, especially familiar to us in perception, that involves the recognition of wholes.

Socrates tells Theaetetus to conceive of a blob of wax "present *in* our souls (191c8, emphasis added)." Differences in the size, purity, and flexibility of the wax underlie the cognitive inequalities among humans that show themselves in differences in memory. The wax block is "a gift from Memory, mother of the Muses"; the imprints in the wax are "whatever we want to remember of the things we see or hear or think to ourselves (191d4–5, d5–7)." Notwithstanding his mention of thinking, the image deals ever more with perception. When Socrates later repeats the cases in which false opinion is possible, he omits the central case wherein someone supposes about things known "that they're things that he doesn't know but is perceiving (192c10)." Socrates omits this case because, as the whole wax-block image requires, perception must somehow be a kind of knowledge; if someone perceives something she in some manner knows it (191e3–5). Socrates thus continues to quietly qualify the earlier refutation of Theaetetus' thesis that knowledge is perception. The initial imprints, on the basis of which we subsequently achieve recognitions, are nothing other than perceptions.[27] Given its concentration on wholes, this rehabilitation of perception should not be surprising. Nevertheless, exactly in this concentration lie the seeds of its inadequacy that Socrates illustrates in his further discussion of the image's capability.

In the subsequent remarkable passage, Socrates adduces the variety of cases in which, on this model, false opinion is, and is not, possible (192a–c6). As many have noted, the passage seems an instance when we are privy to Socrates' speech with himself, when he states out loud the sort of analytical activity that underlies his usually less complicated questions. In total, he adduces seventeen such cases, a total that replicates the number of cases dealt with in Theodorus' consideration of powers discussed much earlier in the dialogue by Theaetetus.

In response to that previous list, Theaetetus discovered a means by which to comprehend these many possibilities. Faced with Socrates' lengthy and complicated list, many commentators have followed Theaetetus' example, categorizing this multiplicity for the sake of intelligibility.[28] Although such efforts are required they should not obscure one significant point made by Socrates' ratiocination: the kind of cognitive activity he thereby demonstrates does not fall within the capability of the wax-block image he has just announced. This

apply only to misidentification. He argues the point, specifically in response to McDowell, in Burnyeat, *The "Theaetetus" of Plato*, 104–5n40. This is not to deny that Socrates does mention thinking (and misthinking) in his account, but these are suggestions of the inadequacy of the image. See, e.g., 191d6–7, 195a8.

27 Socrates does ask Theaetetus whether it is possible regarding the things one does not know that one could suppose "they're things he doesn't know but is perceiving (192c10). But Socrates does not maintain this position himself.

28 Classifications are provided by Burnyeat, *The "Theaetetus" of Plato*, 97; Dorter, *Form and Good*, 98–101; and Polansky, *Philosophy and Knowledge*, 187–90.

image does not comprehend the notion of thinking as speaking. Socrates later makes this inadequacy explicit when he points to the existence of errors involving not only the correlation of perception and thought but also errors in the realm of thought alone, errors in reasoning or discursive analysis. Socrates introduces the aviary image as a remedy for this defect.

I will consider this inadequacy in more detail in the transition to that image. Yet there is a further inadequacy that, being shared by both images, contributes even more profoundly to the partiality of knowledge. Socrates portrays an aspect of the active power of thinking as falling outside both images. I refer to that power by which Socrates can recognize the need to move beyond the wax-block image, by which he recognizes the deficiency of opinion as such. For a portrayal of this power we must rely on the drama of the dialogue, its movement between the two images. We can say that a soul with this power to recognize its own deficiencies, with this capacity for self-relation, must be complex.

Socrates points to such complexity in the present context by telling Theaetetus that the wax block is "in" the soul. It is not, therefore, perfectly contiguous with it. But he lets us see what is at stake in this complexity of soul through his ultimate efforts to deny it. These efforts culminate in the final presentation of the wax block in which Socrates attempts not only to make the wax-block image deny this complexity but, in a related move, to deny it is an image at all. Instead, he treats the image as the simple truth about the soul, with the soul understood in terms of a mechanistic, nonreflective process. There are indications, however, of this complexity prior to that point, and it is useful to trace the development of this presentation.

The image depicts the fitting (or misfitting) of perceptions into previously formed indentations in the wax of memory (191d4–e1). The aspect of the soul that does the fitting remains outside this portrayal throughout. Again, the wax block is *in* the soul. Intellect, the activity of reflection, is distinct from what is known. It is an activity whose effects can be seen. However, it is not clear that it is knowable in the same way that a being's formal structure might be. This difference is evident in how we speak about knowing. Knowledge, for example, is taken to be an achievement, the result of an effort. The term *knowledge* is itself inherently normative, a distinction we withhold from all those contents of the mind that fail to fulfill a set of criteria. The effort that yields knowledge is undertaken specifically by the power of the intellect on the contents of the mind.

The knowledge that results from this effort must at a minimum convey the capacity to designate the kind of thing a being is. This requires us to grasp and articulate what it is, the structure of the being that makes it just the being it is – distinct from some, akin to others. It is through the intellect's activity alone that the knowable becomes something known. Crucial to the present point, it is this difference between the knower and known that requires the treatment of false opinion through the lenses of both being and knowing. For to neglect this distinctive power of intellect would leave us unable even to account for the distinction between truth and falsehood. There would only be that which happens indiscriminately to strike our senses, which is precisely the ultimate result of Theaetetus' initial definition holding that knowledge is perception. Nor would we be able to account even for the simple statement "I know X." This statement, too, envisions an activity, distinguishable from an object, that has the possibility of succeeding in varying degrees.[29] I dwell on this distinction to underscore the character of Socrates' forthcoming speech when, in the conclusion of the wax-block presentation, he portrays the mind as a passive, merely receptive mechanism.

It is this distinction between knower and known that also enables aspects of the knower other than purely cognitive capacities to bear on knowing. For example, Socrates calls attention to the relative "eagerness" with which the viewer assigns perceptions to imprints as playing an important role in cognition (193c2). He could as well speak of the knower's motive, the intent, or view of good, all of which can affect the activity of the knower on the known. Each of these might provide a source of error. In this way, the division between the power of intellect and the contents of the mind presents a persistent source of the partiality of our knowledge.

There is a further issue raised if this division is a necessary feature of the soul. If it is, we can well wonder how we could ever wholly know our own minds. There could, it seems, be no transcendent point from which we could validate our knowledge once and for all, to know that we know and so rid ourselves of error. Each act of knowing would reassert this division. It is in the shadow of this issue that Socrates provides a portrayal of the wax block that aims to eliminate this difficulty by denying the inherent divisions born of the difference between knowing and known.

Now in his last iteration of the wax-block image Socrates attempts a strictly materialistic account of the functioning of the mind, one that abstracts from the soul's power of reflection. He prepares Theaetetus to accept the account by appealing to his desire for beauty, or wholeness, by saying that "having true opinions is a beautiful thing, and being wrong is an ugly thing (194c2–3)." In this materialistic account of thinking the quality of the wax is made to explain thinking and error. Those with the proper kind of wax – allowing for pure, deep, well-spaced imprints – have true opinions. They "quickly sort out, each into its own mold, the things that are called beings, and so it's they who are called wise (194d5–7)." Those with defective wax – impure, too hard or too soft, with little room for imprints – "mis-see and mishear, and mistake most things in their thinking (195a5–9)." They are "without understanding (*amatheis*, 195a9)."

Socrates' presentation enthralls Theaetetus. It provides all that he yearns for. He longs himself to be the knower with the gift of fine wax. He would

[29] On these issues see Stanley Rosen, *The Limits of Analysis* (New York: Basic Books, 1980), 4–18, 36–7.

then know quickly and correctly, readily fitting the being into the correct slot. He could be the one who knows the being as a whole, at once, avoiding the need to engage the challenging questions of the refuters or of Socrates. Theaetetus calls this account, "the most correct things human beings could say (195b1)."

Theaetetus fails to notice that Socrates has obscured the imagistic character of the wax-block image. Images portray, and thus assist in understanding, what we cannot wholly grasp, for example, the workings of our cognitive apparatus. These images or, as we might say, these hypotheses, provide speculative accounts that must then be assessed by the challenging questions characteristic of thinking as speaking. Theaetetus would prefer that we neglect this requirement. Yet Socrates' ostentatious neglect of the status of this image, as an image, serves precisely to bring it forcefully to our attention. This neglect connects directly to the explicit failure to recognize the distinction between knower and known, for it is that distinction that makes the soul's nature as a whole elusive and in need of being portrayed in images – something even Theodorus acknowledged in deed.

Yet if we are attentive to some of the details of Socrates' presentation we see that that distinction is still present, if only implicitly. In particular, Socrates relies on a particularly tortured interpretation of a passage in Homer to substantiate his present account of the wax block. In his reading, Socrates takes as real what is clearly in Homer an image (194c7–9, e1–2).[30] Through this act of interpretation, highlighted by its extravagantly dubious character, he gives prominence to a possibility denied by the overall presentation – namely, the act of interpretation and the latitude of understanding it implies. Were our knowing to have the automatic, unreflective character he describes, interpretation would be neither possible nor necessary. There would be no knower for whom the question of meaning could arise as a question.

It is that same latitude that compels and enables the capacity of image making, expressed in its fullest flowering in the poetic works of a Homer, or a Plato. In this light, a previously mentioned detail takes on added significance. Socrates had referred at the beginning of the wax-block presentation to memory, as the "Mother of the Muses (191d4–5)." To serve in this maternal capacity, memory must differ significantly from the mechanical operation described at the conclusion of the wax-block presentation. The creations of Homer and Plato are possible only insofar as memories can be taken up, reflected on, and transfigured by the power of reflection. However, this use of memories, perfected in the creative genius, epitomizes a possibility each of us has experienced. We each engage in the Muse-ic activity of arranging and rearranging the snapshots in memory's scrapbook in response to shifting purposes. This is a *human* capacity whose power is wholly obscured if memory is only the immediate, mechanical process Socrates describes.

[30] Homer *Iliad* 2.851.

It is not only then that the beings in their complexity enable and compel interpretation and provide a ground for falsehood. Also required for this activity of interpretation is the mind's capacity to reflect. The beings in their complexity are susceptible to being understood in vastly different ways. Their meaning is a question. But that question, what something means, can only be a question to a being for which it can mean, that is, a being with the power of intellect that enables the soul to consider its contents. It is this capacity, I have argued, that also provides an ongoing source of error as it permits latitude in interpretation. This capacity, alluded to by Socrates' very neglect of it, becomes more prominent in the action that follows. Before taking up the aviary image, we must attend to the action that bridges Socrates' first and second images of our cognitive capacity. Familiar by now with the need to treat the dialogue reflexively, the cognitive activity used to recognize the need for, and then construct, this bridge, deserves our close attention. Once again, Socrates' deeds are in our sights.

Garrulity and Shamelessness (195b6–d6)

Socrates brings himself up short. He confesses that he is "disgusted at my own thickheadedness and true garrulity (195c1–2)." Note that this self-critique comes at the very height of Theaetetus' satisfaction with the achievement of the argument (195b1, b8). Thanks to Euclides' editing, we are deprived of any explicit account of the affect of Socrates' self-denunciation on Theaetetus. Nevertheless, in the speeches we can still sense his heart sinking. Theaetetus has just heard an account that satisfies his all-or-nothing conception of knowing, its immediacy, at least for those like him who have the gift of top-notch wax. At the same time, the account "explains" for him the presence of false opinion by attributing it to those who lack this gift. Theaetetus can now embrace his belief in the absolute separateness of opposites regarding knowing without giving up on the possibility of false opinion. It is understandable, then, that as Socrates now voices his self-disgust, Theaetetus' disappointment is palpable. He asks Socrates, rather plaintively: "What? What made you say that? (195b11)."

It is precisely that quality for which he chides himself that compels and enables Socrates' remarks. Garrulity is a quality made possible by, though not simply reducible to, that power of reflection that the materialistic account aimed to suppress. This power, exhibitable but perhaps not analyzable, enables us to ask the questions that the garrulous Socrates inevitably asks: is what he had taken as the whole really the whole? Or is it rather a part of some broader context, some more comprehensive whole, now coming into view, of which it is a part? As evident in Theaetetus' reaction and in the drama of other dialogues, the consequences of this power are not always welcome. A brief consideration of long-windedness or garrulity helps us see all that the drama means here to convey.

This charge of garrulity is found throughout the Platonic corpus. It refers to the inclination, evident in sophists but perhaps especially in philosophers, to engage in high-flying speculation, in idle talk. Given his disappointment at Socrates' unwillingness to accept the pleasing end the argument seemed to have reached, Theaetetus might want to level such a charge. After all, Socrates' garrulity results in the rejection of that "supernaturally" correct view that had dissolved Theaetetus' perplexity (194d8). The Eleatic Stranger captures Theaetetus' frustration in the *Sophist* where he distinguishes between those who dispute endlessly for money and those, like Socrates, who do so without pay, neglecting their own affairs. Their neglect is due to the pleasure they take in this pastime, although "its speaking is heard without pleasure by many of its auditors."[31] Theaetetus knows what he means. The Eleatic terms this activity "garrulity."[32]

Members of the wider community often share such frustration. In the *Statesman*, the Eleatic Stranger connects garrulity with the displeasure Theaetetus feels with other of Socrates' auditors, beyond eager young students. Specifically, the Eleatic alludes to Socrates' fate when he refers to "a talker about highfalutin things, a kind of garrulous sophist" . . . "corrupting different people younger than himself."[33] Witnessing such activity, any citizen "who wants, can and is permitted to draw up an indictment and haul him before a . . . court of law."[34] This description occurs in the context of a discussion about the need for laws to preserve and stabilize the settled convictions of the community.[35] The fear is that Socratic garrulity might open up a horizon, point to a greater whole, from which vantage point the laws will be revealed as partial and so inadequate. Socrates' talk disrupts the efforts of the political community, and of those such as Theaetetus, to comprehend and thus control the world. His garrulity exasperates both.

Yet, in other dialogues, such "idle talk" is characterized as indispensable to philosophic inquiry. For example, in the dialogue of the same name, Parmenides recommends such talk to the then-youthful Socrates.[36] As a young man, Socrates shared Theaetetus' aspiration for the correct answer of the most comprehensive scope. Parmenides recommends such speculation to Socrates even while affirming that the many would regard such talk as idle or merely playful. According to Parmenides, garrulous talk appears to the many as a waste of time because it moves toward no decisive conclusion. But for the philosopher it can play an important role. It can check unquestioned presuppositions and subject them to scrutiny precisely by opening up the vista in which presuppositions can be made explicit. And it seems essential to the philosopher to want to know that he knows – and that he doesn't know.[37]

31 *Sophist* 225d7–9. See also Polansky who associates this activity with Socrates. *Philosophy and Knowledge*, 193.

32 *Sophist* 225d10–11.

33 *Statesman* 299b7–8.

34 Ibid., 299c2–3.

35 I have dealt with this passage in "The Rule of Wisdom and the Rule of Law," 272–3.

36 *Parmenides* 135c8–d6.

37 See Miller, *Parmenides*, 71–3.

Likewise, in the *Phaedrus* the great arts are said to require supplementation by "garrulity and high-flown speculation" about nature.[38] Such speculation serves exactly the purpose previously mentioned – namely, to open up the space to consider the whole in which this current argument resides. The importance that Plato accords this capacity is evident in the form of his writing which demands that we continually ask whether we have in view that whole that unifies the myriad details. As Charles Griswold writes about the reference to garrulity in the *Phaedrus*, "This does not sound much like rigorous method, but it does sound like a Socratic dialogue."[39]

In the context of the *Theaetetus*, what is being described is the power that underlies midwifery. This power enables us to see our opinions as such, to see them as partial, and thus in need of further elaboration in the light of some greater whole. Certainly, the power of ratiocination is necessary for this cognitive activity, but it is not sufficient. We need also to recognize something lacking in argument, to see that with regard to this or that issue there is a *question*. We have been called on throughout the dialogue to use this power, beginning from the abrupt commencement of Socrates' conversation with Theodorus. Here, in the transition between the two images of mind, Socrates exhibits it once again. Its exhibition in this context illustrates the possibility previously mentioned: it is exhibited because it is not simply articulable. Certainly, neither of the images captures it. Nevertheless, this premonitory awareness of the deficiency of wholes, Socrates' knowledge of ignorance, is cognitively decisive for negotiating the persistent discrepancy of parts and wholes. As such, it is the indispensable means and, in the elaboration of its results, the desirable goal of Socratic inquiry. It is an essential aspect of the *phronesis* that comes to us in the *Theaetetus* in the guise of midwifery.

Through Socrates' move beyond the wax block, our knowing is shown to proceed by the dawning awareness that what we took to be a whole is a part of an even greater whole. This awareness stands as a persistent possibility insofar as what we know of the beings always reveals itself on further examination to be partial. And, as Socrates' repeated use of the example of knowing Theaetetus serves to remind us, this characterization applies especially to knowledge of humans, including ourselves. Yet although this insight may be cognitive, one's reaction to it involves other aspects of the soul. It involves awareness but also self-dissatisfaction, an intellectual ability but also a willingness to overcome the disappointment generated by seeing that what was taken to be a whole is only a part. The latitude that attends this power, which provides for the mind's active rather than merely receptive role in knowing, permits normative considerations to enter our knowing. Recall that Socrates joins his reference to garrulity with a sense of self-disgust (195c1). Moreover, Socrates connects the willingness to overcome disappointment at the perceived partiality of an argument with a sense of shame (196d3). He makes this connection in the transition

[38] *Phaedrus* 269e4–270a1.

[39] Griswold, *Plato's "Phaedrus,"* 183.

to a new image necessitated by his self-dissatisfaction. We need to consider the details of this transition to see how shame enters in to the picture.

In addition to the preceding self-condemnation, Socrates also charges himself with thickheadedness, a quality that generates self-disgust. He had used this word to refer to those with overly dense wax. These thickheaded ones could not be included among "the wise" who match perception to imprint with admirable celerity. "But why," Theaetetus asks, "are *you* disgusted? (195c5, emphasis added)." Socrates conjures the imaginary questioner to explain that there are errors other than those arising from the relationship between perception and thought alone. The wax-block image has concentrated on our recognition of wholes, but there are errors pertaining to thoughts alone, matters of reasoning or analysis, that involve relationships between, among, and within these wholes. To exemplify this latter sort of error, Socrates offers the possibility that someone might take five and seven to be eleven rather than twelve (195e9–196a8). If error of this type is possible with respect to the thoughts alone, then false opinion cannot be simply "the swerving of a thought in relation to a perception (196c4–5)."

With the introduction of this possibility, they once again come face to face with the original dilemma: "either there is no false opinion, or it's possible not to know the things one knows (196c7–8)." Socrates makes clear that if one of these is true, the other cannot be: "there's no chance that the argument is going to allow them both (196d1–2)." Strict necessity connects the existence of false opinion and the possibility that we can *not know* the things we know. Theaetetus now calls this an aporia (196c9). The clash between his experience and his desires leaves him no way out, no "passageway" for his inquiry (196c9).

However, the question for Theaetetus, and for anyone reading the conversation, is, what ought to be done in the face of his perplexity? How should we confront our cognitive neediness? Socrates encourages Theaetetus by saying that "one ought to be brave enough for any risk (196d2)." Courage is required to emulate Socrates' example, as he directs his ire not toward the source of the boundary-shattering reflection, but against himself as one who was self-deceived, one who took as a whole that which is not a whole. In this light, it is clear that the battle for Theaetetus' soul occurs on a field introduced at the dialogue's outset: the meaning of courage. One kind of courage, expressed in Theaetetus' willingness to die for his country, is so nobly resplendent as to earn the praise even of non-Athenians. The other, Socrates' intellectual courage, so far from being resplendent, requires the willingness to be shameless.

Accordingly, Socrates now tells Theaetetus that they are to "try to do something shameless" in their pursuit of the argument (196d2–3).[40] Knowing

[40] The root of the word used is *aischun* rather than *aidos*. Bernard Williams, for one, is disinclined to see a difference between the two words. Others do not agree. See Bernard Williams, *Shame and Necessity* (Berkeley: University of California Press, 1993), 194n9. For the controversy concerning the relationship between the two words see the material in Saxonhouse, *Free Speech and Democracy*, 61n9.

that shame and honor are of capital importance to the young and vulnerable Theaetetus, Socrates advises him to learn to be shameless. Previously, Socrates undertook to reorient Theaetetus' shame away from anxiety about community standards toward the requirements of the argument (190e8–191a6). That step now appears as a way station to the present point. Now they are to be shameless, even or especially, in the face of the argument. Their shameless act consists specifically in saying "what sort of thing knowing is" without, however, knowing fully what it is (196d5–6). In a moment of candor Socrates adds, "You don't seem to grasp that the whole discussion of ours from the start has been a search for knowledge on the assumption that we don't know what it is (196d8–9)." In this regard, their inquiry, any inquiry as such, must be shameless. We know enough of the subject to know somehow that we must inquire into it, but not enough to say what it is with such certainty and precision that inquiry becomes unnecessary. Insofar as we inquire, we reside within the realm of partial knowledge. This realm is the home of the question. In his treatment of this second definition, Socrates provides the blueprint of his philosophic home.

With even further candor, Socrates connects this cognitive situation to his conception of human being. Theaetetus asks, "But in what way will you have a conversation, Socrates, if you abstain from these words? (196e8–9)." Socrates responds, "In no way, being who I am (197a1)." This confessional statement deserves our careful consideration. It brings together the twin themes of the passage: the possibility (indeed, necessity) of partial knowledge and its desirability. It proclaims that if we are fully aware of ourselves, such knowledge is the best we can hope for.

To appreciate the import of this far-reaching statement, I want to reflect further on why Socrates characterizes the activity that aims at such a goal as shameless. To this end, we need to revisit the movement of the argument in which Socrates first relocates shame into the realm of intellectual inquiry, and then urges Theaetetus to be shameless. We need first to consider what shame can mean in the context of intellectual inquiry and, next, why we should resist it even there.

Let's begin from Socrates' contrast in the present context between his own behavior and that of the contradictor. The latter would counsel abstaining from such use of words whose meaning we do not fully know (197a1–3). The sophist, it seems, succumbs to the shame that Socrates resists. Generally speaking, we feel shame when in the sight of others (internalized as our own judgment) we fail to live up to some community standard.[41] If this is so, what is the

41 Williams writes, "Even if shame and its motivations always involve in some way or other an idea of the gaze of another, it is important that for many of its operations the imagined gaze of an imagined other will do." Williams, *Shame and Necessity*, 82. Saxonhouse writes, "To feel shame is to live in the minds of others." Saxonhouse, *Free Speech and Democracy*, 76. Her treatment of shame brings out the dependence inherent in those governed by shame, something that is especially important to see in those who believe themselves to be self-sufficient.

source of the shame in the present case? Socrates' reference to himself as one of the "lowly folks" provides a clue (197a4). Presumably, his lesser stature permits, or is a result of, his willingness to do what is shameless. However, in this way he is to be distinguished from other intellectual types, not only the contradictors. For Socrates used this same designation in the Digression to distinguish those he called the "tip-top Philosophers" from philosophy's lowly practitioners (173c7–9). In the Digression, he detailed the numerous ways that these Philosophers differ significantly from himself, presaging his present self-designation as one of the "lowly" ones. At the very heart of the distinction between himself and the tip-top Philosophers lies their haughty contempt for that which is "at their feet," which includes the realm of politics (174a8). Such matters are beneath the Philosophers. To lower themselves to the mundane, instead of flying above the city communing only with the wholes, would cause them intense shame – but, again, shame before what standard?

Their shame is, I think, felt not in the face of their own individual shortcomings but of the limitations of humans as such.[42] Their shame derives from the sense that our knowing does not rise to the standard of omniscient beings who know wholly and all at once, that we unavoidably use words whose meanings we do not fully know. And we do so with reference to the most important things. In their response to this condition, the Philosophers permit their reflections to be shaped by that shame, when they deny those limitations, when they avert their eyes from our neediness.

The line Socrates often quotes from the *Odyssey* expresses his alternative: "It is not good for shame to be present in a needy man."[43] Shame is not good for the one who is needy precisely because it can impede his attainment of good. It can even obstruct the fulfillment or, if taken far enough, the very awareness of that neediness that permeates, and is a spur to, Socratic inquiry. Socrates is acutely aware of his own needy nature, aware that he is treating as wholes such notions as "knowledge" that he knows he does not wholly know. The best he can do is to be aware of his neediness in this regard, knowing what he does not know: thus, the paramount importance of *phronesis*. This is the best course because it preserves the availability of the very great good of remedying this defect as far as humanly possible. Such partial knowledge in this sense is, therefore, preeminently desirable.

42 In this regard, consider Saxonhouse's remarks concerning the act of blushing. She writes, "The gaze of others publicizes our frailties and vulnerabilities and the uncovering of our frailties, what is most private, most distinctly our own, elicits the vivid physiological expression of shame , the blush." Note also Saxonhouse's comments on the reaction of such Socratic interlocutors as Hippothales in the *Lysis* and Alcibiades in the *Symposium* to Socrates' revealing of their inadequacies and vulnerabilities. Their reaction squares with Socrates' discussion of such students in the midwife section. Again, most painful to them, and productive of shame and the desire to run and cover, is the sense of their own lack of self-sufficiency, their lack of power. Saxonhouse, *Free Speech and Democracy*, 73–4.

43 Homer *Odyssey* xvii. 347. See *Laches* 201b1–3 and *Charmides* 161a2–4.

Socrates' shamelessness is the alternative to the Philosophers' pretense that they are gods.[44] And in their sense of shame, the sophist and the tip-top Philosopher ally intellectually with the upholders of the political community.[45] For this reason, Socrates invokes this politically fraught notion of shame in this context. All of them, including Theaetetus, wish to deny our neediness. The heart of the Socratic philosophic revolution lies precisely in his willingness to face this need, a willingness that requires the specifically Socratic brand of courage.

This confrontation compels Socrates to trouble the city as the garrulous philosopher questions its purported self-sufficiency, its claim to know regarding the most important things. But taking seriously the city's claim to know, Socrates does not simply reject it out of hand. Guided by awareness of his neediness, he does not oppose one claim of self-sufficiency with another. Rather, he sees the city's claim as partial, as constituted by law, which, as we have seen, is synonymous with opinion. Through this attention to the city, and to opinion, Socrates remedies the practice of his philosophic predecessors. Unlike them, he does not believe he can fly free beyond these boundaries in the rarefied air of knowledge alone. His remedy derives from the acute self-knowledge that enables him to say with candor, "being who I am. . . . "

The image that follows speaks to that power of reflection that Socratic garrulity requires. Yet the reasoning power expressed in the new image proves to be inadequate in ways that do not permit us to dispense wholly with the first image. Both images, and the powers they represent, contribute to the whole that is knowledge. It is the requirement of these two heterogeneous images that makes *phronesis* indispensable in the consideration of the whole of knowledge.

The Aviary (195d7–200d4)

Socrates' new image of the mind aims to account for the kind of error he had neglected. The mind is to be regarded as an aviary in which birds of knowledge flutter about. He does not, however, leave the wax image completely behind. The aviary image does not dispose of all difficulties.[46] Our task, again, is to locate its inadequacies and consider how these form a part of our cognitive situation.

[44] In this light, Socrates' shamelessness, his awareness of human limits, might be seen as the source of his justice.

[45] The structure of Socrates' comments distances him from this practice of contradiction, for completion of the apodosis would have placed him in the position of being the contradictor. Instead, he makes someone else take up that role.

[46] Both Burnyeat and Sedley recognize that the wax block image is not completely rejected. It returns, e.g., at 209c7 in the third definition. Sedley provides a different explanation of why it is preserved than the one I offer in the text. See Burnyeat, *The "Theaetetus" of Plato*, 102 and Sedley, *Midwife of Platonism*, 139–40 and 140n27.

The example used throughout the aviary is drawn from mathematics. This is perfectly appropriate because mathematics is the paradigm of the kind of cognitive activity Socrates here illustrates: discursive analysis, that comparing and contrasting of beings which depends on our seeing the parts that constitute the wholes we initially recognize. We need to consider, therefore, why discursive analysis is on its own insufficient as an account of our knowing

Socrates' presentation of the aviary image begins with great promise. He abandons the dominant Eleaticism to invoke the notion of potential in relationship to knowledge. The distinction he draws between merely "possessing" knowledge, as opposed to the stronger sense of "having" it, calls attention to several issues that the all-or-nothing principle had presumably settled (197b1–c5).[47] Most obviously, the distinction permits several different senses of knowing, each of them identifiable as such. It also welcomes back the possibilities of teaching and learning earlier dismissed. Additionally, Socrates' distinction seems to promise the recognition of what had previously remained submerged: the active power of mind. The image of the aviary points in this direction. With its emphasis on touch rather than sight, on grasping the birds of knowledge, the image has a role for the activity wherein we take up, regard, and even shape the contents of our mind. Plato was fully aware of a view of the mind as other than passive and wholly receptive.

However, what follows does not explicitly fulfill this promising beginning. Socrates soon reimposes the Eleatic view, apparently closing the door previously opened. Nevertheless, we will have seen through this door and thus are able to extrapolate what a more adequate account of our knowing might look like. His deeds in the course of the presentation again require that we reflect on the nonintellectual requirements of this more adequate account. We begin our look at the aviary image, as so often in the *Theaetetus*, with Socrates' treatment of teaching and learning.

Socrates speaks about "what people call" teaching and learning (198b4). His use of similar phrases alerts us to the possibility that he is using this issue to exemplify the difference between opinion and knowledge inasmuch as what people say may differ from what it is. The definitions he pronounces in this context deepen this impression because of the stark difference between these definitions and his own practice of midwifery. He tells Theaetetus that "teaching" involves the conveyance of information to another, filling someone else's previously vacant enclosure (198a10–b2). It is a definition quite at odds with Socratic midwifery that works on the multiplicity of views already held by the student. Socrates vehemently and repeatedly denied that he in any way fills another's enclosure.

Nevertheless, the alternative practice of midwifery is not wholly missing from the present context. Socrates notes that in addition to the foregoing

47 On this distinction in this context, see Sedley, Midwife of Platonism, 140 and Menn, "The Origins of Aristotle's Concept of *energeia*," 73–5, 81–7, 112–13.

definition of teaching, "there is such a thing as thoroughly understanding these same things *again* by *taking back up* and holding the knowledge of each thing that he'd possessed for some time (198d6–8, emphasis added)." This notion of reconsidering, of reflecting on what we have taken for granted, expresses Socrates' own approach. It takes what was once simply conveyed – those pieces of knowledge, those birds simply possessed within our enclosures – and subjects them to the scrutiny that enables us to grasp them, to truly have and hold them rather than just possess them. Such scrutiny seeks the reasons underlying our opinions. This notion of teaching, a notion congruent with Socrates' own practice, runs athwart teaching understood simply as the conveyance of information.

The lack of readily available names for this Socratic notion of teaching and learning suggests that it is not widely shared (198a2–3, 198e1–2, 199a4–5). Theaetetus calls Socrates' account "strange," the word Socrates had used when describing his fellow citizens' characterization of his midwifery (198e6). This characterization is proof enough that Socrates sees something almost no one else does. He has reflected on the common opinion regarding teaching and learning in a way others are unable and unwilling to do. They remain immersed in *the* false opinion, that they believe they know what they do not. The issue of teaching and learning, of the movement from opinion to knowledge, is used to illustrate the character of that movement. This movement shows in action once again Socrates' "garrulity," the power by which he questions whether what we take to be a whole is a whole. This power eluded the first image that dealt only with the bare recognition of wholes.

For its part, as I noted, the aviary image treats the ratiocinative activity by which we consider the parts of wholes, compare and contrast them, one with another. Such activity, to repeat, takes as its paradigm mathematics, especially counting. Its goal lies in disclosing the parts, the elements of the wholes, which can be treated in the way described owing to their underlying commensurability. The discursive activity portrayed in the aviary image shows the parts that constitute the whole, a demonstration that we take to be an explanation of that whole. Yet such analysis fares no better than the cognitive activity expressed through the wax-block image when it comes to explaining that power exhibited in Socrates' garrulity. For not only can it not provide those initial wholes that are then subject to analysis, on its own it cannot provide the insight that shows the need for analysis. Nor can it enable us to see what a complete examination of a whole in its wholeness might be. This must especially be the case when we are dealing with those wholes, among which is the human whole, whose wholeness is not simply constituted through a summation of their parts.

The existence of this power of insight bears on the sources of false opinion. It means that the soul persists as divided, divided from its contents and so maintaining that latitude, discussed earlier, with respect to the things known. Socrates portrays this latitude in the aviary image by the distinction he draws between number as a piece of knowledge and the art of arithmetic. The latter is regarded not as a piece of knowledge, not as another bird, but as a skill, the activity of the chase (198a7–8).[48] These pieces of knowledge can be arranged and used in a vast variety of ways, as expressed by the great variety of *technai*. What needs to be seen at present, however, is that by separating this skill or art from the pieces of knowledge, Socrates lets us see the freedom we have regarding their use. This freedom does not simply depend on something inherent in the knowledge but also on the knower's intent.

As should by now be clear, by "the knower" we cannot simply mean the power of intellect alone. Precisely insofar as this power requires and establishes a distance from the things known, the space is thereby opened up for the influence of all other aspects of soul on our knowing, whether the desire that impels some few to pursue the argument wherever it might go or those desires that cause others to shrink from this prospect. Because of this latitude again there exists in the character of the knower, taken in all its aspects, a rich source of error. Such error is not simply a matter of inadvertence but more an ingrained source of systematic error. To use Socrates' images, it is less a matter of getting one's shoes on the wrong feet than of a distorting mirror (193c3–4, c7–8). Only such a source of error could explain how so many can persistently err when each has every intention and hope of getting things right. As revealed by the present discussion, the crucial sort of error resides in deception, especially self-deception, rather than simply making mistakes.

It is at exactly this point that, to our disappointment, Socrates reintroduces just such a distorting mirror – namely, the inquiry-squashing all-or-nothing principle. Had he stuck with the acknowledgment of potential we might have had an examination of the active mind that would provide insight into the most debilitating sources of error. Seemingly, that examination will not occur. Yet we should not let disappointment cloud our view entirely. Specifically, we need to be open to the possibility that this examination might continue and in the most appropriate possible way, in a way that might enable Theaetetus to possess, rather than merely have, the requisite knowledge. The examination attends particularly to Theaetetus' deeds. Let me explain why this attention is appropriate.

We have learned that the soul in its dividedness is itself a source of error. But precisely owing to this dividedness its wholeness eludes us. Error, therefore, cannot be remedied simply by providing the comprehensive account of soul. Knowledge of the soul becomes urgently required once we see its role in error. Because of the soul's complex character, such knowledge must be sought, however, not only in speeches about the soul but in the deeds. The dialogue form in general reinforces this insight invoking as it does not only the speeches but also the deeds of individuals, a fact underscored by Euclides' efforts to excise the latter. Although the pervasive theme of the dialogue, the meaning of knowledge, may lend itself to Euclides' attempt to make the conversation

[48] See Polansky, *Philosophy and Knowledge*, 197–8.

wholly abstract, Plato enables us to see that it is more deeply devoted to the very concrete examination of one individual's soul, that individual after which the dialogue is named (145b6–9). As with Socrates' garrulity, there are aspects of the soul best grasped through attending to their exhibition. In Socrates' reversal of the argument, we have an opportunity to examine Theaetetus' and our own deeds. What will be his (and our) reaction as Socrates turns away from the most promising avenue of inquiry?

The immediate result of Socrates' reintroduction of the all-or-nothing principle is that the complexity of both the beings and the soul, which enables there to be false opinion, appear as paradoxes or as what he calls "a more dreadful experience (199c7–8)." Socrates asks, "In the first place, for someone who has knowledge of anything to be ignorant of that very thing, not by means of ignorance but by means of his own knowledge, and next, to have the opinion that this is something else and something else in turn is this, how is that not a load of nonsense? (199d1–4)." In the first he finds it paradoxical that knowledge should be a cause of ignorance. Yet, this is precisely the case with respect to the knowledge of ignorance that Socrates has been exhibiting in his alternative notion of teaching and learning.[49] The second paradox concerns the heterogeneity of the beings that makes them subject to being understood in diverse ways so that any account of them is in some sense partial.

Theaetetus might have reacted by insisting that this is just what Socrates has shown, that these paradoxes are difficulties that must be faced because they are based on a more accurate account of our knowing, one that includes potential. Instead, he succumbs to his attraction to the all-or-nothing principle and regards them as evidence of serious defects with the argument. He thus exhibits the power of a view of good to modify our knowing. He shows how self-deception generates error. By having Theaetetus react in this way Plato continues the examination of error in the most penetrating manner. He directs us to what must be the locus of our most intense scrutiny: the desires and the attendant notions of good that shape and can distort our knowing.

Theaetetus' dismay at this turn of events – that still another image is about to be discarded – prompts him to deliver one of his longest speeches in the dialogue. It is a speech that purposefully avoids invoking that power of intellect, the active mind, that involves the troubling notion of potential. He addresses himself solely to the contents of the mind. Specifically, Theaetetus raises the possibility that there are pieces of nonknowledge flying about the aviary as well as pieces of knowledge (199e1–3).[50] Error, he suggests, occurs when "the hunter" grasps one of these birds of nonknowledge (199e3–4). Theaetetus'

[49] For the view that Socrates himself subscribes to the belief that these are paradoxes, see Sedley, *Midwife of Platonism*, 146–8.

[50] For alternative treatments of Theaetetus' objection, see Cornford, *Plato's Theory of Knowledge*,138; Ackrill, "Plato on False Belief," 399–401; McDowell, *Plato "Theaetetus,"* 224–5; and Bostock, *Plato's "Theaetetus,"* 192.

solution fails to address the core issue of what is in our power. Nor does it even consider his own previous "beautiful" discovery of the active power of soul distinct from its contents (185d6–e9). Wanting to find the source of error only in the contents of the mind, he does not deal with the character of the "hunter," the distinctive power and nature of soul.

In his response, however, Socrates directs attention exactly at "the hunter," the one who "takes hold of a piece of non-knowledge (199e8–200a1)." He speaks, in particular, not about the piece of nonknowledge but about what this one believes about it. Socrates calls attention to the hunter's being deceived, to his thinking that he has knowledge when he does not (200a3–6). But he attributes this outcome not to the contents of the mind but to what the knower "thinks," "knows," and "supposes," all of which refer to ways he is deceived, or self-deceived, just as Theaetetus is now in his resistance to following the argument wherever it might go (200a3, 5, 8).[51]

Socrates has the "skilled refuter," the sophist who peddles the Eleatic paradoxes, transform Theaetetus' solution into an infinite regress. Without attention to the knower's intention and motives – his pretheoretical experience of the world – the aviary's discursive analysis, its thoughts about thoughts, can only lead to further thoughts. The "skilled refuter" tells Theaetetus that his recommendation would require another round of aviaries to account for these knowledges or nonknowledges about knowledge and nonknowledge, and again, aviaries for these aviaries, *ad infinitum* (200b6–c3). The infinite character of this process means that it cannot provide the certainty Theaetetus seeks.

The point is that the criterion of such discursive analysis is logical coherence and such coherence is ultimately not self-validating. Perfectly coherent but wholly fantastic arguments are possible. Plato captures this result with his image of the Philosopher in flight above the world, engaged in reasonings with no discernible connection to the world he inhabits (173e4). At the conclusion of the aviary image, we see the need for ratiocinative activity to be grounded in those wholes impressed on the wax block.

With this outcome, Socrates concludes the consideration of his perplexity involving false opinion. This outcome also helps explain why the lengthy excursus into false opinion was required. The subsequent quick trip into the jury room easily provides the distinction between true opinion and knowledge. Yet this more efficient path is also more dangerous, more likely to leave us in the precarious position of the flying philosopher. Instead, Socrates takes us through false opinion, beginning where we really do begin. In this way, he elicits the prerequisites underlying the existence of false opinion, which rest in the very nature of the beings and of the soul. As such, false opinion, indeed, opinion simply, retains a grip on knowledge. Had Socrates moved at once to the

[51] On this point see F. A. Lewis, "Foul Play in Plato's Aviary: *Theaetetus* 195B ff," in *Exegesis and Argument*, ed. E. N. Lee, A. Mourelatos, and R. Rorty (Assen: Van Gorcum, 1973), 270.

jury room, had he immediately provided the argument distinguishing knowledge from opinion, we might have concluded that the two are simply separable rather than distinguishable but attached. We might then also have mirrored the Philosophers by neglecting the significance of the fact that Socrates begins and concludes the treatment of opinion in the realm of politics. To that realm we now return.

The Jury (200d5–201c6)

Socrates sounds the motto of the *Theaetetus*: they must begin "back again from the start (200d5)." As I have reiterated, to begin again is not to begin simply. Beginning *again*, one can see the importance of the beginning. One can see that initial experience merits further study because it continues to shape our knowing. And that initial experience is shaped by the community each inhabits. This initial experience continues to exert its power because neither the recognition of the wax block nor the reasoning of the aviary has proven to provide comprehensive understanding. Both modes of knowing are required because neither is fully adequate. What becomes necessary, I have argued, is the cognitive capacity that recognizes the need for both. *Phronesis* is needed because epistemology, the knowledge of knowledge that would permit us to transcend once and for all the realm of opinion, is unavailable. In this way, Socrates' images of the mind illuminate a source of the persistently partial character of our knowledge. The complexity of the knower has ruled out any Archimedean point from which we might know with certainty that we know.

Given its apparently unsatisfying conclusion, Socrates judges that the argument has given them a "beautiful rebuke" for investigating false opinion before they have understood the meaning of knowledge (200c7). It is for this reason that they must begin their investigation, "back again from the start (200d5)." Socrates then alludes to the self-awareness I have been discussing as he asks Theaetetus: "What's the most we can say about it [the meaning of knowledge] that would put us least in opposition to ourselves? (200d8–9)." His question reflects the achievement of cognitive humility. He seeks only what will make us least self-contradictory rather than perfectly coherent. The self-awareness inherent in this goal is reflected precisely in his making the avoidance of self-contradiction the touchstone of the inquiry. Such an inquiry is necessarily guided by acute sensitivity to what everyone else in the dialogue, from the Megarians to Theaetetus and Theodorus to "Protagoras," would rather forget: the tension of word and deed that depends on knowledge of ourselves as knowers.

In response, Theaetetus reiterates his definition but with an addendum that unwittingly makes clear the importance of self-knowledge in inquiry. Theaetetus says that "having a true opinion is surely something safe from error at least, and all the things that come from it are beautiful and good (200e4–6)."

His desires for the beautiful and good have animated his inquiry from the beginning. They have dictated what he is willing to regard as knowledge. Yet, despite or because of the enormous influence of these views, Theaetetus has not reflected on them. And so they have led him into impasse after impasse, constantly preventing him from heeding the many alternative signposts Socrates has strewn in his path. The fate of Theaetetus – a lifelong fate as Plato lets us see in showing us the mature Theaetetus – provides the strongest possible warning that serious inquiry must involve sustained attention to those concerns of the heart that are at the heart of political philosophy (142a6–c4).

As is appropriate, Plato conveys this warning above all by the drama of Theaetetus' life. Insofar as the obstacles that impede this effort are not simply intellectual, the scrutiny of one's views of beauty and goodness may be achieved ultimately only by each of us on his or her own. Socrates suggests as much by the proverbial saying he uses to point the way forward (200e7–8). The saying maintains that there are things only known by experience, things known only by and for oneself. He thus points to the irredeemably individual aspect of our knowing, that it cannot simply be a matter of reasoning conveyable to another regardless of experience. But experience must matter because, as Socrates says, contra Thales, what we are seeking may "turn out to be at our feet (200e8–201a1)."

What is at our feet is the political community. The brief and decisive refutation of "knowledge as true opinion" that follows rests on just such a feature of our common experience – namely, the existence of the lawyer's art. This argument provides the closing bookend to the discussion of false opinion that began with similar references to the Digression and so to Socrates' upcoming trial. At the end of Theaetetus' second definition of knowledge we are again in the courtroom. Here, a jury trial is in process, held under the compulsion of the water clock (200b2–3, 172e1). With these images, Socrates connects his own impending fate to the preceding discussion.[52]

His specific point is that the very existence of the art of lawyering testifies that true opinion cannot be identified with knowledge. This claim rests on two diverse distinctions. The first distinguishes between teaching and persuading. With this distinction Socrates makes the point that under the constraints of time, the lawyers are able only to persuade the jurors rather than teach them (201a10–b4). They can do more than inculcate a true opinion about the situation rather than conveying the truth of the matter. On the basis of this distinction it seems the ascent from opinion to knowledge simply requires more time than is available in a jury trial. Conveying the comprehensive truth cannot heed the restrictions imposed by the water clock.

If this were the sole obstacle to the ascent, the realm of politics, of opinion, might, with proper and sustained effort, be left behind. Yet Socrates' second

[52] Lest this be taken as anachronistic, we need to remind ourselves that at the time of the editing of this transcript Socrates knew his fate.

distinction points to a constraint other than time.[53] He maintains that there are things "it's possible to know only by seeing them and in no other way (201b8–9)."[54] On this view, the jury trial results only in true opinion rather than knowledge not because of insufficient time but because it must rely on hearsay.

With this second distinction, Socrates rehabilitates the importance of perception, an aspect of knowing that had been submerged when the aviary image succeeded the wax block. Neither, we should note, is seeing for oneself necessarily limited to visual sense-perception. But we have concluded that reliance on recognition of wholes, whether by sense or intellectual perception, is alone insufficient. Speech or reasoning, that is to say, hearing too is required. To make progress in knowledge, both seeing and hearing, the recognition of wholes and the discursive analysis of them are required. Without discursive analysis, the recognition of wholes remains superficial, ensnared by the opinions we initially receive. Yet discursive analysis alone produces the flying philosopher: reasoning about subjects without a sense of their significance to the one who reasons. Socrates' pair of distinctions reinforces the conclusion drawn from our examination of his inquiry into the possibility of false opinion. Specifically, it is this requirement for both modes of knowing that make our knowledge partial.

The Realm of Opinion

Socrates announced the need to begin again at the beginning and then immediately ushered us into the jury room. At the beginning lies political life because the community is the initial source of our life-shaping views of good – and these views rest on opinion, that is, on partial knowledge. Whether as legislators formulating laws to provide for the future, or as jurors judging guilt or innocence, citizens make life-and-death decisions based on less than comprehensive understanding. These two facts dictate the possibility and desirability of Socratic inquiry. Its possibility follows from the partiality of our knowledge and its desirability from the hope that we might base such significant decisions on something more solid than opinion. Because of their significance, Socrates' recognition of partiality as such is not simply idle talk or garrulity. Such recognition breaks through the boundaries that seek to maintain the community's stance of self-sufficiency, of wholeness, in the most important sense. Such activity, Socrates knows, will be regarded as shameless. He knows

53 For an examination of the tension between these two constraints see M. F. Burnyeat, "Socrates and the Jury: Paradoxes in Plato's Distinction between Knowledge and True Belief," *Proceedings of the Aristotelian Society* 54 (1980): 173–91 and Burnyeat, *The "Theaetetus" of Plato*, 124–7.

54 Here is another example of the rehabilitation of perception. McDowell takes this opportunity to argue once again that, in the *Theaetetus*, Plato "contradicts the most characteristic expositions of the Theory of Forms." See McDowell, *Plato "Theaetetus,"* 227–8.c

too that the indignation it incurs will soon land him in the place to which he has brought us.

The jury room is in a sense Socrates' philosophic home. He cannot, and will not, avoid it. As long as opinion is what it is, only partially overcomeable, that realm which opinion constitutes must always be a focus of the knowledge seeker, if only to free him- or herself as far as possible from its grip. It is the knowledge of ignorance that yields such freedom. The third and final definition of knowledge moves beyond opinion, at least to the extent that it requires inclusion of an additional element. However, from what we have seen, this move is less likely to constitute a transcendence of opinion than a more reflective consideration of the beginning, a consideration of that realm constituted by the necessarily partial character of knowledge. The dialogue has ascended from perception to opinion, but its ultimate destination is not some third autonomous realm. Instead, it leaves the theorist in the realm of opinion, but as a reflective inhabitant of that realm, one aware of its partiality. The excursus through false opinion has made more evident the theoretical underpinnings of this partiality. It has shown, in addition, that the cognitive capacity that makes that partiality available – the *phronesis* whose core is self-knowledge, awareness of our cognitive limitations – is desirable. For through it alone can we avoid the tragedy of self-deception. Socrates employs just this capacity as he now considers the heterogeneous whole that is the third definition.

9

True Opinion and *Logos*

Introduction

Theaetetus offers his third and final definition: knowledge is true opinion plus a *logos*. So understood, knowledge, as a whole, is complex. Insofar as its diverse components' contributions are not simply redundant, knowledge cannot merely be a sum of its parts. It must also possess some unifying principle. The precise meanings of both its parts and this unifying principle are in question. Knowledge itself as an object of knowledge possesses the character evident in every other object of knowledge. So too does every effort to know exhibit the difficulties attendant on knowing in general. The present effort, which takes knowledge as its object, is no exception. The intensely reflexive character of the dialogue reaches a peak in this final definition.

Socrates characterizes Theaetetus' opinion about the meaning of knowledge as a dream. Its dream-like haziness summons the analysis, the *logos*, that occupies much of the forthcoming discussion. In this analysis, the interlocutors aim to grasp that principle by virtue of which knowledge is a whole, not only as a matter of opinion but also in truth. Now, at the end, Socrates maintains, and Theaetetus agrees, that they remain in aporia regarding knowledge. But through this investigation the contours of the aporia become evident. Their investigation does reveal that the objects of knowledge are necessarily complex unities, always both many and one. Moreover, these objects are as such necessarily available to us in diverse ways, just as the distinction between true opinion and *logos* suggests.

This conclusion entails that just so far as our knowing is faithful to the complexity of these wholes it falls short of the apodeictic certainty for which Theaetetus yearns. For this reason, here as elsewhere in the dialogue, Socrates makes the guiding question of their discussion not the possibility of certain knowledge but the possibility of learning, of inquiry. Rather than presupposing any particular outcome, he again lets the character of the object of knowledge emerge from reflection on their activity of seeking it. In this way, Socrates' engagement with his young interlocutor illustrates how one must proceed in the face of this problematic character of knowledge. And it is in this light that we should understand Socrates' concluding invocation of his distinctive art. For with this final definition he confirms that that image of *phronesis*, midwifery, is a permanent requirement of Socratic philosophy.

The Context of the Dream (201c7–202d7)

Theaetetus offers a third definition of knowledge, having recalled what he once heard: "true opinion with a *logos* is knowledge (201c8–d1)." What exactly is meant by *logos* becomes thematic following Socrates' refutation of Theaetetus' dream. At that point, Socrates provides three different definitions of the term: verbal utterance, analytical account, and classificatory account. We will then need to consider whether each successive definition supplants its predecessor or whether we should regard the three senses of *logos* as parts of a broader definition. I will have more to say in what follows on the question of the meaning of *logos* and on its specific meaning in the dream. For now, I want to indicate that, while keeping in mind its several possible meanings, I leave the term untranslated in recognition of these multiple meanings that become thematic as the definition proceeds.[1]

Theaetetus adds to his definition a claim made by its unnamed source: those things of which there is no *logos* are "not intelligible," but those that are susceptible to *logos* are "intelligible (*epistata*, 201d2, d3)."[2] The word

[1] Cornford notes the variety of possible meanings of *logos*. See Cornford, *Plato's Theory of Knowledge*, 142n1. Burnyeat offers an extended discussion of the meaning of *logos* in the dream. He reads back into the dream each of the three senses of *logos* developed by Socrates subsequent to its refutation. He ultimately decides that Plato means to be ambiguous as between the first two – namely, "statement" and "analysis or enumeration." By this intentional ambiguity, according to Burnyeat, Plato means to provoke us "to think for ourselves" rather than rely on "hearsay." Burnyeat, *The "Theaetetus" of Plato*, 136–49. Although I agree that Plato does often, if not always, mean to provoke what Haring calls with reference to our passage "active reading," I must join with Fine, Sedley, and Miller, who hold that the meaning of *logos* in this first section is "analysis." See E. S. Haring, "The Theaetetus Ends Well," *Review of Metaphysics* 35 (1982): 511; Gail Fine, "Knowledge and Logos in the *Theaetetus*," *Philosophical Review* 88 (1979): 370–8; Miller, "Unity and Logos," 91n13; and Sedley, *Midwife of Platonism*," 153–4. This sense is most attractive to Theaetetus because it is most akin to the use of *logos* in mathematical inquiries. The need to consider more closely the precise meaning of *logos*, to consider its several functions, only arises with the refutation of the dream theory, for reasons I discuss in the text. For a summary of the variety of translations, see Chappell, *Reading Plato's "Theaetetus,"* 198–9.

[2] For an overview of speculations regarding the source of the dream, see Chappell, *Reading Plato's "Theaetetus,"* 204–5. One candidate for its origin is Antisthenes. See Cornford, *Plato's Theory of Knowledge*, 144n2; Winifred Hicken, "The Character and Provenance of Socrates' 'Dream' in the *Theaetetus*," *Phronesis* 3 (1958): 133–9. Both Sayre and, in an earlier work, Burnyeat dispute this attribution. Sayre, *Plato's Analytic Method*, 123n59; and Myles Burnyeat, "The Material and Sources of Plato's Dream," *Phronesis* 15 (1970): 108–17. In his

that Theaetetus' source used for "intelligible" is unusual, a point Theaetetus underscores by interrupting himself to affirm the accuracy of his report in this particular instance (201d3).[3] Later in the inquiry, when Socrates and Theaetetus address the notion of intelligibility, they use the standard *gnoston*, translated as "knowable."[4] This initial usage specifies that intelligibility means "availability to *logos*." With the term delimited in this way, its later replacement suggests the possibility at least of an alternative, and perhaps more comprehensive, sense of intelligibility or knowability. Moreover, if true opinion does contribute something to knowledge beyond the contribution of *logos*, a more comprehensive meaning would necessarily be required. That contribution soon becomes evident.

Socrates asks Theaetetus to explain to him this distinction between the intelligible and nonintelligible things. It is a request Theaetetus cannot fulfill. However, he can follow someone else's account (*logos*). Theaetetus' relationship to the dream exemplifies the distinction between recognition and *logos*.[5] His opinion requires supplementation by *logos*. But the *logos* is a supplement, an elaboration, rather than a replacement for this initial opinion. Even when Socrates refers to Theaetetus' initial opinion as "a dream," he does not do so to dismiss it (201d8).

In offering a *logos* of this opinion, Socrates tells Theaetetus to "listen to a dream in return for a dream (201d8)." Although this offer may give the impression that Socrates means to offer an alternative dream to that of Theaetetus, Socrates makes clear that the object of his examination remains Theaetetus' dream throughout (202c5, c7). The dream-like character of Theaetetus' opinion derives from its status as hearsay. Socrates too relates something he "seemed to hear from some people (201e1)." With this dream, we are in the position of the jurors relying on hearsay alone, which conveys, at best, only true opinion rather than knowledge (201b9–c1).[6]

In explaining this dream Socrates speaks first of the primary things, the elements, out of which all is composed, including human beings. On the basis

book, however, Burnyeat allows that Plato may be making creative use of Antisthenes. See Burnyeat, *The "Theaetetus" of Plato*, 164–173. For still another view, see Bostock, *Plato's "Theaetetus,"* 202. In my view, the uncertainty surrounding this question perfectly captures the status accorded it by calling it a dream. It is an opinion handed down from one to the next without scrutiny of its meaning or validity.

3 On the unusual character of the word, see Campbell, *The "Theaetetus" of Plato*, 202n4; Bostock, *Plato's "Theaetetus,"* 202n1.

4 Haring notes that throughout the dream theory Socrates uses words related to *gnosis*. See Haring, "The *Theaetetus* Ends Well," 513n11.

5 On this point, see Amelie O. Rorty, "A Speculative Note on Some Dramatic Elements in the *Theaetetus*," *Phronesis* 17 (1972): 230–1.

6 Haring, Burnyeat, and Polansky make this connection between the status of the dream and the status of the jurors' understanding. See Haring, "The *Theaetetus* Ends Well," 512; Burnyeat, *The "Theaetetus" of Plato*, 129–30; and Polansky, *Philosophy and Knowledge*, 209.

of this initial description some conclude that by "elements" Socrates means the physically simple objects that compose compound physical objects.[7] Lending support to this conclusion is the fact that Socrates regards the elements as perceivable (although this characterization does not obviously support the notion that the elements are atoms).[8] Yet, as several commentators also note, Socrates' subsequent examples, which include number, do not evidently support this narrow definition of the elements.[9]

We must acknowledge that the elements cannot be limited to a materialist conception. How, then, do we explain Socrates' claim that they are perceivable? We can begin by recalling that it was Socrates who confined the meaning of perception to sense-perception alone. He did so in the course of articulating the implications of Theaetetus' initial definition. Yet perception may be understood more broadly to include intellectual perception which in fact better fits with Theaetetus' own experience of "seeing" the right answer all at once. Such intellectual perception becomes all the more pertinent as the examination reveals the object of knowledge to be the "very being" of a thing that is not available to sight. Admittedly, unlike other dialogues, the *Theaetetus* makes no mention of such intellectual perception, or *nous*, for reasons I discuss in the following text. The present point, however, is that Socrates is willing to let Theaetetus' initial opinion appear as a reductionist account of things, with these terms becoming much more inclusive as the examination proceeds. Writing of the ultimate scope of the elements, Amelie Rorty states, "as the dream is told and criticized, the elements may be atoms, points, Forms, physically or logically simple objects – *whatever* elements anyone might suppose could be isolated and named, and then compounded out of letters."[10]

7 Sedley, e.g., under the influence of Aristotle (*Metaphysics* 998a20–b8) sees the need to consider the possibility that by 'elements' Plato might mean either conceptual or physical components. Ultimately, however, he decides on the latter for several reasons among which is Socrates' claim that the elements are perceivable. Sedley does note the tendency of "modern interpreters" to regard the elements as what he calls "conceptual." Sedley, *Midwife of Platonism*," 155–6. However, see Cornford, *Plato's Theory of Knowledge*, 144. Rosen contends that there are two meanings of simplicity in the passage. This conclusion would seem to follow from the forthcoming notion that the compounds taken as unities have the same properties as the simples. See Stanley Rosen, "Socrates' Dream," 164–5.

8 Burnyeat, e.g., wants to argue that the elements are not limited to material objects but finds some difficulty in squaring this view with Socrates' claim regarding the perceptible character of the elements. See Burnyeat, *The "Theaetetus" of Plato*, 181–7. Owing to Socrates' insistence on the perceivability of the elements, Sedley and Sayre want to connect the dream to *Theaetetus* 184–7 and, in particular, to see it as a materialist, reductionist account. Yet just as in that passage, in the present one too the scope of perception is elaborated as the argument proceeds. Sayre, *Plato's Analytic Method*, 120–30; Sedley, *Midwife of Platonism*, 157–8.

9 See the following note for examples.

10 Rorty, "A Speculative note," 235. On the great variety of meanings that attach to elements in the passage, see also Glenn Morrow, "Plato and the Mathematicians: An Interpretation of

These elements, however, are not available to *logos*. We can name them, but to describe them is "out of one's power (201e4)." The inability to provide such a *logos* follows from the elements' nature and from the nature of our reasoning. The former are held to be absolutely simple in nature, hence without parts. Accordingly, any characterization of them, beyond merely pointing at them, must violate their simplicity. As the dialogue has made clear, reason's predicative character presumes the beings' possession of a partite rather than a simple nature. Only beings with parts can both be themselves and have something in common with other beings sufficient to permit the comparison intrinsic to reasoning. Thus, Socrates says even the phrase "this is," goes too far for it attaches to that which is simple something beyond itself, namely being (202a2–5).

The same explanation of the elements' resistance to reason makes clear, conversely, why the compounds are preeminently objects of ratiocination. The things composed of the elements are intertwined elements that can be reasoned about. For reason is nothing but "an intertwining of the names (202b5–6)." Moreover, whoever can provide such a rational account, such a *logos*, of a thing has knowledge of it. As Socrates puts it, this one "has a power over" whatever it is he knows and, moreover, is "in a perfect condition . . . toward knowledge (202c4–5)." *Logos* so understood means an "analytical account." It is a meaning that Socrates later introduces as the second of three senses of *logos* subsequent to the dream's refutation.

This account of intelligibility is sufficient as far as it goes. Yet we can no longer omit consideration of the package in which this account is delivered. We need to consider the opinion of which this *logos* is the articulation, and especially Socrates' characterization of it as a dream.

As I noted, such a characterization underscores the less than rigorously logical nature of this view. Previously, Socrates placed dreaming on a par with illness and madness as exemplifying hallucinatory mental states. In the present context, Theaetetus amplifies this uncertain character of his view by locating its source in hearsay emanating from an unnamed source and by his inability to explicate the view. Yet, again, its dream-like character does not result in its dismissal. Far from it: the dream structures all that follows. The subsequent *logos* is an analysis *of* the dream, an articulation *of* this original insight. Accordingly, if Plato means us to take the interlocutors' inquiry as paradigmatic regarding knowledge then we have to entertain the possibility that an intuition or opinion, dream-like in its lack of rigor, determines the scope of logical analysis.[11] The power-conferring knowledge of *logos* may rest on these less than certain grounds. Something beyond or other than *logos* orients *logos*.

Socrates' Dream in the *Theaetetus*," *Philosophical Review* 79 (1970): 326–7. I cannot agree, however, with Morrow's view that the primary meaning of elements in the passage refers to the basic premises of geometry and arithmetic.

[11] On the importance of the context of analysis see Rosen, "Socrates' Dream," 161–5; Miller, "Unity and Logos," 97, 103–4.

The dyadic formula of this third definition of knowledge indicates exactly the need for this other element of knowledge.

The dream-like status of Theaetetus' initial view, taken together with its content, also bring this definition of knowledge to bear on the ongoing analysis of Theaetetus' soul. This is a mathematician's dream. It possesses the aspirations and shortcomings of that profession.[12] As regards the former, the dream deems knowable only that which is articulable, susceptible to analysis or to the commensuration of reason. More specifically, to use the word that so impresses Theaetetus, what is "intelligible" is that which is countable, that which can be picked out, distinguished, and related. With respect to such objects, the knowledge so gained, in its precision, can grant, as Socrates says, a power over them. It is a hope Theaetetus shares with later thinkers likewise attracted to the mathematicization of knowledge.

The dream belongs to the mathematicians too, however, in its revelation of the limitations of mathematical understanding. Theaetetus, we recall, cannot fulfill Socrates' request to account for the meaning of intelligibility. The mathematician can provide no precise and certain answer as to *why* his view of intelligibility is the appropriate one. In this regard, Socrates places Theaetetus in a situation expressed perfectly in the discussion of knowledge and mathematical understanding in the *Republic* discussed earlier.[13] There, too, Socrates refers to the hypotheses, the foundations of the sciences from which all is deduced, as gained through dreaming.[14] And there too, his characterization carries far-reaching implications for the solidity of those hypotheses on which the practitioners of the *technai* – and especially that paradigm of all *technai*, mathematics – base their reasonings. For the hypotheses are not the subject of examination. Rather, they serve as the unsubstantiated premises from which all ratiocination flows. For this reason, again, the certainty achieved by these practitioners cannot claim to be comprehensive.

This epistemic situation bears most directly on the conflict within Theaetetus' soul. Will he be willing and able to subject the foundations of his chosen

[12] On the connection between the dream and mathematical activity, see Morrow, "Plato and the Mathematicians," 323–4, 330; Polansky, *Philosophy and Knowledge*, 213.

[13] See Morrow, "Plato and the Mathematicians," 323–4, 330; Polansky, *Philosophy and Knowledge*, 214.

[14] *Republic* 533b8. On the connection between hypotheses, intuitions, opinions and dreams, see Burnyeat, "The Material and Sources of Plato's Dream," 103–106; Rosen, "Socrates' Dream," 161–2; Sedley, *The Midwife of Platonim*, 154. The dream is thus linked to "firsts" – in this case, first premises. Note also Cornford's understanding of a true *doxa* as "a complex unanalysed presentation of the whole object." Cornford, *Plato's Theory of Knowledge*, 145. McDowell writes, "the true judgement of, say, a person, might be manifested by the ability to recognize him. Obviously one can have the ability to recognize a person without being able to produce the sort of account of him that is described in the dream theory." McDowell, *Plato "Theaetetus,"* 240. There is widespread acknowledgement that there are diverse modes of cognition in play in this third definition, and that they are necessary components of the whole that is knowledge.

field to scrutiny? Will he treat them not as unquestionable foundations but as "springboards" to truly higher premises?[15] In this concluding definition, the drama of Theaetetus heightens. His soul stands ever more precariously poised between the "downward" movement of ratiocination, of mathematical analysis, and the "upward" movement of dialectics. Perfectly in accord with the practice of his midwifery, Socrates tests simultaneously the mathematicians' approach to knowledge and Theaetetus' own individual situation with the examination of this third definition of knowledge. Caught as he is between the attractions of the deductive certainty of mathematics and the potentially disturbing task of dialectical examination of these premises, there is no better way to examine Theaetetus' soul than to confront this mathematician's dream of knowledge. That confrontation must especially involve the clarification of its status as a dream.

Socrates thus elicits and assesses not only Theaetetus' beliefs but also his motives for holding them. This is evident in his formulation of what the dream's notion of such articulable knowledge will provide. To repeat, Socrates states that the one who knows in this way "has a power over" whatever he knows and that he is "in a perfect condition . . . toward knowledge (202c4–5)." Socrates feeds Theaetetus' hunger for this perfect knowledge that grants control over the world. He also feeds Theaetetus' desire for the recognition that goes along with such accomplishment. Socrates asks whether they have "really gotten hold in this way on this day of something that many wise men also sought after long ago and grew old before discovering (202d1–3)." Perhaps sensing the glory that will be theirs if they achieve what eluded many others, Theaetetus eagerly affirms their discovery. The utter distinctiveness, the novelty of what they have done – "in this way, on this day" – cannot help but thrill him (202d1).

Yet "the wise" that Socrates refers to here seem to differ from the "wise" sophists. The former group, the wise of "long ago," sought ceaselessly without achieving their goal. Nevertheless, despite their failing to possess the knowledge to which Theaetetus now lays claim, Socrates calls them wise. Implied in Socrates' characterization is a distinction between wisdom and knowledge long since rejected by Theaetetus. One can be wise even without possessing comprehensive and certain knowledge.

This distinction is most pertinent to our examination of this third definition of knowledge, and especially to our assessment of its relative success. It is, moreover, a distinction implicitly present throughout the third definition of knowledge, insofar as we wish to distinguish between the problematic character of knowledge and our awareness thereof. On the basis of this distinction, the former need not be held to vitiate the achievement inherent in the latter. It is both the validity of this distinction, and Theaetetus' willingness to make it, with which this last definition is chiefly concerned. Through these concerns,

[15] *Republic* 511b6.

it invokes the explicitly designated object of Socratic philosophy, *phronesis*, which grants such awareness.

Socrates does agree with Theaetetus that it is difficult to see how there can be knowledge apart from "*logos* and a correct opinion (202d6–7)."[16] But Socrates, at least, is not yet clear what this entails for the meaning of knowledge as a whole. His need for clarity leaves him dissatisfied (202d8). This dissatisfaction, the fuel that keeps the conversation going, opposes that desire for honor that would bring the discussion to a halt in a wave of self-congratulation. Without Socrates' self-dissatisfaction, we would have only silence. We would be compelled to settle for what Socrates calls the correct opinion rather than the true, the opinion handed down to us, approved of by our predecessors (202d7). We would be left with hearsay alone.

All these details place us squarely in the atmosphere of Socrates' maieutic practice. As I argued with respect to Socrates' earlier explicit treatment of midwifery, that practice aims to elicit and assess just such correct opinions, and the passions that keep us tied to them. Put otherwise, midwifery brings to light that which is truly first with respect to our knowing, that which shapes our thinking. To use Aristotle's terminology, such *endoxa* are the phenomena from which our knowing begins, dictating how the world appears to us, how we take it to be.[17] If a crucial purpose of midwifery, and thus especially of this last act of midwifery, is to begin again, it must aim to induce awareness of these beliefs.

Reflecting this aim, Socrates places this entire examination in the context of a discursive community; the two interlocutors deal with views that are both explicitly acquired from others and explicitly unexamined, in need of further explanation. At the beginning of every inquiry, and so with this one, there exists not a blank slate but a web of dream-like opinions and hypotheses, which we know only in a certain sense. Contrary to the explicit premise of much of the dialogue, Socrates' *practice* denies that we are wholly ignorant or wholly knowledgeable. As with his conversation with Theodorus, we always begin in midstream.

The theorists especially require the effort to locate themselves in this web. For the theorists' characteristic error consists in thinking that they can extricate themselves from this web with ease. Thus, in their self-deception they believe they soar above those who unfortunately remain entrapped. This presumption

[16] Socrates' question has led many to conclude that this third definition is not rejected completely. See Sayre, *Plato's Analytic Method*, 120n53, 137; McDowell, *Plato "Theaetetus,"* 230; Haring, "The *Theaetetus* Ends Well," 510; Chappell, *Reading Plato's "Theaetetus,"* 200–1. Lending further credence to this conclusion are the numerous times some version of this formula occurs in the dialogues as a definition of knowledge. See, e.g., *Meno* 98a2; *Phaedo* 76b5–6; *Symposium* 202a5–9; *Timaeus* 51e5. Understanding why this can be a formula for knowledge may require, however, that one appreciate the need to replace 'correct' opinion with 'true'.

[17] See Martha C. Nussbaum, *The Fragility of Goodness: Luck and Ethics in Greek Tragedy and Philosophy* (Cambridge: Cambridge University Press, 1986), 243–4.

is most damaging because it precludes the possibility of ever attaining the clarity that should be the theorists' aim. Socrates seeks to provide Theaetetus, and the theoretically inclined readers of this conversation, the opportunity to appreciate just how difficult such freedom is, how far such initial unexamined opinions still inform their knowing.

The effort of elicitation is required precisely because these views are so fundamental we hardly know we possess them. In the present case, for example, Theaetetus would need to come to know why it is that he remembers just this account. He would need to assess why this particular account of intelligibility makes so much sense to him that he is almost incapable of scrutinizing it. Again, the effort is worthwhile precisely because these opinions are so fundamental, structuring our thinking, determining whether we will or will not be satisfied by the account of knowledge that the dream has thus far provided. By spinning out the exact dream that he does, Socrates appeals to the mathematician's hopes. Yet by explicitly referring to it as a dream Socrates provides the path through which Theaetetus might see the limits of his view of knowledge and of the world. He might then be able to consider as wise those who seek without attaining comprehensive knowledge.

Socrates' dissatisfaction maps the direction of the path forward. He locates its source in the distinction between the unknowable and the knowable. This distinction, we recall, provided for the absolute intelligibility of the compounds, as opposed to the elements, insofar as the former are, in their compoundedness, susceptible to *logos*. In what follows, however, Socrates challenges the adequacy of this understanding by loosening the distinction between the elements and the compound. He gives us reason to wonder whether the elements can be regarded as absolutely simple and whether the compounds are not, themselves in some sense, unities. This complexity of the beings proves to require the divergent modes of knowing expressed in Theaetetus' present definition. We need now to consider how the argument unfolds.

Elements and Compounds (202d8–206b12)

When he recalls the distinction regarding intelligibility Socrates uses the more common word for knowability and its opposite (*gnoston*, *agnosta*, 202e1). He indicates that what the speaker must have had in mind with his thoughts about unknowable elements and knowable compounds pertains especially to the letters and syllables of written words. "[L]ike hostages for the argument," these are the paradigms to which the unnamed speaker was referring (202e3, e6–8). The fact that the words in Greek for element and letter, compound and syllable, are the same makes the connection more plausible. Socrates proposes that they take these letters and syllables back up again. More specifically, he asks to "[take] ourselves back up again," apparently referring to the fact that the key example refers to the spelling of their names (203a1–2). But they take themselves up again in the still deeper sense that the discussion revolves around how they learned the letters and syllables, in particular "whether we learned spelling that way or not (203a2)." In this way, Socrates keeps in sight the distinction between the intrinsic knowability of objects and how it is we come to know them, always making the object of knowledge comport with how we really do come to know it. He thus spotlights that point from which we do begin to know.

Directing attention to the first syllable of his own name, Socrates conjures a questioner who asks Theaetetus to say *what* it is (203a7–8). In this way, he designates the character of the object of knowledge, at least so far as to suggest that it should express the "what" of a thing, its distinctive character. Socrates returns to the object of knowledge in the subsequent consideration of the second sense of *logos*. For now, we need to concentrate on Theaetetus' response to the imagined questioner. Theaetetus offers an analysis of the syllable: it is sigma and omega. This, Theaetetus affirms, is a *logos* of the syllable (203a10–11). Then, speaking in his own name, Socrates asks Theaetetus to give a *logos* of sigma. In accordance with the dictates of the dream, which mandate the resistance of the elements to *logos*, Theaetetus balks at this request: "how is anyone going to state an element of the element? (203b2)."

Yet Theaetetus does go on to provide a detailed classification of the various elements. As we see in Socrates' consideration of the third sense of *logos*, this classificatory activity is certainly a kind of *logos*.[18] It is the identification of the elements with letters that most undermines their absolute simplicity and thus their resistance to *logos*. As Theaetetus shows here, we can distinguish letters from one another. They have diverse properties and, as we all know, combine with one another (or not) in diverse ways.[19] None of this would be possible were they absolutely simple.

Just as the resistance of the elements, the letters, to *logos* is more ambiguous than the explicit argument acknowledges, so too is the availability of the compounds to *logos*. Socrates makes this point through his focus on the being, the "what" of the syllable. Specifically, he asks concerning the meaning of the "and" linking sigma and omega. Socrates wants to raise the question as to whether the syllable is an aggregate of letters or a unity, "some *one* look (*mian tina idean*) that has come into being when they've been put together? (203c6, emphasis added)." Theaetetus opts unhesitatingly for the former. Socrates, however, uses the distinction posed by the dream to suggest to Theaetetus that the second might be more accurate. For on the basis of the dream it would have to be the case that, although the syllable can be known – known as the sigma and omega together – the elements cannot. The result would be that one could be "ignorant of each, and knowing neither one he recognizes both

[18] Rorty notes the inappropriateness of exemplifying absolute simples by letters. Rorty, "A Speculative Note," 235. On this point, see also Haring, "The *Theaetetus* Ends Well," 515.

[19] On this use of *logos* as classification see Fine, "Knowledge and Logos," 380; Burnyeat, *The "Theaetetus" of Plato*, 190. This notion is especially crucial to Fine's understanding of the passage insofar as she comes to regard it as decisive to Plato's understanding of knowledge as "interrelated."

together," a possibility Theaetetus finds "dreadful and without *logos* (203d6)." Theaetetus' compound reaction to the possibility of wholes possessing properties not found in their components expresses well the state of his soul. Believing there is no other acceptable way of knowing, Theaetetus finds a thing's resistance to *logos* as at least a concern. It rises to the level of "dreadful" because, as Theaetetus may grasp, if he does not accept this outcome he will have to relinquish the dream.

Yet the abandonment of the dream results also from the notion that the syllable is a unity, "some one form (*hen . . . eidos*) having come out of [the letters], having itself its own single look (*idean mian*, 203e3–4)." As we see in what follows, this possibility proves no more consistent with the dream than the notion just formulated. Before undertaking this examination, Socrates says "one ought to examine [the dream] and not desert in so unmanly a way a great and solemn account (203e8–9)." Theaetetus at this point recognizes the exigencies of the situation (203e10).

Socrates tells Theaetetus that if a syllable is a "single look" it must not have parts. Responding to Theaetetus' uncertainty on this point, Socrates offers again the possibility that the whole is "some one form (*hen eidos*), different from all the parts (204a8–9)." With this formulation, Socrates makes explicit the alternative notion of unity he has been suggesting. It is not the unity or oneness of that which is elemental, absolutely simple. Rather, he returns to the complex unity of mud.[20] Socrates refers to the unity of a whole that is as such in one sense composite but that can also be taken as a unity distinct from its parts. It is this notion of complex unity that is decisive for the rest of the examination of knowledge. The object of knowledge, indeed knowledge itself as such an object, proves to be just such a complex unity.[21]

Theaetetus responds to Socrates' query by explicitly distinguishing "the whole" and "the all."[22] On the one side, he finds the whole possessing a unity

[20] Burnyeat sees the connection between this passage and the earlier one dealing with mud (or 'clay' as he has it). He sees as well that it concerns the status of structure. But, as we will see, he does not take the step of understanding the object of knowledge as a complex unity. See Burnyeat, *The "Theaetetus" of Plato*, 192–3, 199, 202. McDowell notes the need to refer to structure in "an acceptable account" of syllables but thinks that point is missed in this argument. In considering the pertinence of the mud example to the present passage Sedley notes that the definition of mud is "not *simply* a list of empirical components, since 'mixed with' adds a formal relation between the components." Yet, he still holds that the definition "at least gestures towards a reductionist mode of analysis." Sedley, *The Midwife of Platonism*, 162 (emphasis in original). McDowell, *Plato "Theaetetus,"* 241. See also Polansky, *Philosophy and Knowledge*, 230. Desjardins also makes the connection to the mud example (as well as to Theaetetus' treatment of surds or incommensurables.). She does see these as illustrative of complex unity. See Desjardins, *The Rational Enterprise*, 126–8.

[21] My understanding of complex unity is indebted to Desjardins *The Rational Enterprise*, passim and Miller, "Unity and Logos," passim.

[22] On Theaetetus' recognition, see Rosen, "Socrates' Dream," 164; Haring, "The *Theaetetus* Ends Well," 515–6; Desjardins, *The Rational Enterprise*, 156 and n5; Verity Harte, *Plato on Parts and Wholes* (Oxford: Oxford University Press, 2002), 39.

whose being is heterogeneous in relation to its parts; on the other, he finds an arbitrary collection, a mere aggregate, a sum. Everything hinges on this distinction. Theaetetus finally acknowledges wholes not simply reducible to their parts. But will he accept such ontological diversity in the beings once he realizes that it mandates similarly diverse ways of knowing? If he does, then, once again, a further issue arises: can Theaetetus confront the implications of such complexity for those wholes about which he cares most deeply? Again, Theaetetus seems to be aware of what is at stake in this distinction, characterizing himself as "taking a bold risk (204b3)." Approaching the end of the dialogue Theaetetus does show signs of breaking through the self-imposed limitations of his thinking. Our hopes are raised that Socrates will leave as his valedictory one of the few clear-cut pedagogical success stories in the Platonic corpus. Such a portrayal of a soul turned around would be a gratifying Platonic memorial to Socrates.

These hopes quickly vanish. Even worse, as he has done before, Socrates takes measures to suppress the glimmerings of Theaetetus' insight.[23] Knowing we are nearing the end of the dialogue, the end of Theaetetus' time with Socrates as his main interrogator, this last suppression is particularly frustrating. Yet we know too that Socrates chooses to enshrine this conversation whose pedagogical outcome is, to him, uncertain. Apparently, he regards the process of reaching the aporetic conclusion as important in itself, whatever the ultimate success of Theaetetus. For these reasons this last step, however disappointing, merits our careful attention. As always, the dialogue would not serve its function unless it tested our resolve as well.

Through the suppression of Theaetetus' insight Socrates spurs us to think what it is that Theaetetus lacks such that he accepts this suppression. Moreover, Socrates' exertions at just this point highlight the significance of the distinction he obscures. Socrates' tactics compel us to ask whether Socrates demonstrably effaces the distinction between "whole" and "all," or whether, instead, he suppresses the distinction for Theaetetus' and our education. Answering this question is crucial for assessing the notion of knowledge under investigation. For if the latter motive animates the rejection then the distinction abides, as does the notion of complex unity that it reflects.

Socrates begins to obscure Theaetetus' insight by appealing to an example taken from the realm of numbers. He uses the number six to illustrate a

[23] Several commentators recognize that Socrates does suppress this distinction. (The distinction is certainly available to Plato. See, e.g., *Parmenides*. 157c4–e2.) Harte maintains that Socrates' goal is to make the notion that a whole just is its parts more problematic. Left unclear is why he would wish to do so. Haring writes: "Theaetetus will be better off in the long run if his insight [into the distinction between the whole and the all] is postponed." Miller concludes that Socrates suppresses the distinction "to more radically elicit it from us," the readers. As indicated by my treatment of this issue throughout the text, I think these suggestions point in the right direction but need to be understood in the broader political context of the dialogue. See Harte, *Parts and Wholes*, 47; Haring, "The *Theaetetus* Ends Well." 515–6; Miller, "Unity and Logos," 93; and Bostock, *Plato's "Theaetetus,"* 213–4.

collection that is but the aggregate of its parts. Supposedly, the whole does not differ from the all in this case. With this example, Theaetetus need not face that heterogeneity, perhaps irreducible, between parts and wholes. Thus, Socrates implies that whether we count the units totaling six, multiply two times three or vice versa, add four and two, and so on, we are always speaking of the same thing (204b11–c2).

Theaetetus might have responded that even in this case we deal with a whole whose wholeness is something more than the sum of its units. With respect to "six" we have already seen in the example of the dice an instance where its being just that number, located between four and twelve, gives it properties that none of the units has by itself. Similarly, we might well regard the units as the matter of the number, while in the several possibilities of arriving at six we see its formal characteristics.[24] The latter only exist when "put together (203c6)." In this way, even in the realm of number, the problem of the connection between the components and their unity exists. Nevertheless, with Theaetetus' assent, Socrates suppresses the distinction between whole and all with respect to "whatever is made of number (204d1)."

Yet the distinction is even more evident, and more difficult to suppress, as Socrates moves beyond the realm of abstract number. As his first example, Socrates offers the plethron, the Greek equivalent of the mile. As a unit of measurement, it might easily be understood on the model of number. But Socrates then asks, "And it's the same way with the number of the stade (204d7)"? A stade is six plethra. It is, however, more than that. "Stade" came to be the standard word for a racecourse because it is the length of the track at the Olympic Games. As such, it is not merely an aggregate. These plethra, these elements, when arranged in the proper way produce something that none of them is on its own. The whole so produced has qualities not just any plethron or any six plethra possess. It has a certain form, reflective of the human capacity for running and the desire to witness competition. It produces a whole having a certain significance, and even sacredness, that, again, not just any plethron or any random collection of plethora possess. This whole might even elicit reflections on the relationship between part and whole as it makes Theaetetus think of the connection between the individual athlete and his home city.

Such reflections would be even more likely to arise from Socrates' next example, an army. This example appeals to Theaetetus' experience in a similar way. But, again, although it is explicitly presented to exemplify the identity of whole and all, it does just the opposite. Clearly, an army, like a city, should not be identified merely with its individual constituents.[25] We are all familiar, either firsthand or through depictions, with the training required to take mere numbers, raw recruits, and transform them into soldiers. We are familiar as well with the highly organized structure, the precise division of labor, that must be

[24] On this understanding of number, see Burnyeat, *The "Theaetetus" of Plato*, 204–7 and n91.

[25] Many commentators recognize this point. See, e.g., Harte, *Parts and Wholes*, 45.

imposed in order to turn an aggregate of individuals into a fighting unit. This human institution illustrates exactly and emphatically the difference between an all, or a mere aggregate, and a whole. It illustrates as well the persistent tension between the whole and the parts it comprises. This difference, as we know, comes to have a most concrete meaning in Theaetetus' own life – and death.

Socrates presses the assimilation of all and whole further by insisting that the number of constituents is the same as the parts of a whole or all (204e5–6). Yet the foregoing examples should disabuse us of this equation. The raw recruit cannot function as a part of an effective fighting force. The part only appears as a part in light of its contribution to some greater whole. Socrates introduces this possibility to Theaetetus, asking, "But is it possible that a part is the very thing that it is as belonging to anything else whatever than to the whole? (204e11–12)." Unfortunately, Theaetetus now has lost his grip on the distinctiveness of the part-whole relationship, responding, "well, to the all (204e13)." The example of number has done its work on Theaetetus' soul.

However, the other examples remain for his, and our, further reflection. Such reflection would need to confront those perplexities previously considered. Among them is the status of that by virtue of which the whole is a whole. Such a unifying principle would have to be something more and other than the parts in order to provide such unity. For the consequence of that unity is to transform elements into parts. Something of a different ontological status is required in this case. But what exactly it is, how exactly it provides for unity, remains a question. Neither is it then clear what exactly occurs in such a transformation. What happens to that plethron such that it becomes a part of the stade, the site of the Olympic racecourse? How does the individual become a soldier in an effective fighting unit? We might also ask, how do the many versions of Theaetetus become the mature adult? Those perplexities that were imperfectly resolved by the distinction of potential and actual recur.

We know that such perplexities have caused others to persist in assimilating the whole and the all, to deny the notion of potential altogether. Theaetetus does so persist, and when he does, Socrates tells him, "You're battling in a manly way, Theaetetus (205a1)." On the occasion of his discovery of the power of soul, Socrates had called Theaetetus "beautiful." The quality that Socrates now cites seems more closely related to Theaetetus' spirited defense of his own, not Socratic courage but the kind of courage he would later show in defense of his city. Perhaps there is a connection between Theaetetus' later deeds and his rejection of the distinction between the whole and the all. Acceptance of this distinction would strike at the heart of this mathematician's reductionist bent. It would require Theaetetus to acknowledge the potentially irreducible heterogeneity, ontological and cognitive, inherent in wholes that are not simply sums of their parts. This heterogeneity raises the specter that the pure knowledge Theaetetus desires may be unattainable. Behind this desire, I have argued, stands Theaetetus' wish to preserve the pristine character of all wholes he cares about, including but not limited to knowledge. It is this desire that makes him resistant to reflection on wholes such as the army, or more emphatically, the political community, which evinces this problematic relationship of part and whole. Contrary to Socrates' turbulent relationship with Athens, Theaetetus lived, and died, wholly in support of his community's integrity.

Socrates tries again. He does not aim to stifle Theaetetus completely, but to elicit his efforts to learn for himself. Accordingly, Socrates provides Theaetetus with one last chance to see his own way through the identity of whole and all. Regarding an "all," Socrates asks, "whenever nothing is lacking, isn't that very thing all? (205a1–2)." Moreover, about a whole he asks, "won't a whole be that same thing from which nothing is missing in any way? (295a4–5)." The notion of something lacking, however, pertains to a whole in a way that it does not pertain to an "all."[26] As an aggregate, an all is a compilation of whatever elements happen to be included within it. To take Socrates' earlier example, the presence of six units constitutes an all of that number. Remove one of the units and one still has an all, now of five units. The same is not the case with a whole. If one is speaking of an army, and one removes one of its parts, say the artillery, one no longer has a whole. In the light of the whole, there is something missing.

Theaetetus does not walk through the door Socrates has left ajar. Instead, he continues to battle manfully for the identity of whole and all. Socrates' midwifery has done all it can for Theaetetus. It has placed him in the midst of this battle, one that is waged explicitly over the abstract distinction between whole and all but that also reflects the altogether concrete struggle within Theaetetus' soul. Suppressing – but not eradicating – the glimmers of Theaetetus' insight, Socrates makes him fight to see the distinction. Given the character of the obstacles before it, this is the only way Theaetetus can hope to gain clarity about it. Appealing to wholes within Theaetetus' experience, Socrates heightens the tension within Theaetetus between his experience and his yearnings. Socrates' midwifery works on us too. Because he proceeds in this way, we are able not only to reflect on this distinction but also to see the affective dimension of Theaetetus' belief, the existential issues wrapped up in this distinction. These come ever more to the fore as Socrates increases his attention on Theaetetus as a learner.

Socrates now makes perfectly clear to Theaetetus that his mathematician's dream is dead. More specifically, he uses Theaetetus' acknowledgment of the identity of whole and all to place him in a dilemma both horns of which deny the hypothesis expressed in the dream. The reasoning is as follows: if the compound is not the elements, if they are not to be counted as parts of it, then the compound will be, as Socrates says, "a single indivisible look (205c2)." But, as such, these "compounds" must be as partless as any other unity, "without composition" and so, contrary to the dream, as unknowable as the elements

[26] See Ibid., 43.

(205c4–10). Because it was decided that "the parts showed up as the same thing as the whole," then, again contrary to the dream, both the compound and the elements must be equally knowable (205d9–10). Both alternatives reject the dream's vision of unknowable elements and knowable compounds.

In what follows, Socrates examines only one horn of the dilemma. He simply drops comprehensive unknowability. He examines only the possibility of comprehensive knowability. In this examination, he suggests a new hypothesis that has its foundation not in reflection on knowledge but rather on learning. He appeals specifically to Theaetetus' self-reflection, to "the inside knowledge you yourself have from yourself by learning the letters of the alphabet (206a2–3)." Reflecting on this question, he examines the hypothesis that not only the compound but also the element must be knowable in some way. The previous indications of the ambiguity of both the elements and the compound help substantiate this hypothesis.

Socrates elaborates the paradoxical possibility of a complex unity, the possibility that the compound might be both partite and a unity. Such a unity *is* both as a many and as a one. As such, it is also knowable in heterogeneous ways. In developing this thought in the context of the question of learning, Socrates makes explicit the presuppositions of his midwifery, those complexities that must exist insofar as learning is necessary and possible. This approach enables him to confront Theaetetus with the possibility that the object of knowledge requires access by means in addition to *logos*.

Socrates prompts Theaetetus' reflections on himself as a learner by recalling to him what he must have experienced when learning the letters. Socrates says that "in learning them you persevered in nothing other than trying to distinguish each of the letters, itself by itself, by sight and by hearing, in order that their arrangement would not perturb you when they were spoken or written (206a5–8)." Learning requires effort, as is evident in the perseverance to which Socrates calls attention. Apparently, the distinction among and between the letters is not manifestly evident in each case, although such distinctions can be made. Yet if such distinctions can be made then the letters are not perfect examples of the elements, if, that is, the elements are taken to be simples. As I have already stated, that which is simple cannot be distinguished one from another in this way, in a way that identifies their likenesses and differences. Such characteristics cannot belong to that which is perfectly simple. Moreover, these letters are not only to be distinguished but also combined in relation between and among one another – again, something it is not clear that simples can do. Theaetetus' earlier disquisition on the letters pointed to this capacity of the letters to combine with one another. The present point is that even with the letters we may already be thinking of them in some sense as both simple and compound. The meaning of the letters is not self-evident. Effort is required to know them, because they too *are* in heterogeneous ways.

Further reflection on learning reveals that just as the letters are ambiguous so also are the compounds that comprise them. These compounds are, most importantly, the words of which the letters are parts. Socrates conspicuously omits mention of words throughout this discussion. He leaves for Theaetetus reflection on this aspect of his learning. Such reflection might suggest to him why he wished to engage in the analysis of the letters in the first place.

Such reflection would also reveal that the learning of the letters is subsequent to the learning of the larger unities of which they are parts. Prior to learning the alphabet, we learn to speak. Moreover, as Theaetetus indicated earlier, we only fully know some of the letters by virtue of their being combined with other letters in syllables.[27] The syllables and words are the compounds constituted by the letters as parts. Yet, again, we learn these compounds as wholes, as unities, prior to learning the letters. It is, I think, to call attention to this fact that Socrates notes that "the arrangement" of letters in a word might "perturb" Theaetetus (206a7). It is this arrangement, this unity, which is known prior to the analytic learning of the letters. This unity gives direction to the subsequent analysis, to learn what constitutes this particular arrangement.

The other example Socrates offers in this context, learning music, exemplifies the same point. Certainly, the learning of each note, "to what string it belongs" is essential to the learning of music (206b1). However, so is the "arrangement," the order and duration of the plucking of the strings that constitutes a piece of music as a whole rather than simply a series of notes.[28] The overall point is that our experience of learning testifies to the notion that the compounds are also in some sense unities. More importantly, it shows that our knowledge is incomplete if it is confined only to analysis.

Socrates draws a conclusion extrapolating from what "we ourselves have experienced with elements and compounds" to "everything else as well (206b5–7)." His conclusion perfectly reflects the ambiguity we have already seen. It points to the greater knowability of the "*genus*" of elements (206b7, emphasis added). We might ask, which does Socrates mean is more knowable, the elements or the *genus* of the elements? As this question suggests, Socrates' conclusion again provides Theaetetus with a pointer to the problem that he has been circling around. The *genus* of elements is a unity that comprises multitudes – the elements, the building blocks, as Socrates has said, of all things. Yet just insofar as it comprises this multiplicity, insofar as it expresses the elements as a kind, it is also in some sense a unity. Reflection on our learning thus points to such entities, such complex unities, as the objects of knowledge. And, in their complexity, they must be known in similarly diverse ways. For, if they are complex unities they must be known as such.

In finally dismissing the dream, Socrates maintains that if "anyone claims a compound is more knowable, and an element is by its nature unknowable,

[27] On the importance of structure in this regard, see Burnyeat, *The "Theaetetus" of Plato*, 210–11 and n94. See also McDowell, *Plato "Theaetetus,"* 247–8.

[28] See Fine, "Knowledge and Logos," 386; Burnyeat, *The "Theaetetus" of Plato*, 210n94.

we'll consider that, willingly or unwillingly, he's being playful (206b9–11)." Earlier, Socrates made thematic his own playfulness relative to Theodorus. Although Socrates' playfulness is altogether willing, if Theodorus is playful it is only against his will. Theodorus would not affirm the knowability of the compounds and the elements' unknowability out of any desire to jest. If he did do so, it would only be to fulfill a very sober desire: to confine the knowable to that which he could regard as falling within the mathematical domain. Yet someone might well make these claims in an intentionally playful way, that is, in a way that is conscious of the claim's shortcomings. Such a one might do so to teach, to spur reflection on the meaning of knowability and on the diverse meanings this word must necessarily comprehend if the compound and element are both to be supposed knowable. Socrates mentions play in this context because this diversity of meaning enables there to be such playfulness at all. Socrates' willing playfulness reflects the "playfulness" of being itself. The alternatives Socrates offers are either willing or unwilling playfulness, either acknowledging or obscuring this character of being.

Socrates is thus aware, and Theodorus is oblivious, of the complexity of the objects of knowledge and the resultant elusiveness of the whole of knowledge. This complexity demands in addition to true opinion the inclusion of *logos* to which Socrates now turns.[29] Socrates can, and must, turn to examine the role of *logos*, of the analytic reason that is essential to the reasoning of the mathematician, because he has set in place the context in which that analysis occurs. He has brought to light the existence of the complex unities that call for analysis. These looks, these elements, are those unities first available to us in the opinions inseparable from perceptions, which we take in with only minimal awareness. With this discussion of the existence of complex unities, Socrates has prepared the discussion of the complex unity that is knowledge itself. I turn now to the other element in this compound unity.

Logos (206c1–210b3)

Socrates reminds Theaetetus that they must look at "what was set in front of us (206c3)." They must consider the whole definition, which includes *logos* and true opinion (206c3–4). The hypothesis promises that from the combination of true opinion and *logos*, when *logos* "becomes present" with a true opinion, what results is not simply complete knowledge but "the *most* complete (206c4, emphasis added)." The very need to articulate how these diverse elements

[29] On this point, see Desjardins, *The Rational Enterprise*, 157–8; Miller, "Unity and Logos," 95. Desjardins puts the key point with all clarity: "If it is correct to read the *Theaetetus* as attributing to the objects of knowledge *both* simplicity *and* complexity, then one might distinguish between a preanalytic insight or intuition which in recollection apprehends the form as *simple*, and a dialectical analysis which through collection and division apprehends the form as *complex*." See Desjardins, *The Rational Enterprise*, 250n8.

of knowledge fit together into a whole points to one possible source of this step away from perfection. The question is whether we can be more specific than "becomes present" when explaining the relationship between these two components that yields the whole of knowledge.

Socrates proposes that they investigate the multiple meanings of *logos*, which, he asserts, are three in number. Theaetetus accepts Socrates' assertion without objection. The forthcoming argument elucidates the inadequacies of these successive meanings, the inadequacy of one necessitating a move to the next. But inadequacy does not mean *wholly* inadequate, worthy of being jettisoned entirely. Socrates leaves it to us to consider how these partial iterations of *logos* might together constitute a whole. He provides us with a posthumous homework assignment in the relationship between parts and whole.

Socrates first defines *logos* simply as verbal utterance, as speech. So basic is this definition that commentators often quickly pass it by to get to the notions of *logos* that seem more related to the achievement of knowledge.[30] However, we have heard Socrates assimilate speech with thought. And we have seen the import of speech in the conversational character of Socratic inquiry. The character of knowledge itself demands that it be pursued conversationally. Given these facts, this first, admittedly less than wholly adequate, definition of *logos* deserves sustained attention.

At the end of the dialogue, Theaetetus affirms that there was something deeply beneficial about simply uttering what it is he thinks. Because of the mere fact of his utterance, Theaetetus says, Socrates elicited from him more than he knew was in him (210b6–7). Socrates suggests the significance of such utterance in the grounds he provides for moving beyond this initial version of *logos*.

It is, in particular, the awareness of human inequality with respect to knowledge that moves Socrates beyond this initial notion of *logos*. He states, "Then again, everyone has the power to do this sooner or later, to indicate what seems so to him about each thing, who's not mute or disabled from the start; and so all those who have any correct opinion obviously have it with a *logos*, and correct opinion apart from knowledge won't come about any more anywhere (206d8–e2)." Both Socrates and Theaetetus know that utterance alone does not guarantee the attainment of knowledge. Knowledge is an achievement, made so by those obstacles on the side of both knower and known explored in the discussion. Theaetetus, for example, has just gloried in the possibility that they have discovered what no one else before them had despite great efforts. He feels the great honor that comes to the few who achieve knowledge. Moreover, Socrates here appeals to Theaetetus' sense that knowledge cannot be the province of what "everyone has the power to do . . . sooner or later (206d7–8)."

[30] See, e.g., Cornford, *Plato's Theory of Knowledge*, 155; Fine, "Knowledge and Logos," 387; Bostock, *Plato's "Theaetetus,"* 222; Sedley, *The Midwife of Platonism*, 169.

Appropriately, the succeeding notion of *logos*, discursive analysis, exemplifies the kind of reason used by the experts, the select few adepts in any field.[31]

Throughout the dialogue, human inequality connects the problem of knowledge and the inquiry into politics. It elicits in a most concrete manner the complexity of the human whole and the resultant difficulty of knowing ourselves. The present context is no exception. Socrates acts on his knowledge of human inequality, its recognition spurring further understanding of *logos*. Nevertheless, we should not neglect this initial treatment of *logos* as verbal utterance precisely because of the connection between inequality and the difficulty of knowing our wholeness or fulfillment.

We can begin to understand the preceding claim by recognizing that, despite the aforementioned difficulty, the question of our wholeness is one that must be answered for life to proceed. The laws and mores, the foundational opinions of our communities that shape our self-understanding, provide just such an answer. Yet given the vast differences among humans, which make the question of good so difficult, it is not clear that any of these answers perfectly respond to the whole array of human goods. As such, the community may well discourage examination of its answers, its foundational opinions, unsure of whether they can withstand rational scrutiny. The community may well prefer that these opinions remain unarticulated. From these considerations emerges the importance of midwifery's elicitation phase, which, in its insistence on mere verbal utterance of the interlocutor's views, corresponds precisely to this first sense of *logos*.

Given the origin of inquiry, the maieutic task also brings dangers of which Socrates reminds us by his use of the language of his trial in this context. Unlike the action taken against him by Athens, he tells Theaetetus that they must not "condemn" or "denounce" those whose views they find inadequate (206e4, 208b12–c1). The discursive community that Socrates forms with Theaetetus has different criteria for membership than does their political community. This should not be surprising. The two communities provide very different answers to the question of our wholeness. The replacement of the former community by the latter only begins, however, with the expression, the utterance, of the community's principles aloud.

Theaetetus affirms this initial notion of speech as an opinion that "we say (206d6)." Socrates refers to speech in its most basic form as "making one's thinking apparent through sound with phrases and words, molding one's

[31] See Morrow, "Plato and the Mathematicians," 328. Numerous commentators recognize that the next sense of *logos* pertains to competence and expertise. See, e.g., Haring, "The *Theaetetus* Ends Well," 519. Burnyeat, *The "Theaetetus" of Plato*," 211–13. Nevertheless, the way in which this move invokes inequality is largely unnoticed. Burnyeat does remark, however, on the opposition between, on the one hand, knowledge as expertise and, on the other, the modern notion of knowledge as "unequivocally democratic" in being available to all.

opinion into the stream flowing through the mouth as if into a mirror or water (206d1–4)." Socrates' images pose the question left unanswered by this first sense of *logos*: What kind of speech leads to knowledge? Or, to use Socrates' terms, which is the appropriate image – a mirror or water? Speech that flows out of the mouth as if into water would be transient, short-lived. Our words would mingle with the vast stream of all other words, their distinctiveness lost. This image obscures the connection of speech and knowledge. Alternatively, if one's opinion flows through the mouth as if into a mirror then, as witness Theaetetus' experience, one's thoughts become available for reflection. The mirror image preserves the link between utterance and knowledge. It captures the need for those opinions already present inside us to be expressed and then clarified. This is the essential first step of midwifery, gaining awareness that our thinking is shaped by foundational opinions that are controversial and in need of assessment. For this reason, among others, Socratic midwifery insists on the conversational character of inquiry.

We cannot be satisfied to understand *logos* simply as verbal utterance. But what this most basic sense of *logos* does not let us forget is that the subsequent analysis is exactly *of* these initial opinions, these dream-like notions. These wholes give the context for, and thus shape, the forthcoming rational scrutiny.[32] If we join Theaetetus in his eagerness to embrace expertise, rushing past this initial sense of *logos*, we may miss this all-important insight of midwifery regarding the beginning point of reflection in what "we say."

Socrates now moves to the next version of *logos*, which aims to analyze this initial utterance. He attributes the second definition to the same person who declared that first meaning of *logos*, suggesting that perhaps he meant something else by it. The anonymous speaker's utterance, as is true of many significant utterances, requires interpretation. Specifically, it may be that he meant "the one who's asked *what* each thing is should have the power to give the answer back to the questioner by means of its elements (206e6–207a1, emphasis added)."[33]

[32] Compare Fine who holds that the "point of primary interest to Plato, however, is not so much the relevance of context per se as that one must be able to identify the objects of one's beliefs." Ultimately, as indicated above, Fine judges the third, classificatory version of logos as decisive for Plato's view of knowledge. She explicates this version as entailing an "interrelatedness" of understanding which I think is essential to Plato's view of reason. Yet she sees reason so understood as operating within what she calls "a systematic framework" or "the confines of a particular framework, music or medicine, say" or "a particular discipline." But the question then concerns the status of these "frameworks." Without reflection on this question, knowledge remains a technical undertaking, a notion the dialogue aims to put into question. See Fine, "Knowledge and Logos," 392, 396. See also note 13 above. Compare Rosen, "Socrates' Dream," 161. As I argued in my treatment of the Prologue, the *Theaetetus* has emphasized the importance of context from the very beginning.

[33] Among those that insist that the object of knowledge intended here is the "what" understood as the essence of the thing are Haring, "The *Theaetetus* Ends Well," 520; Alexander Nehamas, "*Episteme* and *Logos* in Plato's Later Thought." in *Essays in Ancient Greek Philosophy III*

With this definition of *logos*, we return to the version of *logos* employed in the dream. This enumeration of elements is the kind of analysis that might preserve an arithmetic notion of being such that the summed elements are identical with the whole. Three noteworthy changes, however, prevent the conclusion that we have simply reverted to the dream. First, this is the second sense of *logos*. It follows a first that calls attention to the importance of pre-existing wholes as the objects of analysis. Second, this is the second of three senses of *logos* suggesting that it too is not wholly adequate. Finally, the exact character of its inadequacy is significant. That inadequacy reflects awareness of the vexed relationship between parts and wholes, an awareness that resists the conflation of whole and all ventured in the dream. Versions of *logos* that demand recognition of the irreducibility of wholes surround this second sense of *logos*.[34] The distinction between whole and all resists suppression. It arises again even in Socrates' formulation of the object of knowledge found in his elaboration of *logos* as discursive analysis.

As indicated in Socrates' statement in the preceding text, the goal of this conversational search for knowledge is to find the "what" of each thing, its distinctive character that somehow comprises its components and makes it the kind of thing that it is. Unsure of what Socrates means by this new definition, Theaetetus asks, "*What*, for example, do you mean? (207a2, emphasis added)." Theaetetus' focus on the elements has obscured for him that whole which guides the search. Yet, in his own speech, he cannot help but invoke exactly this question. Were Theaetetus truly to begin again, he might appreciate the natural course of understanding that seeks the what-it-is of each thing. The subsequent argument moves Theaetetus to the threshold of such an understanding.

By way of explanation, Socrates offers the example of a wagon. He uses a quote from Hesiod that conveys the thought that it is not as easy to build a wagon as one might think (207a3–4).[35] The quote notes the "hundred pieces of wood" that would be needed for this project but which, Socrates admits, he "wouldn't have the power to state" nor, referring to Theaetetus, "would you (207a4–5)." Yet both of them clearly know in some sense what a wagon is, enough at least to know some of its elements and generally to recognize one when they see it or hear it used as an example. The wagon is somehow present to them even though they do not know it in the way that the builder of a wagon might. Their analysis thus presumes a whole, a "what," that gives direction and

eds. John P. Anton and Anthony Preus (Albany: State University of New York Press, 1989), 268, 271–2; Polansky, *Philosophy and Knowledge*, 226; Miller, "Unity and Logos," 97. This does not necessarily entail, however, that the object intended is the Form understood as the separate, permanently enduring intelligible – nor, as Miller states, is that understanding necessarily ruled out. Miller, "Unity and Logos," 95n22. It is the case, however, that the terms *idea* and *eidos* refer throughout this passage to immanent characters of concrete things.

34 For two alternative explanations of why this version of *logos* recurs see McDowell, *Plato "Theaetetus,"* 252–3; Sedley, *The Midwife of Platonism*, 170–1.

35 Hesiod *Works and Days*. 456.

boundaries to the analysis. The point is further confirmed when, as his second example, Socrates uses Theaetetus' name and notes that someone inquiring into it would have to ask what it is before proceeding to discuss the analysis of it (207a9–10).

Socrates points to still another aspect of the context of analysis, in alluding to that which determines the proper level of analysis required to claim knowledge. Socrates implies that the one who knows the hundred pieces of a wagon knows it better than does either he or Theaetetus with their meager capacity to name only five such pieces. If such reductionism is *the* criterion of knowledge then certainly the contemporary physicist could exceed the builder by providing the atomic structure of the wagon's materials. Would this count as greater knowledge of the wagon? The same question arises with respect to the next example. Is it so clearly ridiculous, as Socrates claims, to respond concerning Theaetetus' name with syllables rather than letters (207a19–b5)? It may depend on whether one wishes to pronounce or spell his name.

This question of the proper level of analysis – whether the elements are axles or atoms, syllables or letters – stands outside and guides analysis. The answer to this question depends on one's purpose, one's hoped-for good, in knowing. Thus, Socrates says that he and Theaetetus would be "quite satisfied" with the five pieces of the wagon as a list of its elements (207a5). Not wishing to build a wagon, but only to recognize and use it, such knowledge suffices for them. The opinion with which we began our inquiry, the notion of good that shapes our idea of the goal, provides a crucial aspect of the context in which analysis occurs. Such analysis is dream-like unless and until this context is made explicit and is itself scrutinized.

Socrates now answers the question, if one simply desires knowledge of the wagon, what *should* one seek? He twice designates this goal as "the very being" (*autas tan ousian*) of the wagon (207c1, c3). This is the goal that may be reached by going through the elements of the thing as a whole, the whole that is there beforehand. This phrase, "the very being," designates the object of knowledge that becomes available subsequent to analysis. It does not refer simply to that initial whole but to the grasp one has of its wholeness, having examined those parts it comprises. One would presumably then know those parts as parts by virtue of their contribution to the whole that dictates their arrangement. This "very being" is the unity that serves as the ultimate object of knowledge, that unity by virtue of which a thing is what it is.

How does the "very being" stand to its parts? As several commentators note, with Socrates' example of the wagon we are back with the army. That is, we are considering a whole distinct from its parts insofar as the wagon is not fully what it is without the contribution of its structure or form in addition to its elements.[36] The problematic relationship between its parts and the whole

[36] Haring, "The *Theaetetus* Ends Well," 520; Miller, "Unity and Logos," 98.

provide the rationale for moving beyond the second sense of *logos* to the third sense.

Socrates begins his critique of *logos* as analysis by introducing two kinds of error that can arise within *logos* as just defined. The first is when "the same thing sometimes seems to him to belong to one thing and sometimes to something else (207d3–4)." The second is "when he has the opinion that it's sometimes one thing and sometimes another that belongs to it (207d4–6)."

Theaetetus provides examples of each kind of error. He takes these from the time when he was learning to spell (207d10–e3). It is not a time Theaetetus remembers fondly. Socrates asks him whether someone could be considered a knower who makes such errors. Theaetetus adamantly rejects this possibility, twice punctuating his rejection with an oath (207d7, e5). Theaetetus does regard himself as a learner, as someone possessing partial knowledge but on the way to knowing more. Whereas some might take pleasure in reflecting on progress attained, for Theaetetus these thoughts only cause indignation. In his ire, Theaetetus wholly rejects the second sense of *logos*. We, however, should not be so quick to dismiss completely this notion of *logos*. After all, Socrates has just linked it to the attainment of the object of knowledge. Admittedly, perplexities persist regarding that object. Error still haunts inquiry. Yet it is not clear that any meaning of *logos* wholly precludes this possibility, or therefore that the mere possibility of error warrants complete rejection of the second sense of *logos*.

In what follows, Socrates initially highlights only one of the just-mentioned kinds of error, the kind in which one does not recognize the sameness between two wholes. In his example, someone fails to note that "Theaetetus" and "Theodorus" have the same initial syllable. Socrates holds that if one cannot recognize this same syllable when seen elsewhere in a different whole, one cannot be said to know "Theaetetus."

Of utmost significance, Socrates insists twice that this lack of knowledge can result even if one was "holding to the way through it by the letter (208a9, 208b4–5)." The result will still yield "correct opinion with *logos* which one must not yet call knowledge (208b8–9)." The unavoidable conclusion is that "holding to the way through it by the letter," or enumerating the elements in an analytical manner, does not by itself guarantee knowledge. It does not guarantee apprehension of the "very being" as it would have to do if the whole were indistinguishable from the all. Equally unavoidable then is the conclusion that the object of knowledge *is* in a different way than its elements. As such, it is accessible in an equally distinct manner.[37]

37 Fine's understanding of knowledge requires her to dismiss the participation in knowledge of alternative modes of cognition. Fine, "Knowledge and Logos," 269. Haring seems to raise the possibility as an objection but ultimately dismisses it as well. Haring, "The *Theaetetus* Ends Well," 526–7. For other suggestions of the need for diverse modes of cognition see Runciman, *Plato's Later Epistemology*, 40;Polansky, *Philosophy and Knowledge*, 231n26.

It is clear that a thing as a whole, and therefore as a complex unity, would somehow need to partake of both a partite and a unified character. Yet exactly how that movement from the parts to the whole occurs is less clear. This requirement of its being, therefore, leaves a heterogeneity in our knowing between reasoning about the parts and grasping or recognizing the unity, "the very being," that enables us to see them as parts. The picture of the object of knowledge that is emerging specifies what Socrates had earlier suggested in his treatment of mud. We move from an initial recognition of a thing as a whole to the deeper knowledge of it gained through analysis of its parts. Finally, such analysis can result in our grasping its very being, that unity that accounts for its wholeness. The need to move beyond the second sense of *logos* arises from Socrates' desire to direct Theaetetus' attention precisely to the being of the whole as distinct from its parts.

The third sense of *logos* is classificatory in intent, requiring us to compare one whole with another. Such comparisons, as we have seen throughout the dialogue, depend on recognizing those parts of different wholes that are sufficiently similar as to be compared. *Logos* as classificatory depends on *logos* as analytic.[38] The comparisons require a prior analysis of the parts of a single whole, at least if these comparisons have in view the ultimate grasp of the whole. But in what follows we see that Socrates' final destination for Theaetetus is the beginning. Thus he finally focuses instead on the initial recognition of the whole.

In his discussion of the classificatory *logos*, Socrates emphasizes what he had omitted in the discussion of the errors permitted by analysis – namely, the difference between wholes. If, as I have maintained, the three senses of *logos* are interdependent, none simply dispensable, the question becomes why Socrates wishes to culminate his discussion of *logos* with this classificatory version, a version focused especially on ascertaining the differences between wholes.

We must first note that Socrates leaves the impression with Theaetetus that classificatory *logos* has wholly supplanted the two previous versions. In addition, although it too is found wanting, it is not said to permit errors as did analytical *logos*. Of the three meanings of *logos* Socrates makes this last one the relatively most attractive to Theaetetus. If Theaetetus is not inclined to jettison reason entirely, it is the one that he will take with him from this memorable conversation with Socrates. Socrates' tactic in this context is intelligible in terms of the psychic needs of Theaetetus and his kindred theorists. With this third sense of *logos*, Socrates can emphasize, above all, the initial recognition of a whole in its distinctiveness that permits and calls for analysis, rather than the movement through analysis to the "very being" of this whole. Again, with this third sense of *logos*, Socrates means to move Theaetetus back to the beginning,

[38] On this point see Miller, "Unity and Logos," 92–3 n.16. Miller makes the point in the course of responding to Fine's contention that classificatory *logos* becomes the one true meaning of *logos*.

to have him discover for himself the distinction between the initial grasp of the whole and the analysis thereof. It is just this distinction that makes knowledge as a whole complex. Following too from this goal are Socrates' efforts in this context to blur repeatedly and ever more blatantly the distinction between the initial whole and its ultimate version that follows on analysis.

Socrates introduces the need for this third sense of *logos* as a way of providing a part that has been left out of a whole. In explaining it he says it is "[j]ust the thing that *most people say*: having some sign to say in what respect the thing in question differs from all things (208c7–8, emphasis added)." This view of *logos* represents a widespread understanding; it is what "most people say (208c7)." Socrates finds this use so prevalent because the initial recognition of the variety of beings in their differences from one another provides the basis of knowing common to all. Sedley recognizes this fact when he calls this third definition "the most commonplace and therefore *un*philosophical of those considered."[39] He maintains, moreover, that it "captures a very low-level and familiar criterion of knowledge."[40] In this assessment, he echoes Burnyeat who writes that with the third version of *logos* "mundane knowledge has come back into focus."[41] It is, Burnyeat adds, an "admirable account . . . of what the ordinary man means when he talks of knowing people and things."[42] As such, it hardly rises to the level of a self-conscious use of *logos*. Thus, Socrates speaks here initially of a "sign" rather than a *logos*. This is surely not the province of the theorists alone.

Related to this "democratizing" third sense of *logos* is the way in which Socrates dismisses the previous view. Referring to the second sense of *logos*, Socrates says, "So as it seems, our wealth was a dream (208b11)." The previous notion of *logos* permits the mathematicians' dream that all can be known through analysis. As in that dream, we could be lulled into neglect of the necessary preknowledge of the wholes. But the dream's form of *logos* no longer stands alone. Moreover, even more explicitly than the first, with this third sense of *logos*, especially in its emphasis on the comparison and differences between and among wholes, the initial wholes cannot be forgotten.

To exemplify what he means, Socrates first refers Theaetetus to the sun, *the* perceivable, recognized or identified as "the brightest of the things going across the heavens (208d2–3)." Socrates deals here with individuals.[43] These

39 Sedley, *The Midwife of Platonism*, 174.

40 Ibid. Sedley adds that it is "only when a method is added for achieving that differentiation that this account of knowledge will become philosophically adventurous." Ibid. My quite different interpretation of the import of this "commonplace" view is indicated in the text.

41 Burnyeat, *The "Theaetetus" of Plato*, 219.

42 Ibid., 222. My interpretation of this "return to the mundane" differs also from Burnyeat's.

43 See, e.g., Haring, "The *Theaetetus* Ends Well," 522; Miller, "Unity and Logos," 105; Cornford, *Plato's Theory of Knowledge*, 154, 161–3; Polansky, *Philosophy and Knowledge*, 231. Cornford maintains, in accordance with his overall interpretation that the use of individuals

individuals are also wholes available immediately through perception. They are not those wholes that, following intense analysis, stand as the culmination of intelligibility. The difference proves important in what follows. Socrates says that "for some people" grasping this distinctiveness is to grasp a *logos*. Yet, clearly, this cannot be the case for more than a very few people. What he is speaking about here occurs without a *logos*. To have determined that the sun is the brightest thing in the sky leaves significant work for a *logos* to contribute in its role in achieving knowledge. With his next move, Socrates focuses exactly on the status of such initial wholes vis-à-vis subsequent analysis.

Socrates characterizes his own situation regarding the knowledge of knowledge. With respect to such knowledge, he likens himself to someone viewing "a sketch made of shadings (208e7–8)." Such a sketch would appear as a whole image from one perspective. Yet when viewed too closely, when analyzed, it breaks down into apparently unrelated elements (208e9–10).[44] When glimpsed at first from afar the sketch appears as a whole, as *what* it is. Yet, on closer inspection, it is constituted by parts that do not clearly yield the whole. To know the sketch as a whole, to know its very being, one would have to know the contribution of both.

This whole is available to the artist. He knows what he wished to portray and how the parts, the shadings, should be arranged to constitute it. However, as regards knowledge, we are in the position of Socrates, the position of the viewer. We take in the initial look, the initial whole, which, as Socrates says, appeared "to make some sense" to him (208e10). Still, on the basis of this look alone we have not yet clearly determined how the parts of this whole are not simply elements but parts, that is, how they constitute that whole. With analysis alone we reside between two unities, between these two versions of wholeness.

Theaetetus expresses uncertainty regarding the meaning of Socrates' example. In his reply, Socrates tells him "I'll show you, if I'll be able to (209a1)." In question is Socrates' assessment of his own powers, and those of Theaetetus. Socrates had begun the examination of this third definition of knowledge with a reference to the question of our powers (201e4). The entire investigation into the meaning of knowledge is undertaken so that Socrates might know one specific thing: Theaetetus' soul. In these, the dialogue's culminating passages, Socrates returns to the issue of knowing Theaetetus, this particular individual, to exemplify his point.

rather than Forms is supposed to be spotted by the Platonist as the fatal flaw in the argument. Polansky argues that the argument works equally well for Forms or individuals. My position is that Socrates means to move Theaetetus, and other theoretically inclined auditors, to appreciate the importance of first looks – not as the last word but as shaping subsequent inquiry. I.e., Socrates returns his interlocutor to the beginning but now with the possibility of reflection on that beginning.

44 On such painting, see Burnyeat, *The "Theaetetus" of Plato*, 229, 348n62.

Socrates tells Theaetetus: "When I have a correct opinion about you, if I get hold, in addition, of your *logos*, I'll recognize (*gignosko*) you, but if not, I'll have the opinion only (209a1–3)." Clearly, *logos* is not required for mere recognition understood as identification. Socrates recognized Theaetetus prior to the analysis of his soul, which the subsequent dialogue has provided. If such a *logos* were required, it would not be clear that Socrates could even now recognize Theaetetus. Recall that Socrates hedged his prophecy about Theaetetus with several qualifications. Additionally, in his concluding remarks, Socrates urges Theaetetus to a gentleness that already characterizes his disposition (210c2–3). We might well wonder at the end of this conversation whether Socrates yet possesses a complete *logos* of Theaetetus' soul.

Socrates continues to play on this distinction between recognition and analysis. He says that a "*logos* was a putting into words of your differentness (209a5)." Yet, surely, to put this differentness into words it first must be recognized. Socrates asks, whether when he had "only an opinion" he was "touching on something else in my thinking, but not on any of those things by which you differ from everything else (209a7–8)." Theaetetus should answer that in fact he was "touching on" evidence of Theaetetus' distinctiveness. Stated otherwise, he should acknowledge the existence of that initial look that Socrates recognizes and that provides the occasion for the "*logos* of differentness" to which Socrates refers.[45] Socrates' present argument seeks to elicit this acknowledgment from Theaetetus and like-minded theorists. Doing so, they would become aware of the context that shapes their theoretical activity.

To his credit, Theaetetus' response to Socrates' question does evince a hint of hesitation, and so a glimmer of such acknowledgment: "It *seems* not (209a9, emphasis added)." Furthermore, in his rejoinder Socrates shines a light on the decisive point by urging Theaetetus, "Come on then, by Zeus. How in the world in such a case, did I have an opinion about you any more than about anyone else whatever (209b2–3)"? If the distinction between recognition and analysis is blurred in the way that Socrates has done, it is not at all clear how this could be. But with his oath, Socrates points to just where Theaetetus needs to exert resistance to the momentum of this argument. Socrates' oath should prompt Theaetetus to concentrate on exactly what midwifery takes as its focus: the initial looks, or opinions, which in themselves and in their inadequacy, provide analysis with its direction and purpose.

In the subsequent exchanges, Socrates concentrates even more emphatically on Theaetetus, especially on his face and its features. Zeroing in on the source of the recognition of Theaetetus' distinctiveness, Socrates refers first to the analysis of the parts of Theaetetus' face simply as parts of *a* face (209b4–6). As such, this analysis will not make him think of Theaetetus "any more than

45 In thinking of the character of such looks, Burnyeat's characterization is helpful. He calls it "a Gestalt of numerous distinctive features in relation to each other" – taken in, I would add, all at once. Ibid., 229–30.

of Theodorus, or of the least of the Mysians, as the saying goes (209b6–8)."[46] They might conjure up just any human. He even maintains that Theaetetus' squashed-in nose and popped-out eyes do not serve to distinguish Theaetetus alone, although they must seriously narrow the field to those of this type (209b10–c3). Willing, perhaps, to use any means to jar Theaetetus into the importance of the initial looks, Socrates is only now completely explicit about Theaetetus' ugliness.

What Theaetetus fails or refuses to see is that both of these inadequate differentiations of him presume a previous recognition. Consider the phrases Socrates uses to introduce these attempts. With respect to the first, Socrates begins by saying, "For put it that I'm thinking that this is Theaetetus . . . (209b3–4)." With the second, he says, "if I think of the one who . . . (209b10–c1)." In both cases, there is already a previous recognition of Theaetetus as this distinctive one that precedes the necessarily subsequent analysis. This recognition is available as a unity, as something grasped at once in a perception. To drive this point home, Socrates even rehabilitates the wax-block image at exactly this point to convey what occurs in such recognition; the perception deposits "a memorial by imprinting it in me (209c7–8)." Socrates then draws this conclusion: "Therefore, correct opinion too would be about the differentness of each thing (209d1–2)."

Everything is now in place for Socrates to confront Theaetetus with a dilemma. This dilemma depends on Theaetetus' reluctance to appreciate the difference between the wholes as initially grasped and as known subsequent to analysis, between the initial look of a thing and its "very being." The dilemma is this: if we already have grasped the thing in its differentness, simply by seeing it as this thing, what then does the *logos* add? Through our initial look, we have already ascertained, in some sense, the thing as a whole, the thing in its difference from other things. Yet the third sense of *logos* was supposed precisely to explicate the thing in its differentness. It now, therefore, seems redundant. Or, as Socrates soon says, "it turns out to be a completely ridiculous requirement (209d6)." However, if Theaetetus flees from the horn of redundancy, he collides with the horn of circularity. For if *logos* does supply knowledge of differentness, then, Socrates says, "it's totally silly, when we're inquiring about *knowledge*, to claim that it's a correct opinion along with a *knowledge* of differentness (210a7–8, emphasis added)." We will have defined knowledge by reference to knowledge, and so not defined it at all.

There is, however, a way out of this dilemma. We can see its traces through closely considering Socrates' explanation of why the definition is redundant.

46 The reference to the Mysians can be an indication of the role that experience (and so embodiedness) plays in determining the boundaries of knowledge. Can Socrates, or anyone, claim to know all the inhabitants of every far-flung land? See Ibid., 231. In light of the Mysians' low standing, Socrates may also be attempting to appeal to Theaetetus' desire for distinction in order to get him to reflect on differentness.

As we see in what follows, the impasse to which Socrates has brought the argument does not appear so desperate if we insist on the distinction Theaetetus neglects.

Socrates characterizes the addition of *logos* as simply piling one opinion on top of another. We already have recognized the thing's distinctiveness. What more need be added? – hence the charge of redundancy. Yet Socrates' own words suggest what the *logos* does add to this initial recognition. As he repeatedly says, the *logos* aims "to get hold of" what differentiates the thing (209d9, e3, e7, 210a5). This phrase – "to get hold of" – also used when Theaetetus discovers the power of opinion, refers to that active capacity by which the mind reflects on those looks that impress themselves on our "wax." By this usage, Socrates points exactly to the distinction between the initial activity of recognition, on the one hand, and the analysis of that which is recognized, on the other. Initial recognition of a thing leaves us far from truly "getting hold" of it. We get hold of a thing, come to know its "very being," only through strenuous efforts. Once we express the thing encountered in our experience, these efforts require the analysis of the thing's elements, and the subsequent comparison to other wholes that depends on this analysis. Only at that point, after engaging *logos* in these diverse but related ways, might we be able to grasp the being as what it is in its unity.

Again, the one pervasive deed of the dialogue makes the point. Socrates' own examination of Theaetetus provides no clearer example of the distinction to which his words point. Even once Socrates recognized Theaetetus, having picked him out from the approaching trio, he proceeded with the analysis of Theaetetus' soul. This analysis, prosecuted through *logos*, through conversation, is anything but redundant to that initial look. It enables Socrates to know Theaetetus if not completely then at least in a more comprehensive way than provided by that initial recognition. Such analysis proceeds through eliciting the "elements" of Theaetetus' soul, the opinions that constitute his outlook, the traits that constitute his character. And, as Socrates exhibited most explicitly in the midwife passage, his investigation also involves comparing Theaetetus with other students who have come to the midwife in various stages of pregnancy. The need for *logos*, and the extent to which it adds to this initial look is evident in its difficulty, and in the time and attention Socrates has expended on it. This entire conversation bespeaks the inadequacy of that initial recognition of Theaetetus and the need to move toward a grasp of Theaetetus' "very being" through *logos*. If *logos* is redundant then so is the dialogue as a whole.

We see the same pattern in Socrates' continual commentary on the "dilemma" he has introduced. That commentary also depreciates *logos*, but it does so in terms that belie this depreciation. He compares the addition of *logos* to a useless going around in circles, and he quotes a proverbial saying to this effect. Rather, he half-quotes it, comparing the appeal to *logos* to the "twirling of a baton or a bat, *or whatever the saying is* (209d10–e1, emphasis added)."[47] Again, Socrates' manner of expression requires consideration. His hesitation about the saying indicates precisely what *logos*, the activity of "getting hold of" the opinions, adds. Such proverbial sayings, implanted there by those who raise us, shape our understanding. They possess the cognitive status that Socrates' apparently offhand remark – "whatever the saying is" – connotes; we are only dimly aware of them. Unless and until they are brought to light, elicited and assessed, our lives are not fully our own. If *logos* is nothing but a useless going around in circles then so must be Socrates' lifelong practice of maieutics.

Socrates makes the same point in his conclusion of the argument. This activity of *logos* – "to get hold in addition of those things that we have, in order that we might understand the things we have opinions about" – seems, Socrates says, "to have a completely true-born resemblance to someone who's lost his sight (209e4–5)." Yet this subjection of critical opinions to *logos*, dismissed as the activity of the blind, may be just what is required to approach knowledge. This would only occur, however, to one who took this step, one who subjected these initial opinions to scrutiny. Such a one would see the difference between these initial looks and "what is." She would see that although such rational scrutiny can look like the activity of the blind, because it requires a seeing in the mind alone, it is crucial to attaining knowledge. Perhaps, to the "true-born," the noble of birth, this activity of questioning these opinions seems foolish. After all, these constitute the bounds of that community that grants the nobles their elevated status. To examine these opinions might suggest their inadequacy. However, one who did not care about a reputation for strangeness might nevertheless persist in such inquiry. If this *logos* is but a kind of blindness then the laws of every, and any, community must suffice for the guidance of life.

In the foregoing ways, the dialogue shows that, with respect to knowledge, *logos* is anything but redundant. Its contribution in this regard is as distinct as the intricate conversation of the *Theaetetus* is from Socrates' initial glimpse of Theaetetus. However, the question of the definition's circularity remains. In light of the indispensable contribution of *logos* to knowledge, why should we not conclude that *logos* is not only necessary but also sufficient for knowledge? Here, again, the dialogue as a whole provides an answer.

The ultimate object of knowledge is the "very being" of the thing in question. This "very being" constitutes the unity, the wholeness, of the thing in light of which the parts are parts. A prominent theme of the dialogue, however, concerns the discrepancy between parts and whole. To use the terminology of this third definition, a "whole" differs from an "all." The dialogue indicates that access to this ontological diversity requires similarly diverse cognitive means. *Logos*, analysis of the parts, is required to approach the wholeness of a being

47 On the possible meaning of this image, see Benardete, *Being of the Beautiful*, I.182, 190n87; Chappell, *Reading Plato's "Theaetetus"*, 231.

but that wholeness is grasped by other means. Therefore, although necessary for knowledge, *logos* is not sufficient.

In other dialogues, Socrates does concentrate on this ultimate object of knowledge. And he refers to *nous*, the cognitive capacity by which the ultimate whole in its unity may be grasped.[48] Yet in the *Theaetetus*, he is relatively quiet about this ultimate object, and absolutely silent regarding *nous*. The way out of the dilemma Socrates poses lies in seeing and acknowledging ontological and cognitive heterogeneity. However, Socrates wishes Theaetetus to see that heterogeneity as it emerges from the difference between logos and the *initial* looks or wholes. These wholes too differ from *logos* and thus provide the context in which logos operates, just as this third definition analyzes the mathematician's dream. Socrates wishes to induce in Theaetetus, and those like him, an appreciation of how these initial looks shape his theoretical activity, and of their particular inadequacy that calls for such activity. Theaetetus, and those like him, are much more in need of recognizing the ground beneath their feet than in gazing at the sky above.

Theaetetus does approach such an acknowledgment of these differences. In his initial reaction to Socrates' claim that this third sense of *logos* is ridiculous in its redundancy, Theaetetus sensed that Socrates was conflating what should be distinguished. He sensed, in particular, that "to recognize" is precisely different from "[taking] hold of knowledge." For at just that point Theaetetus responded with a question that returned Socrates to an earlier exchange in the argument, an exchange where Socrates was asking a question that obscured the capacity of the initial opinion, the look, to convey differentness (209e6). If he were to pursue this line of inquiry Theaetetus would need to scrutinize the basis of the difference that, his earlier question suggests, he now only very dimly recognizes. Yet his very reaction to the difference comprised by the complex definition of knowledge does exhibit a nascent sense of the diverse sorts of knowledge in play. It exhibits his need "to get hold of" these opinions "in order to understand" the things he has opinions about. If he did, he might then appreciate the difference between these ways of knowing, between the initial recognition of a difference and the analysis of its underlying basis through *logos* that moves toward a grasp of its true wholeness or unity.

Theaetetus, however, is not yet ready to take that step. He is not yet ready to appreciate the life-shaping power of those initial looks. Again, to elicit such appreciation in the theorist is an overriding purpose of the dialogue. To avoid

48 On the significance of the absence of *nous* in the *Theaetetus*, see Rosen, "Socrates' Dream," 161–2, 166–7. Nicholas White has recognized this same lack in the dialogue. He takes it as an indication of the need to complete Plato's picture of cognition with an examination of such intellectual perception in the *Seventh Letter*. I agree with the need for such an effort but share some of the misgivings about White's particular discussion expressed by Bostock. See Nicholas P. White, *Plato on Knowledge and Reality* (Indianapolis, IN: Hackett Publishing Company, 1976), 179–215; Bostock, *Plato's "Theaetetus,"* 258–260. See also on this issue Miller, "Unity and Logos," 108–110.

the fate of the flying philosopher, Theaetetus, and those like him, must reflect further on the discrepancy between the relationship between these disparate parts of knowledge and their unity in knowledge as a whole. As Socrates indicates in the concluding passages of the dialogue, what Theaetetus has yet to attain is the kind of self-knowledge that makes this step necessary and possible.

Socrates explicitly rejects this third definition of *logos*. The argument, he claims, has led them to an impasse, an aporia. Down one road stands redundancy, down the other circularity. We have seen, however, a third alternative, one that awaits Theaetetus' discovery on a further study of Socrates' text. The alternative is that all wholes, all objects of knowledge, including knowledge itself, are complex unities. Again, the ontological diversity that undergirds this complexity demands equally diverse modes of knowing. It demands, first, the grasp of beings as wholes both immediately and ultimately, but also that discursive analysis by which we ascend from that immediate apprehension to the ultimate grasp of a thing's "very being." Socrates does not simply mislead Theaetetus in deeming the result of their investigation aporetic. For knowledge so understood *is* a problem, the character of the relationship between its parts and the whole remaining a question. In this light, with this final dilemma, Socrates gives Theaetetus a great gift. Working through the charges of redundancy and circularity, he can come to understand the true character of that which he seeks.[49]

Given such complexity, a complexity shared by knowledge and knowledge's objects, the crucial cognitive capacity is that by which we consider parts in light of the whole, and vice versa – precisely the cognitive capacity required to make one's way through the world of the Platonic dialogue. By means of this capacity, we are always aware of the other-than-seamless connection between the parts and the whole and aware too of the significance of this issue for our lives. *Phronesis* is always necessary.[50] We have taken a road that leads

[49] For a treatment of the fruitfulness of the dilemma, see Miller, "Unity and Logos, 102–4.

[50] Sedley verges on recognition of the need for such a capacity when he interprets a passage in the *Meno* that is immediately subsequent to the famous statement regarding calculation of the cause to which I have previously called attention. See *Meno* 98a1–b5. In the passage, Socrates says he is sure that correct opinion differs from knowledge. Yet, why it so differs, he says, is a matter of guesswork. Sedley writes: "Whatever he may mean by 'guess' in this context, it inevitably falls short of anything that could be called 'calculation', or indeed of anything that could be thought adequate to underwrite a knowledge claim." Sedley goes on to say that Socrates thus "invites the killer question: if not mere guesswork, what *is* the required cognitive relation between the knowing subject and the extra something?" I agree that the answer to this question will not be a matter of calculation. But I am more hesitant to dismiss guesswork as of no worth, especially Socrates' guesswork. This is exactly how he characterized his assessment of souls in discussing his midwifery. *Theaetetus* 151b4. There, as here, such guessing may be all that is possible. It is a great achievement, both intellectual and ethical, to come to grips with this fact. The appropriate response is not to lament the absence of calculation but to make one's guesses, one's judgments, in each case as wise as possible. Sedley, *The Midwife of Platonism*, 177–8. On guessing, see Roochnik, "Self-Recognition,"43.

us to see that the nature of knowledge itself calls for *phronesis* or wisdom as a capacity necessarily distinct from knowledge. Accordingly, at the end, Socrates returns to the most striking image of *phronesis* within the dialogue. Once again, and finally, he appears in the guise of the midwife. In the manner of the truly Socratic return to the beginning, we can now more fully appreciate the appropriateness of the image.

10

The Wisdom of the Midwife

Introduction

At the outset, I claimed that only through careful attention to the political content of the dialogue could we understand Plato's examination of the meaning of knowledge in the *Theaetetus*. Such attention enables us to see more clearly that, and why, knowledge is a problem. It allows us to appreciate as well the ongoing significance of that problem for the practice of philosophy. Because that significance persists, consideration of political life remains a requisite of philosophic inquiry.

The rationale for this requirement derives ultimately from the importance of the question of human good and the enduring perplexities surrounding its determination. We have access to the range of issues surrounding this question especially through the cognitive capacity called *phronesis*. The same considerations that make political inquiry central to philosophy designate wisdom, philosophy's object, as *phronesis*. In the *Theaetetus*, Socrates clothes *phronesis* in the garb of midwifery. He formulates this practice in recognition of the problems that attend philosophic inquiry and the existential significance of those problems. This being the case, Socrates' maieutics stands already as an achievement of *phronesis*. It is also the means to its further acquisition. Accordingly, in the concluding passages of this his valedictory, Socrates leaves for Theaetetus, and for any potential Socratic philosopher listening in, a picture of his strange, perplexity-inducing activity. In this final act of midwifery, he lets the wise midwife stand as the image of his life, available for any willing and able to emulate.

Back to the Beginning: Midwifery and the Political Context of Knowledge (210b4–d4)

Socrates makes clear that the entire preceding discussion was an example of midwifery. He asks Theaetetus, "Then are we still pregnant and in labor with anything about knowledge, dear fellow, or have we given birth to everything? (210b4–5)." Socrates' question expresses the central conceits of the midwife image. The image draws its power from the undeniable fact that human development has not only a physical but also a psychic aspect. With respect to both, that which is only latent, only present potentially, must develop if we are to achieve maturity. Moreover, both physically and psychically we require the assistance of others to become and to be what we are. The image incisively captures the latency and dependence that characterize the path toward human fulfillment.

Taken together, these characteristics, latency and dependence, determine the beginning point of the path to psychic fulfillment. Far from being blank slates, already present within us is a set of opinions through which we view the world. In other dialogues, Plato has Socrates trace these opinions to the soul's presumed prenatal existence. No such mythic presumptions are present in the *Theaetetus*. Here, the intrepidly earthy midwife recognizes these opinions as sown by the political community. When he notes his fellow citizens' reaction to his challenging questions, Socrates leaves no doubt of this source.

The pretheoretical context of human life is, most decisively, political precisely because of our dependence. Just as nature does not see to our unassisted physical development, neither does it provide for our spontaneous psychic development. Put otherwise, the incomplete determination of our biological inheritance requires the formation of humans by the deeds of other humans. In this sense, both midwifery and politics respond to the "lapses" of nature, each attending to the psychic requirements of human development. Working the same ground, however, they soon conflict, bringing all the well-documented dangers to the midwife.

This political origin accounts not only for midwifery's dangers but also for its two-phase structure. The community's education is so comprehensive and so deeply engrained that it requires great effort even to elicit, to bring to awareness, the offspring within us of its laws, written and unwritten. The kind of conversation employed in this association provides further testimony of the community's hold on the psyche. Socrates employs as his primary tool the challenging, refutative conversation required to break through the walls of the old community.

Have we given birth to everything? Theaetetus' response to Socrates' question gives a sense of the density and height of these walls: "yes we have, by Zeus, and I at least have said more on account of you, than what I used to have in myself (210b6–7)." Socrates' sustained interrogation has elicited views from within Theaetetus that he did not realize he possessed, views that would have remained latent without the midwife's ministrations. These foundational opinions permeate our understanding to the point that we are hardly aware of them as beliefs susceptible to examination, much less to doubt. However, it is not only obliviousness that obstructs the path to their examination. These opinions, these notions of good, engage admonitory passions that also impede such scrutiny. Theaetetus' oath, triumphantly affirming the exhaustiveness of the examination, provides one more example of the work of these passions. Only once the delivery, the elicitation of these opinions, has been accomplished can the midwife and patient embark on the second phase of midwifery, the critical assessment of these opinions.

The theorist may well believe that he easily escapes the shaping hand of the community. But beneath the apparent cosmopolitanism of Theodorus and Protagoras the political passion grips them even more firmly because of their blithe disregard of its power. Socrates concentrates on the political beginning of inquiry with these interlocutors precisely because of their inclination to neglect the power of such opinions, and especially of the passions that underlie them, to distort inquiry. As was evident in the case of the conflict between the fluxists and stabilists, theoretical inquiry unaccompanied by political reflection becomes indistinguishable from politics.

The very form of the *Theaetetus*, beginning with its unusual Prologue, highlights the importance of the initial context of inquiry. Moreover, with his repeated calls to go back to the beginning, Socrates seeks to make such reflection imperative for the philosopher. In trying to understand the motive for Socrates' recommendation, we should note that he urges a movement of thought evident in authors nearer our own time. Thinkers such as Nietzsche, Husserl, and Heidegger likewise see the need to rethink the pretheoretical context of theory.[1] For these more recent thinkers that need arises from the judgment that the prevailing form of what is called rationalism is dogmatic, that it partakes of Theodoran self-forgetfulness in its unsubstantiated belief regarding its need and its possibility. One reason that Socrates considers, and reconsiders, the beginning follows from this same judgment: the life of reason as it comes to him remains unsubstantiated. Without connection to pretheoretical life, theoretical inquiry floats in midair. It is in this case a way of life, to quote Theodorus, chosen "for some reason or other (165a1)."

Socrates was acutely aware just how questionable is the notion that "making speeches every day about virtue" constitutes the preeminent human activity.[2] The paucity of those devoted to this activity alone makes it questionable. The cost of such devotion, illustrated in Socrates' case, makes it even more so. However, as I have argued, the ire of his fellow citizens is ultimately only the by-product of Socrates' response to an even deeper source of questionableness – namely, that the very object of the theoretical life, knowledge, is a problem.

[1] See, e.g., Nietzsche, *Beyond Good and Evil*, 9–32; Edmund Husserl, "Philosophy as Rigorous Science," in *Phenomenology and the Crisis of Philosophy*, trans. Quentin Lauer (New York: Harper and Row, 1965), 83–7, 119–20, 280–2, 295; Husserl, *The Crisis of European Sciences and Transcendental Phenomenology*, trans. David Carr (Evanston, IL: Northwestern University Press, 1970), 315–34; Heidegger, *Being and Time*, trans. John Macquarrie and Edward Robinson (Oxford: Basil Blackwell, 1973), 32–5, 98–9, 122–49.

[2] *Apology* 38a2.

Especially given its risks, how can we justify a life devoted to such an elusive object? For Socrates, the goodness of his own life becomes a question.

Socrates' awareness of the partiality of his, and everyone's, knowledge, dictates that he must consider, and not only consider but also confront, the most powerful alternative answers to this question. For the reasons indicated, these are preeminently the answers provided by the political community. Socrates cannot afford, therefore, to emulate the practice of the Philosopher who does not know his own neighbor. Too much is at stake. For the sake of his own well-being, Socrates must turn the focus of philosophy to political life.

Socrates sees, too, that he must confront these alternatives by an approach that recognizes their power. He does not regard himself as entirely exempt from the influence of the passions to which these views respond. By his own report, he also yearned for the kind of comprehensive knowledge that lures Theaetetus. Socrates was himself a pre-Socratic; he had to become Socrates. He thus appreciates the need to impose an external challenge because it may not always be forthcoming from within himself. Socrates' maieutic practice reflects his realization that, even for him, knowing is not the activity of a disembodied being. We do not inhabit the perfectly free world of words alone dreamed of by Theodorus.

In these concluding passages, Socrates acknowledges this imperfect distinction of theory and practice when he tells Theaetetus that an alternative view of knowledge may alter his character; "not supposing that you know things you don't know" may render Theaetetus more "moderate (210c3–4, c3)." This intertwining of belief and passion explains Socrates' participation in the kind of conversations in which Plato depicts him engaging. Socrates is interested in the interlocutors and themes of these conversations, especially insofar as they are challenging or "refutative," because his own most decisive choice requires the closest and most challenging assessment. Theodorus' life, a life of the intellect based ultimately on little more than a whim, stands as a cautionary example. The failure to subject his own life of reason to rational scrutiny would earn Socrates a place right next to Theodorus in the pantheon of self-forgetfulness.

Socrates' examination of his own way of life requires, then, acute sensitivity to the way in which passions and desires affect the plausibility of arguments. Especially important in this regard is the assessment of the competing desires that animate diverse ways of life. Aware of the questionable character of his chosen way of life, he must assess with particular care those desires that stand in closest proximity to his own desire to know. Only thus can he prevent himself and others from confusing ways of life that seem to be next of kin but are in fact profoundly at odds. For this reason, with the delineation of his distinctiveness in the *Theaetetus*, Socrates is at pains to distinguish the desire to know from the desire for certainty, his own way of life from that of the Philosopher. In this distinction, which is ultimately one between wisdom and knowledge, resides Socrates' deepest defense against the charge of dogmatism.

Yet it is just this charge that has been persistently leveled at Platonic thought. For well over a century, we have been taught that Plato's dogmatic rationalism is the edifice lying now in pieces before us.[3] I referred in the preceding text to contemporary thinkers' concern for pretheoretical life, evoked by what they regard as an unfounded devotion to reason. That devotion originates, purportedly, in the Platonic dialogues. I have argued, however, that the *Theaetetus* belies this judgment in several related ways. By itself, the motive animating Socrates' practice of midwifery just discussed makes such a judgment difficult to sustain. More generally, the dialogue casts doubt on this charge through the portrayal of Socrates' distinctly nondogmatic approach to the question of the meaning of knowledge that reveals knowledge as a problem.

Through this approach, Socrates seeks to discern the conditions of what he experiences himself and others doing every day. He assesses arguments not in terms of some preexisting notion of metaphysical truth but rather by asking whether they can account for our own experience. It is perplexity about our lives – or as Socrates puts it in a more encouraging fashion, wonder – that gives rise to philosophy. The arguments by which we hope to respond to those perplexities must not deny the conditions that generate them. The explanation must preserve the reason for the initial perplexity.

In accordance with this procedure, nowhere in the *Theaetetus* does Socrates presuppose what the object of knowledge must be. Instead, that object emerges out of how we really do come to know, its character determined by what we experience ourselves doing in connection with knowing. Socrates asks after the conditions of inquiry: how is it that we learn? How can we possess only partial understanding? How can we err? He makes the nondogmatic character of his approach all the more pronounced by his silence regarding the famous doctrines directed exactly at these questions. These doctrines, of the Forms and of Recollection, do mandate a certain understanding of the object of knowledge. For this reason, their inclusion would encourage exactly that inclination in his interlocutors, immediate or remote, that Socrates aims to forestall.

The theorists, or potential theorists, whom Socrates addresses, would like nothing better than to have Socrates provide them with a theory of knowledge, one that resolves all issues in its vision of an unchanging, eternal object of knowledge. We see this desire in Theaetetus' wish to be counted among those "who are and have been the great and wondrous men" from whom Socrates here distinguishes himself (210c5–6). The "great and wondrous men," who are anything but barren in their claim to know, are always around. They will always be seen as great and wondrous, as attractive, because of this claim. Those devoted to knowledge must find this claim especially difficult to resist. Wishing to possess their object in all wholeness and purity, they cannot be detained by attention to the political context of knowledge. The theorist is

[3] See Friedrich Nietzsche, *The Birth of Tragedy*, trans. Walter Kaufmann (New York: Vintage Books, 1962). See also pp. 210–15 in the preceding text.

least likely to give credence or even attention to the views of those he regards as his intellectual inferiors. Rather, the theorist is most likely to desire, and to see as attainable, comprehensive and certain knowledge. Such a devotee of knowledge desires the theoretical certainty, in whatever form, that can remove all doubts. The subsequent career of the Forms bears this out. Despite the qualifications, hesitations, and outright critiques that always accompany this notion, it does after all come to be regarded as The Theory of Forms. Especially in the present context, the theoretically inclined, those who understand themselves to be oriented on knowledge, would have heard this presentation and gone to work deducing its myriad consequences.

I do not mean to suggest that the Forms are simply a dispensable part of Socrates' thought. A crucial aspect of the argument in the *Theaetetus* is that there are intelligible wholes not simply reducible to their components. Yet how exactly to characterize these wholes is a question – and the *Theaetetus* leaves it that way. Accordingly, not only the Forms, as his accusers claim, but also the qualifications and critiques that accompany them should be regarded as part of Socrates' understanding. Socrates aims this presentation at those that are drawn to neglect the qualifications and embrace the comprehensive theory. Accordingly, he spotlights the danger he is trying to avoid by omitting this doctrine altogether. In this his intentional legacy, the absence of the Forms where we would most expect them provides the occasion for a question, a pause in the theoretician's headlong rush beyond the mundane, the rush to lose him- or herself in theory untethered to life.

Through this nondogmatic approach, the object of knowledge emerges in all its complications as the complex unity considered in Chapter 9. Knowledge is, and remains, a problem. In this light, the much-criticized rationalism is, at best, a caricature of the life of reason led by Plato's Socrates. I suggest that it is in light of this problem that we should understand the permanent need for political inquiry as a guide for philosophy.

Throughout the dialogue, Socrates expresses the problem of knowledge in terms of the vexed relationship between parts and wholes. The difficulty of knowing a human as a whole provides the equally pervasive exemplar of that relationship, in its most vexed and most compelling form. Near the dialogue's conclusion, Socrates once again calls attention to the difficulty of understanding the human whole with his reference to an example of the problem, the recurring issue of the meaning of human beauty. He states that he practices his art among "the young and well-born, all those, that is, that are beautiful (210d1–2)." Taking Theaetetus as one such subject of his art, we must conclude that the beauty to which Socrates refers is not a simple notion. Nor are the complexities of the human whole resolved in a certain grasp of the beings in general. The last definition of knowledge makes clear that all beings as wholes reflect the complex unity that characterizes the human whole. Moreover, this ontological diversity requires similarly diverse means of apprehension, so that the more accurately we reflect their diversity the more difficult is it to achieve certainty. This inverse relationship between accuracy and certainty substantiates the concluding sense that the meaning of knowledge is an aporia.

It is just this character of the problem of knowledge that demands political inquiry as an enduring requirement of philosophy even after its goodness has been demonstrated. For the conflicts endemic to political life express most vividly this perplexity of human wholeness in which the problem of knowledge is most seriously expressed. And it is of the utmost importance that the philosopher remains aware of the problematic character of knowledge. Sustained attention to the enduring issues of politics would keep the being and significance of such wholes before the philosopher's mind. It would forestall the intimately related temptations, still present, to reduce nature to either absolute stability or absolute flux, both of which make life inexplicable. Such awareness is the antidote to dogmatisms of every kind – including those that would efface the difference between dogmatic rationalism and the life of reason Plato portrays with his Socrates – because it encourages constant vigilance over the unavoidable latitude in our understanding that permits passion to shape inquiry. In this regard, the political heart of Socratic inquiry proves comprehensively pertinent to all subsequent inquiry into every issue.

These observations should make us hesitate before affirming Theaetetus' judgment regarding the fruitlessness of Socrates' efforts. In doubting Theaetetus' judgment, we take our bearings from Socrates' deeds. The dialogue's culmination in aporia does not cause Socrates to reject the art of midwifery that led to this outcome. At the end, he identifies himself with his mother's practice as firmly as ever – and rightly so (210c6–7). The theoretical premises that substantiate his midwifery derive precisely from that complexity of wholes, evident in both the beings and the soul, that constitutes the problem of knowledge. That complexity, and the problematic character of knowledge to which it leads, calls for, and is alone available to, *phronesis*, to wisdom understood as the cognitive capacity that discerns the elusive harmony between parts and wholes. Far from being fruitless, Socrates' conversation thus yields the understanding that enables him to designate and define the object of his distinctive philosophic practice.

A further demonstration of this conversation's fruitfulness occurs when Socrates recommends that the formula for this wisdom – "not supposing that you know things you don't know" – can and should guide Theaetetus' life, as it has guided his own (210b11–c4). He thus recommends this way of life to all those who, he hopes, might subsequently read the text of this conversation. By this act, Socrates indicates that he has provided in the conversation of the *Theaetetus* what his predecessors did not: a reasoned defense of the life of reason. In so doing, he has exhibited precisely how reason might inform our choices of good. He has provided *the* example of how theory can be connected to life. He has provided us as well the measured guide for such a life – a most fruitful outcome.

We might also expect Socrates' philosophic inquiry into politics to provide guidance not only for philosophic practice but also for political life. Such guidance is, I think, available, but again it may be disappointing in its direction. In particular, the *Theaetetus* conveys two considerations that bear significantly on the relationship between political theory and political practice. First, Socrates does not undertake the rational scrutiny of politics *primarily* to install reason as the guide for political life. Second, those perplexities uncovered by this scrutiny give pause regarding the possible scope of such rational guidance. To recall a point from Socrates' account of his midwifery, comprehensive eugenics remains outside our ken. For this reason, the prescriptions that would most properly flow from the philosopher to the political community would take the form of doubts about the possibility of that perfect peace, the object of Theodorus' hopes, in which these perplexities would be dissolved. Such well-founded doubts can be fruitful indeed insofar as they preserve politics as a realm of deliberative adjustment of enduringly diverse views of good.

Yet, admittedly, from the standpoint of the Theodoran theorist this entire harvest does not appear quite so bountiful. Knowledge *is* a problem. The practical guidance that the knowledge of ignorance can give to practical life seems at best indirect, consisting largely of counsels of moderation regarding our aspirations. The remaining question for Theaetetus, and for us, is whether to regard such an acquisition as good. In this regard, the conclusion of the dialogue appears as another piece of the midwife's art. How should we respond to the dialogue's explicitly aporetic outcome?[4] Will we succumb to disappointment? Or will we recognize that the outcome is most accurate and therefore to be valued?

Theaetetus unhesitatingly opts for the former (210b10). His reaction is understandable. Socrates' way will perhaps always be strange. It appears neither great nor wondrous. Moderation lacks a certain splendor. Moreover, his claim of ignorance does bear a certain resemblance to the blind leading the blind. Clearly, his way does not promise to supply those things that earn admiration either from a political community or from Theodoran theorists. Aligning himself once again with his mother, reminding us also of his reputation as a corruptor, Socrates at the end recalls the shameless character of his pursuit.

Yet "shame is not good for a needy man." All of the preceding considerations must give way to this judgment when we recognize that we are needy in a most decisive way – namely, with respect to our knowledge of that which is truly good. This neediness sets Socrates on his final path. He concludes the dialogue saying, "But now there's something I need to go and face in the court-yard of the king-archon, in response to the indictment which Meletus has drawn up against me (210d2–4)." Socrates' impending obligation is not unforeseen. The meaning of knowledge that calls for midwifery made his walk to the courtyard

4 As I indicated in Chapter 1, it is around this question that the variety of interpretations of the dialogue revolves.

of the King inevitable. It is because Socrates has appreciated the importance of the ground under his feet, the importance of the beginning, that he can both answer the question "why theory?" and must face the authorities in Athens. Both outcomes are rooted in the philosophic inquiry into political life. Both arise from Socrates' awareness of his neediness regarding knowledge of what is good. Insofar as we too share in Socrates' neediness, the wisdom of the midwife counsels us to inform all our reflections with inquiry into political life. If we hope to satisfy that same decisive need, we must join with Socrates as he walks to the courtyard of the King.

Bibliography

Ackrill, J. L. "Plato on False Belief: *Theaetetus* 187–200," *The Monist* 50 (1966): 383–402.

Ahrensdorf, Peter J. *The Death of Socrates and the Life of Philosophy*. Albany: State University of New York Press, 1995.

Allen, R. E., ed. *Studies in Plato's Metaphysics*. New York: Humanities Press, 1965.

Annas, Julia. "Plato the Sceptic," in *Oxford Studies in Ancient Philosophy*, suppl. vol., eds. James C. Klagge and Nicholas D. Smith (Oxford: Clarendon Press, 1992), 44–61.

______. *Platonic Ethics, Old and New*. Ithaca, NY: Cornell University Press, 1999.

Bartlett, Robert C. *Plato "Protagoras" and "Meno."* Ithaca, NY: Cornell University Press, 2004.

Benardete, Seth. *The Being of the Beautiful*. Chicago: University of Chicago Press, 1984.

Benitez, Eugenio and Livia Guimaraes. "Philosophy as Performed in Plato's *Theaetetus*," *Review of Metaphysics* 47 (1993): 297–328.

Berger, Harry, Jr. "Plato's Flying Philosopher," *Philosophical Forum* 13 (1982): 385–407.

Blondell, Ruby. *The Play of Character in Plato's Dialogues*. Cambridge: Cambridge University Press, 2002.

Bolotin, David. "The *Theaetetus* and the Possibility of False Opinion," *Interpretation* 15 (1987): 179–93.

______. *Plato's Dialogue on Friendship: An Interpretation of the "Lysis," with a New Translation*. Ithaca, NY: Cornell University Press, 1989.

______. "The Eleatic Stranger and Parmenides in Plato's *Sophist*" (lecture, St. John's College, Santa Fe, New Mexico, January 14, 2004).

Bostock, David. *Plato's "Theaetetus."* Oxford: Clarendon Press, 1988.

Bradshaw, David. "The Argument of the Digression in the *Theaetetus*," *Ancient Philosophy* 18 (1998): 61–8.

Bruell, Christopher. *On the Socratic Education: An Introduction to the Shorter Platonic Dialogues*. Lanham, MD: Rowman and Littlefield Publishers, 1999.

Burger, Ronna. *The "Phaedo": A Platonic Labyrinth*. New Haven, CT: Yale University Press, 1984.

Burkert, Walter. *Greek Religion*. Cambridge, MA: Harvard University Press, 1985.
Burnyeat, Myles. "The Material and Sources of Plato's Dream," *Phronesis* 15 (1970): 101–22.
______. "Plato on the Grammar of Perceiving," *The Classical Quarterly* N.S. 26 (1976a): 29–51.
______. "Protagoras and Self-Refutation in Plato's *Theaetetus*," *Philosophical Review* 85 (1976b): 172–95.
______. "Socratic Midwifery, Platonic Inspiration," *Bulletin of the Institute of Classical Studies* 24 (1977): 7–16.
______. "The Philosophical Sense of Theaetetus' Mathematics," *ISIS* 69 (1978): 489–513.
______. "Socrates and the Jury: Paradoxes in Plato's Distinction between Knowledge and True Belief," *Proceedings of the Aristotelian Society* 54 (1980): 173–91.
______. "Idealism and Greek Philosophy: What Descartes Saw and Berkeley Missed," *Philosophical Review* 90 (1982): 3–40.
______. *The "Theaetetus" of Plato*. Indianapolis: Hackett Publishing Company, 1990.
Campbell, Lewis. *The "Theaetetus" of Plato*. 1861. Reprint, New York: Arno Press, 1977.
Chappell, Timothy. *Reading Plato's "Theaetetus."* Indianapolis: Hackett Publishing Company, 2004.
Cherniss, Harold. "The Relation of the *Timaeus* to Plato's Later Dialogues," in *Studies in Plato's Metaphysics*, ed. R. E. Allen (New York: Humanities Press, 1965), 339–78.
Clay, Diskin. *Platonic Questions: Dialogues with the Silent Philosopher*. University Park: The Pennsylvania State University Press, 2000.
Cole, A. T. "The Apology of Protagoras," *Yale Classical Studies* 19 (1966): 101–18.
Cooper, John M. "Plato on Sense-Perception and Knowledge (*Theaetetus* 184–186)," *Phronesis* 15 (1970): 123–46.
Cornford, Francis M. *Plato's Theory of Knowledge*. Indianapolis: Bobbs-Merrill Company, 1957.
Cropsey, Joseph. *Plato's World: Man's Place in the Cosmos*. Chicago: University of Chicago Press, 1997.
Davis, Michael. *The Poetry of Philosophy: On Aristotle's "Poetics."* Lanham, MD: Rowman and Littlefield Publishers, 1992.
Descartes, Rene. *Discourse on the Method*, in *Selected Philosophical Writings*, trans. John Cottingham, Robert Stoothoff, and Dugald Murdoch. Cambridge: Cambridge University Press, 1998a.
______. *Meditations on First Philosophy* in *Selected Philosophical Writings*, trans. John Cottingham, Robert Stoothoff, and Dugald Murdoch. Cambridge: Cambridge University Press, 1998b.
Desjardins, Rosemary. *The Rational Enterprise: Logos in Plato's "Theaetetus."* Albany: State University of New York Press, 1990.
Diels, Hermann and Walther Kranz, eds. *Die Fragmente der Vorsokratiker*. Berlin: Weidmannsche, 1954.
Dorter, Kenneth. *Form and Good in Plato's Eleatic Dialogues: The "Parmenides," "Theaetetus," "Sophist," and "Statesman."* Berkeley: University of California Press, 1994.

Farrar, Cynthia. *The Origins of Democratic Thinking: The Invention of Politics in Classical Athens*. Cambridge: Cambridge University Press, 1988.

Fine, Gail. "False Belief in the *Theaetetus*," *Phronesis* 24 (1979a): 70–80.

______. "Knowledge and Logos in the *Theaetetus*," *Philosophical Review* 88 (1979b): 366–97.

______. "Conflicting Appearances," in *Form and Argument in Late Plato*, eds. Christopher Gill and Mary Margaret McCabe (Oxford: Clarendon Press, 1996), 105–33.

______. "Relativism and Self-Refutation: Plato, Protagoras, and Burnyeat," in *Method in Ancient Philosophy*, ed. Jyl Gentzler (Oxford: Clarendon Press, 1998), 137–63.

Ford, Andrew. "Protagoras' Head: Interpreting Philosophic Fragments in *Theaetetus*," *American Journal of Philology* 115 (1994): 199–218.

Fowler, D. H. *The Mathematics of Plato's Academy: A New Reconstruction*. Oxford: Clarendon Press, 1987.

Frede, Michael. "Observations on Perception in Plato's Later Dialogues," in *Essays in Ancient Philosophy* (Minneapolis: University of Minnesota Press, 1987), 3–8.

Galston, William. *Liberal Purposes: Goods, Virtues, and Diversity in the Liberal State*. Cambridge: Cambridge University Press, 1991.

Gonzalez, Francisco J., ed. *The Third Way: New Directions in Platonic Studies*. Lanham, MD: Rowman and Littlefield Publishers, 1995.

Gordon, Jill. *Turning toward Philosophy: Literary Device and Dramatic Structure in Plato's Dialogues*. University Park: The Pennsylvania State University Press, 1999.

Griswold, Jr., Charles L. *Self-Knowledge in Plato's "Phaedrus."* New Haven, CT: Yale University Press, 1986.

______, ed. *Platonic Writings/Platonic Readings*. New York: Routledge, 1988a.

______. "Plato's Metaphilosophy: Why Plato Wrote Dialogues," in *Platonic Writings, Platonic Readings*, ed. Charles L. Griswold, Jr. (New York: Routledge, 1988b), 143–67.

Hackforth, R. H. "Notes on Plato's *Theaetetus*," *Mnemosyne* 10 (1957): 128–40.

Hadot, Pierre. *Philosophy as a Way of Life*, trans. Michael Chase. Malden, MA: Blackwell, 1995.

Halperin, David M. "Plato and the Erotics of Narrativity," in *Methods of Interpreting Plato and His Dialogues, Oxford Studies in Ancient Philosophy*, suppl. vol., eds. James Klagge and Nicholas D. Smith (Oxford: Clarendon Press, 1992), 93–129.

Haring, E. S. "The *Theaetetus* Ends Well," *Review of Metaphysics* 35 (1982): 509–28.

______. "Socratic Duplicity: *Theaetetus* 154b1–156a3," *Review of Metaphysics* 45 (1992): 525–42.

Harrison, Jane. "Plato's Prologue: *Theaetetus* 142a–143c," *Tulane Studies in Philosophy* 27 (1978): 103–23.

Harte, Verity. *Plato on Parts and Wholes*. Oxford: Oxford University Press, 2002.

Heath, Thomas. *Greek Mathematics*. New York: Dover Publications, 1963.

Heidegger, Martin. *The Basic Problems of Phenomenology*, trans. Albert Hofstadter. Bloomington: Indiana University Press, 1982.

______. *Introduction to Metaphysics*, trans. Gregory Fried and Richard Polt. New Haven, CT: Yale University Press, 2000.

______.*The Essence of Truth: On Plato's Cave Allegory and "Theaetetus,"* trans. Ted Sadler. New York: Continuum, 2002.

Hemmenway, Scott R. "Philosophical Apology in the *Theaetetus*," *Interpretation* 17 (1990): 323–46.

Herrmann, Fritz Gregor. "Wrestling Metaphors in Plato's *Theaetetus*," *Nikephoros* 8 (1995): 77–109.

Hicken, Winifred. "The Character and Provenance of Socrates' 'Dream' in the *Theaetetus*," *Phronesis* 3 (1958): 126–45.

Hobbes, Thomas. *Leviathan*, ed. Michael Oakeshott. New York: Collier Books, 1962.

Howland, Jacob. "Re-reading Plato: The Problem of Platonic Chronology," *Phoenix* 45 (1991): 189–214.

______. *The Paradox of Political Philosophy: Socrates' Philosophic Trial*. Lanham, MD: Rowman and Littlefield Publishers, 1997.

Kahn, Charles H. *Plato and the Socratic Dialogue*. Cambridge: Cambridge University Press, 1996.

Klagge, James and Nicholas D. Smith, eds. *Methods of Interpreting Plato and His Dialogues, Oxford Studies in Ancient Philosophy*, suppl. vol. Oxford: Clarendon Press, 1992.

Kirk, G. S and J. E. Raven, *The Presocratic Philosophers*. Cambridge: Cambridge University Press, 1957.

Klein, Jacob. *A Commentary on Plato's "Meno."* Chapel Hill: University of North Carolina Press, 1965.

______. *Plato's Trilogy*. Chicago: University of Chicago Press, 1977.

Kraut, Richard. "Introduction to the Study of Plato," in *The Cambridge Companion to Plato*, ed. Richard Kraut (Cambridge: Cambridge University Press, 1992), 1–50.

Lee, Edward N. "'Hoist with His Own Petard'": Ironic and Comic Elements in Plato's Critique of Protagoras (Tht. 161–171)," in *Exegesis and Argument*, eds. Edward N. Lee, A. Mourelatos, and Richard Rorty (Assen, The Netherlands: Van Gorcum, 1973), 225–61.

Lesher, James H. "Parmenidean *Elenchos*," in *Does Socrates Have a Method?*, ed. Gary Alan Scott (University Park: The Pennsylvania State University Press, 2002), 19–35.

Lewis, F. A. "Foul Play in Plato's Aviary: *Theaetetus* 195B ff," in *Exegesis and Argument*, eds. E. N. Lee, A. Mourelatos, and R. Rorty (Assen: Van Gorcum, 1973), 262–84.

Locke, John. *Two Treatises of Government*, ed. Peter Laslett. Cambridge: Cambridge University Press, 1988.

Long, A. A. "Plato's Apologies and Socrates in the *Theaetetus*," in *Method in Ancient Philosophy*, ed. Jyl Gentzler (Oxford: Clarendon Press, 1998), 113–36.

Lutz, Mark. *Socrates' Education to Virtue: Learning the Love of the Noble*. Albany: State University of New York Press, 1998.

Lyons, John. *Structural Semantics, An Analysis of Part of the Vocabulary of Plato*. Oxford: Blackwell, 1969.

Madigan, Arthur S. J. "Commentary on Witt," in *Proceedings of the Boston Area Colloquium in Ancient Philosophy, vol. XI*, eds. John J. Cleary and William Wians (Lanham, MD: University Press of America, 1995), 267–72.

Maguire, Joseph P. "Protagoras – or Plato?," *Phronesis* 18 (1973): 115–38.

McDowell, John. *Plato "Theaetetus."* Oxford: Clarendon Press, 1973.

______. *Mind and World*. Cambridge, MA: Harvard University Press, 1996.

Menn, Stephen. "The Origins of Aristotle's Concept of *energeia: energeia* and *dunamis*," *Ancient Philosophy* 14 (1994): 73–114.

Miller, Jr., Mitchell. *The Philosopher in Plato's "Statesman."* The Hague: Martinus Nijhoff, 1980.

______. *Plato's "Parmenides": The Conversion of the Soul.* University Park: The Pennsylvania State University Press, 1986.

______. "Unity and *Logos*: A Reading of *Theaetetus* 201c–210a," *Ancient Philosophy* 12 (1992): 87–111.

Modrak, Deborah. "Perception and Judgment in the *Theaetetus*," *Phronesis* 26 (1981): 33–54.

Morrow, Glenn. "Plato and the Mathematicians: An Interpretation of Socrates' Dream in the *Theaetetus*," *Philosophical Review* 79 (1970): 309–33.

Nails, Debra. *The People of Plato: A Prosopography of Plato and Other Socratics.* Indianapolis: Hackett Publishing Company, 2002.

Nehemas, Alexander. "*Episteme* and *Logos* in Plato's Later Thought," in *Essays in Ancient Greek Philosophy III*, eds. John P. Anton and Anthony Preus (Albany: State University of New York Press, 1989), 267–92.

Nietzsche, Friedrich. *The Birth of Tragedy*, trans. Walter Kaufmann. New York: Vintage Books, 1967.

______. *Beyond Good and Evil*, trans. Walter Kaufmann. New York: Vintage Books, 1989.

Nussbaum, Martha C. *The Fragility of Goodness: Luck and Ethics in Greek Tragedy and Philosophy*. Cambridge: Cambridge University Press, 1986.

Owen, G. E. L. "The Place of the *Timaeus* in Plato's Dialogues," in *Studies in Plato's Metaphysics*, ed. R. E. Allen (New York: Humanities Press, 1965), 313–38.

Page, Carl. "Philosophy and the Outlandishness of Reason," *Journal of Speculative Philosophy* 7 (1993): 206–25.

Palmer, John. *Plato's Reception of Parmenides*. Oxford: Oxford University Press, 1999.

Plato. *Platonis Opera*, ed. E. A. Duke et al. Oxford: Clarendon Press, 1995.

Polansky, Ronald. *Philosophy and Knowledge: A Commentary on Plato's "Theaetetus."* Lewisburg, PA: Bucknell University Press, 1992.

Press, Gerald A., ed., *Plato's Dialogues: New Studies and Interpretations*. Lanham, MD: Rowman and Littlefield Publishers, 1993.

______. *Who Speaks for Plato? Studies in Platonic Anonymity*. Lanham, MD: Rowman and Littlefield Publishers, 2000.

Renaud, Francois. "Humbling as Upbringing: The Ethical Dimension of the Elenchus in the *Lysis*," in *Does Socrates Have a Method?*, ed. Gary Alan Scott (University Park: The Pennsylvania State University Press, 2002), 183–98.

Robb, Kevin. "*Asebeia* and *Sunousia*. The Issues behind the Indictment of Socrates," in *Plato's Dialogues: New Studies and Interpretations*, ed. Gerald A. Press (Lanham, MD: Rowman and Littlefield Publishers, 1993), 77–106.

Roochnik, David L. *Of Art and Wisdom: Plato's Understanding of Techne*. University Park: The Pennsylvania State University Press, 1996.

______. "Self-Recognition in Plato's *Theaetetus*," *Ancient Philosophy* 22 (2002): 37–51.

Rorty, Amelie O. "A Speculative Note on Some Dramatic Elements in the *Theaetetus*," *Phronesis* 17 (1972): 227–38.

Rosen, Stanley. "Socrates' Dream," *Theoria* 42 (1976): 161–87.

———. "Dynamis, Energeia, and the Megarians," *Philosophical Inquiry* 1 (1979): 105–19.

———. *The Limits of Analysis*. New York: Basic Books, 1980.

Ross, W. D. *Plato's Theory of Ideas*. Oxford: Oxford University Press, 1953.

———, ed. *Aristotle Metaphysics*. Oxford: Clarendon Press, 1970.

Rue, Rachel. "The Philosopher in Flight: The Digression (172c–177c) in Plato's *Theaetetus*," in *Oxford Studies in Ancient Philosophy, vol. 11*, ed. C. C. W. Taylor (Oxford: Clarendon Press, 1993), 71–100.

Runciman, W. G. *Plato's Later Epistemology*. Cambridge: Cambridge University Press, 1962.

Ryle, Gilbert. "Logical Atomism in Plato's *Theaetetus*," *Phronesis* 35 (1990): 21–46.

Sachs, Joe. *Plato's "Theaetetus."* Newburyport, MA: Focus Publishing Company, 2004.

Salkever, Stephen. *Finding the Mean: Theory and Practice in Aristotelian Political Philosophy*. Princeton, NJ: Princeton University Press, 1990.

Santas, Gerasimos X. *Socrates: Philosophy in Plato's Early Dialogues*. London: Routledge, 1978.

Saxonhouse, Arlene. *Free Speech and Democracy in Ancient Athens*. Cambridge: Cambridge University Press, 2005.

Sayre, Kenneth. *Plato's Analytic Method*. Chicago: University of Chicago Press, 1969.

Schleiermacher, Friedrich. *Introductions to the Dialogues of Plato*, trans. William Dobson. New York: Arno Press, 1973.

Sedley, David. "Three Platonist Interpretations of the *Theaetetus*," in *Form and Argument in Late Plato*, eds. Christopher Gill and Mary Margaret McCabe (Oxford: Clarendon Press, 1996), 79–103.

———. *The Midwife of Platonism*. Oxford: Clarendon Press, 2004.

Sextus Empiricus. *Vols. I and II*. trans. R. G. Bury. Cambridge, MA: Harvard University Press, 1933.

Silverman, Allan. "Plato on Perception and 'Commons'," *The Classical Quarterly* N. S. 40 (1990): 148–75.

———. "Flux and Language in the *Theaetetus*," in *Oxford Studies in Ancient Philosophy, vol. XVIII*, ed. David Sedley (Oxford: Oxford University Press, 2000), 109–52.

Spinoza, Benedict. *Theological-Political Treatise*, trans. Samuel Shirley. Indianapolis: Hackett Publishing Company, 1998.

Stern, Paul. *Socratic Rationalism and Political Philosophy: An Interpretation of Plato's "Phaedo."* Albany: State University of New York Press, 1993.

———. "The Rule of Wisdom and the Rule of Law in Plato's *Statesman*," *American Political Science Review* 91 (1997): 264–76.

———. "Tyranny and Self-Knowledge: Critias and Socrates in Plato's *Charmides*," *American Political Science Review* 93 (1999): 399–412.

Strauss, Leo. *Natural Right and History*. Chicago: University of Chicago Press, 1968.

———. *The City and Man*. Chicago: University of Chicago Press, 1977.

———. "On Classical Political Philosophy," in *The Rebirth of Classical Political Rationalism*, ed. Thomas L. Pangle (Chicago: University of Chicago Press, 1989a), 49–62.

______. "The Problem of Socrates: Five Lectures," in *The Rebirth of Classical Political Rationalism*, ed. Thomas L. Pangle (Chicago: University of Chicago Press, 1989b), 103–83.

Taylor, A. E. *Plato: The Man and his Work*. London: Methuen, 1926.

Tomin, Jules. "Socratic Midwifery," *Classical Quarterly* 37 (1987): 97–102.

Tschemplik, Andrea. "Framing the Question of Knowledge: Beginning Plato's *Theaetetus*," in *Plato's Dialogues: New Studies and Interpretations*, ed. Gerald A. Press (Lanham, MD: Rowman and Littlefield Publishers, 1993), 169–78.

Umphrey, Stewart. *Complexity and Analysis*. Lanham, MD: Lexington Books, 2002.

Velkley, Richard. *Being after Rousseau*. Chicago: University of Chicago Press, 2002.

Vernant, Jean-Pierre. "Death with Two Faces," in *Reading the "Odyssey": Selected Interpretive Essays*, ed. Seth L. Schein (Princeton, NJ: Princeton University Press, 1996), 55–62.

Versenyi, Laszlo. "Protagoras' Man-Measure Fragment," *The American Journal of Philology* 83 (1962): 178–84.

Vlastos, Gregory. *Plato "Protagoras."* Indianapolis: Bobbs-Merrill, 1956.

______. *Socrates, Ironist and Moral Philosopher*. Ithaca, NY: Cornell University Press, 1991.

______. "The Socratic Elenchus: Method Is All," in *Socratic Studies*. Cambridge: Cambridge University Press, 1994.

Waterfield, Robin. *Plato "Theaetetus."* London: Penguin, 1987.

Waymack, Mark H. "The *Theaetetus* 172c–177c: A Reading of the Philosopher in Court," *Southern Journal of Philosophy* 23 (1985): 481–9.

Weiss, Roslyn. *The Socratic Paradox and Its Enemies*. Chicago: University of Chicago Press, 2006.

Wengert, R. G. "The Paradox of the Midwife." *History of Philosophy Quarterly* 5 (1988): 3–10.

White, Nicholas P. *Plato on Knowledge and Reality*. Indianapolis: Hackett Publishing Company, 1976.

Williams, Bernard. *Shame and Necessity*. Berkeley: University of California Press, 1993.

Williams, C. J. F. "Referential Opacity and False Belief in the *Theaetetus*," *The Philosophical Quarterly* 22 (1972): 289–302.

Witt, Charlotte. "Powers and Possibilities: Aristotle vs. The Megarians," in *Proceedings of the Boston Area Colloquium in Ancient Philosophy, vol. XI*, eds. John J. Cleary and William Wians (Lanham, MD: University Press of America, 1995), 249–66.

Woodbury, Leonard. "Parmenides on Naming by Mortal Men: Fr. B8. 53–56," *Ancient Philosophy* 6 (1986): 1–13.

Zuckert, Catherine. *Postmodern Platos*. Chicago: University of Chicago Press, 1996.

Index